Separate Societies

Separate Societies

Poverty and Inequality in U.S. Cities

SECOND EDITION

WILLIAM W. GOLDSMITH AND
EDWARD J. BLAKELY

Foreword by
PRESIDENT BILL CLINTON

 TEMPLE UNIVERSITY PRESS
Philadelphia

TEMPLE UNIVERSITY PRESS
Philadelphia, Pennsylvania 19122
www.temple.edu/tempress

Library of Congress Cataloging-in-Publication Data

Goldsmith, William W.
  Separate societies : poverty and inequality in U.S. cities / William W. Goldsmith and
Edward J. Blakely. — 2nd ed.
    p. cm.
  Includes bibliographical references and index.
  ISBN 978-1-4399-0291-2 (cloth : alk. paper) — ISBN 978-1-4399-0292-9 (pbk. : alk. paper) —
  ISBN 978-1-4399-0293-6 (e-book : alk. paper)
  1. Urban poor—United States. 2. Inner cities—United States. 3. Urban renewal—
United States. 4. Regional planning—United States. 5. United States—Social policy—
1980–1993. I. Blakely, Edward J. II. Title.

HV4045.G65 2010
362.50973'091734—dc22   2009053615

⊛ The paper used in this publication meets the requirements of the American National
Standard for Information Sciences—Permanence of Paper for Printed Library Materials,
ANSI Z39.48-1992

Printed in the United States of America

2 4 6 8 9 7 5 3 1

Contents

List of Illustrations and Tables

TABLES

Foreword to the Second Edition

Our founders championed equal opportunity for all, knowing it was not a reality, but understanding that as a driving aspiration, this American Dream could keep us moving forward no matter what the future held. While there will always be a gap between where we are and where we want to be, every generation of Americans must always work to narrow it.

Today the gap is too large and the American Dream is out of reach for too many. Bill Goldsmith and coauthor Ed Blakely have long held that the most effective way to increase opportunity is to ensure that the poor are brought into the fabric of our communities. In the first edition of *Separate Societies,* Goldsmith and Blakely showed that the isolation of low-income individuals had exacerbated inequality and they outlined policies to remedy it.

My administration's domestic agenda reflected these views in our efforts to create more jobs and new businesses, reduce economic inequality, improve access to housing and quality education, and make our streets safe. We made important strides; however, many of these gains have since been erased. In the first decade of the new millennium, median wages have decreased, the number of families without health insurance has risen, and the number of people working full-time but still falling below the poverty line has increased.

As we confront these problems once again, we must look at the evidence. What went wrong, and most important, how can we get back on the right track?

How can we effectively uplift populations that are often scattered and frequently forgotten? How can our efforts achieve the greatest impact on those at risk with the money we have to spend on them? In the broadest sense, how can we turn our good intentions into concrete, positive results?

In their new edition of *Separate Societies,* Goldsmith and Blakely address these *how* questions. After careful analysis of the issues that face us, they outline alternatives for state and federal policies and offer suggestions for how community groups and everyday people can make a difference. The authors argue that when governments and local organizations keep a careful eye on how new strategies are working, we can improve education, renew neighborhoods, ignite economic engines, and alleviate persistent inequalities in our cities.

We must build a country where no person is abandoned, where we pull people in instead of pushing them away, and where we all share the responsibilities, benefits, and sense of destiny. This begins by bringing opportunities to those who have the fewest—and who need them the most. That's what I tried to do as president and what I do now through the work of the William J. Clinton Foundation. Bill Goldsmith and Ed Blakely show us how to begin.

—President Bill Clinton
November 2009

Acknowledgments

Many people contributed to this book. First, we owe a debt of gratitude to all the administrators and activists in city halls and neighborhoods who have fought against poverty and inequality, and told the tales. We are also grateful for ideas and comments from our colleagues on the city planning and urban studies faculties at UC Berkeley, Cornell University, The New School, and the University of Southern California. We are deeply indebted as well to numerous Cornell graduate students: Kevin Waskelis found and organized reams of data; Anna Read and Vishwesh Viswanathan labored tirelessly on the final tables and figures, collected materials for the text, and contributed to the analysis; and Leah Coldham and Jonathan Wellemeyer worked with patience and skill on the final text, notes, and references. Anna Read prepared the index. Other Cornell graduate students, including Claiborne Walthall, Elizabeth Murphy, Avery Ouellette, Matthew Hendren, and Joy Chen, worked on earlier stages. During the publication process Lynne Frost and Kimberley Vivier were extremely effective with fact checking and copyediting. We thank them all. Finally, we are indebted to Douglas Band and Trevor Zimmer on President Clinton's staff for facilitating our request for his foreword.

1

The End of an Era

Divided We Fall

When we published *Separate Societies* in 1992, American cities were troubled by failing economies, severe racial segregation, and desperate neighborhood conditions. These problems had preoccupied politicians, social activists, and scholars since the 1960s. We contended that if left unattended, city problems would impair national social and economic life. We looked to the federal government to enable solutions ranging from inner-city revitalization to dramatic changes in welfare and workforce development. Although proposals like ours found their way in whole or in part, by accident or design, into aspects of welfare reform, job training, and urban renovation in the 1990s, for the most part the government ignored the cities. Starting in 2000, the Bush administration acted toward cities with profound hostility. Because city-regions form the base of the new global economy, the whole nation today pays a high price for these anti-city policies.

Through the first decade of the twenty-first century, so-called urban problems affected not only the poor but everyone, and not only cities but suburbs, too. Inequality worsened along with isolation and separation. Better-off people built a Fortress America, insulating themselves in suburban districts and city enclaves.[1] Tax breaks, subsidies, and unregulated greed enhanced the market gains of the wealthiest households, fantastically increasing their social exclusiveness and threatening to destroy any sense of national unity that might lead to improved access and extended opportunity. After a spree of unprecedented financial failures of the world's largest firms, the Wall Street collapse required the federal government to intervene. Leading up to the collapse, standing as testament to the earlier lack of accountability, formal rules favored neglect over inclusion. Beneficiaries of the political arrangements tolerated failed health care for millions, collapsed schools for minorities, poor neighborhood maintenance in cities and inner suburbs, and exacerbated racial inequality. Balkanized patterns of metropolitan growth not only harmed the underprivileged but held back the nation, spreading competitive weakness, environmental irresponsibility, and broad social discontent. Whether the Obama election signals a sufficient turnaround seems doubtful. A slightly improved Department of Housing and Urban Development and a new but weak Office of Urban Affairs in the White House enhance the government's abilities, but they will not suffice to tackle the long accumulation of city and metropolitan problems.

In spite of suburbanization of Black and Hispanic populations in recent years, extremely large groups of people, who typically have very low incomes, still reside in what may properly be called ghettos or barrios—restricted areas where households are confined, where neighborhood conditions are poor and services are inadequate, and where children are likely to attend dismal, failing schools. The numbers astound: in each of 25 large central cities, half of them in the West, at least 100,000 Latinos live. Together they add up to more than 10 million residents. At the same time, in each of 33 cities at least 100,000 African Americans live, who add up to another 10 million. The big-city districts in which these Black and Latino people live are mainly in the Northeast, the Midwest, and the South. Combined, we get 63 cities and more than 23 million people. Many more Latinos and Blacks live segregated in other large cities as well, those with populations under 100,000.[2]

Among big-city minority residents, some are perfectly well off, as part of the middle class with good incomes, sending their kids either to magnet schools or to private schools and enjoying the benefits of city life. But the vast majority struggle with low incomes, bad services, dangerous neighborhoods, and discriminatory behavior from public officials, rental agents, real estate agents, mortgage bankers, and Whites in general. Things are *not* as bad as they used to be. Opportunities for advancement that used to be closed are now open to Blacks, Latinos, Asians, immigrants, and others. Many dangers have abated. But huge numbers of people remain excluded from opportunity, relegated to bleak futures, feeling trapped in Black ghettos, Latino barrios, and even poor Asian enclaves despite legislation requiring fair housing in every state.

This set of persisting, perhaps even worsening, urban problems is what motivated us to write a second edition. In the first edition, we sensed that progress might come. During the economic boom of the 1990s, our hope held, as some progress was made, now mostly evaporated. Yes, the United States has now elected a Black president, and top-ranked Black, Latino, and Asian advisers populate elite circles in education, industry, government and even—although very rarely—high finance. Meanwhile, however, in large swatches of metropolitan America, legacies of slavery and Jim Crow persist, made worse by bad treatment accorded immigrants from Latin America and elsewhere. Millions of Americans are still underpaid, underhoused, and underserved. The country has not moved toward solutions but instead has extended city problems into the suburbs. Now the term *inner suburb*, like the term *urban*, means poverty, crime, and neighborhood decline. (Note that most minority persons now live in the suburbs, and the suburban poor outnumber the poor in the cities.)

As such overbearing issues as climate change, war, global economic competition, and continuing threats of severe economic downturns challenge U.S. political institutions, few commentators bother to note the persistence of urban problems. New York's Mayor Michael Bloomberg complained during the Obama–McCain presidential campaign, "[Most] Americans now live in urban areas—our nation's economic engines. But you would never know that listening to the presidential candidates. At a time when our national economy is sputtering, to say the least, what are we doing to fuel job growth in our cities, and to revive cities that have never fully recovered from the manufacturing losses of recent decades?"[3]

Even in research on urban studies and planning, study after study focuses on the elements of positive change—in politics, race relations, real estate markets and residential choices, and school enrollment. Many studies support Mayor Bloomberg's notion that cities are the engines pulling the national economic train. These engines have been fueled by the arrival of immigrants, shifting cultural and aesthetic preferences in favor of city life, and even by the cityward moves of people under economic pressures of rising costs of commuting to work. The optimistic emphasis in these studies is understandable, but it is not sufficient. For millions, change has been too slow and too halting, or not at all, and that lack of change, we claim, threatens progress on most other national issues.

The history is important. Through the last half of the twentieth century, city residents bore many of the nation's burdens. Over decades, the economy shifted from manufacturing to information, counterbalanced by joblessness and low pay in retail and services. Global pressures changed the structure of industry and forced workplaces to move. Central cities with their nearby factories, railheads, and shipping yards fell into disrepair, and city housing that had been located near the plant or factory lost its advantage. The locus of jobs and power moved to the suburban fringe, so that critics eventually spoke of old, dead cities replaced by new and lively boomburbs, edge-cities, and other sprawled configurations, as though the periphery contained the essence of metropolitan life.

In 1992, against bleak evidence of global economic trends and these troubling urban consequences, we argued that the time had come for well-off suburban majorities to acknowledge their privileges and correct the unequal distribution of opportunities that weighed so unfairly on the least advantaged people of color. We favored judicial decisions such as *Mt. Laurel*, which instructed New Jersey suburbs to accept their "fair share" of affordable housing, and *Gautreaux*, which forced the Chicago public housing authority to place eligible families in suburbs as well as city neighborhoods. Although we suggested that suburban economic superiority was a chimera and that suburban social isolation from cities was costly even for the national economy, we did not press the issue. We kept our focus on the poverty of city neighborhoods and their plight, and we sought economic options and political opportunities for city revival as a means to reduce economic and social inequality.[4]

Now, after two terms of Bill Clinton centrism followed by two frightening terms of George W. Bush conservative radicalism, we find the entire nation burdened by the decay and hopeless poverty of some city neighborhoods and a growing number of inner suburbs. As the mortgage crisis brings home, not only do central cities suffer, but so do entire metropolitan areas, even the well-off suburbs that felt so protected. Metropolitan inequalities that pile unjustifiable burdens on the poor have become threats to all, even to national politics.[5] Cities are crucial not only because so many Americans live in them, not only because inequalities appear so vividly in them, but also because in this time, the world's first urban-majority century, our metropolitan economies, ecologies, and societies offer views into the future and should suggest key options for progress. Thus metropolitan well-being should serve as both barometer and sustainer of national prosperity.

In this book we argue that although compassion for the poor and the needy has not generated solutions, the self-interest of the privileged ought to. Some political and economic leaders have already begun to note the gains that would be available to middle-class communities and even the wealthy if they would promote reductions in inequality. This book explores such options for cities, suggesting that broad national gains would derive from a successful attack on metropolitan inequality.

The United States, we argue, cannot continue with the metropolitan policies of the Bush administration, relying on the unfinished business of the Clinton administration. The national penalties that come down from a continuation of this metropolitan trajectory are already being paid in costly currency. These penalties fall beyond the city line, to include not only the obvious failures, but also hugely expensive prisons, an unskilled and unmotivated labor force, an infrastructure of isolation, and distorted real estate markets. The penalties also include public schools that are less and less able to prepare young people for productive careers and good citizenship. These schools deprive stigmatized immigrant and racial groups, stimulating resentment among the very people who need to be incorporated into our rapidly changing economy. Further penalties include profound environmental damages caused by a rising consumerism based on endless sprawl and a political system that fails to account for ruin of natural resources or to curb global warming and excessive use of fossil-fuel energy. Finally, the penalties include the corrosion of politics, so that democracy becomes less and less real for the many Americans who languish at the bottom of a spreading base of poverty, propping up an ever steeper social pyramid of wealth. When added up, these multiple penalties impose heavy costs indeed—which we argue can be attributed in good part to the way the nation mismanages its urban and metropolitan affairs. The toll is paid by every one of us.

Three measures vividly indicate national failure: the prison population is now gigantic, household incomes are grossly unequal, with the wealthiest 1 percent of Americans taking ever larger portions of the total, and voter participation is low, as large numbers of Americans ignore a political process that reaps them no reward.

The U.S. prison system, outsizing those of even Russia and South Africa, incarcerates the world's largest portion of any national population. In absolute terms, U.S. prisoners make up far and away the largest imprisoned group in the world, numbering nearly 2.5 million men and women. Add in parolees, disenfranchised ex-convicts, and their damaged families, and the numbers grow to include millions more.

U.S. household and family wealth holdings and incomes are by far the most unequal among developed nations, and poverty rates are the highest. Income inequality is particularly pronounced in comparison with other rich nations after accounting for taxes and public services such as medical care, transit, social housing, and social security. In every U.S. metropolis, one can actually *see* the inequality, by moving block by block on almost any radial, from the city center to the suburban outer edge. U.S. inequality puts the country "in league not with our putative economic peers, Canada, Europe and Japan, but with Brazil, Mexico and Russia, countries 'in which adults have the right to vote, but real political power is wielded by a relatively narrow, and rich, segment of the population.'"[6] The divisions in U.S. cities have long called up images of the Third World.[7]

In the presidential election of 2004, 62 million citizens voted for George W. Bush, another 59 million for John Kerry, but more than 95 million stayed away from the polls. That is, more than 44 percent of the nation's adult citizens did not vote. In the 2008 landmark election, with the largest turnout in decades, Barack Obama won nearly 67 million votes, and John McCain more than 58 million, but still more than 80 million adult citizens did not vote. Nearly 38 percent of the potential electorate stayed home. In other democratic, highly developed nations, France and Germany, for example, such massive absenteeism is unheard-of, and fewer than 20 percent typically miss their chance to vote. Moving around any U.S. metropolis, district by district, keen observers can easily identify the middle class and wealthy areas where the vote will be high and the poor areas where it will be low. At one extreme, the very rich have entered a new golden age. In 1980, just prior to the Reagan presidency, incomes for what we might call ordinary families, everyone except the richest 10 percent, averaged just under $31,000 (in 2006 inflation-adjusted dollars). In the subsequent quarter century, that ordinary family's income did not rise; it *fell* by $72. Meanwhile, the incomes of super-rich families (those in the top one hundredth of 1 percent) *rose* dramatically, from $5.4 million on average to $29.6 million.[8]

Societies have struggled over acceptable degrees of inequality for centuries, ever since the creation of the nation-state. As the sociologist and historian Immanuel Wallerstein has written: "The great political question of the modern world, the great cultural question, has been how to reconcile the theoretical embrace of equality with the continuing and increasingly acute polarization of real-life opportunities and satisfactions that has been its outcome."[9]

Americans have long dealt with this inconsistency between democratic theory and unequal reality by avoidance, as they hide behind the isolating divisions that organize their lives in metropolitan areas. Municipalities manipulate their boundaries and multiply segmentations, thus perpetuating some of America's most troublesome legacies. But as pressures repeatedly arise from below, avoidance becomes impossible. People who live in poor and underserved city neighborhoods and increasingly in decaying inner suburbs resist their fates. While dominant social actors, economic institutions, and political parties try to frame the debates and reinforce boundaries to ensure exclusion, people who are excluded and who belong to oppressed groups refuse to go along. As their social movements gain traction, the whole system moves. As Wallerstein says, at some point and under sufficient pressure, those holding power typically admit new beneficiaries, and the balance of power shifts, but only marginally. In the United States (and increasingly in the rest of the world) people and social groups on all sides find themselves fighting through these sorts of struggles in the crucibles of large metropolitan areas.

To be sure, not all these problems are home grown in U.S. cities. Immigrants arrive at U.S. shores as a result of rapid technological change, the spread of the information economy, astonishing expansion of communications capabilities, and the constant lessening of transportation costs. Others come because the global military and political imbalances resulting from the collapse of the Soviet Union left the United States with no serious competitor to impose restraint and no one else for others to blame. Finally, even the most powerful nation no longer finds anywhere to escape. When the new economic octopus squeezes its arms around the globe, they compress people and their activities from all places, denying isolation as an option for anyplace, including America, even partially or temporarily. Employment in all highly developed countries, and even in mid-range countries, has shifted from manufacturing to services, leaving rust-belt decay worldwide, as plants shut down and factory jobs disappear, move elsewhere, or downgrade to high-technology, low-skill work. Although in some ways the U.S. national economy has responded more flexibly than others, so that regional shifts of business investment and internal migration of the workforce have eased or at least masked the distensions, the changes are still dramatic and costly. Although regional economies have grown in the sun belt and the gun belt, attracted by weak unions, fresh fields for investment, good weather, and Department of Defense contracts, many regions that previously manufactured autos, steel, appliances, and other heavy industrial goods have long been collapsing. For the nation to compete successfully in the tough global marketplace, people and places must figure out how to share benefits and burdens more fairly. If we do not act now, divided we will continue to fall.

To make matters worse, U.S. practices and pressures now threaten other rich nations that had chosen wisely to limit inequality by means of social democratic reforms, which they introduced and expanded in the last half of the twentieth century. Even in those western European cities that planning theorist Manuel Castells once pointed to as oases of peace in a world of conflict, levels of inequality are rising, due in part to alterations in the global economy that others have made under U.S. pressures and in service to U.S. corporate interests.[10] In the United States itself, the bad effects are greatly magnified.

The details of U.S. metropolitan inequality have changed over the years, but solid improvement is hard to find, as troubled cities not only mirror a troubled national society but sometimes cause the trouble. Everywhere, city regions encounter difficulties, especially as they confront disparities that separate poor from middle-class and wealthy neighborhoods and municipalities. Although in some cities poverty has diminished, the improvement has often come at the expense of inner suburbs, which in large metropolitan areas now house more than half the poor. Although new immigrants have greatly altered the racial, ethnic, and cultural mix that makes up many metropolitan areas, even helping with revival of a few central cities, most central cities remain deeply troubled. The old and simple model of urban-suburban doughnut with poor center and well-off suburbs no longer fits everywhere, but the more finely grained metropolitan model with a less predictable checkerboard pattern is hardly to be celebrated. Ethnic and racial residential patterns have become less standardized and more varied as metropolitan areas have spread and become geographically highly complex; nevertheless, neighborhood by neighborhood, jurisdiction by jurisdiction, urban apartheid remains, separating rich from poor and especially minorities from Whites. Although the new federal welfare program was built on the promise of better access to paid employment, the replacement of guaranteed family incomes (AFDC) by temporary assistance (TANF) has instead driven many poor women and their dependent children still deeper into economic isolation.[11] At the same time, gated communities and other forms of residential withdrawal are on the rise. The 2000 Census found that 6 percent of all Americans then lived in homogenous suburban enclaves surrounded by walls, 3.4 percent of them with electronic gates or guards. Uniform levels of wealth and homogeneity of race comprise the dominant features of these new socially isolated compounds. Homeowners in communities with controlled access have a median income 43 percent higher than the income of the typical American homeowner.[12] All indications show that the number of these fortress-mentality communities is on the rise.

A national pathology is emerging, as we argue in this book, but it reveals opportunity. Cities and their metropolitan areas serve as bellwethers, early warning systems that foretell or illustrate problems of national scope. They serve also as laboratories for social, environmental, and economic change, allowing experimentation that can lead to innovation. Metropolitan areas can operate as city-states, with integrated economic activity and internationally competitive production, allowing quick feedback from corporate and political decisions, crucial for innovation in the nation's knowledge-based economy. As the cities succeed or fail, so the nation prospers or declines.

Sustainable Global Change, National Dilemmas, Local Reform

Our pessimistic structuralist views on metropolitan inequality and social separation can be painted to recede into the background only if we find positive, optimistic options. Such reframing is the rationale for this book. Even though separation and rising poverty have led to political incapacity, they also signify a positive potential. The breakdown of the old and rigid metropolitan pattern of poor central cities of color surrounded by rich rings of White or lightly integrated suburbs is still far from fluid and equal, but the changing arrangements show how people refuse and reject the old categories. New patterns provide new spaces for innovation. The growth of gated communities and the fencing of privatized residential zones give good cause for worry, but the revival of city neighborhoods and the energies of immigrant communities give cause for hope. Less privileged residents ask questions about who has access to which parts of the territory, where and for whom living arrangements are safe and comfortable, and which children get to attend good schools. They ask who has access to the best places to work and who pays for services and who receives them. With these questions they challenge not only the status quo but the entire pattern of metropolitan development. Pressures from below to reduce separation, inequality, and poverty furnish key parts of a new vision and strategy that the nation needs in order to deal with rising global competition. In our view, policies to restructure the economy, reorganize the metropolis, protect the environment, and reduce poverty and discrimination should work hand in hand, and they should stimulate beneficial national change, sustainable change.

But how can local or metropolitan innovation result in national change? Throughout the book we provide what we hope is persuasive evidence, but here for a preview we offer a few illustrations. The first example is in some ways reminiscent of the Progressive era, from 1900 to 1920, when U.S. cities were reshaped by social policies aimed at getting rid of slums. Illustrating this progressive approach in today's world, the city of Burlington, Vermont, repeatedly elected an administration that fashioned new programs, including a city health plan, a community land trust furnishing five hundred units of permanently affordable housing, and funds to help house the lowest-income residents in partnership with local nonprofit organizations.[13] After more than two hundred years of casting its Electoral College votes for Republicans (one of only two states to vote against Franklin D. Roosevelt in his landslide election in 1936), Vermont has now voted Democratic in the last ten presidential elections, and it has sent an independent socialist first to the House of Representatives and then to the Senate. Thus has municipal reform projected its (still limited) potential onto national affairs.

A much earlier example, in the mid-twentieth century, suggests in a different way how a local innovation might lead to lessened metropolitan inequality and then to beneficial national changes. After the Great Depression and World War II, as both workers and manufacturers sought to stabilize incomes and boost production, union leaders in heavy industry proposed regional pension funds. The United Auto Workers union in Toledo had a plan for Ohio to distribute pension costs across the numerous small plants in auto parts, electrical appliances, and plastics, a plan that would have allowed workers to move retirement benefits as they changed jobs and allowed employers to share the risks. Technically, this plan had much to recommend it, as the insurance principle would protect workers against the unexpected and the much expanded pool of workers would reduce costs and volatility for employers. A year later, in negotiations with General Motors, UAW president Walter Reuther envisioned an even broader plan, one that would share risks still more widely. This time, too, the technical benefits offered efficiencies for the industry and broad medical coverage for many of the region's households. The stimulus for both proposals came from directly affected people who lived and worked in the area. The idea was that workers and firms would see the mutual benefits.

Fast-forward to the first decade of the twenty-first century. Problems of health coverage and industrial costs have grown well beyond the metropolitan boundaries of Toledo and Ohio or Detroit and Michigan. Some large employers no longer meet their pension obligations, and many smaller employers offer no health or retirement benefits at all. Unfunded pension plans constitute a national crisis, and tens of millions of households live without health insurance. Where does the stimulus for universal health insurance arise today? Again, it arises where business, citizens, and government see their mutual interests served locally. The first serious moves are being made by the states of California and Massachusetts, which are dominated by a small number of very large metropolitan areas.

What happened with the earlier UAW proposals? The reactions of the manufacturers were solidly hostile. They "were terrified ... [and] organized a trade association to stop the [1949] plan ... [and] actually said 'This idea might be efficient and rational. But it's too dangerous.'" The corporations felt these plans had the potential to empower employees far too much for the comfort of investors and managers.[14] Charles Wilson, known nationally first as the president of GM and later as secretary of defense, did not merely oppose the plan for GM, but he upped the ante, bribing the UAW by offering the "treaty of Detroit," with generous employee health benefits and pensions paid for by the company.[15] Pension plans did gain national attention, but via separate agreements, firm by firm, not spread as regional or national programs as intended. Virtually all workers in unionized firms—and many others—came to be covered by pension benefits, but in separate contracts. And after Henry Kaiser started a group health plan for workers in the area where his firms were located, this approach to group-membership health care spawned an entire industry that insures millions of working and retired Americans. But in spite of such corporate innovations in response to local pressures, moves for national progress were defeated. Without progressive national legislation, recurring problems overwhelm the corporations, and people without insurance overwhelm the cities.[16]

In our view, persistent urban and suburban poverty has been generated not simply by transformations in the structure of global and domestic economies. It has been generated also by a particular set of American political responses, which have reduced American opportunity, guiding the nation from stability to instability, as corporations operate globally but residents compete ever closer to the bottom of the world economic ladder. The alternative, competing at the top as the Scandinavians do, has been ruled out. These political responses are not always conscious, but neither are they inevitable, forced by autonomous events. They may be rooted in history, pressured by economics, and dependent on past politics, but they are choices nonetheless. Because they are choices, they can be changed. The collapse of New Orleans after Hurricane Katrina offers a good example. Governments at every level from the city to the White House responded ineptly, as their work was hampered by the damage done by earlier decades of poverty, discrimination, and inequality. The bankruptcies of corporate pension systems leave whole regions without wherewithal, and the collapse of subprime housing mortgages leave millions of strapped homeowners without options. Our argument is that as the problems push up to the national level, they may force leaders to recognize metropolitan crises as threatening to the nation as a whole.

There is plenty of stress to go around. Starting from the 1980s, and perhaps earlier, when the squeeze tightened from the global economy, public institutions were disinterested and unprepared to relieve the inevitable difficulties that confronted the poor. Corporate redeployment and government economizing ensured that city labor markets would turn sour, especially for basic jobs. The federal government cut funds for cities and poor people, and they reduced guarantees for benefits and services. Federal budget reductions hit hardest on public jobs and services first in central cities, later in inner suburbs. The tax revolt was managed by a new reactionary politics that coalesced after thirty-five years of White, middle-class suburban isolation. In the scramble to survive the lowered incomes and neighborhood decay that came after shutdowns, contractions, layoffs, and budget cuts, nearly everyone with any money or power tried to escape the city and inner suburbs and get ahead. Those with less were left behind and increasingly separated physically, occupationally, and socially from the main society. California's decline provides a telling example. Dominated by metropolitan Los Angeles and San Francisco, which comprise 70 percent of the population and are the second and fourth largest metropolitan areas in the country, the giant state passed its infamous Proposition 13 in 1978. This law hamstrings local governments with severe restrictions on property tax growth, thus denying adequate funding for anything but the most essential services, like police and fire protection. Proposition 13 found broad electoral support in suburban voters who ignored the needs of cities, in the process ignoring their own needs just down the road. The result is tragic. The Golden State tarnished as it fell from top national positions in education and transportation in the 1970s, to the very bottom (just above Mississippi and Louisiana) on such diverse rankings as student test scores and spending on highway maintenance.[17] The state may win top prize for prison expansion, hardly something to brag about.[18]

It is our argument that politics and economics can be reshaped, not only to respond more positively to worldwide events, but simultaneously to attack problems of domestic urban poverty. Such reshaping, we believe, will begin soon because the pressures resulting from urban segmentation, inequality, and isolation are spreading and will force not only community-level influentials and politicians to respond but also national institutions. Small businesses and neighborhood organizations, union locals and branch plants, civil rights associations and school reform groups, and many others find need for change. Multilocal coalitions, we argue, should be formed to press for reallocation of federal resources in favor of domestic needs and for redirection of the national economy in favor of workers and common citizens. Again, California provides an example, but this time a positive one. Stimulated by pressure from environmental advocates and its massive urbanized population, California now leads the nation in energy regulation and pollution-control policies, as it requires even out-of-state suppliers to utilize clean electric power-generating plants. The nationwide dissatisfaction with domestic affairs that played a role in the widespread Republican defeats in the 2006 midterm elections spread more heavily in 2008. If metropolitan and federal energies could be combined, then a successful attack might begin, to simultaneously undo problems of severe urban poverty and reorganize the national political economy.

The metropolis is not a passive recipient in this process. Reshaping the metropolis into a new vehicle for human and physical resource development is the best course for national economic revitalization. At the national level, action to reduce poverty will unleash new human capacity. At the local level, human resources can be reformed. Because problems of poverty are apparent and threatening, local authorities, local political institutions, and community organizations can be turned seriously to the task of dealing with poverty. As central city officials know, regardless of their politics or color, on their own they cannot succeed. But through cooperation with surrounding municipalities, and then state and national coalitions, and by means of other influences on national politics, local politicians can move toward success. New policies should be directed toward strengthening such possibilities. This is our central thesis.

We advance our arguments in five chapters. In this chapter we examine theories of inequality and poverty, explore concepts of race and racism, propose national requirements for urban success, and introduce basic theories. In Chapter 2 we document the appalling conditions of poor and minority people in central cities and inner suburbs, examining those conditions in relation to inequalities in the national distributions of income and wealth. In Chapter 3 we analyze the connections between the structure and movement of the new global economy, the regulatory options taken by the federal government, and the dilemmas of the poorest Americans. There we note how major corporations use tightly centralized control systems to manage widely dispersed, globalized markets and

production facilities. In Chapter 4 we extend the arguments and see how changing industrial patterns have worsened the structure of opportunities facing most
Americans in cities and inner suburbs, leaving increasing numbers of people in
precarious and poorly paying jobs or without jobs. We also look at the privatization of public assets that has shifted the burden for provision of public goods
from all users to the poor and the lower middle classes. Simultaneous dispersal
of jobs and centralization of management have removed good jobs and left
behind minorities and women and their children. With limited social contact
outside their embattled neighborhoods and with weakened social contracts tying
them to the larger community, these people have fallen into a poverty that is
persistent and leaves few routes for escape.

In Chapter 5 we lay out options for better federal policies, identify sources of
political support, and focus on new roles for local governments and community-
based organizations, finding what is innovative about them and what constrains
them. There we argue that people will take the initiative to transform national
politics only through local reconstruction and newly organized politics, involving grassroots and neighborhood groups in new ways. Our institutions need to
rechannel resources toward this domestic crisis. In the end, democratic participation and politics will have to give direction to the economy, or the nation
will stay divided politically and immobilized. We believe the sources for change
are to be found in coalitions formed from below.

A tension pervades this book, a conflict between two findings. On the one
hand, powerful global economic forces play a major role in determining the life
chances of American citizens. On the other hand, the situation of the poor—
which we see as threatening everyone with economic, social, and environmental
challenges—can be radically improved only through a staged process of local
empowerment, the formation of new political coalitions, and the consequent
reformulation of a national agenda.

At one extreme, we show pessimism about structural arrangements such as
globalized competitive markets, and we display deep concern that global economic forces should be better understood by the nation's policymakers. They
must learn how global affairs contribute to poverty in American cities, and they
must be able to trace more general inequality, job loss, and household instability through to the ways American corporations behave in a newly expanded,
more competitive, and highly integrated world market. People active in social
movements—those people working directly to alleviate the handicaps of poverty,
improve neighborhoods, and repair severed social connections—also need to
understand these connections. With a clear grasp of the structural impediments
to their programs, they will better be able to use moral arguments and to keep
sight of what, in the long run, they intend as improvements in our cities.

At the other extreme, we show optimism about the potential good influence
of human agency, through social movements, political action, and the like.
Changed local governments and coalitions of local forces should demand much
from Americans and their elites. Chances for challenging and improving federal

policy may seem remote. After all, it is not easy to violate the structural integrity of these global economic and political arrangements. But as urban planning theorist Peter Marris wrote years ago in *Community Planning and Conceptions of Change*, small changes in thinking sometimes lead to large changes in institutions. Or as André Gorz, the German leftist-turned-green, put it in his book *Strategy for Labor*, since nearly all social change comes via reform and not revolution, one must seek "non-reformist reforms," reforms that will empower, giving rise to pressure for more reform.

Despite the enormous concentrations of economic power, despite the remoteness of the decisions that determine the fate of a factory or a neighborhood, despite the subservience of political institutions to the requirements of corporations, despite the ideological manipulation embodied in control over newspapers and television, even despite the Supreme Court's sharp turn to the right, the system only works, as Marris wrote, because most people, most of the time, choose to go along with it. Thus our interest in collective resistance, in expansion of political participation, and in bridging the class and race boundaries that now keep sections of each metropolis separate from each other. The outpouring of electoral support for Barack Obama in November 2008 indicates high hopes. If federal efforts can support local innovations, we see enormous potential for causing change in the system.

Fighting Poverty, Expanding Social Inclusion, Enhancing Capability

Throughout this book, even though we would prefer to use broader concepts of social inclusion and exclusion, we often define poverty and inequality in *absolute money* terms. If a household or a family has too little money for buying the necessities of life, then, as the U.S. Census and the Bureau of Labor Statistics certify, they are *poor*. International institutions also use benchmark numbers in this way, to count the number of poor people. In China, Indonesia, Nigeria, and elsewhere, for example, less than two dollars per day per person may denote severe poverty.

The Human Development Index, reported annually in the United Nations' *Human Development Report*, combines measures of income, literacy, and life expectancy. This complexity makes the HDI a better indicator than income alone. Oddly, the international discussions have had little effect in the United States, where the official poverty line is still defined as it has been for forty-five years, equal to three times the money required for a family or household to purchase a decent basket of food. This absolute standard, updated annually for food-cost inflation, is rooted in a study by Mollie Orshansky published in the *Social Security Bulletin* in 1963. Even as an absolute poverty standard, this line, defined in Orshansky's article "Children of the Poor," is subject to various problems of interpretation. Although adjusted for household size, the standard fails to acknowledge taxes paid, public services provided, and special needs of particular

;. It fails to account for the fact that the income required to be above
cities could be as much as twice that required in rural areas, or in
ɒoston much higher than in St. Louis. It also fails to account for the fact that
acceptable household expenditures today may cost not three but six times as
much as food. All in all, the U.S. poverty line understates considerably the financial requirements for escaping poverty.

More commonly throughout the world, scholars and policymakers discuss
relative poverty, the positions different groups occupy as compared with others.
Experts examine how household money income is *distributed*, and when possible
they extend the examination to measure social inclusion and "capability." Such
ideas have been around at least since Adam Smith published *Wealth of Nations*,
in 1776. Smith noted, for example, that to win social respect, people need the
ability to take part in community affairs, so they must be able to dress well
enough to appear comfortably in public. To buy material to sew clothing appropriate for their society, they required adequate incomes. Today, to take part in
community affairs in the United States, members of most households require
access to a car, money to keep it repaired, and money to buy gas. The updated
poverty line does not measure relative levels and does not adjust sufficiently for
rising "social" needs. Such particulars often go unmentioned, but as we see in
Chapter 2, they can be powerful.

Europeans focus on relative poverty à la Adam Smith, to consider a household *socially excluded* (officially *poor*, using U.S. terminology) if its income is
below half the national median income. Below this level, the Europeans say, a
household cannot maintain a standard of living that the society regards as mini-
mally acceptable. If the income of a family or household is marginally higher,
between 50 percent and 60 percent of the national median, then the European
Union declares the family to be at "risk of poverty." This shift of attention from
absolute levels to relative distribution has the effect of redefining poverty constantly in terms of the nation's well-being. In another echo of Adam Smith, the
EU also requires its anti-poverty agencies to consider nonmonetary factors,
including problems of social isolation, low levels of participation, various forms
of disrespect and discrimination, and lack of social services and support. National
standards and official requirements are one thing, of course, and reality another.
But the adoption in European social policy of these relational and more inclusive
standards to measure social exclusion improves sharply on the rigidity of the U.S.
approach, which still measures absolute money poverty. European social scientists, statisticians, and governments have discussed these differences for more
than twenty-five years now.

Economist and Nobel laureate Amartya Sen and philosopher Martha Nussbaum expand these broader and relational notions of poverty and exclusion a
step further and speak of the *capabilities* of individuals and households. Nussbaum posits ten Central Human Capabilities as standards for measuring a society's achievement in eliminating poverty, supporting social justice, and encouraging full human functioning. Although she directs her remarks toward poor

Third World nations, her list of fundamental entitlements includes many items that should be of concern everywhere: a long life, bodily health, nourishment, shelter, and reproductive rights; protection against violence; the ability to use senses, imagination, and thought; an emotional space that allows for association; freedom from fear and anxiety; the ability to exercise practical reason, including liberty of conscience and religion; the freedom to assemble and speak politically; the dignity of nondiscrimination; and the right to property and protections against search and seizure.[19] As we turn our focus to shortcomings in U.S. cities, we find many of these entitlements missing. For example, a majority of children who attend public schools in the country's largest school districts fear daily encounters with violence. These districts are nearly all in central cities. The children are so anxious that they frequently stay away and miss school, contributing to their own failures. Narrow poverty measures cannot capture this sort of problem, so we need other measures.

Even when defined simplistically and narrowly, in terms of absolute money income, poverty in a modern society like the United States is a complex phenomenon, and it can be difficult to explain. Advocates of differing approaches to dealing with poverty, and by extension with social exclusion and lack of capability, hold three, usually competing but sometimes overlapping, ideas about the *causes* of poverty. These ideas direct attention to the behavior of the poor, to liberal public policy, or to economic structure. In other words, these divergent explanations of poverty call attention either to the individual and his or her personal or family problems, to temporary circumstances that may be corrected by public assistance, or to flaws in basic social structure and politics.

In the first concept, theorists view *poverty as personal pathology.* Poor people suffer from the defects of their own (pathological) activity. Policymakers and others who subscribe to this *behavioral* view concentrate on psychological and motivational inadequacies. The best known city-focused statement may be Edward Banfield's 1968 book, *The Unheavenly City.* Proponents used to argue that poverty arises because a permissive welfare state generates a large group of nonparticipants, marginal people, bums. The original, often more generous and sympathetic conceptualization of these ideas referred to a Culture of Poverty. Originating in social anthropology, this idea was aimed at the complexities of modernization and urbanization in former colonies and developing countries of what was called the Third World (after the Western industrialized nations, the First World, and the Soviet bloc, the Second). Some social scientists thought that family poverty was persistent because parents and communities passed on wrong values and attitudes to new generations.[20] Although subsequent researchers convincingly refuted these ideas, the notion has been repeatedly reused and adopted in superficial ways by conservatives (and especially neoconservatives) in advanced, industrial countries, most of all in the United States. These notions disconnect the plight of the poor not only from the responsibilities of others but also from the impediments of the situation. They do not allow room for thinking about either social exclusion or powerlessness. At worst, these ideas can be used to make allowances for racism, sexism, and selfish individualism, offering little to counteract the ethnocentric, reactionary logic of the street, thus blaming the victim. Some comments sting with stereotypical racial disdain, as they ignore the difficult, respectful lives of hardworking but poorly paid maids, health care aides, porters, and menial workers of all sorts: "Lower-class blacks lacked industry, lived for momentary erotic pleasure, and, in their mystique of soul, glorified the fashions of a high-stepping street life."[21]

Although neoconservatives still carelessly invoke the Culture of Poverty, the notion and its suggestion that the poor are irrational (and therefore to blame for their own problems) has been refuted and outmoded by excellent formal studies and criticism. These studies properly put the major blame for poverty not on poor individuals but instead on social structure, situation, and lack of opportunity.[22] A tradition in fiction testifies to the obstacles imposed on rational and well-organized poor people, obstacles missed by those who subscribe to demeaning stereotypes. Novelist James Baldwin long ago led us to imagine how a city's police and courts can entrap and then condemn innocent people. In Baldwin's story *If Beale Street Could Talk,* the main character is a young New York sculptor named Fony. Fony's dilemma is that in spite of his talent, honesty, and enterprise, he cannot escape the punishment inflicted by authorities who adopt the negative stereotype of the young Black man. We find this story repeated over and over by perceptive writers, and we find it verified in research, and—most unfortunately— we find it reported often in the daily press. The unrelenting hostility to Latino immigrants by one Long Island political leader encouraged community toughs to administer beatings and even to commit murder.[23]

In the United States, inequality almost inevitably involves race, especially in cities. Even though many Whites are poor, Blacks, Latinos, and American Indians, as well as some immigrant groups from Asia, *on average* have much lower incomes. "Since 1968, the year Martin Luther King Jr. was assassinated, the income gap between Blacks and Whites has narrowed by just three cents on the dollar." Median per capita income in 2005 was $16,629 for Blacks and $28,946 for Whites.[24] In the lower reaches of each income group, poor Blacks and Hispanics are drastically worse off, earning only about 10 percent of White incomes. Throughout the book, we need to work through the thicket of race and class.

Racism, when it functions structurally, does not require actively racist individuals to cause discrimination but can be perpetuated by institutions, systems, and policies. Thus conventional police behavior in New York City emasculates Fony catastrophically, and none of his friends or loved ones can marshal enough power to defend him against the standard bureaucratic practices that augment the original damage, even though at first it is inflicted by a single individual, just one bad cop. Despite the oft repeated misconception that racism no longer exists, substantial research and reporting of popular experience show that racism is alive and well.[25] Most Whites see racism solely as "prejudice," biased actions taken by actively racist individuals, but people of color also see racism as "systematic and institutionalized," as an element of inequality. Whites and people of color often do not agree even on what the word "racism" means.[26] While overt racism has become much less prevalent and racial discrimination and segregation are finally illegal, Whites often fail to recognize that a modern form of racism exists—what Lawrence Bobo calls "laissez faire racism," a subtle force that "relies upon the market and informal racial bias to recreate . . . structured racial inequality."[27] Since Whites do not experience this kind of discrimination and, moreover, may have limited interaction with people of color, they have few opportunities to acknowledge and understand racism comprehensively.[28] Many Whites also resist discussion of race and racism because they believe such discussion itself to be a racist activity. They cling to "colorblindness"—the idea that because we should all be judged equally regardless of race, we should refuse even to notice or discuss difference. Our society's oversimplified rhetoric on race takes Martin Luther King Jr.'s dream—that we should "some day" judge our fellow citizens "by the content of their character, not by the color of their skin"—to mean that in the present we should feign obliviousness to racial differences and hope they go away. This attitude immobilizes dialogue about the ways in which race and racism continue to diminish the life chances, health, and prosperity of many people of color. This philosophy also causes many Whites to oppose constructive efforts to treat people differently, including those who attempt to redress de facto inequality.[29] Thus the Supreme Court, in pursuit of a "colorblind constitution," turned *Brown v. Board of Education* on its head. *Brown* had finally outlawed school segregation, perhaps most famously prompting President Dwight Eisenhower to send federal troops to protect Black students as they entered Little Rock High School in 1957. When Seattle and Louisville proposed popular and modest programs for desegregation fifty years later, the Court said no, rejecting *Brown*'s logic of scrutinizing racially conscious municipal policy and instead striking down exceedingly modest school integration plans because they would use "measures that take explicit account of a student's race."[30]

Oppressed or unfortunate people themselves throw up obstacles that reinforce false stereotypes. Positioned at the bottom, where the society itself is most unfair, they sometimes behave in ways that appear to be—and often are—self-destructive. To reject the stereotype, one must argue that these oppressed people can imagine or find no other choice.[31] In the extreme, as Jonathan Kozol argues in *Rachel and Her Children,* many of them (the big-city homeless in this case) end up themselves believing they are worthless because that is how they are treated. Homeless populations have a "culture" that is related not to the street, as though they live there by unconstrained choice, but to the social networks in which they must operate. In some cases, the homeless are refugees from institutions, so they use the street as a point of congregation. They want to be free, in full view so as to be offered some protection, rather than institutionalized and brutalized. In other cases, homelessness dictates a lifestyle difficult to overcome through the use of only the external remedies of shelter and food. The underlying personal reality is very difficult. These people are not worthless, and most often they behave reasonably, given the limited range of accessible options, their restricted backgrounds and skills, and the dangers inherent in experimentation, such as seeking a new and distant job.[32]

Elements associated with the notion of a culture of poverty still play a role, in practical matters as well as in theory. To help move into the mainstream those people whose "adaptive" behavior increases their own (and others') difficulties, caring institutions and individuals must provide assistance. Behavior modification, for example, can help control drug addiction and alcoholism (but these problems are not confined to the poor). Whatever the utility in particular cases, however, this sort of behavioral approach is not a fruitful path for our discussion. As we argue, it is more useful for us to examine ways to change the situation, not to change people's attitudes. We agree with William Julius Wilson that we should not "postulate that ghetto-specific practices become internalized, take on a life of their own, and therefore continue to influence behavior even if opportunities for mobility improve." We believe, along with Wilson, that more equal access to better jobs and other improvements in the structure of equality would cut down on counterproductive behaviors and "would also make their transmission by precept less efficient."[33] Even the neoconservative researcher Lawrence Mead reminds us that poor people are not lazy: "The poor accept work along with other mainstream social norms. . . . They do not contest the work principle. They are not radicals seeking social change. There is simply a larger gap between their professed norms and actual behavior than there is for most people. The inclination to avoid demeaning labor is hardly confined to the disadvantaged."[34]

This leads us to the second view, also quite common, which holds that *incident and accident cause poverty.* Those who hold this view think cutbacks in social subsidies cause the growing problems of the poor. Thus advocates of social responsibility resist reductions (or promote expansion) of national and local resources devoted to the promotion of equity and equality.

Throughout much U.S. history, certainly from the end of World War II until the 1970s, it was not unreasonable to envision rising tides, lifted boats, and an ample supply of life preservers or safety nets to rescue those "accidentally" thrown overboard. In the views of Presidents John Kennedy and Lyndon Johnson throughout the 1960s, federal programs should assist people with very poor skills, those suffering the bad luck of illness or accident, people in declined rural areas, and a few in inner-city neighborhoods. Optimism and increasing affluence accompanied this social and political sense of responsibility The struggling poor, trade unions, neighborhood organizations, and aggrieved victims of racial and ethnic discrimination kept pressing their demands. In a continuation of the tendency toward social democracy (and social inclusion) from the 1930s, interrupted temporarily by the reactionary anti-Communism of the late 1940s and 1950s, what some call the American Social Contract provided not only good salaries and benefits for union members in industry and for public employees, but also transfer payments, gradual expansion of entitlements, and the elaboration of public services and protections for most workers, along with a steadily increasing share of economic output to labor rather than capital. Programs were generally effective in dealing with the problems of the elderly or of married couples or families who were socially or physically isolated. These programs limited (but did not eliminate) poverty, led to expectations of further improvement, and even included some caps on extravagance, such as progressive taxation. (The top marginal federal tax rate for the richest filers was above 90 percent until 1963, at about 70 percent until the early 1980s; it dropped to 35 percent by 2004, with larger reductions still on estate taxes and capital gains taxes.) With public policies directed at the provision of safety nets, poverty still existed, but it was less onerous and it was perceived as temporary. The opportunity structure was seen by many to be strong enough to allow energetic people to move into decent, rewarding life conditions.

Exponents of this incident/accident view tend to think public programs can remedy poverty easily, rather mechanically, by the provision of short-term or extended relief. In recent decades, sad to say, the evidence has been mostly negative, in good part because political difficulties have led to limitations on funding and maintenance for such programs. As the economy was being restructured and the nature of public policy changed to respond to global economic challenges, budgets tightened and legislatures slashed funds. Reductions began with the Nixon administration in the early 1970s, with ups and mostly downs continuing through Presidents Gerald Ford, Jimmy Carter, Ronald Reagan, and George Bush senior. The Clinton administration made the most dramatic single move when it dismantled the family safety net. Established by the Social Security Act in 1935, Assistance for Families with Dependent Children (known as AFDC, originally AFC, or just "Welfare") was replaced in 1997 by Temporary Assistance for Needy Families (TANF), which imposed stiffer work requirements and a five-year limit on relief payments. The G. W. Bush administration proposed drastic reductions and implemented cuts for most social supports and transfer programs. TANF funds for child care fell 20 percent, from $4 billion in 2000 to $3.2 billion in 2005. Increased restrictions, such as the requirement of getting a job no matter what, have lowered rolls. The 2008 budget proposal included heavy cuts in social service block grants and no increases for child care and development block grants. Early Obama education budgets reversed the downward slide,[35] but congressional resistance and fiscal pressures persist.

Throughout the entire period, few programs worked successfully to remove families from poverty. Even disability payments and unemployment benefits have strict limits, and conservatives continually target them for cuts. The chief historical successes are the long-term, large-scale reduction in poverty among the elderly that resulted from Social Security pensions and, much later, improvements to health from Medicare and Medicaid benefits. The White House threat of 2005 to privatize, weaken, and diminish Social Security guarantees was turned back, neoconservatives transferred the focus of their budget-cutting attention to Medicare and Medicaid, and then they lost the national elections of 2006 and 2008.

In the liberal, macrosocial view that constitutes mainstream thinking, poverty simply reflects temporary weakness in the economy, to be corrected by (also temporary) public generosity. This view is based on the correct observation that a strong demand for labor, to create numerous and well-paid jobs, is a necessary basic factor in any fight against poverty. These approaches recognize the importance of generous unemployment insurance and health and retirement benefits. The political right wing has successfully challenged these benefits, so that many aspects of the U.S. response to globalization of the economy work against a persistent and strong demand for labor. These problems lead us, later in the book, to advocate simultaneous battles for better economic policy and against budget cuts that tolerate poverty and the growing isolation of impoverished communities. The severe demands of the recession of 2007–2009 and the Wall Street meltdown may make such improvements more rather than less possible, but the raw situation presents serious problems. Underemployment (discussed in Chapter 3)— adding up the officially unemployed, those who have given up and stopped looking for jobs, and those who work part time but want full-time work—causes poverty, and it rises and falls with the economy.

In the third and most comprehensive view, observers see *persistent structural poverty*. In this view, to which we subscribe, with important reservations to be explained below, certain patterns of large-scale socioeconomic arrangements create poverty and prevent its alleviation. Some arrangements create more poverty than others, and developments in the United States have moved for some years in the wrong direction. Students of the international economy mark the beginnings of a new era for the United States with the advent of an intensified global capitalism, beginning as early as the mid-1960s. Wall Street banker C. Douglas Dillon, after all, cut the top marginal income tax rate from 91 percent to 70 percent while he served as President Kennedy's secretary of the treasury in the early 1960s. President Nixon gave formal end to postwar global rules when he took the United States off the gold standard in 1971. President Reagan cut top tax rates further, to 50 percent and again to 38.5 percent in 1982 and 1987, respectively. Since then the rate has settled at about 35 percent, and the Bush II administration provided gifts to those who hold enormous wealth, by cutting taxes on corporations, estates, and investments. More recently, with further challenges to the dollar's stature as the global currency, the rise of Chinese commodity exports, the shift overseas of manufacturing and even service jobs (one portion of "outsourcing"), and the autonomy of transnational financial empires, a globalized economy has become ascendant. The most agreed-on date for a sharp shift in direction is 1973 or 1974, after the first global oil price shock, when a new world economic pattern began to take hold. The effects of these changes were unmistakable by the late 1970s, when global difficulties led the Carter administration to cut back on urban aid. Since then global change has accelerated, and metropolitan fortunes across the United States have more and more depended on international flows of goods, services, finance capital, and corporate investment, and finally even on the international movement of people.

Perhaps the most striking feature in the minds of many Americans is the federal government's unwillingness—or inability—to exercise clear and independent influence so as to turn the domestic economy in redistributive directions. Part of this reluctance stems from the increasing difficulties confronting the Treasury Department and the Federal Reserve in their use of Keynesian economic tools to control inflation, unemployment, and interest rates simultaneously. The old relationships no longer hold, largely because the United States is now much more integrated into a global economy, with numerous powerful nations participating indirectly in the U.S. domestic economy. Part of the balance of power now lies with foreign markets, corporations, banks, and governments, as well as with U.S.-based corporations themselves operating overseas. Foreign central banks and even central banking authorities, such as the Chinese, who hold claims on the Treasury, can now manipulate U.S. economic forces in the same way that U.S. multinational corporations, the Treasury, and the Federal Reserve System have for many years manipulated others' economies.[36]

This globalization of the American economy has forced massive changes in the industrial structure of U.S. cities, reinforced by federal policy and in most cities only weakly resisted by local politics.[37] Patterns of international migration have changed, and so have labor markets. With few exceptions, minority populations in central cities and inner suburbs find themselves more than ever victimized by poverty, marginalized and exploited, pushed aside when they are not needed or employed at low wages when they are. Rising credentialism excludes those who lack formal education and training from good jobs, and anti-immigrant (or anti-Latino) politics reinforces the discriminatory effects. An uneven and undependable labor demand has always threatened the poor, but the global changes of recent years have made the market even less forgiving.[38]

In today's difficult world, poverty isolates a growing group of racially distinct Americans who are socially disconnected from the greater society, educationally handicapped, and institutionally victimized not only by labor markets but by the social-welfare and penal systems. Severe poverty is built into the economic and political structure, generated by three interrelated forces. The first is a set of long-term, intergenerational arrangements that disconnect some people from the mainstream society, mainly through lack of employment, resulting in physical, social, and political isolation. The second force arises from educational and social handicaps that prevent potential employees from entering the transformed high-tech, high-touch workforce, where technical and office skills and personal presentation are preeminently important. The third force is institutionalization by welfare, prisons, and related bureaucracies that victimize and stigmatize the poor and make them dependent on public charity rather than help them participate in generating resources for themselves or their families. All three of these forces are buttressed by changes in national policies in response to a global economic integration that makes national actions less effective and less evidently useful for private corporations. In these changed circumstances of a rising and desperate poverty, residual assistance has become insufficient and inappropriate. A more direct and structurally appropriate set of polices has to be forged, aimed at the root problem and not just at its manifestations.

The Effects of Inequality—Risk and Citizenship

The poor suffer directly from inequality. In their poverty they suffer loss of health, social respectability, self-regard, and many opportunities to enjoy life. In association with these problems, and reinforcing them, they suffer from stress.[39] These evident effects constitute central topics in this book. But the nonpoor suffer also, because inequality spoils the society for all. Highly unequal societies must invest heavily in systems that neither enhance productivity nor improve living but merely provide protection. Highly unequal societies spend heavily for exclusion and repression, to pay for police, prisons, judicial systems, and gated communities. They spend even for new transportation and housing infrastructure as part of a pattern of physical avoidance. Examples from Brazil and other extremely unequal developing countries show what can happen when big cities organize themselves mainly to protect rich people from the poor, using high walls for physical exclusion, fences as key architectural elements, and armed guards as a standard requirement for urban design.[40] In the United States, internally unequal when compared with European social democracies, such patterns for exclusion and protection have become more common—and more costly and more corrosive.

The nonpoor majority also suffer, although less directly, through a general, nationwide loss in productivity, as the poor, with inferior educations and low skills, cannot contribute much to the economy. The low-income majority suffer additionally, as the unequal society fails to make general provision for such things as universal health insurance, thus driving up costs, uncertainty, and anxiety for all. Large numbers of recent college graduates in the United States, for example, even many who are members of the upper middle class or expect soon to be, find themselves unable to afford health insurance, risking financial disaster from illness or injury. At least in concept, these costs and losses are measurable in monetary terms. Further losses, almost impossible to quantify, arise because of the unpleasantness or even dangers involved in a society with great disparities of well-being. Although some might argue that the rich take pleasure from their isolation and their chance to purchase deference from a low-wage servant class, surely the middle class endures unpleasantness in the perception (if not also the reality) of endangerment, the need to avoid problematic zones of the city, and the invidious contrasts that demean their ordinary lives and incomes compared with those of the much advertised and celebrated upper class. One may find displeasure even in the certainty of a steady job if it requires work as part of an increased force of repressive police and jailers. One aspect involves an emergent form of local politics, of small-town support for prison construction, in anticipation of new jobs for jailers and new contracts for local suppliers. Indeed, in economically depressed areas, such as the decayed resort area in New York's Catskill Mountains, the only revived towns are those near prisons, where guards, their families, employees of supply firms, and even prisoners' families make up a new (and ethnically noticeable) population.

Finally, theory and tentative evidence suggest that inequality harms even the health status of the nonpoor. British epidemiologist Richard Wilkinson makes such claims most forcefully, providing international health statistics to suggest that among rich nations, as inequality rises, health status falls for all. Wilkinson and his colleagues identify three major psychosocial risk factors through which social inequality contributes to illness even for the nonpoor: low social status, including weak control over one's affairs; weak social affiliations; and high stress in early life.[41] Yale economist Jacob Hacker points to risk itself as a deep economic problem in the United States, a problem that may afflict not just the poor or minority persons but the majority:

Economic risk is a lot like a hurricane. Hurricanes strike powerfully and suddenly. They rip apart what they touch: property, landscape, and lives. They are common enough to affect many, yet rare enough still to shock. And although they can be prepared for, they cannot be prevented. Some people will inevitably suffer and require help; others will be spared. Recovery is inevitably traumatic and slow. And so it is with families whose lives have been touched by economic risk. What happens in an instant may change a life forever.[42]

The highest risks fall on the poor. Just as Hurricane Katrina inflicted unequal burdens, so do Hacker's increased economic risks add burdens in the absence of protective social guarantees. Given their low status, weak control, and loneliness, it is easy to imagine the poor becoming sick. Ample evidence demonstrates that low status causes bad health. As one would expect, rich industrial countries provide clean water and sanitation generally, so the health disadvantages of poverty have been strongly mitigated. In most advanced Western democracies, national health systems extend this good effect. In the United States, however, as suggested by Michael Moore's movie *Sicko,* health status is tied to income. To take but one example, while life expectancy for White men in the United States was 75.3 years in 2003, for much poorer African American men in Harlem, who on average have much lower incomes *and* inferior health care, life expectancy was below 65, lower than that of Bangladesh. It is not just a matter of people over 60 having different chances of aging into their golden years, but a situation of pervasive community influences. For Black males in Harlem, higher infant mortality and homicide rates exert a huge influence in bringing down the average.[43]

What Wilkinson and Hacker argue in their separate accounts, however, is broader still. High inequality and the attendant growth of risk carry penalties for whole populations. The individual and family costs are borne not only by the poor but by members of all social classes. These burdens are on the rise, and they affect everyone, crushing expectations even for children of the middle and upper class: "Over the last generation, we have witnessed a massive transfer of economic risk from broad structures of insurance . . . onto the fragile balance sheets of American families. . . . The Great Risk Shift has dashed . . . expectations, transforming the economic circumstances of American families *from the bottom of the economic ladder to its highest rungs.*"[44]

Although researchers continue to debate statistical findings that show such effects of social inequality on physical health, and especially on the health of the well-off, the broader deleterious effects of social inequality would seem not in doubt. People in subordinate positions at work, without much control and subject to the close authority of others, suffer feelings of hostility and stress—leading to bad health effects.[45] Given that employment instability across the economy spreads widely the risk of losing one's job, income, and status, these effects threaten many who are not poor. Even homicide rates, which account mainly for killing among associates, friends, and relatives, seem to rise with greater income inequality. A cross-section study comparing all U.S. states and Canadian provinces shows close correlation, with murder rates rising as inequality increases in state or provincial distributions of income.[46] Similarly, homicide rates vary internationally along with measures of inequality: the higher the income inequality, the higher the murder rate.[47]

Finally, inequality corrodes political participation and the effectiveness of democracy. As Justice Louis Brandeis said: "We can have a democracy in this country, or we can have great wealth concentrated in the hands of the few. We cannot have both." In the United States, as we have seen, only 60 percent and 62 percent of the eligible adult population actually voted even in the presidential elections of 2004 and 2008, respectively. In off-year elections voting rates fall as low as 42 percent, and in special elections such as those for local school boards, voting rates are sometimes vanishingly small, frequently in the single digits. Among the rich, nearly everyone votes, at least in presidential elections, but the rate drops steadily with income. Among the poorest 20 percent of adults, fewer than 40 percent typically vote in presidential elections, leaving six of every ten *not* voting, thus negating their putative citizenship.[48] These measures ignore the large numbers of resident noncitizens and ineligible felons, neither of whom can vote. Voting rates exhibit racial bias: 30 percent of eligible African Americans and 40 percent of Latinos are not registered. More than 5 million felons cannot vote. Nonparticipation impoverishes politics overall: agendas are set without the involvement of significant segments of the population, and decisions are taken without their agreement.[49]

Notions of Race and Ethnicity

Race is central to the way things turn out even if race is now excluded as a target and constitutionally denied as an element of public policy. Americans celebrate their multiculturalism, but the mixing is superficial. Although formal discrimination against middle-class men and women of color has diminished markedly, in every metropolis nearly all residential areas remain profoundly divided by race. Americans care deeply about race. On March 23, 2007, the *New York Post* printed two front-page items centered on what Columbia University law professor Patricia Williams calls biologized abnormality. The first offered "a stunning mother–child portrait" of the "magical" interracial adoption by White actor Angelina Jolie of a child from Vietnam. The second reported a Park Avenue fertility clinic blunder that "left a family devastated—after a black baby was born to a Hispanic woman and her White husband." The doctor said not to worry, the child will "lighten up," but the parents did worry, suing the company that fertilized the mother's egg with the wrong sperm.[50]

Biologists and anthropologists conclude that race is an almost empty physiological concept, void of real scientific meaning, hardly measurable, insignificant. As the Jamaicans say, we are "one blood," whatever the superficial differences, such as skin color. Genetic codes of individuals may be useful for tracing ancestry, perhaps to connect family trees with the continents of forebears, but statistical variations *within* "racial" groups make nonsense of any but the most superficial "racial" identifiers. True as these firmly scientific statements are, based on genetics, they fly in the face of social experience. Any comprehensive view of the U.S. metropolis must account for something commonly called race or ethnicity. With the crucial exception of indigenous First Peoples or Native American Indians, all others in the Americas (not just the United States) trace their recent ancestry to other continents, other cultures, languages, and "racial" groups. Consistent with this historical reality, publicly promoted conceptions of the United States typically entail an ideology of newness, inclusion, and diversity. Various authentically American "races," ethnicities, and historical cultures express themselves daily. In one familiar ideological representation, to be American is to be an amalgam of others. The resident population in nearly every U.S. metropolis displays wide ethnic and "racial" diversity, an unusual situation internationally.[51] Race may not exist in genetics, but racial variety is a bedrock American social reality.[52]

Given that each of these perceptions is supported with broad and deep evidence—race does not exist but at the same time race lies at the center of the structure of U.S. society—how can one proceed? The answer, available to thoughtful scientists and social scientists at least since the work of W.E.B. DuBois in the early twentieth century, calls on the idea of social construction. Social groups, especially dominant social groups, have "constructed" race, manufactured it, so to speak, as a *social category*. Although no one can define race or measure race, all Americans know perfectly well what "it" is. This knowledge complements the observation that *minority groups*—those whom "Whites" categorize as *not White*—play key roles in the U.S. metropolis.

Cities—in this case we refer to those places people have come to call "inner cities" or "central cities," especially the most populous of them—have long been identified as places for "minority" populations to live, people whom statisticians used to label with the pejorative "non-White." Those minorities (Black, Hispanic/Latino, Asian, Native American Indian, and now, in the newest Census categories, people who check off multiple identifiers, including many recent immigrants) have grown to constitute significant *majorities*. When they are counted together, they numerically dominate half the largest cities.[53] In ten big U.S. cities minority

persons make up between three-quarters and nine-tenths of the residential population.[54] As minority populations have grown, non-Hispanic White populations
have practically stood still or even shrunk, except in those very few cities that
receive heavy European immigration. This demographic evidence alone reveals
a severe city/suburb "racial" divide.[55]

At the same time, persons of color are moving to suburbs in large numbers,
so that about half the minority persons who live in the largest 102 metropolitan
areas now live in suburbs, that is, outside the municipal boundaries of the central
city. By 2000, the suburbs themselves on average were already about one-quarter
minority, and the growth continues. What this minority suburbanization *means*
is a question we address later in the book, as we grapple to interpret ever more
complex metropolitan patterns of land use. For now, we observe that three geo-
metric facts—growing or even stable metropolitan populations, declining densities, and fixed central city boundaries—*must* combine to push people beyond
the central municipal boundaries, therefore to the suburbs. If densities decline
rapidly, which they have, then this suburbanizing push is strong. The result: more
than 70 percent of all Americans now live in the suburbs, and suburbs contain
the majority of jobs, classrooms, stores, and most other institutions and activities. In the absence of strict racial prohibitions, these three facts of urban growth
have caused minority populations to locate in the suburbs.[56] Questions arise: Has
the suburban dream arrived for minorities? Is the U.S. metropolis multicultural?
Two answers are necessary.

In spite of massive minority suburbanization, racial differences still dictate the
layout of many metropolitan areas. At the metropolitan scale, a simple suburb/
city distinction often remains appropriate, but not always. The suburbs, too, have
fragmented spaces, many as badly isolated as inner cities are from their suburbs.
Gary, Indiana, for example, originally built by Judge Gary to move his U.S. Steel
Corporation and its unruly workers away from the union-supporting streets of
Chicago, functions today as a suburb of Chicago, a component of the metropolis,
yet it is not White. Instead, it is dark skinned, 90 percent African American and
Hispanic.[57] At the same time, considering the Gary area with its surroundings as
a separate metropolitan area, we find that only 17 percent of *its* suburban population is minority, while the great majority of its suburbanites are White.[58] If this
double segregation is not apartheid, what is? The courts no longer enforce such
racial separations, or segregations, but so many other institutions encourage the
separations that they persist. They are so built-in, normal, and expected that
many people hardly notice. In metropolitan areas throughout the country, city
and suburban populations contrast sharply by race. In Boston the city is 34 percent minority but the suburbs only 9 percent. In Rochester, New York, the city is
55 percent minority but the suburbs only 8 percent. In St. Louis the contrast is
47 percent versus 16 percent, and in Knoxville it is 20 percent versus 5 percent.
These cases show minority concentrations from three to seven times as high in
the cities as in the suburban rings combined—these concentrations *after* such a
strong trend toward suburbanization of minorities that a leading demographer

tried to coin the term "melting-pot suburbs."[59] As illustrated by the Gary case, when measured with finer geographical divisions of neighborhoods and individual suburbs, segregation statistics rise dramatically. Some very poor suburbs look like the worst neighborhoods in the old core city, saddled with the problems that plague the bottom of the U.S. social order, in places where so many minority persons must reside—problems such as drug sales, gangs, and crime.

In other metropolitan areas, those where minority populations have greater weight overall, the city-to-suburb contrasts are lessened but hardly absent. In New Orleans before Katrina the city was 71 percent minority, the suburbs 30 percent. In Atlanta the city versus suburb concentration of minority persons is 67 percent versus 33 percent. In both cases, however, as local observers well know, neighborhood-by-neighborhood and block-by-block racial segregation is very high. In metropolitan areas with the heaviest immigration of Asians and Hispanics (including Los Angeles, New York, Chicago, Washington, and many southwestern metropolitan areas) minorities are suburbanizing rapidly, and in a few of these areas, where immigrants are proportionately very numerous, minority populations are of similar proportions in city and suburbs. In Phoenix, for example, minority persons, overwhelmingly Hispanic, constitute 37 percent of the city population and 30 percent of the suburbs.[60]

Throughout U.S. history, from the subordination of Indians, through the enslavement of Africans, through the exclusion of Asians and various spasms of "ethnic" European immigration, the country has constituted its class structure on the experiences and construction of racial difference. Since the beginning, Whites as householders, small business owners, and later corporate managers have employed racial and ethnic distinctions to extract productive energy from subordinated residents and employees alike. Municipal governments, nearly always dominated by Whites, have everywhere enforced social distinctions that protect White-only residential areas against intrusions by people of color and provide superior public services to Whites.[61] Federal laws, from the constitutional allocation of three-fifths of the slaves to be counted for purposes of representation, to Jim Crow laws segregating public facilities in the South and private real estate nationally, to the Supreme Court refusal today to recognize de facto school segregation, have likewise enhanced the privileges of Whites and kept them isolated and insulated from people of color. Now, in the twenty-first century, schools and prisons—two of the nation's premier institutions of social inequality—have become even more thoroughly racialized. As we see in each subsequent chapter, analysis of inequality in U.S. cities cannot proceed without consideration of race, and vice versa.

A Broad View—Extending the Separations

We take a broad view to observe how national industry, the domestic economy, and politics have become entangled internationally. Global-scale social and technical transitions have combined with ever more complicated domestic politics to reverse long-term national trends. Positive tendencies toward the reduction of poverty and social exclusion, equalization of resource distribution, and augmentation of the middle class, incomplete though they were from the late 1930s through the 1970s, have turned negative. Economic and political forces no longer combat poverty, *they generate poverty*—and in turn that poverty and the social inequality of which it is part further complicate and compromise many attempts to solve both domestic and international troubles in the economy, the environment, and politics.

To arrive at this broader view, which connects neighborhood, city, metropolis, and nation with international conditions and events, we see poverty and inequality in several dimensions, which we try to capture in a single word, *separation*. By this usage of *separation* we mean to include ideas of social segmentation, economic division, and sharp geographic isolation. We see separation as a matter not just of degree, but of kind, a process like the melting pot in reverse. It is like phase transition, or symmetry breaking, in physics. As water gets colder, it changes gradually, by degree, but then suddenly the homogeneous substance gets too cold to survive, and some of the water turns into ice. In the later years of the twentieth century, American society was like water just above freezing, dangerously near a point where it might dissociate into separate parts.

In the first decade of the twenty-first century, some chunks of social ice seem already to have formed and drifted off, separated from the main fluid of social life. The 2.5 million men and women who fill U.S. prisons and jails, by far the largest prison population in any country, are disproportionately poor, Black, and Latino, frozen out by a racially biased "War on Drugs."[62] Other persons of every race, but disproportionately Blacks and Latinos, are locked into low-wage jobs or the informal cash economy without benefits or prospects of advancement, facing high risks of being poor, living in a neighborhood with weak municipal services, sending kids to a lousy school, or even being homeless. Many poor men and women looking for a way out have gone into the military, only to hit a dead end, sometimes literally. U.S. troops have been sent to wage unpopular and unwinnable wars overseas, as political ineptitude has enabled unseen enemies to manipulate anti-American symbols. More privileged citizens and officials, in their ignorance, hostility, and negligence, isolate and denigrate not only the prisoners and the returned warriors, but also the warriors' old neighborhoods, thus further harming the people left behind.

U.S. industry in every form faces huge challenges from abroad, just as U.S. communities face challenges from burgeoning immigration, but neither the nation's diplomacy nor its domestic policy seems up the task, so business firms and communities freeze up and fail. Many bastions of industry, such as the major auto firms and airlines, teeter on bankruptcy or actually fail. Their fragility became evident to all in the Wall Street debacle of 2008–2009 and its lingering aftermath.

U.S. consumers have the highest levels of debt in peacetime history, yet economic policies leave growing numbers of bankrupt individuals and families adrift. American families are stressed to unprecedented degrees. Many households send more members into the workforce to try to maintain an acceptable standard of living. Between 2000 and 2005 millions of families refinanced their homes to maintain lifestyles rather than invest in education or economic improvement. They used borrowed funds for repayment of other debts and consumer spending, as well as home improvements, taxes, and risky investments. Already in 2006 foreclosures were up 43 percent from 2005, and later they exploded. The holes in the real estate market push families to the brink.[63] The subprime mortgage crisis has hit minority homeowners with special force, wiping out what for many was their first chance at accumulating family capital.

Despoliation of natural resources grows apace, and as global warming continues, scientists predict increasingly violent weather fluctuations, leading to more natural disasters. These crucial problems have found response not in thoughtful analysis by leading politicians and corporate leaders but in degenerative and oversimplified "culture wars," both at home and abroad. Such national failures, we contend, connect intimately to a failure to grapple with metropolitan problems and an inability to make the most of metropolitan opportunities. The Obama election might have provided a chance for serious reflection and reconsideration, but the pressure of other events, domestic and international, has kept urban problems off the president's appointments calendar.

We find it unsettling how often Americans (we include ourselves) unconsciously allow the use of segmentation, inequality, and isolation to hide poor people, objectify them, and rationalize their conditions. As the poor are thus separated, poverty removes itself, and poor people become more distant from the nonpoor. This distance itself makes inequality more palatable to those who are better off, and the separation further increases. Social distance reinforced by geographical isolation is the new metropolitan form. As metropolitan areas have grown and segmented in formal ways, and as individualized technologies of the automobile and the internet connection have spread the nonplace realms of social connection, residential groups from elderly singles to households with schoolchildren find themselves not only removed from others but typically ignorant of the conditions of their fellow metropolitan residents. Suburbanites fear inner-city neighborhoods, their fears surely abetted by racial differences. It works the other way, too. In Portland, Oregon, city planners found that even where issues of racial and class separations were largely absent, most city residents knew nothing about their suburban neighbors on the rural boundary, the needs of those people and their communities, their interests, their lifestyles. For the most part, they did not know, really, of the others' *existence*. How much the worse, when differences of race and class are prominent. The fear of others rises as the constant barrage of crime reporting depicts people of color as perpetrators but fails to show that most victims are of the same color as their attackers, and that most live in the same desperate neighborhoods, distant from the middle-class enclaves.

Perhaps more than ever before, in the early years of the twenty-first century, American leaders have found these separations to be pushed on them by the force of events. As they attempt what sometimes seems very difficult, to promote competition in an ever more globalized economy, they find it convenient to ignore at least this one set of domestic concerns. Neighborhood isolation makes it more acceptable to make negative political use of differences in race, social background, and place. In turn these practices then build on discrimination against poor and minority persons in offers of employment, the assignment of status, and the distribution of income. These practices also encourage discriminatory provision of housing, public services, and neighborhood quality. The various inequalities then further extend the separations. Cleveland mayor Michael White suggested in 1991 that the majority in America wanted to leave the city behind: "Big Cities are becoming a code name for a lot of things," he said, "for minorities, for crumbling neighborhoods, for crime, for everything America has moved away from."[64] City Year, like a domestic Peace Corps, objectifies the population of the inner city as if it were the population of an underdeveloped country. Now minorities, neighborhood decay, and crime have spread from the city to the so-called inner-ring suburbs. Although some areas enjoy improved situations, in which poor residents have moved away from neighborhoods previously overwhelmed by poverty, the overall situation has hardly improved. Rather, the very poor have been reshuffled, sorted into a different geographical pattern, still out of work or with too-low pay, some of them still doing drugs, drinking, or selling drugs, still causing their neighbors problems and unable to solve their own. Often the emptier neighborhoods, in which the poorest residents are left behind, have become still worse. Neighborhood murders, called "the rage thing" by the Milwaukee police chief in 2006, already seem to have reversed citywide declines. Murder rates that had begun to fall in the early 1990s have since reversed and risen in Boston, Philadelphia, Kansas City, Milwaukee, Tulsa, Charlotte, Houston, Nashville, and San Francisco.[65]

We are witnessing the ruins of the affluent society.[66] In the 1952 anti-utopian novel *Player Piano*, Kurt Vonnegut imagines an America divided in two. At the top, a tiny group of managers, engineers, and technocrats use their brains and positions to guide the future and protect their privileges. At the bottom, an underclass of "wreaks" and "wrecks" do the dirty, dull, and unskilled work; serve in the repressive army; or just hang around, unemployed, drinking, miserable. Fifty years earlier H. G. Wells predicted an even sharper class division in *The Time Machine*, with the underground vestiges of the English working class devouring the above-ground vestiges of their rulers. Is it possible that these writers foresaw real, not fictionalized, futures? Will the exaggerated inequalities that now separate top professionals and business executives from ordinary employees and them in turn from the underemployed constitute a prominent component of the future? Is America beginning to retreat, divide in two or three? Is the nation eroding the middle-class gains of a half century, tearing up the foundations of the future? If evidence about the depth of division rending the middle class is worrying, then at the *bottom* of the social class structure the evidence of debilitating poverty, isolation, and exclusion is conclusive. These are not questions anymore of race alone. The Black and Latino middle classes are becoming as distant from the ills of poverty as the White middle class. As a result, those with limited resources find few capable champions who empathize with their plight.

We see divisive dichotomies everywhere in American society, but especially in the metropolis. Corporations build magnificent office towers where they manage worldwide networks of factories, offices, sales rooms, and high finance. These global headquarters rise above the latest "public" squares, the enclosed, air-conditioned, publicly subsidized but privately owned atriums, like the one in Trump Towers on Fifth Avenue in New York City. Even the sidewalks and parks are sometimes privatized, with municipal functions of policing, cleanup, and event scheduling given over to municipally sanctioned business improvement districts.[67] In adjacent neighborhoods, families live in welfare hotels and homeless people live on the streets. Cities and suburbs maintain their familiar divides, in some ways hardened. Detroit's suburbs sharply isolate themselves from the city, as viewers know from Eminem's movie 8 Mile, where the divide shows up along a single, wide street. In Michigan and across the country, from the population-losing Northeast to the expanding South and Southwest, gated and guarded communities sit close to decrepit, decaying suburban slums.[68] Although the minority neighborhoods that are now sprinkled through the suburbs shatter the oversimplified picture of poor cities with rich suburbs, those suburbs themselves are often in trouble. Literally thousands of acres of abandoned malls dot the landscape, empty but for cheap stores selling secondhand goods, venues for alienation and violence, dragging down their neighborhoods.[69] Meanwhile, ever farther out, contractors sell McMansions with three or four times the square footage of a typical city home, so that the nation's most successful home-building developer worries that his huge profits depend on dangerously deepening inequality.[70]

These geographic barriers and municipal separations find counterparts in skewed economic power. In 2006, top officers of the largest corporations took home compensation averaging nearly $15 million, up more than 9 percent from the year before. And they give up less to taxation. Whereas in 1955 the top four hundred taxpayers paid 51 percent of their income to the IRS, fifty years later they paid only 18 percent.[71] According to Forbes, the best-paid CEO in 2005 was Terry Semel, who "earned" more than $230 million at Yahoo.[72] The average CEO made 411 times the average worker's pay. Meanwhile, the average wage paid to the lowest-level working Americans continued to fall or at best stagnate: from 1979 to 2005 the lowest-income fifth of families saw their inflation-adjusted wages decline by 1 percent, as some of the largest global corporations paid salaries below a living wage to many of their American workers.[73] Both inside and outside the corporate sector, problems of unemployment, low-wage work, and dependency afflict people who live in poor, minority neighborhoods.

Alternative Metropolitan Images

If one looks worldwide to find cities that do succeed—in terms of productivity and competitiveness, social life and social peace, and in their ability to adapt appropriately toward environmental sustainability—one discovers that successful cities are nearly always supported by national societies that provide six kinds of guarantees to citizens, or even to all residents, citizens and immigrants alike. These guarantees *reduce inequality.* The six guarantees are *social* rather than individual, and they are organized by politics, not the market. Contrary to the widely accepted rhetoric, dominant since Ronald Reagan's conservative political victory in 1980, a rhetoric that has openly celebrated *private* success as provided by the market, these guarantees seek *collective* success, even if they sometimes utilize market mechanisms. Especially in the urban realm, the neoconservatives mislead with their enthusiasm over unregulated markets, privatization, and the advantages of social inequality.[74] Even following the market debacle of late 2008, many economists still cling to their ideological blinders, ignoring limitations on their notions of efficiency when they confront requirements of social welfare and social and environmental efficiency.[75] Ideologists misrepresent failures and ignore contrary evidence. The fact is, cities prosper not when national leaders irresponsibly loosen regulation of businesses and greedily reduce guarantees to citizens and residents, but rather when leaders enhance those guarantees by providing broader support to cities' economies and societies. Cities prosper when they can regulate business effectively and when they can efficiently offer social supports to their residents, so that human needs are met for majorities, not only for those in families or households with incomes sufficient to pay. Good cities thrive when those needs are seen nationally as *social* responsibilities rather than private obligations.

We noted earlier that Manuel Castells once wrote of western European cities as islands of peace in a sea of global turmoil. This figure of speech is still appropriate. Consider the images one typically conjures of any of these well-functioning European cities, then add Japanese cities, surely one or more in Canada, perhaps even Singapore and Hong Kong. In each of these cities one sees a *highly regulated* panorama, a result of many decades of *collective* efforts. In these cities, collective decisions provide a basis for good private decisions. Even in popular photographic images of these cities, one frequently sees evidence of elaborate *social* decisions—such as systems of collective transit with excellent and speedy subways, large numbers of well-tended public open spaces, zoned limitations on building heights, and extensive schemes of social housing, financed through publicly designed programs. If these physical manifestations appear so prominently in these good cities, it may be worth asking how they got there, why they work so well, what it is in a city's functioning that *prevents* the appearance of deep failures. In the United States, even the language of politics requires some adjustment if we are to be able to figure these things out.

Many social theorists of the Western tradition have reflected on the connection between the individual and society. Adam Smith, the eighteenth-century political economist, Max Weber, the nineteenth-century historian and sociologist, and Karl Polanyi, the twentieth-century historian, all noted the connection. Modern interpretations tend to sever this connection. From Weber comes the notion that even when a person acts rationally, the advantage may be thwarted by a broader social irrationality. As a family chooses a location for housing, for example, it might wish to avail itself of public transit but be denied the option. The family will thus make a privately "rational" choice involving ownership and use of an automobile, because collectively the system is irrational, as it fails to operate bus lines, quite probably because zoning regulations have specified neighborhood densities too low to make bus operations efficient. The family's individually rational decision thus reinforces the social irrationality. From Polanyi comes the idea that markets never operate in the abstract, but rather function always embedded in a set of social rules, such as a prohibition against child labor, or the limitation of the work week to forty hours, or the specification of a minimum wage. Conservatives often claim falsely that Adam Smith proposed that only the unfettered invisible hands of many would lead to efficiency and happiness, as producers compete in uncoordinated markets totally without regulation. This now popular interpretation maintains that private economic activities, selfishly pursued for individual gain, always work for everyone's benefit, as they are coordinated by an abstract market via adjustments in supply and demand. This is the version argued by conservatives such as the late Nobel laureate economist Milton Friedman and pushed by ideologues at right-wing publicity mills such as the Heritage Foundation. But Smith never made such arguments. He was a radical thinker, for sure, and he did argue against *undue* regulation of international trade by national governments in the eighteenth century, but he never argued away the collective responsibilities of governments, and he never thought that privileged individuals should be able to protect their advantages against the common good.

The importance of these collective, social responsibilities stands out clearly in the six kinds of *national* guarantees that throughout western Europe have led cities and their metropolitan areas to prosper. In nearly every case, these guarantees provide for health care, housing, education, transit, income security, and public spaces and facilities. Although in practice even in the United States more public money is spent on these guarantees than most observers credit, public rhetoric commonly acknowledges only one of these guarantees, and that one increasingly grudgingly—for public schools and state universities. In theory, it is generally believed in the United States that any resident, or certainly any citizen, *should* be able to expect good instruction for his or her children in public schools and opportunity for inexpensive attendance at a college or university. The other five collective, social guarantees are *not* considered fully legitimate even as targets for public action in the United States.[76]

Against the finding that these six guarantees lead to urban sustainability and economic and social success, trends in U.S. politics, society, and economy have moved in precisely the opposite direction. National guarantees have shrunk just as they have come more into need, as markets have spread across borders not only for finance, raw materials, and consumer goods, but also for industrial ownership and control, for managing chains of production. Consistent with this rampant globalization, supporters of privatization hold the upper hand, shifting control from public authorities to private companies over everything from water supply, to prisons, and even to warmaking. Exploding immigration advances the corporate agenda, reinforced by remarkable, highly visible changes in the U.S. urban landscape. These three expanding phenomena—globalization, privatization, and migration—have abstract qualities, but they also have mechanical, technical qualities that make them appear inexorable. Finally, Americans face the threat of three less tangible, but no less influential, trends: an increase in religiosity and nativism, a growing enthusiasm over rising inequality, and recklessness about the dire ecological effects of rampant consumerism.

In the chapters that follow, all these trends are seen to connect—as both causes and effects—with the way urbanization and metropolitan growth have been abused by private corporations and managed and mismanaged by federal agencies and state and local governments. Our argument makes the case for better urban policy and better metropolitan management as one of the most effective and efficient ways to promote equality, provide opportunity, and recover our national sanity.

2

Separate Assets

Race, Gender, and Other Dimensions of Poverty

The brief "American Century" of diminishing inequality, the post–World War II decades, finished long ago. Ever since the mid-1970s, global competitors have transformed the nation's economy and politics, and since the severe downturn of 2008, the nation has faced disintegrating traditions of social solidarity. In the mid-twentieth century there was a common belief that all Americans shared an economic destiny. The wealth of the nation would flow to all citizens who displayed diligence and thrift. This belief lasted perhaps forty years, and then, after four decades of progress, the basic social contract that connects people and opportunities began to tear. Whereas in the earlier period citizens generally (and accurately) expected economic improvement, now most cannot. False and temporary relief came with the dot-com bubble and mortgage balloon, but those artificial reprieves have ended.

The first decade of the new century has finished, and economic prospects are bleak. Public officials seem unable to face up to the most pressing problems of the poor. Willing to allocate resources to giant institutions like banks, bond houses, and auto manufacturers, leaders still expect poor people to survive on trickle-down. Neither economic growth nor public subsidy works to solve the problems of poor people. The failures are perhaps best revealed by severe inequalities in the distributions of income and wealth. We use a series of basic facts about these distributions to construct a platform from which we can view the middle class, the poor, and, most important, those who are very poor and thrown together near the centers of metropolitan areas. Only after framing this evidence can we interpret their problems. In

, as background for subsequent chapters, we thus display the statisti-
sions of poverty.

nation of plenty, Americans face surprisingly wide-ranging poverty. At
rn of the century the highly respected Luxemburg Income Study estimated
17 percent of Americans were poor, almost double the Census Bureau esti-
ate, then just under 9 percent.[1] By either count, things then got worse—for
2008 the Census increased its estimate to 13.2 percent, with worse to come.
Economists of every political persuasion agree that inequality has risen for at
least thirty years.[2]

Some of the poorest people, disproportionately African American and Latino, have lived for years tightly concentrated into inner-city areas. Neighborhoods of the poor have transferred population recently from the historically most segregated cities into the close-in suburbs and sometimes beyond, but even in the suburbs, as we see in Chapter 4, the poor live in relative isolation from the middle class, and most people of color live isolated from Whites. In newly poor suburban neighborhoods, as in long-poor city neighborhoods, problem involve lack of family resources, inadequate public services, homelessness and poor housing, crowded or poorly run schools, and inadequate police protection.

Americans rarely see poor people in plain sight, and then usually in just a few places—elderly women working evenings at McDonald's, Wal-Mart clerks without health insurance, young men in a sidewalk line for the soup kitchen, children signing up for free school lunch, or beggars on the corner. Aside from such passing observations, most middle-class Americans avoid the poor, whom they find frightening or repugnant. Exceptions include anti-hunger campaigners and poverty activists working on Living Wage campaigns or with Justice for Janitors or similar organizing efforts, but such efforts have been few, small, and fragmented. Barack Obama worked as a community organizer in Chicago and later on a legal case for ACORN, which assists poor neighborhoods nationwide to organize, so at least the White House is aware.

Even when residents in rich industrial societies such as the United States and Canada do perceive the poverty that surrounds them, they are not so likely to perceive the *inequality,* because various social and psychological mechanisms hide it from view. Inequality encompasses much more than poverty. People who earn enough to escape poverty and avoid physical deprivation may be hurt socially and damaged psychologically by their *relative* lacking. The terms *rich, middle class, working class,* and *poor* are slippery but important social distinctions that mirror social stigma and signal psychological harm. People who experience the downsides of inequality may suffer health problems and reduced life expectancy. Inequality can reinforce more tangible deprivations such as lack of food, housing, medication, or hospital treatment. People reveal feelings of unfairness, disrespect, and stress in many situations of inequality, as noted at the end of Chapter 1.

In many countries, traditions of social debate pit political parties against one another ideologically, raising inequality issues for open contention, but public debate in the United States rarely takes note of inequality. When things get so wildly out of hand that the stock market collapses, Democrats and Republicans alike speak of the unbridled greed of bonus-taking bankers, but not otherwise, whereas British Labor Party leaders commonly point to the greed of people near the top of the income distribution. *The Economist,* a conservative British magazine, uses the terms *bosses* and *workers,* aware of the conflicts inherent in the struggle involved in distributing income. Elsewhere in rich, industrialized western Europe, large voting blocs have long elected socialists and Communists, who put distributional disputes at the forefront. Americans tend not to acknowledge that the private market creates inequality as it allocates wages, salaries, profits, and rents, and they forget that paltry public expenditures will be insufficient to make up the gaps. Still, these controversial topics never lie far from the surface, and when the gaps become extreme, people pay attention. Focusing on the top of the distribution, for example, the press informs the public about court cases that involve fraud, war profiteering, or the stockholder disputes that accompany such events as financial collapses, budget overruns, and contested corporate mergers. Journalists report with relish when big-time abusers like Ponzi investor Bernard Madoff, Enron's chief Kenneth Lay, or WorldCom's Bernard Ebbers lose not only their millions of dollars but their social status as well. Complaints arise over multimillion-dollar bonus payments by banks and corporations when they are supported by direct federal subsidy. Because such events reveal so vividly a kleptocracy that grossly overpays its members in the form of profits and rewards to corporate executives, the abuses cannot stay hidden. Still, the political system works quietly to safeguard the more quotidian inequalities, keeping them hidden, thus putting limits on open discussion. Even in the Wall Street disasters that exploded in 2008 and 2009, the White House and Congress seemed unwilling to challenge the high rollers. The man initially leading the rescue effort, Treasury Secretary Henry Paulson, himself amassed $700 million in salary and bonus payments while head of Goldman Sachs, and hardly anyone notices.[3]

At the bottom end of the income distribution, inattention prevails as well. When the Clinton administration reneged on the New Deal's promise of support for needy families, protest was limited. Either many liberals went along, showing new tolerance for acceptance of inequality, or they did not even notice. Ending more than sixty years of guaranteed federal welfare payments, the president signed the 1996 Personal Responsibility and Work Opportunity Reconciliation Act. The act's title signals denial of collective burden, as it marks poverty as a "personal responsibility," a sharp reversal from Franklin D. Roosevelt's New Deal, in which *social* collapse was seen as the major cause of personal, family, and community poverty. The new law proposes no longer to relieve people who are poor or to provide them with well-paying jobs, but rather to solve their individual poverty by forcing them to work at the bottom of the wage scale by limiting the number of months they can take benefits, whether or not they find work. The new law undermines a potentially stable form of remedy, and it blames badly behaved individuals, not such community shortcomings as a failed school system, shortage of decent-paying jobs, or poorly served and undersupported neighborhoods. On all sides, the U.S. political system encourages excessive incomes at the top yet permits growing misery at the bottom.

Two public questions about incomes serve to raise income distribution issues in an unusual way, relating them to our argument about separation. The questions reveal and define the concerns of two distinct social groups, with distant viewpoints. The first question has to do with judges' salaries—is the bench underpaid? The second has to do with hourly pay, minimum wages, and welfare—how low must incomes be to keep American workers competitive? These questions illustrate the myopia identified by John Kenneth Galbraith, the economist and ambassador, as he mused about the strange ideology that justifies such contrasts, an ideology that argues that higher incomes should be offered the rich, lower wages to the poor, in both cases as incentives to work.[4]

Among America's opinion makers there was only one answer to the first question, and very little debate: we must make up the salaries that federal district judges have lost to inflation in the last decades. In early 1989 the chief justice of the Supreme Court made the extraordinary move of holding a press conference to call for higher judicial salaries.[5] Even Congress, politically unable at the time to raise its own salaries, made it clear that judges' salaries should be higher. The case was readily made by columnist Anthony Lewis: "In the metropolitan areas where most federal judges sit, it is difficult to provide good housing for a family and to put children through college on $89,500 a year. And by the standards of the legal profession, the figure is extremely modest."[6] Some worried that the independence of the judiciary was threatened by low salaries. According to economists and other observers, judges were deeply disadvantaged compared with other attorneys, whose salaries are much higher.

In 1989, $89,500 a year would have been a fortune for most families: adjusting the figure for inflation to 2008 yields about $153,000 a year. Two decades later a similar controversy simmered regarding salaries of New York State judges. The chief judge worried about a demoralized judiciary that might threaten "work stoppages, slowdowns or recusals." "An emotional Chief Judge Judith S. Kaye said . . . the judiciary will not remain 'docile in the face of the shabby treatment' it is receiving from officials of other governmental branches and is prepared to sue to get judges their first raises in more than eight years."[7]

For the majority of Americans, these debates over compensation for judges, legislators, and other lawyers miss the mark. Across the country, only one in twenty households, even with two adults working, can equal the earnings of a New York State judge. Fully half the households in the country take home less than one-quarter as much money as a federal judge.[8] By European standards, which designate the poor as those who get less than half the median income, either the judges are doing extraordinarily well or many people are doing badly. The judges have lost earning power compared with the very rich, but nearly everyone has also suffered against that standard, and the majority have lost much more. According to studies by the Internal Revenue Service: "Between 1979 and 2003 . . . the share of overall income received by the bottom 80 percent of taxpay-

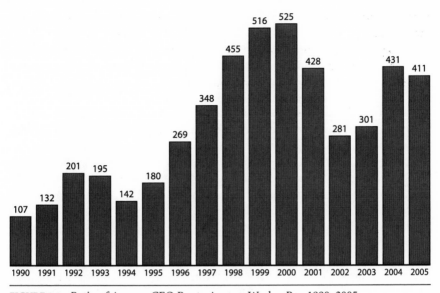

FIGURE 2.1 Ratio of Average CEO Pay to Average Worker Pay, 1990–2005
Source: CEO Pay Charts, United for a Fair Economy. Available at http://www.faireconomy.org/news/ceo_pay_charts.

ers fell from 50 percent to barely over 40 percent. The main winners from this upward redistribution of income were a tiny, wealthy elite: more than half the income share lost by the bottom 80 percent was gained by just one-fourth of 1 percent of the population, people with incomes of at least $750,000 in 2003."[9]

What about the second question, on keeping wages down to keep workers globally competitive? Most Americans depend on wages and salaries. One measure of inequality is the ratio of executive salaries to average wages. CEOs in the United States average two to three times the pay of their British, French, Canadian, and German counterparts. But the really big gap separates U.S. CEOs from workers, who are cheaper than their international counterparts. In 1990 U.S. CEOs earned just over 100 times the average earnings of their employees. Nearly a decade later, in the Patriot Corporations Act, Congress proposed limits to excess at the 1990 level. By 2000 the ratio had risen to more than 500 to 1. Figure 2.1 shows the ratio of CEO compensation to average worker wages from 1990 to 2005. Had workers' wages increased at the same rate as CEO compensation, the average worker would have earned $108,000 in 2005, rather than $28,000, the actual average.

Given the palpable unfairness of severe income inequality, the miserable situation of households with low incomes, rising health costs, failing schools, and myriad other penalties of inequality and poverty, one hastens to ask, What drives the society to such outrageous results? The problem builds in part because the global economy has grown more interconnected and the U.S. position has become less powerful. No one aims directly either for an unequal distribution of income or to make other people poor, but when businesses respond to high-pressure competition, then markets push wages down and drive under-employment up, causing inequality to expand. The problem grows in part because society has withdrawn restraints on this built-in tendency of markets to create inequality, adopting the pretense of fairness in what Cornell University economist Robert Frank calls Richestan, the unregulated, winner-take-all society.[10] We do not take votes in favor of inequality, but narrow individual interests and convincing political advertising lead to votes against measures to reduce inequality. Leaders reject progressive income taxes, minimum wages fully indexed to keep up with inflation, extensive universal benefits for retirement and health care, subsidies for transit and housing, and adequate funding for public schools, child care, and public squares and parks. In their reluctance to endorse these and similar endeavors, Americans fail to resist the forces that expand inequality. These forces wreak havoc on cities.

Elsewhere in the book, we explore the forces that cause inequality to expand. We also explore the consequences of inequality and poverty. In this chapter we take on a simpler task, to outline and describe the phenomena themselves. How extensive is inequality, how is it shaped? Who is poor, and how poor? How does income inequality differ from wealth inequality? How does inequality affect productive human assets and social capital?

Distributions of Income and Wealth— The Great U-Turn

When the Bureau of Labor Statistics still provided its "low-budget" definition of poverty, more than one-third of American families had incomes too low to help them maintain "a sense of self-respect and social participation."[11] Although average incomes have risen, the inequalities have not diminished nearly three decades later. The distribution of income is highly skewed, the range of poverty is quite broad, and households at the bottom are extremely poor. According to the most widely accepted international income study, done long before the Wall Street meltdown of 2008–2009, the United States is in a bad way:

> Comparative cross-national poverty rankings suggest that United States poverty rates are at or near the top of the range when compared with . . . other rich countries. . . . America's elders . . . have poverty rates that are high, particularly on relative grounds. In most rich countries, the relative child poverty rate is 10 percent or less; in the United States, it is 21.9 percent. What seems most distinctive about the American poor, especially poor American single parents, is that they work more hours than do the resident parents of other nations while also receiving less in transfer benefits.[12]

Adequate public support for health care, housing, transit, child care, and retirement comes as a set of standard-issue social benefits in all other wealthy industrial democracies, everywhere in western Europe as well as Japan, Australia, New Zealand, and Canada. The main protection from poverty in the United States is income from employment, but it falls short. According to a former Ford Foundation executive, once head of the New York City Human Resources Administration, inadequate employment was the key in 1989, and its burden fell most heavily on select groups: "For whites and minorities alike, the inability to get well-paid work is the most common proximate cause of family poverty. The poverty falls most visibly on women and children, especially on women alone bringing up children. The problem is highly concentrated in isolated districts of metropolitan areas, where minority people are segregated, [many] living in isolated pockets of such intense poverty that they are cut off from the world of work and independence."[13] The dependence on jobs continues fifteen years later, and as Nobel Prize–winning economist Paul Krugman writes, the isolation has worsened: "Living in or near poverty has always been a form of exile, of being cut off from the larger society. But the distance between the poor and the rest of us is much greater than it was 40 years ago, because most American incomes have risen in real terms while the official poverty line has not. To be poor in America today, even more than in the past, is to be an outcast in your own country."[14]

In the United States, most goods and services must be purchased, and the income for purchases comes almost entirely from salaries or wages, which depend on employment. Employment rises and falls with the economy, with global competition, and with changes in regulation. Wealth is the accumulation of unspent previous income, including inheritance. People with no wealth, low wages, or no wages tend to be at the bottom of both distributions, of income and wealth. Programs to redistribute income exist in the United States to provide food stamps and school lunches, housing subsidies, health benefits, and negative income taxes, as well as retirement payments from Social Security, but these programs fail to reach many households in need, and even for those who receive benefits, the provisions are often insufficient. The redistribution of wealth is not on the U.S. political agenda.

Statisticians assess the relative well-being of segments of the population in many ways. Family or household income is the most common measure, compiled from different sources, aggregated in different ways. All the measures, however, tend to tell the same story: in broad contours, incomes are highly unequal and disparities have been getting worse. It was not always that way. For about twenty-five years following World War II, U.S. economic growth and redistributive policies reduced disparities.

In 1947 the average household in the top income quintile (the top 20 percent ranked by income) received thirteen times as much as the average household in the bottom quintile. Three decades later, by 1979, inequality had diminished, so that incomes of the top group averaged eleven times those of the bottom group.[15] Despite strong periods of economic growth since the late 1970s, however, the trend reversed and disparities have worsened. By 2003 inequality had risen, so that the ratio was fifteen-to-one. By 2005 inequality was at the highest level since

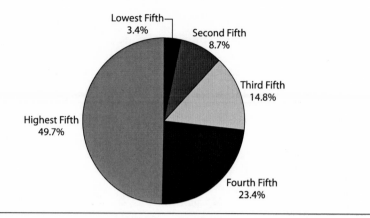

FIGURE 2.2   Income Share by Household Quintiles, 2007

Source: U.S. Census Bureau, Current Population Survey, Annual Social and Economic Supplements, Historical Income Tables—Households, Table H-2. Share of Aggregate Income Received by Each Fifth and Top 5 Percent of Households, All Races: 1967 to 2007. Available at http://www.census.gov/hhes/www/income/histinc/h02AR.html.

before the Great Depression. The gap between the rich and the rest has stretched wide: the top 300,000 people, as a group, earn as much as the bottom 150 million, a ratio of 500 to 1.[16] Political economists Bennett Harrison and Barry Bluestone noted the reversal in trends, blamed a hollowing out of the middle class as the result of corporate responses to the collapse of the manufacturing sector, and gave the reversal its name, the Great U-Turn.[17]

Figure 2.2 shows the 2007 before-tax distribution of income. The largest share, half, goes to the top fifth (quintile) of the households, while the smallest share, only 3.4 percent, goes to the same number of households in the poorest quintile. The richest 5 percent of households (not shown) take home 21 percent of the income.[18]

The poorest fifth's share of aggregate household income has fallen persistently since 1976, and shares of the next three-fifths have also fallen. In other words, relative incomes have fallen for four out of five households, while they have risen for only for one in five. Even within that top 20 percent, the gains are fantastically concentrated, with the top 1 percent of families getting the most. As evidence shows later in this chapter, even larger specific inequalities occur by race and ethnicity, as well as gender. Figure 2.3 shows how the average inflation-corrected income of each quintile has grown (or declined) from 1967 on. This *real* value (that is, purchasing power after removing the effects of inflation) hardly changed for the bottom 60 percent of households. Incomes increased modestly, by half, for the second-highest quintile. Average income for the lowest quintile grew by $2,732, approximately a third, between 1967 and 2005. For the highest quintile, incomes grew by more than $71,000, that is, by 80 percent.[19]

Wealth is even more excessively concentrated. By "wealth," economists mean the value of things people own—corporate stocks, bonds, savings and checking accounts, cash, and real property, including factories, shops, offices, and equip-

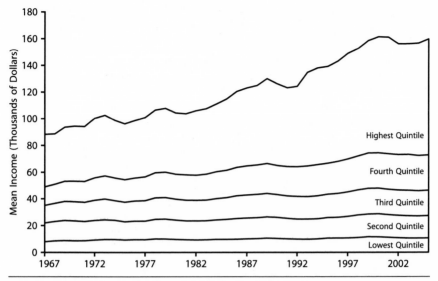

FIGURE 2.3   Mean Income by Household Quintiles, 1967–2005

Note: Income in 2005 CPI-U-RS adjusted dollars.

Source: U.S. Census Bureau, Current Population Survey, Annual Social and Economic Supplements, Table A-3.
Selected Measures of Household Income Dispersion: 1967 to 2005. Available at http://www.census.gov/hhes/www/
income/histinc/p60no231_tablea3.pdf.

ment, as well as homes, cars, and other personal assets.[20] "Net worth" counts these assets minus debt.

In 2004, when the wealthiest 1 percent of households received 16.9 percent of all income, those households held nearly double that portion of all net worth (34.3 percent) and even more of all net financial assets (42.2 percent). Stated differently, these extremely affluent households own more than 34 times the average share of wealth and more than 42 times the average share of investment resources. The top 10 percent of households holds 71.3 percent of the wealth (the top four groups on left and right in Figure 2.4). These few people are the winners. At the losers' end of the distribution, the greater part of the people, amassing 80 percent of households, hold only 15 percent of the net worth, mainly in owner-occupied housing. This concentration of wealth at the top has increased for decades, and the excesses of the first years of the twenty-first century led Krugman to talk of the New Gatsby.[21]

Table 2.1 provides more detail on ownership by wealth class. The vast majority of households, if they have any wealth at all, hold it in vehicles and homes. When these and similar assets, like furnishings, are excluded, the remaining categories in the economist's measure of wealth are called *productive* assets. These assets "produce" income as a privilege of ownership, in the form of profits, dividends, interest, and rent. Economists refer to these returns as *unearned* income, in distinction to wages and salaries, which come as payment for work. Unearned income accrues with huge disproportion to a tiny, wealthy minority, as rewards

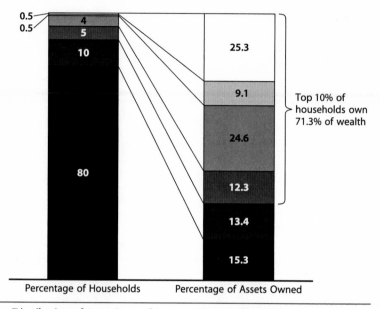

FIGURE 2.4 Distribution of Asset Ownership across Households, 2004

Source: Lawrence Mishel, Jared Bernstein, and Sylvia Allegretto, *The State of Working America*, 11th ed., ch. 5: "Wealth: Unrelenting Disparities" (Ithaca, N.Y.: ILR Press, 2008–2009). Available at http://www.stateofworking america.org/swa06-ch05-wealth.pdf.

to owners of capital, to those who hold the power of the purse, who can enjoy the fruits of exploitation.

From 1962 on, all but the very top groups have experienced steady declines in their shares of financial assets, while the top group has run away with the store. By 2004 the average household in the top one-half percent had cornered 50 times

TABLE 2.1 HOUSEHOLD OWNERSHIP OF WEALTH, 2004

Wealth class	Percentage of asset class held, by wealth class				
	Common stock excluding pensions*	All common stock†	Non-equity financial assets‡	Housing equity	Net worth
Top 0.5%	29.5	27.6	38.8	8.1	25.3
Next 0.5%	9.7	9.3	10.3	4.4	9.1
Next 4%	28.6	28.4	23.1	19.9	24.6
Next 5%	13.3	13.5	9.3	13.5	12.3
Next 10%	11.0	11.9	9.3	19.5	13.4
Bottom 80%	7.9	9.4	9.1	34.6	15.3

Source: Adapted from Lawrence Mishel, Jared Bernstein, and Sylvia Allegretto, *The State of Working America*, 11th ed., ch. 5: "Wealth: Unrelenting Disparities" (Ithaca, N.Y.: ILR Press, 2008–2009).

*Includes direct ownership of stock shares and indirect ownership through mutual funds and trusts.

†Includes direct ownership of stock shares and indirect ownership through mutual funds, trusts, IRAs, Keogh plans, 401(k) plans, and other retirement benefits.

‡Includes direct ownership of stock shares and indirect ownership through mutual funds, trusts, and retirement accounts, and net equity in unincorporated businesses.

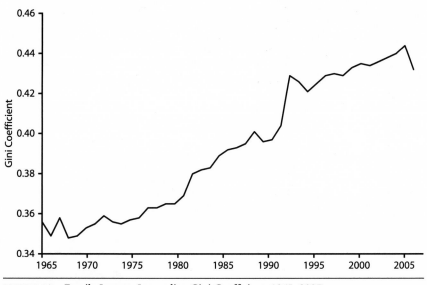

FIGURE 2.5   Family Income Inequality, Gini Coefficient, 1965–2007

Note: Families as of March of the following year.

Source: U.S. Census Bureau, Current Population Survey, Annual Social and Economic Supplements, Historical Income Tables—Families, Table F-4. Gini Ratios for Families, by Race and Hispanic Origin of Householder: 1947 to 2007. Available at http://www.census.gov/hhes/www/income/histinc/f04.html.

its proportionate share of wealth. A larger group, the top 10 percent, held about 80 percent of all common stock. At the same time, the bottom 80 percent of the households held only 10 percent of financial assets.[22]

Analysts often use aggregate, single-indicator measures of inequality to interpret the data with a snapshot. These measures indicate how far the distributions deviate from some idealized (and unrealistic) standard, such as uniformity or perfect equality. Because reliable time-series are not available for wealth holdings, we use income figures. The most widely used statistic, called the Gini coefficient, has generally worsened in the last half century, and studies reveal that overall inequality in the United States has remained high in comparison with other advanced, industrialized nations. The U.S. distribution improved with some fluctuation until the late 1960s. Looking at the longer term in more detail (Figure 2.5), we see that inequality has worsened fairly steadily since 1968, most drastically in the early 1980s and early 1990s.[23]

As this collection of statistics begins to suggest, even the myth of a solid American middle class turns out to be not particularly well supported by the data. In 1967, for example, 55 percent of *full-time* workers did not earn enough by themselves to purchase a lower-middle-class living standard. Twenty years later, in 1986, a family of four, with one adult working outside the home, the other at home with young children, needed at least $21,000 to purchase the "lower-middle" consumer basket of goods and services. Half the country's full-time workers still earned below this standard, without supplementary income from a working spouse. Sixty percent of African American men *with full-time jobs* in 1986 fell below this middle-class standard.[24] Given the increases in inequality of income and wealth over the subsequent two decades, the early warnings by social scientists of the shrinking of the middle class were prescient. Although they encountered doubters still in 1988, Harrison and Bluestone had it right when they called this change the "Great U-Turn."

In many households today, two adults work, thus squeezing into the middle class. But with broad economic difficulties adding to maldistributed income in the first decade of the twenty-first century, damages to the middle class have spread. The debt-to-income ratio among middle-class households is the highest it has been since the late 1980s, and in spite of more stringent legal prohibitions, families much more commonly declare bankruptcy. In 2002, long before the Wall Street meltdown, 2 million people filed for bankruptcy, and among these people, married couples with children were overrepresented (1.5 million families in 2002). Of the parents who filed for bankruptcy, nearly all would be considered middle class.[25] Many other families, with only one worker, or on low wages, or with no full-time or permanent worker at all, fall below these minimal middle-class standards.

Race/Ethnicity and Gender

Throughout the book, when we speak of differences by ethnicity and race, we most often contrast African Americans, Latinos (Hispanics in the Census), and Whites, adding information about various other groups when available data make comparisons possible. For the most part, we are constrained by available statistics, which give fairly complete and historical information about African Americans and Whites, less about Hispanics, and still less about other minority persons, including Native Americans, Asians, or recent immigrants from a wide variety of nations and ethnicities.[26] We are eager for more comprehensive statistics to be collected that better reflect America's burgeoning diversity, but for present purposes three factors compensate. First, most poor people in the United States are White. Although this book focuses on minority populations living in segregated urban neighborhoods, these populations share many economic problems with impoverished suburban, small-town, and rural Whites. Second, the problems of African American and Latino poverty are so serious and manifold that any examination is likely to raise issues pertinent to other groups. Such a focus will fail to identify Vietnamese or West African or Pakistani immigrants or Asian Americans or American Indians, or any other group whose problems might be measured with precision, but our data will help to suggest areas for questioning.

Third, for various historical reasons, anti-color racism, applied with increasing severity to those with darker skins, registers most notably in the United States in the situation of African Americans. We do *not* claim that racism is absent in the experiences of other minorities in America—to the contrary, ample evidence shows broad and painful affects of racism on all who are deemed "minority" per-

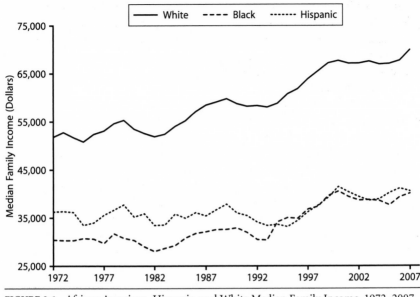

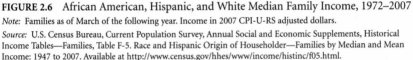

FIGURE 2.6   African American, Hispanic, and White Median Family Income, 1972–2007

Note: Families as of March of the following year. Income in 2007 CPI-U-RS adjusted dollars.

Source: U.S. Census Bureau, Current Population Survey, Annual Social and Economic Supplements, Historical Income Tables—Families, Table F-5. Race and Hispanic Origin of Householder—Families by Median and Mean Income: 1947 to 2007. Available at http://www.census.gov/hhes/www/income/histinc/f05.html.

sons. Nor do we claim that others' experiences with racism are the same as those of African Americans or Latinos, or suggest that poor Whites do not suffer from prejudice. Indeed, each case is remarkably distinct, none somehow "better" or "worse" than the others. And not all harmful prejudice is racial—discrimination and violence directed at gays and lesbians is a case in point. What we *do* claim is that by exploring the (more readily available) information about African Americans and Latinos, we will be enlightened—and that this information can corroborate and augment findings from other, more detailed studies. Some have said that rising numbers of immigrants in the metropolis will lead the country to an integrated, racially mixed, and less discriminatory society. Unfortunately, as more astute observers of racial issues have found, many arrivals at U.S. shores, even many immigrants of color, absorb and then practice anti-Black racism themselves, as a way of learning the U.S. rules of progress.[27]

The figures on overall distributions of income and wealth that we have just observed for the general population, unequal as they are, obscure the larger gaps that divide racial and ethnic groups from each other. African American and Hispanic family incomes, for example, always low compared with White family incomes, fell relatively still lower from the early 1970s to the early 1990s. Although the relative position of these minority families then improved marginally after that, they slipped subsequently. As Figure 2.6 shows, by 2007 minority incomes remained below 60 percent of White family incomes.

Figure 2.6 contrasts the midpoints of the income distributions, in which African American and Hispanic families earned about $40,000 versus $70,000 for Whites in 2007 ($77,000 for Asians).[28] At lower incomes the gap is widest: in 2006, for example, incomes of the poorest 20 percent of African Americans families were only half the incomes of their poor White counterparts (these details are *not* shown in Figure 2.6).

Poor families of every race are disproportionately headed by women. Put differently, female-headed families are disproportionately poor. It does not help that women still suffer from discrimination, getting paid less even for literally the same work. Conservatives argue that women choose lower pay, opting out of competitive jobs, but the evidence suggests otherwise. Economist Heidi Hartmann explains: "If a woman knows a field is unfriendly . . . she is unlikely to go into it. . . . Choices are not made in a vacuum."[29]

Gender inequalities are compounded for African American families, which are more likely to be headed by women. As Figure 2.7 shows, for example, of all African American families with incomes of $10,000 or less, nearly four of five (78 percent) are headed by women. At those low incomes, women head two-thirds of the Hispanic families and half the White ones. At the upper end of income distribution, female-headed families are rare.

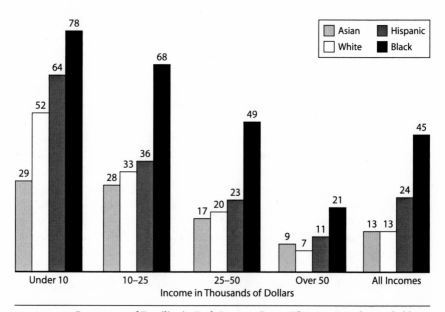

FIGURE 2.7 Percentage of Families in Each Income Group That Are Female Headed by Race, 2007

Note: Families as of March of the following year.

Source: U.S. Census Bureau, Current Population Survey, Annual Social and Economic Supplements, Table FINC-01. Selected Characteristics of Families by Total Money Income in 2007. Available at http://pubdb3.census.gov/macro/032008/faminc/new01_000.htm.

Looking at wealth rather than income, and summing for all racial and ethnic groups, we find that households headed by a single adult, who is nearly always a woman, on average, hold only about a fifth of the wealth of married-couple households, $20,000 compared with $100,000 in 2002.[30]

Income inequalities *among* African Americans are greater than they are among Whites. Disparities have worsened (since 1975), most dramatically among African Americans. This tendency toward minority division into middle class and poor finds expression in the separation of middle-class Black suburbs from inner-city poverty districts, discussed in Chapter 4.[31]

Measures of *wealth* holdings reveal much larger gaps separating Whites, on the one hand, from African Americans and Hispanics, on the other. Whites by nearly any measure have vastly larger holdings of stocks, bonds, cash, and real property, including houses, appliances, and automobiles. This chasm by race and ethnicity appears unbridgeable without dramatic public effort. Deepening the chasm still more, the housing crisis beginning in 2007 drastically eroded the modest housing assets of minority mortgage holders. Just before the crisis, in New York City in 2006, for example, subprimes accounted for 32 percent of all mortgages on one-to-four-family dwellings, and these mortgages were concentrated in Black and Hispanic neighborhoods. (Subprime mortgage payments are much more volatile and ultimately more costly, therefore unfair and more likely to lead to collapse.) Even middle-class and wealthy minority home buyers were more likely than White home buyers with similar incomes to have subprime mortgages.[32] The picture was similar nationally, and these mortgages tended to be wiped out by the crisis.

In 2002, White households had median net worth of $87,000, sixteen times the median wealth of African American households and eleven times that for Hispanic households. (These figures represent not only enormous inequality but an intense relative worsening, since comparable disparities fourteen years earlier were only about half as high, with White households then only eight to ten times as wealthy as minority households.) Excluding home equity, the median holding for Whites in 2002 was $19,000, while for Blacks and Hispanics the comparable average wealth holdings were vanishingly small. As Figure 2.8 indicates, giant wealth gaps similarly divide female-headed from married-couple households. When race and gender combine, even small cushions vanish, as female-headed Black and Hispanic households own virtually nothing.[33] To make the inequality still worse, poor minority households rarely have relatives or neighbors with high income or wealth, so they encounter much more difficulty in weathering economic downturns.[34]

Wealth differences are especially marked at the lower levels of the national income distribution, which includes most African American and Hispanic households. For African American and Hispanic households in the lowest U.S. income quintiles, for example, wealth holdings are infinitesimal. One-quarter of all African American families have no productive *or* personal assets; that is, they

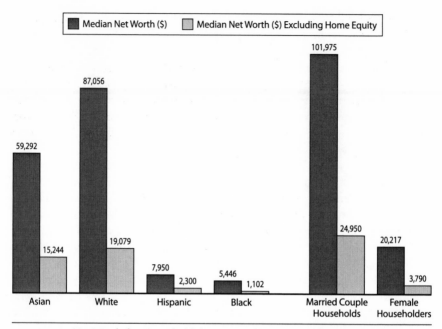

FIGURE 2.8 Net Worth for Households by Race and by Type of Household, 2002

Note: In 2002 dollars.

Source: Alfred O. Gottschalck, "Net Worth and the Assets of Households: 2002," U.S. Census Bureau, Current Population Reports, Household Economic Studies, report P70-115, 2008. Available at http://www.census.gov/prod/2008pubs/p70-115.pdf.

have no net wealth, or worse, they have net debt. Nearly 42 percent of African American families have net assets (including real estate) worth less than $10,000, whereas only 15 percent of White families are this asset-poor. The proportions owning assets worth $100,000 or more is reversed—from less than a fifth of Black families to more than half of White families.[35]

Indexes of Poverty

To be poor is to live in inadequate housing in overcrowded neighborhoods with bad schools and few or no recreational facilities; to be mired down in an atmosphere of hopelessness, of enduring agony over one's children, of poor health, rampant crime, price-gouging in local stores, job discrimination, political under-representation, police brutality, and constant insults—not least in the local welfare office. The emotional, psychological—and physical—impact of such conditions can only be imagined (or read about) by those who have not experienced them directly.[36]

Unlike some other calculations, those relating to poverty have no intrinsic value, no meaning on their own. They exist only in order to help us make them disappear from the scene.... With imagination, faith and hope, we might succeed in wiping out the scourge of poverty even if we don't agree on how to measure it.[37]

These comments on poverty come from remarkably different perspectives. Douglas Dowd, a professor of economic history, wrote the first passage in a 1997 book highly critical of conventional views. He focuses on the poor who live in marginal central neighborhoods, but his ideas apply equally to troubled suburbs, small towns, and rural America. Mollie Orshansky, the federal statistician who pioneered the official U.S. poverty measure, wrote the second passage thirty years earlier, in 1966, to plead for attention to the needs of poor children, rural and urban alike. Over the years many others have argued in similar ways. Michael Harrington's *Poverty in America*, published in the 1950s, led President John F. Kennedy to raise poverty as a national political issue, and after Kennedy's assassination in 1963, President Lyndon Johnson initiated the War on Poverty.

Through the last half of the twentieth century, as poverty became an ostensible target of public policy worldwide, international differences led to questions of definition and measurement. How is poverty to be defined, for example, when the most severely poor people in the United States would be materially wealthy in many parts of Asia or Africa? What of comparisons with western Europeans that show most Americans enjoying a superabundance of material goods? More than half (56 percent) of all U.S. households, for example, have two or more cars, and huge majorities (including many who are deemed poor) have home appliances like dishwashers, clothes dryers, and large-screen televisions. Houses and apartments are large, and consumption of energy breaks all limits. As averages rise, so do consumption levels even for the poor. If people consume at high levels, detractors from aid programs ask, how can they be poor? The first answer is this: Their *relative* deprivation, compared with neighbors in the metropolitan area or with Americans more generally, matters a great deal.

Second, the society may require high consumption or it may provide alternatives, not just leaving it to individual choice. For example, most European cities are arranged so that people journey to work by transit, walking, or biking. European cities are built densely, and transit is available and relatively inexpensive, so commuters do not need to use a car. In Amsterdam only 40 percent commute by car. In U.S. metropolitan areas, on the contrary, majorities have no choice but to use autos, because residential densities are too low to support transit. In Atlanta 95 percent commute by car.[38] In the same vein, although smaller apartments arranged more densely would encourage transit, they are typically not available. Americans are taught by example, by the media, and by advertising to regard them as inferior—the "relative" issue—and financial considerations restrain developers from building them, either because they appear to be unprofitable or because municipal regulations stand in the way.

Further complicating matters of measurement, the official poverty line has been set especially low. Although the poor may always have been with us, it was only with the War on Poverty in the 1960s that public authorities took notice, when federal agencies began defining and measuring poverty, just as they had begun to define and measure unemployment in the 1930s. The official poverty line was originally defined as three times the minimum cost of food. The other two-thirds would pay for rent, utilities, transportation, clothing, medicine, and all other necessities. To settle on that food budget, dieticians put together menus to meet essential nutritional requirements at the lowest prices. The original poverty line was set 40 percent *below the low budget* of the Bureau of Labor Statistics. As we noted earlier, the idea was to mark the ground floor level for "a sense of self-respect and social participation."[39] Although the government adjusts the poverty budget line annually to reflect price changes, the line remains too low for payment of necessary expenses. In 2007 the line, set by the Social Security Administration (SSA), ranged from $10,210 for one person to $20,650 for four people, and up to $34,570 for a family of eight. Surveys show that these stringent standards understate what most Americans think a family needs to escape poverty. Compared with the "living wage," which nearly one hundred cities and counties now stipulate as minimum pay for businesses that sign municipal contracts, the official poverty line falls far short. For a single worker in Ithaca, New York, for example, the 2009 *living wage* for a single person required $23,104 ($11.11 per hour, $1,925 per month), double the official poverty line.

The official poverty line is not only stringent; it is also inaccurate, missing items on both sides of the household budget ledger, the income side and the cost side. The budget aims to count money income, but neglects various cash benefits, including the EITC (earned income tax credit), as well as noncash transfers such as food stamps, housing subsidies, and school lunches. The official measurement also neglects various inescapable spending needs, including income taxes and social security and Medicare taxes, as well as child support, medical insurance, and child care. During the long dot-com and housing bubbles and even in their aftermaths, exploding housing costs have gone beyond budgeted items, with unaffordable increases in real estate prices, property taxes, and rents, especially in many gentrified inner-city neighborhoods that previously provided low-rent options for the poor. The Urban Institute, a premier national center for research on urban affairs, marks low-income families or households as those below *twice* the official poverty line. By that measure, one-third of families with children are low-income. In four of five of these families, the adults have jobs.[40]

Despite its many shortcomings, the official poverty line works well to measure change over time. As the solid-line SSA count in Figure 2.9 shows, the number of officially impoverished people declined dramatically through the 1960s, since then increasing substantially, except during the 1990s. In round numbers, in 1960 there were about 40 million poor people, falling to 24 million by 1969, staying low for a decade. Then came the Reaganesque U-turn. By 1994 the number had risen back to nearly 40 million. By 2000, improved labor markets and perhaps Clintonomics pushed the number back down but only part way, to 32 million. Then—responding to worsening market conditions and Bush II economics—the count headed back up. Perhaps as a symbolic beginning for the twenty-first century,

FIGURE 2.9 Poverty Rate and Number of People in Poverty, 1960–2007

Note: Numbers of people in thousands, as of March of the following year.

Source: U.S. Census Bureau, Current Population Survey, Annual Social and Economic Supplements. Historical Poverty Tables, Table 2. Poverty Status of People by Family Relationship, Race, and Hispanic Origin: 1959 to 2007. Available at http://www.census.gov/hhes/www/poverty/histpov/hstpov2.xls.

from 2000 to 2007 the U.S. population grew by only 6 percent, but at the same time the number of poor people grew by 20 percent, by 5.7 million people.

The poverty *rate*, indicating with the dashed line in Figure 2.9 the proportion who are poor, dropped by half in the 1960s, from well over 20 percent to about 11 percent in 1973. The rate stayed stable through the 1970s, rose sharply to 15 percent in the early 1980s, fluctuated for a decade, then fell to its lowest point in a quarter century, 11.3 percent, by 2000. After that, the rate rose very moderately, until the recession pushed it to 12.5 percent by 2007, then higher. Over the half century, major upsurges in the poverty rate occurred during the Reagan, Bush I, and Bush II administrations, thus seeming to contradict the neoconservative assertion that tax cuts would stimulate economic waves that would wash incomes toward the poor. If economic policy of the 1960s floated all boats, as Democratic president Kennedy claimed, then the policies of supply-side and tax cuts mainly floated luxury liners, catering to the wealthy, such as Republican president George W. Bush's political "base," with rowboats for the middle class. Left to drown have been families in poverty, especially those headed by women and minority persons.

Perhaps the best summary information is for families with children.[41] The lower dashed line in Figure 2.10 shows poverty rates for families with kids dropping from 1960 to 1970, then rising to stay high through the mid-1990s, then

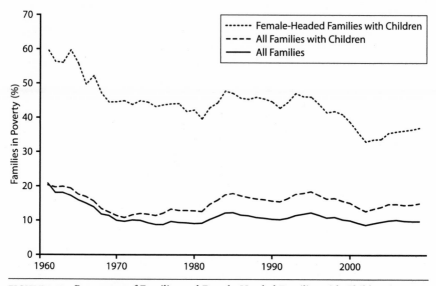

FIGURE 2.10 Percentage of Families and Female-Headed Families with Children in Poverty, 1960–2007

Note: Numbers of families in thousands, as of March of the following year.

Source: U.S. Census Bureau, Current Population Survey, Annual Social and Economic Supplements. Historical Poverty Tables—Families, Table 4. Poverty Status of Families, by Type of Family, Presence of Related Children, Race, and Hispanic Origin: 1959 to 2007. Available at http://www.census.gov/hhes/www/poverty/histpov/hstpov4.xls.

down again to 2000, then back up. A roller coaster, but with long-run improvement. For *women* with children, a subgroup we discuss below, the rates are much worse, as the top line on the chart shows, but the improvements are more marked. Poverty rates for female-headed families, horrifically high historically, decline steadily from about 1960 until 1979, then increase during the 1980s, to drop again until 2000 to a historic low. Still, that relatively low figure is high, reminding us that a full third of women alone with kids fall below the official poverty line, and the numbers continued to rise with the heavy recession.

Since seven out of every ten American families are White (69 percent in 2007), a large portion of the poor are White as well. As Figure 2.11 indicates, the 2.9 million White families (excluding those few headed by men) made up 38 percent of all poor families. The 1.6 million poor Hispanic families (again, excluding those headed by men) made up 22 percent. Black female-headed families (1.5 million) made up 20 percent. Given large numbers of Whites in poor families who are eligible for welfare, one wonders about the cynicism that lies behind the persistent racist stereotype of the Black welfare queen, the one that played such a large role in Ronald Reagan's campaign for the presidency in 1980. Another way to look at family poverty is to ask what proportion of any social group is poor.

Looking at Table 2.2, we see that poverty rates for families vary considerably by race and family type. Looking at the extremes, we find that in 2007 only

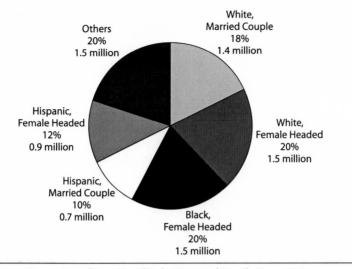

FIGURE 2.11 Proportion of Poor Families by Race and Family Type, 2007

Note: Numbers of families in thousands, as of March of the following year.

Source: U.S. Census Bureau, Current Population Survey, Annual Social and Economic Supplements, Historical Poverty Tables—Families, Table 4. Poverty Status of Families, by Type of Family, Presence of Related Children, Race, and Hispanic Origin: 1959 to 2007. Available at http://www.census.gov/hhes/www/poverty/histpov/hstpov4.xls.

3.2 percent of White married couples were poor but 38.4 percent of Hispanic female householders were poor, a rate exactly twelve times as high. The rate for Black women householders is 37.3 percent, virtually the same.

An alternative view of American poverty is revealed by flipping these coins to their other sides, looking at women and poverty. In 2007 families with children were three times as likely to be poor as those without children, 15 percent as against 5 percent. Of female-headed households with children, 28.3 percent are poor. If we add the near-poor mothers and children, these high rates depict abandonment of the society's most vulnerable members.

TABLE 2.2 POVERTY RATES BY RACE AND FAMILY TYPE, 2007

	Percent below poverty level			
	Married couple	Male householder with no wife present	Female householder with no husband present	All families
All races	4.9	13.6	28.3	9.8
White	3.2	10.3	20.7	5.9
Black	6.8	25.7	37.3	22.1
Asian	6.6	7.6	16.1	7.9
Hispanic	13.4	15.3	38.4	24.9

Source: U.S. Census Bureau, Current Population Survey, Annual Social and Economic Supplements, Historical Poverty Tables—Families, Table 4. Poverty Status of Families, by Type of Family, Presence of Related Children, Race, and Hispanic Origin: 1959 to 2008. Available at http://www.census.gov/hhes/www/poverty/histpov/hstpov4.xls.

The Elderly

When we consider the elderly, we find dramatically different historical trends. The incomes of the elderly improved long ago as a direct result of Social Security retirement benefits, mainly the payment of monthly income to retired persons and subsequently Medicare and Medicaid payments for health care. Census statistics show that the rate of poverty fell drastically in just thirty years, from more than a third of all elderly people in 1959 to just over a tenth in 1989, where it has remained with minor fluctuations. This decline in poverty demonstrates that specific and well-targeted national policies can make a difference. Although Social Security benefits faced budget-cutting threats by Ronald Reagan and privatization threats by George W. Bush, Gray Power advocates and later a Democratic Congress resisted. Great disparities remain nonetheless. Elderly African Americans remain three times as likely to be poor as do elderly Whites, and poverty rates for elderly Hispanics still fluctuate greatly with the business cycle because many do not receive Social Security and are thus dependent on employment, often at part-time, low-wage jobs.

Earning Poverty: Working Hard, Falling Short

Many poor people have jobs. Working poverty starts with low-wage jobs, falling purchasing power, intermittent employment, and involuntary part-time work. A study of conditions in 2003 by the Bureau of Labor Statistics shows that low-wage work pervades the economy. More than 20 percent of all those who worked at least 27 weeks in the year were poor, and in the large and growing service sector, more than 30 percent of the workers were poor.[42] In 2006, of the adults in low-income working families (up to double the official poverty line), only 37 percent had health insurance on the job, and 42 percent had no health coverage at all.[43] In 2008 working families constituted nearly 40 percent of Food Stamp recipients.[44]

Measurement of working poverty introduces new complications. Researchers at the Mobility Agenda use a social-inclusion approach, akin to the European use of relative incomes for measuring poverty, defining low-wage work as the bottom of the wage distribution. As the cutoff, they take two-thirds of the pay for a job held by a typical male worker. In 2006 the median wage for men was $16.66 per hour, so low-wage work was defined as $11.11 or less per hour, just under $23,000 for a full-time year.[45]

However they are defined, low-wage jobs are often uncertain and impermanent, and most workers in these jobs do not get unemployment insurance when they get laid off because eligibility rules exclude them.[46] Sales clerks, janitors, house cleaners, child-care attendants, restaurant workers, and others in low-wage occupations are not likely to get paid time off for illness, paid vacation days or holidays, pension payments, or job training. They are less likely to be well protected with safety rules and equipment and less likely to have job flexibility, allowing time to care for a sick child, visit a school, or exercise some control over the pace of work.[47]

Working poverty has increased, caused by political as well as economic forces. Under great pressure from conservatives who used the pernicious politics surrounding the "culture of welfare," and unwilling to confront and reject the false assumption that unskilled people can always overcome poverty by getting jobs, the Clinton White House and Congress in 1996 disabled welfare as a last resort, requiring aid recipients to find jobs and then lose the dole. Many parents went to work, mostly because they faced the new requirement to work, but eager as well to believe the rhetoric that gave promise of better services and new benefits that would boost take-home pay sufficiently to compensate for commuting and various other costs. But with low-paying jobs or part-time jobs requiring little education and few skills, workers do not earn enough to meet everyday costs of living, as Sheila R. Zedlewski, Ajay Chaudry, and Margaret Simms note:

> Low-income working families face the greatest risks in today's unpredictable economy. The loss of a job, a cut in work hours, a serious health problem, or a rise in housing costs can quickly push these families into greater debt, bankruptcy's brink, or even homelessness. Few have an economic ladder to climb because the wages of less-skilled workers have on balance either stagnated or fallen over the past two decades. Most cannot save for a rainy day when earnings can't be stretched to cover even the everyday basics. Most do not receive group health insurance coverage from their employers or qualify for unemployment insurance if they lose their jobs. Neither employers nor the government gives them much of a safety net.[48]

Working poverty used to be the norm, which is why we talk about "working stiffs," but it no longer is. Although significant pockets of oppression persist, the country developed a dominant middle class through the long postwar boom, and by 1975 the norm had moved up.[49] The economic boom stimulated a steep improvement in wages that produced the reductions in family and household inequality documented above, and expectations rose. The downturn then came as a disappointing reversal. A glance at one well-paid segment of the workforce, factory production workers, shows how they formed part of the increase and then part of the U-turn: "In the two and a half decades from 1947 through 1973, the inflation-adjusted hourly earnings of an average production worker in private employment rose more than 70%, or about 2.1 percent a year. During the next fourteen years, from 1973 through 1987, average real hourly earnings *fell* 5.4%, or about 0.4% a year."[50]

Wages did not just fall, they split into two—part of the middle class did well, but another part did not. Through the 1980s men shifted from middle-wage and

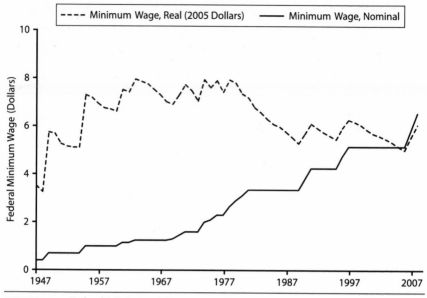

FIGURE 2.12   Federal Minimum Wage, 1947–2008

Source: Data360, Federal Minimum Wage—Nominal vs. Real. Available at http://www.data360.org/dsg.aspx?Data
_Set_Group_Id=762.

high-wage jobs to low-wage jobs. African American young men (aged 25–34)
shifted especially sharply; the proportion that earned only poverty-level wages
rose 151 percent from 1979 to 1989.[51]

Since 1980, bottom-level wage rates for all workers have stagnated in comparison with wages at the top. One way to trace the bottom is to look at the federal minimum wage. Many states have higher minimum-wage standards, but the
federal level marks a political bottom line.[52] A family of three or four with one
employee, if the breadwinner earned the minimum wage, was no longer able to
stand above the poverty line after 1981. By 1989 the minimum wage had fallen
so far that it was comparable in buying power to its 1956 level.

As Figure 2.12 shows, the real value of the hourly minimum wage (the top
line, in 2005 currency) rose through the 1950s and then fluctuated between $7
and $8 for about fifteen years. The wage then headed downward through the
Reagan, Bush I, and Bush II terms, with two minimal adjustments during the
Clinton years. By 2006, just prior to the long-overdue congressional adjustment,
the minimum wage had fallen to only 63 percent of its 1978 value. Even after the
adjustment, it was only at 75 percent of the 1978 value.[53]

Wage declines were perhaps most severe for those who shifted from production work to service jobs, the factory worker flipping hamburgers. Others with
less well paying jobs to begin with have increased in number, to constitute a growing proportion of the workforce.[54] Between 2002 and 2006 the number of low-
wage jobs increased by 4.7 million, to nearly 30 million, 22 percent of all jobs.

TABLE 2.3   MYTHS VERSUS FACTS: LOW-INCOME WORKING FAMILIES, 2006

Myth	Fact
Low-income families do not work.	72% of low-income families work.
Low-income families do not work hard.	The average annual work effort for low-income working families is 2,552 hours, roughly one and one-quarter full-time jobs.
Low-income working families are headed by single parents.	52% of low-income working families are headed by married couples.
Low-income working families are headed by immigrants.	69% of low-income working families have only American-born parents.
Low-income working families have very young parents.	89% of low-income working families have a parent between the ages of 25 and 54.
Low-income working families are overwhelmingly minority.	43% of low-income working families have White, non-Hispanic parents.
Low-income working families are dependent on public assistance.	25% of low-income working families receive food stamp assistance.

Source: Adapted from Brandon Roberts and Deborah Povich, "Working Hard, Still Falling Short," Working Poor Families Project, October 2008. Available at http://www.workingpoorfamilies.org/pdfs/NatReport08.pdf.

The number of low-income working families, with incomes up to twice the poverty line, grew by 350,000, to 9.6 million from 2002 to 2006, to include more than 28 percent of all working families. These families have 21 million children under age 18.[55] In spite of these figures, myths abound, as we can see from Table 2.3. In 2005 about 35 million men and women worked in the kind of jobs listed in Table 2.4. Near the bottom of the wage scale, nearly 2.3 million of them were waiters, men and women both, about half of whom earned less than $14,000 in the year.

Underemployment and Poverty

The Bureau of Labor Statistics (BLS) now provides six indices to count the unemployed, not only in the narrow sense but also to add the numerous people who would work but for one reason or another cannot. The BLS adds "marginally attached workers," persons who have recently worked and want jobs now but are neither working nor looking for work. Discouraged workers are a subset. The BLS then adds those who work part-time but not by choice. Some years ago, to get a total it termed "*under*employment," the BLS added still one more large category, full-time workers who earned a very low wage.[56] Finally, many commentators argue for at least partial inclusion of the more than 2 million persons who are incarcerated. In December 2009 the official unemployment rate stood at a seasonally adjusted rate of 10 percent. Adding in "marginally attached" and involuntary part-time workers, we arrive at a minimal estimate of what many now call *under*employment, which stood at 17.3 percent, more than 70 percent higher than the *un*employment rate. The BLS measures are defined in Table 2.5, and the

TABLE 2.4   LOW-WAGE OCCUPATIONS, NUMBER OF WORKERS, AND WAGE RATES, 2005

Occupation	Total employed	Median hourly wage ($)
Retail sales persons	44,344,770	9.20
Cashiers	3,481,420	7.82
Office clerks, general	2,997,370	11.09
Laborers and freight, stock, and material movers, hand	2,363,960	9.91
Combined food preparation and serving workers	2,298,010	7.11
Waiters and waitresses	2,274,770	6.83
Janitors and cleaners, except maids and housekeeping cleaners	2,107,360	9.32
Stock clerks and order filers	1,625,430	9.66
Nursing aides, orderlies, and attendants	1,391,430	10.31
Receptionists and information clerks	1,088,400	10.65
Security guards	994,220	9.98
Landscaping and groundskeeping workers	896,690	9.94
Maids and housekeeping cleaners	893,820	8.21
Food preparation workers	880,360	8.19
Packers and packagers, hand	840,410	8.36
Cooks, restaurant	791,450	9.54
Home health aides	663,280	9.04
Cooks, fast food	631,190	7.25
Tellers	599,860	10.24
Personal and home care aides	566,860	8.34
Child-care workers	557,680	8.20
Helpers and production workers	528,610	9.80
Counter attendants, cafeteria, food concession, and coffee shop	501,390	7.60

Source: Adapted from Heather Boushey, Shawn Fremstad, Rachel Gragg, and Margy Waller, "Understanding Low-Wage Work in the United States," March 2007. Available at http://www.mobilityagenda.org/lowwagework.pdf.

TABLE 2.5   ALTERNATIVE MEASURES OF LABOR UNDERUTILIZATION

Measure	Definition
U-1	Persons unemployed 15 weeks or longer, as a percent of the civilian labor force
U-2	Job losers and persons who completed temporary jobs, as a percent of the civilian labor force
U-3	Total unemployed, as a percent of the civilian labor force (official unemployment rate)
U-4	Total unemployed plus discouraged workers, as a percent of the civilian labor force plus discouraged workers
U-5	Total unemployed, plus discouraged workers, plus all other marginally attached workers, as a percent of the civilian labor force plus all marginally attached workers
U-6	Total unemployed, plus all marginally attached workers, plus total employed part time for economic reasons, as a percent of the civilian labor force plus all marginally attached workers

Source: U.S. Bureau of Labor Statistics, Labor Force Statistics, Household Data, Table A-12: Alternative Measures of Labor Underutilization. Available at http://www.bls.gov/webapps/legacy/cpsatab12.htm.

FIGURE 2.13 Unemployment Rates, 1979–2008

Note: U-3 and U-6 measures are defined in Table 2.5. Plotted data are seasonally adjusted rates for December of each year.

Source: U.S. Bureau of Labor Statistics, Labor Force Statistics, Household Data, Table A-12. Alternative Measures of Labor Underutilization. Available at http://www.bls.gov/webapps/legacy/cpsatab12.htm.

historical trajectories of official unemployment and underemployment appear in Figure 2.13.

As we see in Chapter 4, both unemployment and underemployment rates for central-city residents tend to be very high, worse in industrially troubled regions of the country and worst of all for African Americans, Latinos, young workers, and those without college educations. In 1982 central-city African American men had a 23.4 percent unemployment rate, while the comparable rate for central-city Whites was 9.5 percent. Comparing central-city Blacks with suburban Whites in Detroit and St. Louis in 2003, we find Black city unemployment rates of 15.3 percent and 14 percent, respectively, and White suburban rates of 5.2 percent and 4.4 percent.[57] Even when levels of education are held comparable, African American men are unemployed at much higher rates than White men. In December 2008 the nationwide African American and Latino unemployment rates (U-3) were 11.9 percent and 9.2 percent, respectively, when the rate for Whites was 6.6 percent. Employment options in central-city minority areas and some inner suburbs have reached new lows with the economic collapse of 2008–2009.

Intermittent work, a frequent reason for low annual earnings, is most concentrated among minority women and young African American men, amplifying the higher unemployment rates of younger workers and their greater difficulty in obtaining full-time work at any wage. In contrast, older women and older minority persons were more likely to have full-time, full-year employment but still with low wages.

Although some economists argue that racial discrimination today plays a small role in the labor market, there is ample evidence that considerable bias still exists. As Thomas Boston points out, race-related earnings differentials result from discrimination at three stages of the labor market.[58] At the final stage, minority workers on average get less pay for the same job. Even after accounting for differences in age, education, region, job experience, family size, and other factors, and in spite of much improvement as a result of civil-rights and equal-pay legislation, wages in many occupations for African Americans are still lower than for Whites. One stage earlier, and of more consequence, discrimination unfairly reduces incomes by limiting access of minority workers to preferred lines of industry, where jobs are better and pay higher.

Worse yet, at the first stage of labor allocation, African American and other minority workers "are disproportionately concentrated among [bad] occupations," even after controlling "for job-related attributes, age and other demographic differences."[59] In each sector of the economy (e.g., manufacturing), White adult wages average significantly higher than African American wages. In similar ways, Hispanic workers earn less per hour than White workers. Two sets of occupational comparisons appear in Table 2.6, men versus women, and for minority workers, Blacks, Asians, and Latinos compared with each other and (implicitly) with Whites. The table does *not* display differential wages across race and gender, but it does display median wages for each occupation and the distribution of occupational employment by race and gender. For example, nearly 3 million persons worked in architecture and engineering in 2007, with a median hourly wage of $31.14. More than twice as many people, close to 8 million, worked in food preparation and serving or related occupations, with a median hourly wage of $8.24. Of all the architects and engineers, 86.5 percent were men and only 13.5 percent were women; of these men and women, 5.1 percent were Black, 6.1 percent Asian, and 8.2 percent Latino—leaving roughly 80 percent White. In contrast, 56 percent of the food workers were women, and 38.5 percent were Black, Asian, or Latino. Women and minority persons held the high-wage jobs in very small numbers and the low-paid jobs in great disproportion. The three minority groups count as about 30 percent of the total employees but hold about 22 percent of the management and professional jobs. They hold more than half the grounds and buildings jobs and nearly 44 percent of the health-care jobs. Women are concentrated most highly in health-care support (approximately 89 percent), as nursing/medical technicians, in personal care, and in teaching. The largest number of women by far work in sales and offices, where wages are low.

These and other data suggest that industrial and occupational changes related to restructuring, international competition, and corporate reorganization have combined to reinforce already-segmented labor markets, leading to increased unemployment, underemployment, and nonparticipation, these in turn leading

TABLE 2.6 GENDER AND RACE IN THE LABOR MARKET: WAGE RATES BY OCCUPATION, AND DISTRIBUTION OF EMPLOYMENT BY GENDER AND RACE, 2007

Occupation	Total employed (in thousands)	Median hourly wage ($)	Men	Women	Black or African American	Asian	Hispanic or Latino
				Percent representation among those employed			
Total employed (over 16 years of age)	145,362		53.3	46.7	11.0	4.8	14.0
Management, professional, and related occupations	52,761		49.2	50.8	8.3	6.3	7.1
Management	15,852	40.60	62.6	37.4	7.2	5.2	7.5
Business and financial operations	6,207	26.87	43.8	56.2	9.4	6.5	7.9
Computer and mathematical	3,676	33.21	43.3	56.7	9.0	7.1	6.7
Architecture and engineering	2,931	31.14	86.5	13.5	5.1	6.1	8.2
Life, physical, and social science	1,307	26.59	53.9	46.1	7.1	12.0	4.7
Community and social services	2,293	17.87	39.7	60.3	19.0	2.5	8.9
Legal	1,671	33.54	48.1	51.9	7.0	2.8	6.6
Education, training, and library	8,605	20.47	26.0	74.0	9.2	3.8	7.5
Arts, design, entertainment, sports, and media	2,820	19.28	52.2	47.8	6.1	4.1	8.3
Health-care practitioners and technical	7,399	26.17	25.4	74.6	10.2	8.0	5.9
Service occupations	24,451		42.8	57.2	15.9	4.6	20.2
Health-care support	3,212	11.45	11.2	88.8	25.8	4.2	13.6
Protective service	3,047	16.11	77.2	22.8	19.1	1.8	10.9
Food preparation and serving related	7,824	8.24	44.0	56.0	12.1	5.4	21.0
Building and grounds cleaning and maintenance	5,445	10.18	59.8	40.2	15.0	2.8	33.4
Personal care and service	4,923	9.50	21.6	78.4	14.7	7.4	14.2
Sales and office occupations	35,544		36.8	63.2	11.5	4.2	12.3
Sales and related	16,295	11.41	50.5	49.5	9.7	4.7	11.7
Office and administrative support	19,249	13.91	25.2	74.8	13.0	3.7	12.8
Natural resources, construction, and maintenance occupations	14,806		95.8	4.2	6.9	1.9	25.0
Farming, fishing, and forestry	988	8.94	78.9	21.1	4.5	1.7	39.3
Construction and extraction	8,667	17.57	97.5	2.5	6.3	1.4	29.6
Installation, maintenance, and repair	5,152	18.04	96.1	3.9	8.5	2.8	14.5
Production, transportation, and material moving occupations	17,800		77.6	22.4	14.6	3.8	20.4
Production	8,973	13.53	70.3	29.7	12.2	5.2	21.1
Transportation and material moving	8,827	12.65	69.0	31.0	16.4	2.5	19.7

Source: U.S. Bureau of Labor Statistics, Household Data and Annual Averages 11, "Employed Persons by Detailed Occupation, Sex, Race, and Hispanic or Latino Ethnicity" and "Occupational Employment and Wages," May 2007.

to lower earnings. Past and current discrimination against minorities and women in labor markets concentrate the hardship. White men face considerably better structures of opportunity than any other group, but corporate reorganization has entailed a disruption of the lives and incomes of many White men as well. Nevertheless, in an attempt to enhance flexibility, companies parcel out abuse to others, those most at risk in the society. People of color, especially women and youth, remain the most vulnerable groups in the labor market. It is hardly surprising that layoffs in the 2008–9 recession have hit minority workers so hard. One of the most striking effects of this social regression is growing inequality from region to region and especially from city to suburb. Later, in Chapter 4, we analyze these issues in detail.

Women at Work

Women at work earn only three-quarters of what men earn per hour. Although in the last several decades women in the labor force have made progress toward economic equality with men, they are still less well paid and much more likely to be poor. Women's earnings have long influenced family poverty, and over the years their earnings have become increasingly important to family incomes, so even though the wage gap has diminished, its importance has increased. In 1979 wives contributed 16 percent of the income of the average middle-quintile family with children, for example, but by 2000 their contribution had risen to 29 percent.[60] If women are paid less, these contributions are not only harder to get but more limited. For work at home, as critical economists have pointed out now for many years, women receive no salary.[61]

In the paid labor force, women earn less for various reasons. Their occupations pay much less: women predominate among the 3.6 million secretaries and administrative assistants, 2 million cashiers, 1.5 million health aides, and more than 4 million child-care workers, customer service representatives, waiters, and personal appearance workers. Even in management and professional jobs, women tend to be nurses and technicians rather than doctors, and to be teachers and social workers rather than lawyers and top executives, and these occupations draw much lower salaries. But even when women work in the same occupation as men, they get paid significantly less, subject to various forms of discrimination and segregation added to the fact that they are newer, with less experience.

For single women, the wage gap in paid work is even more crucial. Single mothers bear a double burden, as they work in poorly paid occupations, must support families with just one income, and tend to work fewer hours. Their poverty rates, as we have seen, are particularly severe. In the 1980s, among single mothers who worked, 53 percent were unable to earn above poverty-level incomes, generally because their work was intermittent or their wages low.[62] In 2007, although only 6.7 percent of married couples with children were poor, 37 percent of single mothers with children were poor, *a rate more than five times as high.* Single-mother families accounted for more than 60 percent of all families in poverty.[63]

African American, Latina, and Native American women do worse, as wage rates and poverty rates remain tremendously influenced by race and ethnicity. Racial discrimination and occupational segregation weigh heavily. Surveys in the 1980s found African American employees most heavily concentrated in four occupational categories: services; handlers, equipment cleaners, helpers, and laborers; transportation; and machine operators, fabricators, and laborers. Hispanic employees were most heavily concentrated in similar occupations. These occupations tend to be the lowest-paying.[64] Asian American women are "disproportionately represented in low wage jobs such as garment work, high-tech contract assembly work (for example, in Silicon Valley), and domestic work." Compared with median earnings for White women in 2002 ($30,900), those of African American women and Hispanic women were substantially lower ($27,600 and $23,200, respectively). Poverty rates reflect some of these labor market differences. In 1999, 25 percent of Native American women, 24.1 percent of African American women, and 22.5 percent of Hispanic women were poor, in contrast to 9.0 percent of White women. Among Hispanic women, rates vary as well: Cuban women earned $27,700 in 1999, Mexican women $22,100, and Central American women only $19,900.[65]

Who Are the Poor? A Summary by Gender and Race

Two tree diagrams of U.S. Census data for 2007 provide a summary view of poverty numbers. The first diagram (Figure 2.14) is organized initially by gender, the second (Figure 2.15) by race and ethnicity. Together they show that the burden of poverty falls heavily on women with children and disproportionately on African Americans and Latinos/Hispanics. In the first diagram, one finds that more than 14 million families are headed by women, nearly 10 million with children. Of these families with children, 36 percent (3.6 million) are poor; of these poor, female-headed families, 36 percent are White, 38 percent are African American, and 25 percent are Hispanic. Of the married couples, just under half have children under 18 years of age. Of those couples with children, 7 percent (1.8 million) are poor, and 78 percent of those poor families are White. The burden on women with children—White, Black, or Hispanic—is clear. All these dismal figures, from 2007, may be expected to have worsened with further effects of neoconservative budget cuts and then the economic crisis.

Alternatively, in Figure 2.15, one can see that of the 9.3 million African American families in the United States, 2 million (22 percent) are poor. Proceeding down the tree, 80 percent of those poor, African American families have children, and 88 percent of those families with children are headed by women. Of the 10.4 million Hispanic families, 2 million (19 percent) are poor, 90 percent with children. Half these poor Hispanic families with children are headed by women.

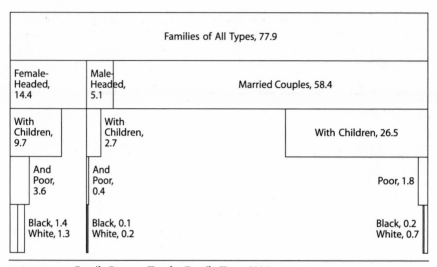

FIGURE 2.14 Family Poverty Tree by Family Type, 2007

Note: Numbers of families in millions, as of March of the following year.

Source: U.S. Census Bureau, Current Population Survey, Annual Social and Economic Supplements, Historical Poverty Tables—Families, Table 4. Poverty Status of Families, by Type of Family, Presence of Related Children, Race, and Hispanic Origin: 1959 to 2007. Available at http://www.census.gov/hhes/www/poverty/histpov/hstpov4.xls.

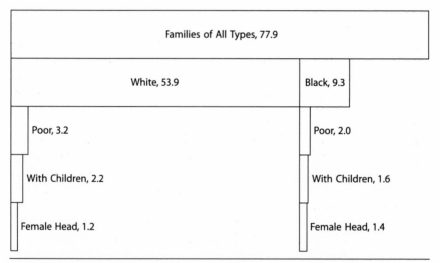

FIGURE 2.15 Family Poverty Tree by Race, 2007

Note: Numbers of families in millions, as of March of the following year.

Source: U.S. Census Bureau, Current Population Survey, Annual Social and Economic Supplements, Historical Poverty Tables—Families, Table 4. Poverty Status of Families, by Type of Family, Presence of Related Children, Race, and Hispanic Origin: 1959 to 2007. Available at http://www.census.gov/hhes/www/poverty/histpov/hstpov4.xls.

In contrast, this family poverty tree reveals that a much smaller portion of White families are poor (6 percent), though they also tend to have children at home (69 percent) and to be headed by women (59 percent).

Health Care, Hunger, Homelessness, and Persistent Poverty

Health care figures prominently in debates over domestic policy. At one extreme, things look good as U.S. scientists win Nobel Prizes in medical research, but at the other extreme they look bad, with high infant mortality and low life expectancy. The contrasts are vivid. With massive expenditures on research and development, new equipment and facilities, and medical personnel and administrators, health-care activities have burgeoned. The elderly population has expanded and with it the need for more services. As activities have increased, insurance companies have raised premiums out of reach. The most severe problems are concentrated on the poor, most of whom are among the 45 to 50 million people without insurance: "At 16 percent of gross domestic product (GDP), U.S. health spending is double the median of industrialized countries and since 2000 has been growing more rapidly than before. Yet the United States is the only major industrialized country that fails to guarantee universal health insurance; coverage in this country is deteriorating, leaving millions without affordable access to care. The U.S. health system also is not the best on quality of care, nor is it a leader in health information technology."[66]

As we saw in Chapter 1, large corporations for decades led opposition to the sorts of national insurance plans used by every other rich industrialized nation. They felt these plans to be too invasive, but now they face the private reality of mushrooming costs. Small or marginal firms, typically opposed to the higher levels of taxation required for collective health services, find the private purchase of insurance unaffordable. For individuals, the problem extends beyond affordability, to include keeping a job. Noting a common incident, a student intern in Baltimore reported a patient who "worried that I will lose my job if they find out about my blood pressure."[67] Like many others, this patient cannot afford complicated health care, and his employer does not provide it. But neither does the employer want the liability of a sick worker.

Many Americans, like their counterparts in other wealthy industrial countries, enjoy the privilege of good health coverage. Their insurance plans provide medications at low cost and the benefits of close professional attention and advanced procedures. Some people are still treated by private physicians, and others enroll with clinics operated by a consortium of doctors or even with giant groups like Kaiser, in which doctors work as employees and patients receive treatment from a hierarchy of specialists. The result for these privileged people mirrors the situation in countries with well-running systems of national health care.

Indeed, the U.S. health-care system seems rigged throughout to benefit the middle class, public employees, unionized workers, and the rich, who reap benefits

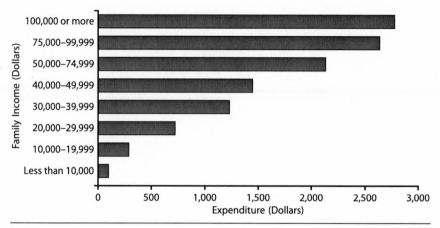

FIGURE 2.16 Federal Tax Expenditure on Health by Family Income, 2004

Source: John Sheils and Randall Haught, "The Cost of Tax-Exempt Health Benefits in 2004," *Health Affairs, Web Exclusive,* W4.106, February 25, 2004. Available at http://content.healthaffairs.org/cgi/content/abstract/hlthaff.w4.106.

of good treatment and low costs. People holding steady jobs full-time with well-covered employers, for example, pay for health insurance and marginal medical costs via salary deductions deposited into tax-free savings accounts. As Figure 2.16 shows, the resulting tax relief increases tremendously with income. Although health failings are more intense for the more than 40 percent of families with incomes below $30,000, their tax benefits averaged well below $725 in 2004. Families with high incomes, on the other hand, received benefits averaging $2,650 or more, almost four times as much.

Parallel biases in favor of those with higher incomes affect research expenditures, quality of clinics and hospitals, and even emergency treatment. More than $94.3 billion is spent annually on private medical and pharmaceutical research, for example, much of it oriented to dealing with problems such as allergies, hair loss, and sexual dysfunctions, as well as on drugs and procedures more likely to be available only to those with higher incomes. Not only do the poor not receive the latest and best drugs, but increasingly they are segregated in a tiered medical delivery system that puts them in hospitals and care systems with the least well trained and least-experienced practitioners. Private hospitals assign physicians according to the patients' health-insurance status. By every measure of physician quality including patient relationships, the poor do not get the best care in the system.[68] More ominously, large and very selective hospitals are beginning to turn away low-income noninsured patients. Aurora St. Luke's in Milwaukee, for example, tries to deflect the problem, claiming that it will continue to see complicated patients who meet their profiles for service and that affiliated hospitals only a few miles away will see indigent patients.[69]

Those without the coverage of medical insurance include people who have lost their insurance as the economy tightens, young workers and others who

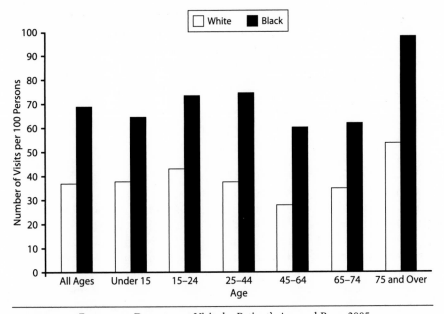

FIGURE 2.17 Emergency Department Visits by Patient's Age and Race, 2005

Source: Eric W. Nawar, Richard W. Niska, and Jianmin Xu, "National Hospital Ambulatory Medical Care Survey: 2005 Emergency Department Summary," Centers for Disease Control and Prevention, National Center for Health Statistics, Advance Data from Vital and Health Statistics, no. 386, 2007. Available at http://www.cdc.gov/nchs/data/ad/ad386.pdf.

work "flexibly" and often change their jobs, or those who simply lose their jobs with worsening industrial fortunes and regional declines. Those who are lucky, who do not have accidents and do not fall ill, avoid the need for medical care. But even the lucky ones worry about their health-care prospects. When the unlucky suffer injuries from accidents or get sick, they either forgo treatment or rely on services for the indigent. Elderly poor patients rely on Medicaid, with its financial penalties. Others depend on the vagaries of various federal programs and state, local, and charitable institutions, few of them dependable and most of them extremely costly for the society that pays the bills. Among the most common solutions is use of emergency rooms in public hospitals. The numbers of emergency room visits is startlingly large, averaging—over the entire population—nearly one ER visit per capita every two years.

As Figure 2.17 shows, African Americans use emergency rooms almost twice as frequently as Whites. Presumably much of that difference is due to lower incomes, lower-paying jobs, and higher unemployment. A look at food-security data in the discussion that follows suggests that race and income indeed play interconnected roles.

Lack of insurance not only burdens the emergency care system but also causes people to postpone and reduce treatment, thus leading to less effective treatment in the end. Some who are ill do not seek treatment at all. Some, in overburdened emergency rooms, wait too long for attention, for hours or even days. Some get treatment too late, their conditions leading to complications or potentially avoidable illnesses. All these bad consequences of unaffordable private health care lead not only to worse health for the poor but to higher costs to the society at large, for more expensive health facilities, more extensive and more specialized treatments, and lower productivity. Whatever the mix of causation for poor care, extra illness, and high costs—including discrimination by race/ethnicity, low household income, underprivileged neighborhood location—lack of health care or poor health care contributes to illness and to premature death.

Certain kinds of lifestyles can lead to poor health, and unhealthy lifestyles may be encouraged by poverty and neighborhood isolation. Whatever the causes, poor Americans drink more alcohol, smoke more cigarettes, and eat more fatty foods than the middle and upper middle classes, and these proclivities make them sicker. It is increasingly "uncool" among the wealthy to smoke anything other than marijuana or a good contraband Cuban cigar, and although a general reluctance to smoke may have moved down to the middle class, this good health choice has not yet moved much lower.[70] Among the most damaging results of the lifestyle of the poor is obesity, spreading worldwide but in the United States becoming epidemic. One in three army volunteers in 2008 was turned away because of weight problems.[71] Obesity leads to increased hypertension, diabetes, and even respiratory problems, known to be higher in minority groups. The multiple and overlapping effects of race, income level, and neighborhood combine so that African Americans, Native Americans, and some Asians have higher rates of obesity than Whites. Alarming levels and increases in the 1990s appear in Figure 2.18.

Obesity is not merely a personal problem but a neighborhood problem as well. In poor neighborhoods food choices are limited and healthy food options harder to indulge. Once again race comes into play. "More than a third of African American women report no leisure time physical activity," according to the U.S. Centers for Disease Control.[72] Neighborhoods (connected to poverty) would seem to be at the root of this problem. Researchers examining variations in obesity community by community found that residents in "neighborhoods in which at least one-quarter of the residents are Black face a 13 percent increase in the odds of being obese compared with residents of other communities."[73]

What does all of this mean? Poor people have long been at the bottom of the health pyramid, during the industrial revolution suffering from life expectancies only half those of the rich, but history shows that society has implemented collective improvements that allow the poor to catch up, perhaps mainly in self-defense. When communicable diseases were rampant and the rich were unable to insulate themselves, new vaccines were delivered universally, in good part to protect the rich. Over the centuries it is only with social advances such as municipal provision of clean water and sanitation and public regulation guaranteeing clean food that the health and longevity of poor people has increased. When

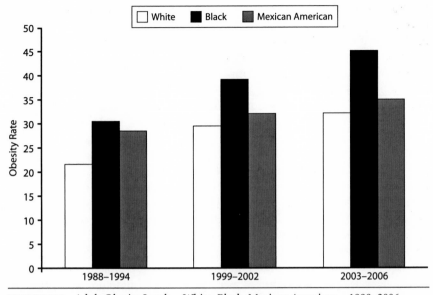

FIGURE 2.18   Adult Obesity Levels—White, Black, Mexican American—1988–2006

Source: Centers for Disease Control and Prevention, Health Data Interactive, Risk Factors and Disease Prevention. Available at http://205.207.175.93/hdi/ReportFolders/ReportFolders.aspx?IF_ActivePath=P,24.

authorities feared that rats could carry diseases from tenements to middle-class neighborhoods, tenements were razed to make way for cleaner dwellings. When housing is a public health matter, its provision may ensure survival of the rich. If the society can fund research and treatment for the "private" problems of breast cancer and heart disease, what about the "public" health threats of obesity, poisonous air quality, and toxic poisoning?

As poverty has become more widespread, residential segregation, workplace segmentation, and other aspects of geographic isolation have made it less visible. In an odd turn, however, the extremities of poverty have become more visible as illiteracy has thwarted job applicants, hunger has extended breadlines, patients have overwhelmed emergency wards, and beggars have become part of the urban landscape. Perhaps most noticeable are homeless people. A 2004 report by the National Law Center on Homelessness and Poverty counted 3.5 million people homeless for one or more nights in the course of the year, approximately 1 percent of the U.S. population. Children form the fastest-growing group among the homeless. Between 170,000 and 330,000 children under 18 were homeless each night, not including runaways. Missing from all these counts are families doubled up with relatives, friends, or others, growing numbers especially in rapidly expanding and high-rent metropolitan areas. The numbers above all refer to good economic years long before the 2008–2009 meltdown. Daily reports suggest great increases in homelessness, tent cities, doubling up, and of course foreclosures and evictions.

Information on hunger is equally damning. Each year the Economic Research Service of the Department of Agriculture conducts a nationwide survey on food security—ERS asks families and households whether they get enough to eat.[74] If households have incomes higher than 185 percent of the federal poverty line *and* say they never run short of money for food *and* say they always get enough food of the kinds they want to eat, then they are food-secure. If they do run short, they are called food-insecure. Nationwide, 11 percent of households in 2004 and 12 percent of persons were not food-secure, that is, they went hungry some of the time. This statistic undercounts because the survey misses homeless people. In 2006, 15.6 percent of households with children experienced food insecurity.[75] The ERS found that more than 5 million children under age 12, one of every eight children in the country, then suffered from substantial food shortages because of poverty. Another 6 million children were close to the margin, either hungry or risking hunger.[76] Hungry children are more likely than others to suffer from fatigue, irritability, headaches, and related health problems.

Poor people are the hungriest. Even if we ignore those who are homeless, one-third (33.2 percent) of poor households (below 130% of the poverty line) were hungry, as were 40.6 percent of poor households with children. Among poor White households, the figure was 30.5 percent; for Black households, it was notably higher, at 39.8 percent, with Hispanic households in between, at 33.5 percent. Significantly, hunger rates for *poor* households are higher in central cities.[77] We return to these city-suburb differences in Chapter 4, to suggest why the city poor are hungrier than their suburban counterparts, whether households in inner suburbs suffer similarly, and how the race of the household matters.

Illness and even death result from poverty, homelessness, and hunger. As reported by the Centers for Disease Control, after a century of improvement, trends for improvement have stagnated:

> Infant mortality is one of the most important indicators of the health of a nation, as it is associated with a variety of factors such as maternal health, quality and access to medical care, socioeconomic conditions, and public health practices. The U.S. infant mortality rate generally declined throughout the 20th century. In 1900, the U.S. infant mortality rate was approximately 100 infant deaths per 1,000 live births, while in 2000, the rate was 6.89 infant deaths per 1,000 live births. However, the U.S. infant mortality rate did not decline significantly from 2000 to 2005.[78]

Infant mortality in the United States is the highest in the First World, and it ranks last among twenty-three industrial countries. Worldwide among developed countries, the United States was ranked 29th in 2004, tied with Poland and Slovakia. Things have gotten worse: the United States was ranked 12th in 1960 and 23rd in 1990. Among new mothers, Black women have the highest infant mortality, with rates at 13.6 per 1,000 live births, compared with Whites at 5.5. Puerto Ricans, American Indians, and Alaskan Natives also have rates above average, while other Latinos, Asians, and Pacific Islanders have rates the same as those of Whites or somewhat lower.[79]

The three Hs hit home—health, hunger, and homelessness. When broken down in detail by race and ethnicity, the already ominous figures become more troubling. As we have seen, high proportions of African Americans and Latinos have always lived below the poverty line, and many more not far above, so they are more vulnerable. Similar or even worse situations confront Native Americans and some Asian American or immigrant subgroups. Minority households have rates of poverty two to three times as high as those of Whites.

Most poor people are officially poor only temporarily. As economist Michael Zweig points out in a study published in 2004: "While in any given year 12 to 15 percent of the population is poor, over a ten-year period 40 percent experience poverty in at least one year because most poor people cycle in and out of poverty; they don't stay poor for long periods. Poverty is something that happens to the working class, not some marginal 'other' on the fringes of society."[80]

Nevertheless, of the many people who pass through poverty, a significant number remain poor for long periods of time, and many researchers have argued that—under certain circumstances—poverty gets passed on from parents to children, or even from neighbor to neighbor. Poverty afflicts not just people but their places.[81] Bruce Katz, director of the Brookings Institution Metropolitan Policy Program, in his introduction to the 2008 Brookings–Federal Reserve report on concentrated poverty, points to the places where persistent poverty is so frequently a serious problem. "Not only does concentrated poverty affect the big, older inner cities in the North that are the subject of so many classic studies, but it also exists within smaller cities of the South and West, immigrant gateways, struggling areas of Appalachia and the Delta, and Native American lands." Katz adds, "The negative consequences ring familiar across places big and small; urban and rural; industrial and agricultural; African American, White, Latino, and Native American."[82] In most of the metropolitan situations we examine in this book, concentrations of poor people involve Blacks and Latinos, and persistence of poverty is a circumstance forced onto them and their children.

As Zweig's data confirm, most poor people struggle through, eventually becoming not "poor." In this period of economic crisis, as millions lose their jobs, their savings, and their homes, the experience of poverty becomes more widespread and the damages from poverty become more well known. Even in the United States, where the cult of individualism reigns, deep recession or near depression causes people to become aware that it makes no sense to assign blame for poverty to the victims of systematic failures beyond their control.[83] Nevertheless, for outsiders, for those who are not usually poor, the guilty parties *are* the persistently poor places and families—the ghettos and barrios themselves, and the underpaid or unemployed people who live in them.

Long-term poverty afflicts a significant number of households, and it puts huge pressures on communities. A considerable number of people who fall persistently below the poverty line live in households with intact families, or where the householder is disabled or elderly, or where the householder works a sub-stantial part of the year. Even to outsiders, these people look like the "deserving" poor. But because within cities the long-term poor are most often located in high-poverty areas, African Americans and Latinos disproportionately among them, stereotypes are common.

A minority of the persistently poor often have problems that come close to the pejorative stereotypes, suffering from welfare dependence, long-term unem-ployment, or failure to complete high school. Because African American families are overrepresented among the persistently poor, misuse of the data allows racist stereotyping of the country's poorest people. In fact, most poor African Ameri-can families, including those who have been poor over the long term, are poor for the same reasons that White families are: lack of well-paid work, only one employee in the family, normally a woman, and little useful education, even for those who have finished high school. Children are highly overrepresented among the persistently poor of all races.

Deep separations divide Americans. The bad situation of the persistently poor in inner-city neighborhoods continues, connected to skyrocketing prison popu-lations, and the problems have spread to inner suburbs. Barriers of race, ethnic-ity, and income continue to erode the social fabric of our cities and undermine our national economic well-being.

Once we account for race and ethnicity, household demographics, and physi-cal isolation, we have the basis for "explaining" most of the inequality of urban incomes that the statistics show. Large numbers of Americans are poorly educated and underskilled, suffer from discrimination, and are in turn hampered by low self-esteem. Many African Americans remain isolated from mainstream Ameri-can jobs, education, culture, and economic life, and so do many Puerto Ricans, Chicanos, and Central Americans, other immigrants, and women who manage families alone. These groups form the base for urban poverty.

Social, economic, and geographic separations mirror and extend the divisions that have been deepening even among better-off Americans, as the middle class has been shedding members into a more and more affluent portion at the very top and a harder-struggling group of workers and unemployed adults below.

Sophisticated and experienced observers from the Third World are shocked when they see in U.S. cities scenes that display familiar sorts of distinctions. The gap between well off and very poor confronts these visitors when they see beggars outside elegant city shops and restaurants or when they hear of neighborhoods that are dangerous to visit. These observers have learned to live with but not to notice such distinctions in the big cities of Asia, Africa, and Latin America. The present danger in the United States is that we are creating a bottom level, like that taken for granted by some in the Third World, with no access to the top. As the next two chapters show, our social institutions now guarantee this result. This is not what America should be about.

3

Separate Opportunities

Competition versus Inclusion—
The International Dimensions
of American Urban Poverty

In the twenty-first century some U.S. metropolitan areas operate from high in the global economic order and others function near the bottom, but they all find themselves zooming up, down, and around, as if they are riding an international roller coaster, constantly ducking obstacles thrown in the way by new contenders from overseas. The Chicago mayor and his economic development director travel to Japan to entice investors, and it will not be long before major U.S. cities have secretaries of foreign affairs, as does São Paulo. Meanwhile, small cities in the southern or midwestern United States propose English-only legislation, fearful at their first heavy encounter with immigrants—a January 2009 ballot measure in Nashville almost made English the official language, and in Missouri the previous November, a constitutional amendment for official English passed by a margin of 86 to 14.

Journalist and author Thomas Friedman thinks the new global arrangements yield a flat earth. The high interconnections are revolutionary, and they radically change the context, but from most cities' perspectives, the earth is anything but flat. Some cities sit off the roller-coaster tracks, abandoned at the bottom, while others ride high, powerfully linked to subordinate places worldwide: "With the revolution in transportation technologies ushered in with the introduction of the jumbo jet, the supertanker, and the container ship, manufacturing firms have been able to move their operations farther and farther away from where their products are actually consumed. Now, with such revolutionary telecommunications technology as high-speed Internet, mobile phones, and satellite links, all kinds of business services—from banking

es [and] teleconferencing [to] online technical assistance—can be coordi-
ed and delivered from nearly anywhere on earth."[1]

Some see the world as flat, but the most successful cities stick up like mountain peaks, as their enterprises create the technology and infrastructure of communication, invent new products, manage far-flung operations, and offer the
high life. Yet in this competitive world even these cities face challenges. All struggle to mitigate internal inequalities as they feel the effects of a globalization led
by giant banks, corporations, and compliant government allies. The stakes are
high, and the game is rigged. In every metropolis the poor are merely pawns.
Powerful interests have set rules that permit imports from foreign sweatshops,
assist companies to move production offshore, reduce taxes and regulations on
speculators and leave them free to move their assets abroad, and encourage people to consume excessively at home. The offshoring firms avoid paying taxes even
though they receive services and subsidies from public agencies and protection
from the military, thus expanding public deficits.

This system reduces human beings to consumers, who when they spend,
purchase imported goods and generate huge international debt imbalances. They
are encouraged by advertisers and admonished by the government to spend
unproductively.[2] The system bulges with instability. The easy money led many
to ignore the problems that follow unregulated growth, unmitigated borrowing,
and uneven development. Some observers anticipated the bad news to follow,
saw the roller coaster heading too fast down the tracks. In January 2007, nearly
two years in advance of the crash, North Dakota senator Byron Dorgan spoke a
warning: "At the moment, there's a great yawn about all this, but one day when
everything collapses, people will ask: Why didn't we do anything."[3]

In order to meet outside competition, metropolitan business elites demand
that municipal leaders support the construction of *competitive cities,* making
them more attractive for investors and top managers and more efficient for
production and commerce. The elites want their cities to replace decadent
industry with redeveloped waterfronts and to build new recreation facilities.
They want hotels and high-end restaurants to attract tourists, gussied-up downtowns to attract residents to shops and theaters, and high-end services to be
offered to themselves and their office staffs. In their operations, business leaders
want to avoid strong unions, cut expensive programs for social services, and
reduce high levels of taxation. To no one's surprise, corporations exert their
pressures so as to enhance profitable operations in the face of outside competition, and such pressures are hard for politicians to resist. Coalitions of business
firms, labor unions, and even neighborhood organizations form local alliances
in favor of economic growth, to persuade otherwise opposed groups that their
interests are mutual, and to convince skeptics that local or regional economic
growth must be the paramount goal.

Almost inevitably, as cities try to take steps along the global-competitive
path, they trip over snags growing out of the ordinary inequalities of the labor
market. Corporations pay their executives and professionals extremely well, and

cities serve downtowns and other business areas well. But ordinary workers earn much less, and cities, unlike well-off suburbs, do not serve their ordinary neighborhoods well. Business groups push for economic growth, but residents, local leaders, and political representatives make demands for neighborhood services. They create pressure for *inclusive cities*, with changes that would make things *more* equal, not less. Even if residents support growth coalitions, they still want safe and clean streets and sidewalks, competent schools that teach their children, affordable rents and mortgages, and good jobs that provide a living wage. These things require municipal expenditures, which can come only from expanded budgets, which dictate higher taxes. But capacities are limited. In middle-class suburbs residents may complain, but they often meet the fiscal demands rather easily. In the cities and in some less affluent suburbs things are more problematic, especially since tax revenues are often based on declining property values.

Deep contradictions and opposing forces thus confront cities and their surrounding metropolitan areas, as the rules of competition make it more difficult to promote inclusion. Many urbanized areas—and not only in the United States—face such conflicts, which arise from the very nature of market-dominated societies. Increasingly, many cities with their surrounding areas also confront the daunting experience of economic decline, loss of status, and increased dependency. When a metropolis faces such conditions, success at global competition becomes ever more crucial, but it also becomes less likely.

With corporate decision makers ever more susceptible to stimuli from overseas, the push and pull of global market competition brings about industrial changes. The new economy generates migration, influences patterns of land use, arranges and rearranges residential neighborhoods, and finally, affects not only how people are paid and where they live but the way they are housed, transported, and provisioned with municipal services. In the most starkly obvious picture, one can see in every U.S. metropolis a pair of opposed interests, fully *separate societies,* one rich and the other poor, one suburban and the other urban, one white and the other minority. As the next chapter shows, reality is more complex than such a sharply bifurcated pattern, with profound inequalities appearing in geographic patchworks. International intrusions have led to broad regional rearrangements of industry, leaving many metropolitan areas economically stagnant, with suburbs still stable but central cities, inner suburbs, and some fringe areas in decline, city people stranded without jobs, and various municipal governments unable to collect sufficient taxes.

City halls cannot fund the public services needed by the additionally unemployed or increasingly poorly paid workforce. Fiscal shortcomings make the city still less attractive for reinvestors, thus aggravating a cycle of self-reinforcing decline. With circular causation the downward spiral is extended by the legacy and continued practices of employment discrimination, housing exclusion, and school segregation. Even unincorporated places on the fringes of previously booming areas in Florida or California feel the pressures. Once-vital small central cities such as Utica or Elmira in Upstate New York or Youngstown, Ohio, or large cities like St. Louis were hit first by long-run industrial change and migration of business and population to growing parts of the nation, and second by global economic changes drawing manufacturing plants, trade, and employment overseas. Many U.S. cities have lost their main employment base and now seem half ghost towns, deserted by the middle class, surrounded by still viable suburbs, but collapsing at the centers. Such cities are sometimes said to be "specializing" in health care, drug rehabilitation, and social services, but these activities make little sense as metropolitan export bases or "growth" generators.

Some see the glass half full; others, half empty. From one set of perspectives, as markets expand internationally, corporations can operate in freer ways and entrepreneurs can avoid constraints that would limit their innovative activities, so globalization enhances both productivity and democracy. Arguing this case, corporate lobbyists once generated wide support from those who believe everyone would benefit, and until the recession that began officially in December 2007 these promoters encountered little opposition. Hyper-neoconservatives such as Francis Fukuyama propounded wild optimism about the wonders of free markets.[4] They cited stale arguments to warn anew against the hazards of centralized planning, as though the cold war were still being fought. They recycled once cogent critiques by Friedrich Hayek and others, exaggerating so as to turn solid analysis into flim-flam, railing against all government activity, supporting the anti-tax movement's malign efforts to slash the public sector.[5] Even after the stock market crash of the 2008–2009 recession, most politicians have difficulty openly rejecting the right-wing rhetoric that falsely ties freedom and prosperity to deregulation. This rhetoric survived the 1980s presidency of Ronald Reagan to be vigorously revived by President George W. Bush, Vice President Dick Cheney, and their political allies, and in spite of changing political fortunes, critics still hesitate to point directly enough at the disruptive nature of weakly regulated corporations, banks, and markets.[6] Long ago some of the most enthusiastic adherents of "supply-side" economics acknowledged that they cynically used smoke and mirrors to create myths that allowed their leaders to shift tax burdens away from the rich.[7] Nevertheless, right-wing politicians and their talk-radio allies continue to condemn tax payments and government services as the ultimate evils.[8]

The voting majority that elected Barack Obama would seem to reject these views, but even after widespread revulsion against the multimillion-dollar bonuses paid to bankers, whom most people blame for the crisis, the Washington break with the old neoconservatism is tentative. Apparently very few are willing to admit in public what economist Bruce Scott of the Harvard Business School pointed out in 2007: "The one thing that you can say is that capitalism is going to relentlessly produce inequality of income, and eventually that is going to become incompatible with democracy."[9] Mountainous transfers of fictitious wealth triggered the Wall Street disintegration of 2008 and 2009. Yet the very leaders of deregulation, those who prompted the paper-value explosions and transfers of wealth, later moved to occupy positions of authority in the Obama government. If these officials hesitate to implement sufficiently radical changes, they will be unable to limit the drastic inequalities that make the market downturns so much more painful for the poor and for minority persons.[10] One of the worst effects is the growth and deepening of poverty, which extends bread lines, overtaxes homeless shelters, and dislodges communities as it destroys families and individuals. These damages hit poor city neighborhoods particularly hard.

In the previous chapter we detailed the proximate driving forces of poverty as underemployment, falling real wages, and a badly skewed income distribution. In this chapter we look at how pressures in the global economy threaten to overwhelm the domestic economy, creating the context for the transformations we observe. U.S. policy has moved to include the domestic labor pool inside the global workforce, not only weakening domestic labor but preventing it from finding a new perch in the American economy, given labor's isolation from those who control American politics. Even after the Obama election, evidently with strong support from labor, top cabinet and agency appointments appear less than accepting of many labor demands. The underlying problems, of workers without skills and income distributions with great inequality, remain hidden.

High on the list of the concerns of many leaders—along with war and climate change, but relegating poverty problems to the sidelines—is the U.S. response to global economic and financial pressures. Such global concerns push issues of cities and metropolitan areas near the bottom of the list. Even the most progressive activists in the Obama campaign and in the administration say little if anything about problems of cities or problems of poverty. The Obama transition team's document on urban policy does pose the possibility of a dramatic shift, as it suggests that the nation might celebrate rather than denigrate cities, and it acknowledges poverty as a problem, but its proposals seem remedial rather than fundamental. Nowhere do the proposals measure up to the challenges that cities face as they confront a drastically changed international economy. We return to these themes when we address questions of governance in Chapter 5.

This chapter has five main sections:

- In the first two sections we observe that in the game of industrial restructuring, the bad cards have been dealt to labor. U.S. industry has responded to reorganized global markets by reducing wages as a short-term measure to meet competition. Corporations have worsened working conditions and laid off workers, thus increasing unemployment and pushing up poverty. Unskilled men and women especially, including many minority workers, all trying to get on the bottom rung of this economic ladder, have discovered that the rung has been sawed off and shipped overseas.
- In the third section we explore the relocation of industrial activity, and we ask how different theories have tried to understand that transformation. As industrial composition has shifted and places of employment have moved, labor has been stranded and workers and their families have been impoverished.

- In the fourth section we briefly examine components of international economic reorganization. We focus on international trade and saturated domestic markets. These changes have cut into the profits of U.S. firms, which in turn have moved to downgrade labor.
- Finally, we look at the globalization of finance and regulatory systems. We find increased instability, rising speculation, and high levels of debt. Each of these erodes the capacity for the sound domestic policy that is required to fight poverty.

As we have seen in Chapter 2, although real wages grew continuously from the end of World War II until the early 1970s, they declined precipitously in the 1980s and continued their decline after 2000. Worse yet, many workers are unable to find full-time or steady work, or any work at all. Minority persons and women suffer additionally from discrimination. It is our argument that these worsened conditions result from inappropriate public policy in the face of the restructuring of industry, shifts in labor demand, and the weakness of workers against employers. Sharp shifts in worldwide patterns of economics and politics laid the basis for rising poverty, and layoffs and low wages then combined with untimely and ill-designed political shifts and fiscal withdrawal to cause the growth of poverty. These troublesome trends occurred before the financial meltdown, to be exacerbated by it.

The competition that accompanies increased "openness" of national economies, with less restricted trade, labor, and capital flows, has placed pressure on governments and firms to restructure their operations according to international technological, commercial, and regulatory conditions rather than national ones. New technologies and practices have played a critical role in restructuring the global economy and in reorganizing occupational patterns, urban economies, and whole regions. These changes, in turn, have led to a reshuffling of national priorities so that low-skilled labor has become far less valuable to firms, except at bargain-basement low wages.[11] Perhaps the most astonishing result of all is that persistent and even expanding poverty in recent years has mirrored ever-increasing salaries at the top echelons, as business entered competitive markets on international terms but without any national strategy to include ordinary workers.

Under these circumstances, policymakers ought no longer to think that problems of poverty issue solely from local or even national pressures. As Matthew Drennan notes, "Just as a city is not a sufficient unit of analysis of an urban economy, neither is a nation."[12] Although we do not agree with Hazel Henderson that "what's happening in Washington is less important than the globalization processes" or that "the [White House] is as much being buffeted around as the government of any other country," we do think poverty grows in part because of the failure of governments to respond properly to international economic pressures. As Henderson wrote years ago, "The inability of governments to manage domestic economies because of the enormous capital flows, along with these globalization processes, is one of the key drivers."[13]

Whereas once the United States was highly insulated from international economics and politics at least during peacetime, by the beginning of the 1990s it had become merely one among equals in the industrial world, even if still the leading one. And where the United States once could manage the Third World with gunboat diplomacy, even seizing foreign customs offices so as to collect tax payments on the dock or sending in the Marines, as it did in Grenada, the Dominican Republic, and Panama in the late twentieth century, it now has little choice but to suffer penalties when bankrupt nations appear to pose threats or fail to pay their debts. The U.S. economy is still mainly domestic, and it need not fear three ultimate financial indignities: it has not suffered hyperinflation, it has neither declared bankruptcy nor suffered insolvency, and it has not been forced to accept formal directives from the International Monetary Fund. Nevertheless, the country now endures grave problems that derive in large part from its unwillingness to manage properly its ever more intense and interconnected economic relations with other countries. One great symbol of limitations on U.S. freedom of economic action comes from China's massive holdings of U.S. debt. Many of these difficulties lead to public incapacity to deal with poverty at home.

In one way, globalization is like sustainability—the meaning is hard to pin down, and each speaker or writer seems to have a different idea. Still, at the root of nearly every discussion of globalization is the idea that international connectedness has not just increased by degree but changed in nature. Faster telecommunications, broader spans of financial control, and increased transport capacity have brought a global economy into existence. Unlike sustainability, however, which nearly everyone favors even without agreement on its meaning, globalization has proponents and opponents. Among mainstream economists and many corporate leaders, who define globalization narrowly and mainly in terms of expanded trade, the new global economy is altogether a good thing. Others worry that the integrated economy brings various costs, such as the transfer of political control to multinational corporations, broad reductions in national autonomy, or uncontrolled trade in weaponry.[14] One major concern is exacerbated inequalities. Dani Rodrik, an international economist at Harvard's Kennedy School, challenges "the people who talk incessantly about trade and its importance," warning that the country needs to adopt a "social insurance agenda as part and parcel of that process," much as European nations have done.[15] According to David Autor, an economist at MIT: "The consensus until recently was that trade was not a major cause of the earnings inequality in this country. That consensus is now being revisited. . . . There is agreement that outsourcing abroad, in particular, is potentially a source of real downward pressure on employment and wages."[16] The Hamilton Project, founded by President Clinton's treasury secretary, Robert Rubin, whose protégés dominate the Obama economics team, accepts the social insurance agenda, but only grudgingly, "to soften the backlash."[17] Noting lost jobs and reduced wages, Hamilton Project director Jason Furman put it this way: "People are more likely to support free trade if it does not have the intense personal downside that it so often has today." Ben Bernanke, the chairman of the

Federal Reserve, first appointed by George W. Bush, notes threats to "the liveli-hoods of some workers and the profits of some firms," warning that "the unequal distribution of the economy's spoils could derail the trade liberalization of recent decades.... [Policymakers should] insure that the benefits of global economic integration are sufficiently widely shared."[18]

Three features dominate the current situation: America is less influential in worldwide economic affairs, the international economy itself is less stable, and the landscape of domestic industry has been transformed. In these circumstances, and given the more complete interpenetration of U.S. and world markets, it would be almost impossible to eradicate poverty by relying on old-fashioned domestic economic policies, employment and training programs, or efforts that focus on jobs alone. Policies must face up to America's new place in the world, but they have not. David Raney, a city planning professor turned labor organizer, finds the effects of globalization most telling in the frustration of workers who would organize unions and neighborhood groups. Globalization, he finds, exports factory jobs, undermines worker incomes, and raises urban real estate prices, thus damaging people at the workplace and at home.[19]

As we will see, corporate strategies to meet international competition have resulted in disinvestment, de-skilling, relocation abroad, and retreat into finan-cial rather than productive activities. They have also resulted in extraordinary levels of spending beyond our means. Up to the financial crisis, saving rates in the United States dropped practically to zero, or even turned negative, and the failure to pay our way resulted in heavy international debt. Corporate changes, undertaken in part to deal with the pressures of globalization, are inadequate, temporary responses to longer-term, more ominous global economic trends. The changes are private, uncoordinated, conflictive, and unsuccessful. The strategies themselves generate new difficulties, such as fiscal crises for particular places and massive unemployment for certain social groups within the United States. Not least among these problems is the pushing out of large numbers of people from the labor market, the victims of the previous chapter, who find fewer and fewer opportunities for good jobs.

Industrial managers and union officials long ago broke their mutual-admiration contracts, and the high wages of organized factory workers and many other employees have been hacked away. After years of progress with technical innovation, product development, advertising, and big assembly lines, American industry faces decline. Many industries reached the top of the curve of mass consumption and production and the peak of their technological superiority in the 1970s, which they then followed with cutbacks, shutdowns, job loss, and capital flight. Where U.S. leading-edge technological dominance was once the rule, it is now the exception. The superprofits that reward technological leader-ship and fatten domestic wages now belong to industries in other countries. U.S. shares have declined in science and innovation, as measured by publications in professional journals, patents, Nobel Prizes awarded to researchers, and numbers of students pursuing graduate-level work in science and engineering. In 1983

U.S. scientists wrote 61 percent of the articles in *Physical Review,* for example, but by 2003 that share had declined to only 29 percent. Officials at the National Science Foundation and the National Academy of Engineering credit "the ebb and flow of globalization," saying that "the rest of the world is catching up," and "science excellence is no longer the domain of just the U.S."[20]

The transformation began as the energy ran out of U.S. postwar hegemony. Briefly stated, after the full force of the still-limited American welfare state was spent, with its Keynesian regulation of the economy, high wages, supportive labor legislation, and extensive public services, rising expenditures began to outstrip tax resources.[21] Services could not be provided without huge public deficits on top of higher taxes, many of them to support the warfare state. The Treasury financed the Vietnam War with deficits, and inflation kept moving up and up. To stem inflation, conservatives began to snip the threads of the social safety net; then they slashed. Reactionary politics attacked liberalism: in California in 1977 there was Proposition 13, which drastically limited property taxes and therefore undermined the financial basis for education, public services, and a multitude of locally supported public programs. Prop 13 was pushed by a tiny but influential group of property owners, but it was supported by large majorities of voters. In Massachusetts, Proposition 1-1/2, passed in 1979, similarly strangled municipal efforts to deliver expected services. In New York City the corporate officers who directed the Municipal Assistance Corporation temporarily resolved the city's bankruptcy by installing an austerity program similar to those approved by international lenders to balance the books of insolvent Third World countries.

Excepting comparatively wealthy suburbs, almost everywhere else schools, public services, and maintenance of facilities were neglected, budgets left stagnating or reduced. Ronald Reagan, Margaret Thatcher, and other ultraconservative ideologues led an almost global reaction against using public resources to meet domestic human needs, as political leaders, corporate managers, and other well-paid people fought to increase their wealth by lowering taxes as the path to economic recovery. In the United States the Reagan juggernaut was adapted in more subtle terms to corporate reality with the presidency of George H. W. Bush. During the entire three terms of Reagan and Bush, the people who could least afford the dismantling of an already weak welfare state were required to bear the burden of a drastic economic overhaul.

Some respite from the conservative onslaught occurred during the presidency of Bill Clinton, but the respite was limited in scope and duration, as the administration compromised its liberal mission and then suffered defeat in Congress with the 1994 Republican Revolution, which ended forty years of Democratic Party dominance of the House of Representatives. The neoconservative Contract with America disabled a potentially progressive White House after it had been in power only two years.

As pointed out in Chapter 2, workers' incomes did rise and poverty did fall in the 1990s, from 15 percent to 11 percent. When George W. Bush entered the White House after being in effect appointed by the Supreme Court in 2000, his

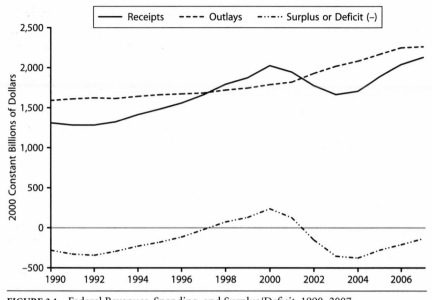

FIGURE 3.1   Federal Revenues, Spending, and Surplus/Deficit, 1990–2007
Source: U.S. Office of Management and Budget, Budget of the United States Government, Historical Tables, Table 1.3. Summary of Receipts, Outlays, and Surpluses or Deficits (–) in Current Dollars, Constant (FY 2000) Dollars, and as Percentages of GDP: 1940–2014. Available at http://www.whitehouse.gov/omb/budget/Historicals/ (accessed 2008).

administration was joined by a compliant Congress, and the poverty rate stopped improving. After the disastrous attacks of September 11, the warfare-state budget went back into deficit. Simultaneously, authorities weakened regulations, diminished labor protections, and lessened various taxing powers of the federal government, despite the need for funds to pay for billowing war expenditures in Iraq and Afghanistan and despite the rising dependency ratio, reflecting more retirees for every active taxpaying worker, which requires adjustments in funding for Social Security and health programs. As during the Reagan administration, public spending rose despite anti-government rhetoric and drastic reductions in tax revenues, so that public debt increased. Figure 3.1 shows that annual real outlays from 1991 to 1999 increased at an arithmetic average of 1.0 percent, while from 1999 to 2007 they increased on average more than three times as steeply, by 3.3 percent. In the first eight years revenues rose more quickly than outlays, but in the second eight years they did not.[22]

Although the financial and employment collapses of 2008–2009 suddenly added depth to many problems, they had built up over many years. Even while pundits and economists loudly denied that the economy was in trouble, the country entered recession officially at the end of 2007. Long before the recession was confirmed, a front-page article in the business section of the *New York Times* in March 2008 asked whether the "lean" economy was turning "mean." The article looked back a few years: "Even as job growth accelerated in 2005 and 2006 before slowing last year, it was not enough to return the country to its previous level. Some 62.8 percent of all Americans age 16 and older were employed at the end of last year, down from the peak of 64.6 percent in early 2000, according to the Labor Department."[23]

The terms hark back not just to 2005 but much longer, to at least 1994, when economist Bennett Harrison published a book called *Lean and Mean,* remarking on one of the changes that had already broken the nation's middle-class consensus.[24] The next section examines several decades of technology change, corporate decisions, and globalization, to see how they have affected the labor force.

Restructuring for Whom?

The first recession of the twenty-first century hit the U.S. labor force hard, especially manufacturing. As the Congressional Budget Office (CBO) reported in February 2004: "The manufacturing sector of the U.S. economy has experienced substantial job losses over the past several years. In January 2004, the number of such jobs stood at 14.3 million, down by 3.0 million jobs, or 17.5 percent, since July 2000 and about 5.2 million since the historical peak in 1979. Employment in manufacturing was its lowest since July 1950."[25]

The CBO attributes those job losses to the recession, but also to shifts in demand away from manufactured goods, increases in productivity, competition from overseas producers, and changes in the way workers are used in manufacturing. Specialists debate how much of the job loss to attribute to the changing structure of the industry and how much to foreign competition (much of that from U.S.-owned firms), but no one disputes that changes in the global economy influence both trade and the structure of domestic industry. Analysts at the Economic Policy Institute find trade to have a powerful effect, with service-industry gains insufficient to make up for manufacturing losses. Already by 2003 the damages were severe: "The growing trade deficit in manufacturing goods accounts for about 58% of the decline in manufacturing employment between 1998 and 2003 and 34% of the decline from 2000 to 2003. . . . It is unrealistic to think that [service growth offsetting manufacturing loss] can be sustained in the long run."[26]

What do these changes bring to the poor? By 2009, with deeper recession, losses for a broad spectrum of Americans had become much more serious, and the public had little energy left to worry about the poor. After all, reasonably paid factory workers, office employees, and retails clerks had already lost hours, wages, or entire jobs, and the deep recession struck them harder. But things were already bad for the poor: "If you look at the numbers, the 1990's was a bad decade for young black men, even though it had the best labor market in 30 years."[27] In New York City, for example, even in the boom years from 1990 to 2000, between 300,000 and 500,000 people crowded themselves into tiny, unsafe spaces in illegal housing units. A survey found 114,000 such units, in buildings cut up like nineteenth-century tenements. Yet with each downturn the ranks of the poor grew and the situation turned bleaker. Randy Albelda, an economist at the University

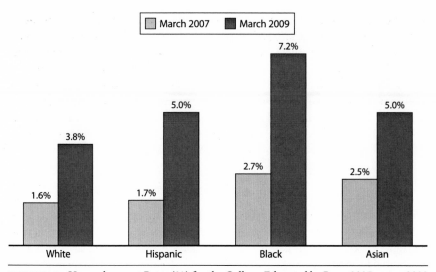

FIGURE 3.2   Unemployment Rates (%) for the College-Educated by Race, 2007 versus 2009
Source: Algernon Austin, "Among College-Educated, African Americans Hardest Hit by Unemployment," Economic Policy Institute, Snapshot for April 22, 2009. Available at http://www.epi.org/economic_snapshots/entry/snapshots_20090422/.

of Màssachusetts, said in March 2008 that "the labor market for low-income women is so poor that it's almost a hoax."[28] In November the Richmond *Times-Dispatch* reported that "from income to unemployment to health care to home-ownership, Hispanics and African-Americans lag significantly behind whites."[29] And by February 2009 the *New York Times* editorialized: "This is the reality: Jobs are being cut and unemployment is rising in virtually all sectors of the economy ... At the same time, families' housing values and retirement savings have been pummeled."[30] That reality hits the poor particularly hard, and it also hits minority groups hard. We saw in Chapter 2 that low-skilled Black men suffer very high unemployment rates compared with Whites. As Figure 3.2 shows, even for graduates of four-year colleges, unemployment hits minority persons hardest. The unemployment gap is large for Hispanics and Asians, but particularly for Blacks.

Like families and individuals, U.S. firms found themselves less insulated from international market pressures than they were earlier, as they confronted the post-1970 collapse of international economic rules, increased competition, rapid technological change, and the emergence of new trade patterns and higher volumes. Industrial relocation can offer only a partial response to international changes, given the rise of new competitors, increasing import penetration, globalized financial interpenetration, and market saturation. As an alternative to relocation, corporations choose internal restructuring, designed to enhance flexibility, increase profits, cut costs, reduce risks, and gain markets. Numerous business texts, self-help management books, and the business press have commented on the process. The restructuring of an industry may include the reorganization of corporate ownership, changes in organizational structure and style, and alteration of occupational and employment relations. Several consequences of restructuring are pertinent to our study of poverty in American cities. Jobs are lost, wages are cut, and occupational changes are implemented in order to reduce payroll size. There are changes in the way profits are made and consequently the way investments occur. Public policies reinforce and echo industrial restructuring efforts. New and less generous employment relations, uncharacteristic of the post–World War II period, become dominant. (This last consequence of restructuring is discussed below in the section on labor segmentation.)

Changes in the composition of industries directly affect employment opportunities—in more formal terms, industry and occupation both change. New types of jobs and the decline of traditional industrial employment have caused dramatic shifts in occupational categories, wages and benefits, and promotional ladders. Mixed with segmentation of the labor market by race, gender, and age, these shifts lead to marked changes in the structures of opportunity. As we see in Chapter 4, these deficiencies operate locally to harm city dwellers especially. Two trends—the shift from manufacturing to service jobs and the disappearance of middle-income jobs—have expanded the structures of disadvantage and reduced job opportunities.

The relative decline of manufacturing jobs and the absolute rise in service jobs have dramatically worsened the opportunities available to blue-collar workers. Manufacturing work in relatively large firms in many sectors (such as steel, rubber, plastics) and in many occupational lines was historically more secure and better paid than comparable work in service industries.[31] Moreover, manufacturing industries traditionally had internal labor markets, with some upper-level jobs generally filled by current employees moving up in the firm. Once employed, even in an unskilled, "entry-level" job, a worker had good opportunities for raises and some chance for promotion; foremen were recruited on the assembly line. Service industries, in contrast, have lower wages and a radically different entry structure. Retail trade, hotels, and restaurants offer much lower pay, and even the finance sector pays only 84 percent of manufacturing. Service industries, such as finance and health care, also have highly stratified occupational distributions and limited mobility, with many barriers between low-wage, low-skill jobs at the bottom and high-paid professional and managerial jobs at the top. Internal labor markets and promotional ladders are uncommon in most service industries, and union pay scales, with cost-of-living increases, are almost unheard-of. Bus "boys" do not become assistant managers, nor do they organize to demand higher wages.

Efforts to increase union shares in the labor force have amplified in the twenty-first century, but expansions have been modest and must be measured against earlier long-term reductions, which were dramatic. Union membership peaked in 1979, at about 21 million. By 2003 the number had fallen below 16 million, down to only 11.5 percent of employed workers. As a percentage of nonagricultural employment (a measure that solves the statistical problem caused

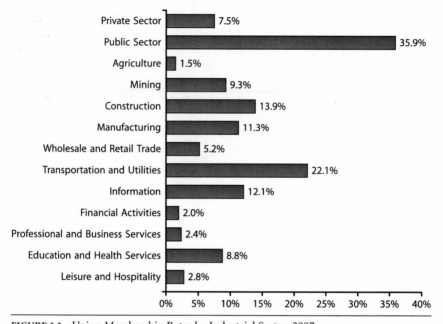

FIGURE 3.3   Union Membership Rates by Industrial Sector, 2007
Source: U.S. Bureau of Labor Statistics, Labor Force Statistics from the Current Population Survey, Household Data, Annual Averages, Table 42. Union Affiliation of Employed Wage and Salary Workers by Occupation and Industry. Available at http://www.bls.gov/cps/cpsaat42.pdf.

by long-term shrinkage of agriculture's share of the workforce), union membership peaked above 35 percent in 1945, staying high for a decade, but the rate then fell steeply, down to 12.1 percent in 2003. Rates began to rise slightly late in the decade, as 311,000 new union members were added in 2007 and another 428,000 in 2008, the largest annual increase since the Bureau of Labor Statistics began counting in 1983, but even after these increases unions enrolled only about 7.6 percent of private sector workers.[32] Even in industries with strong unions, long-tenured workers have been insulated from new hires, who enter with lower wages scales and receive sometimes drastically reduced benefits, and new operations, such as JetBlue Airways or Mercedes, Honda, and Hyundai plants in Alabama, avoid unions altogether.

The distribution of occupations differs greatly from sector to sector. Manufacturing workers are heavily concentrated in one middle-income occupational category, operations and maintenance. This is a result of many years of successful negotiations, strikes, and related union struggles in the most highly developed sector of the economy. Service occupations vary more widely, but as a rule they offer lower-paying jobs and their workers less frequently join unions. Figure 3.3 shows the very low union membership rates for services (including retail and wholesale trade, finance, business services, hotels, and restaurants), contrasted to manufacturing. In 2007 just over 22 percent of the workforce in transportation and utilities, over 13.9 percent in construction, and 11.3 percent in manufacturing belonged to unions, totaling more than 4 million union members. Only 2.4 percent of professional and business service workers belonged, fewer than 2 million union members. These historic differences fit everywhere but the public sector, where unions have been strong and where even service workers have pushed up their wages and benefits. Looked at from the other side, 7.5 percent of private sector workers belong to unions, but they make up just over 51 percent of union members. In the public sector 35.9 percent of workers belong to unions, well over 40 percent in local governments.

These union disparities between manufacturing and services and between public and private generate different patterns of income inequality. The growth of manufacturing employment in the 1950s, 1960s, and even the 1970s, with reduced inequality in earnings for men, led to reduced inequality of family incomes. With few exceptions, cities with higher proportions of manufacturing jobs had lower levels of inequality for both men's wages and family incomes. The high levels of working-class incomes became a staple of American can-do ideology. One explanation for the subsequent emergence of severe inequalities and the worsening income distributions noted in Chapter 2 is the decline of manufacturing and the concentration of service-sector employment in two highly separated wage groups, professional and unskilled, the spread resulting directly in bifurcated earnings and more inequality. Additional trouble comes from a new source: manufacturing itself. As part of global restructuring, the manufacturing sector has developed more highly separated employment pools, leading to growing internal polarization. Polarization has resulted from such changes as the downgrading of manufacturing processes and the development of two-tier wage systems, allowed by deregulation and by the failure of weakened unions in response to competition from cheaper labor—and more efficient operations— especially overseas. All these changes contribute to growing inequality.[33] Much of this inequality is manifested in old urban industrial areas with large out-of-work African American labor forces.

Even as employment has grown, these changes have badly eviscerated the middle class; when employment shrinks, damages intensify. As we saw in Chapter 2, several groups persistently get low pay: most women, part-time workers, and temporary workers, added to many workers in year-round, full-year positions with minimal skill requirements. A look into the future brings little optimism. Table 3.1 displays anticipated employment growth for the decade up to the year 2016, with estimates made more than two years before the financial meltdown. The Bureau of Labor Statistics anticipated a 10.4 percent increase in jobs overall, but in bifurcated sets of occupations, with about 5 million new professional jobs and about 6 million new service and sales jobs. In the long, detailed list of BLS occupations, only eight job categories expand substantially, by 100,000 new jobs or more. Four of these occupations pay well, and four do not. Computer engineers, computer systems analysts, software engineers, and network analysts require advanced education, and they will add 611,000 jobs.

TABLE 3.1   EMPLOYMENT BY OCCUPATION GROUP IN 2006 AND PROJECTED FOR 2016

Occupation	Employment number*		Percent distribution		Change 2006–2016	
	2006	2016	2006	2016	Number*	Percent
Total	150,620	166,220	100.0	100.0	15,600	10.4
Management, business, and financial	15,397	16,993	10.2	10.2	1,596	10.4
Professional	29,819	34,790	19.8	20.9	4,971	16.7
Service	28,950	33,780	19.2	20.3	4,830	16.7
Sales	15,985	17,203	10.6	10.3	1,218	7.6
Office and administrative support	24,344	26,089	16.2	15.7	1,745	7.2
Farming, fishing, and forestry	1,039	1,010	0.7	0.6	−29	−2.8
Construction and extraction	8,295	9,079	5.5	5.5	784	9.5
Installation, maintenance, and repair	5,883	6,433	3.9	3.9	550	9.3
Production	10,675	10,147	7.1	6.1	−528	−4.9
Transportation and material moving	10,233	10,696	6.8	6.4	463	4.5

Source: Adapted from Arlene Dohm and Lynn Shniper, "Occupational Employment Projections to 2016," *Monthly Labor Review* (November 2007). Available at http://www.bls.gov/opub/mlr/2007/11/art5full.pdf.
*Numbers in thousands.

Personal and home care aides, home health aides, medical assistants, and human service assistants require only on-the-job training and will add more than a million jobs. Workers in these jobs will get low pay, just like retail clerks or hotel and food-service workers—the May 2007 BLS survey found that retail trade paid 64 percent of the median for manufacturing, and hotel and food services paid only 51 percent. African American and Latino workers are almost absent in the high-wage occupations, but they are heavily overrepresented in the low-pay occupations, for which a high school education is usually enough.[34]

During early restructuring, in the shift from manufacturing to services in the six years from 1979 through 1984, 11.5 million American workers lost their jobs because "their plants or businesses closed down or moved, their positions or shifts were abolished, or not enough work was available for them to do."[35] Of these 11.5 million workers, nearly half, 5.1 million, had held their jobs for at least three years and thus were counted as displaced by the Bureau of Labor Statistics. Another 4.3 million workers were displaced from 1985 through 1989. More recently, in the three years from 2005 through 2007, 8.2 million workers lost their jobs, of whom 3.6 million were long-tenured. As of January 2008, a third of the displaced workers were either officially unemployed or had dropped out of the labor force after not finding new jobs. Nearly half (45 percent) were reemployed at lower wages, and a quarter lost more than 20 percent. One in four had been employed in manufacturing.[36] As a BLS analyst wrote: "Worker displacement is often considered a symptom of poor economic times. While large job losses are expected during recessionary periods, far fewer are expected during expansionary ones. Data for the 1980s show . . . displacements . . . common even during years of rapid economic growth."[37]

Calculations a quarter century ago by the U.S. Office of Technology Assessment, for 1984, suggested that increases in imports and decreases in exports exercise a tremendous negative effect on employment, the losses then running as high as 25 percent in some industrial sectors.[38] Absolute net losses were then estimated to be approximately 26,000 jobs for every $1 billion of direct U.S. investment that left to go overseas.[39] The loss or gain of jobs in sectors that export or compete with imports was particularly important since these jobs tend to be higher paid than those in the rest of the economy. Most employment loss comes from gradual reductions, not from complete, physical factory shutdowns. In addition, as we see in the next chapter, the severity of dislocation is much greater in highly specialized places, particularly in old manufacturing areas in central cities, the Northeast, and the Upper Midwest. With the mortgage crisis, dislocation has also spread to the areas in which the real estate bubble was the most puffed up. A further complicating factor is that shifts represent demographic changes in the population, including the entry and then maturing of the baby-boom population and varying tides of immigration. Displaced blue-collar workers do not find it easy to obtain employment either in high-end manufacturing or in high-pay services, and they are likely to be unemployed for prolonged periods. Moreover, even ordinary service jobs require more public contact, which encourages more social (and racial) discrimination than the old manufacturing employment structure.

The urban regions surrounding the Great Lakes have experienced sobering declines. In a series of studies of one of these regions, Upstate New York, Rolf Pendall and his colleagues have found lagging personal incomes and troublesome occupational shifts. The regional declines affect dozens of cities, including Buffalo, Rochester, and Syracuse. Even in the 1990s, while things were improving nationally, Upstate poverty rates grew for families, individuals, and children; concentrated poverty expanded; and Black and Hispanic residents found themselves highly isolated.[40]

Overall, then, ignoring special cases such as New York City, San Francisco, and Boston, where the dot-com, high finance, and real estate booms were so visible before the busts, service job expansion did not compensate for manufacturing job loss. The transition is difficult and costly for the individual worker and the society, and it is unfairly biased. Manufacturing jobs, for example, have traditionally provided better opportunities for African American men to gain middle-income earnings than have other occupations; the decline in these jobs in particular has disproportionately hurt their employment opportunities.[41] In essence, the ways into the labor market are increasingly difficult and frustrating for the least qualified workers.

The drop in real wages discussed in Chapter 2 has been one consequence of the shift to lower-paid service jobs, of union concessions forced by corporate threats of relocation, shrinkage, or shutdown, and of declining industrial sectors. Real wages grew continuously from the end of World War II until 1973, and for most workers they have risen only slightly, stagnated, or declined ever since, as we saw in Chapter 2.

In many respects, the growth of the service sector is a consequence not so much of a decline as of a changed industrial order.[42] The connection between services and the goods-producing sector means that the growth of services represents a fundamental transformation in the way production occurs. "Indirect" labor increases while "hands-on" labor decreases; a more complex industrial society emerges instead of a postindustrial one. Those who work with their hands and backs are not only disadvantaged; they are positively discriminated against.[43] As *The Economist* wrote during the boom in 2006: "Virtually everywhere, even as profits surge, workers' real incomes have been flat or even falling. In other words, the old relationship between corporate and national prosperity has broken down. . . . Globalization has also shifted the balance of power in the labor market in favor of companies. It gives firms access to cheap labor abroad; and the threat that they will shift more production offshore also helps to keep a lid on wages at home."[44]

Beating Labor to Pay for Bad Management: New Patterns of Work

As we observed earlier, a bifurcated labor force has emerged—a two-tiered wage structure with many workers poorly paid in unstable, dead-end jobs while others are employed in jobs with stability, opportunities for upward mobility, and high pay. Racism and sexism amplify and complicate the separations, sometimes freezing out minorities and women even from the less desirable jobs. We see in Chapter 4 how these cleavages show up by neighborhood and city zone. Indeed, divisions in urban labor markets often match discrimination in housing markets.[45]

We turn now to look directly at jobs and how they are allocated. Although textbooks often deny or gloss over sharp discontinuities in labor markets, in fact labor markets have always been broken into segments arranged on the basis of race, gender, and other characteristics not related to job performance.[46] In line with changes in the global economy and U.S. adaptations to it, we find labor segmentation by race and gender sometimes to be deepened. The automation of white-collar industry encourages resegregation up and down the occupational hierarchy, with women and minorities once again restricted from access to top- and middle-management positions.[47]

Public austerity, privatization, deregulation, and growing use of non-union subcontractors for government work have resulted in new forms of labor segmentation and increased competition among workers within segments.[48] In some cases, existing patterns of segmentation—which protected workers' rights—have been reduced. The use of non-union labor has risen in the private sector, with lower wages, benefits, and security, and civil-service wage standards have been undermined, even in federal jobs. Two distinct labor markets have been created within the public sector, a realm of employment in which minorities and women had in the past achieved substantial gains.

Corporations have pursued four strategies to counter the declining profits that have resulted from increasing competition: reduction of the number of workers on the payroll; increase in financial profits through speculation and investments; intensification of pressure on governments to support the restructuring of industry through more favorable monetary, fiscal, and regulatory policies; and reorganization of production to create new terms of employment. These last two strategies are less well studied than job displacement and financial speculation, which we treat in subsequent sections. They are, nevertheless, particularly important to the geography of U.S. poverty, since emerging patterns of work tend to move labor disputes outside the traditional range of union activities.

Besides relocating their plants to non-union areas, corporations have benefited from the government's reluctance and even refusal to enforce social legislation designed to protect workers. In the 1980s we saw such federal anti-union activities as President Reagan's dismissal of the air controllers and the destruction of their union, PATCO; the reversal of earlier pro-labor findings by new appointees, so that the National Labor Relations Board (NLRB) restricted industrial organizing; and long lags in NLRB action on complaints by unions that managers had used unfair labor practices, despite increased complaints registered with the board. Twenty years later President George W. Bush manifested his hostility to unions in similar ways, but the Obama administration promises change. Just after taking office in 2009, Vice President Biden announced: "Over the last 100 years the middle class was built on the back of organized labor. Without their weight, heft and their insistence starting in the early 1900s we wouldn't have the middle class we have now."[49] Pressures from unions on the Obama administration may yield improvements in federal governance of labor relations, but early indications are negative, and the economic crisis adds burdens to business budgets already subject to global competition. Pressures from both sides are sure to persist.

Individual firms increase their flexibility to respond to intense competition by engaging in new patterns of work. Work patterns have been found to differ among manufacturing oligopolies whose operations are capital-intensive, oligopolies that are labor-intensive, and service firms that are competitive. In each industry type, firms have worked out special strategies to increase what is now euphemistically called labor flexibility.[50] This flexibility diminishes the opportunity structure for the worker while increasing the options for the firm, allowing easier layoffs and reassignments, adjustments downward in wages, and so forth.

Capital-intensive oligopolies, generally large manufacturing firms with extensive work sites, have created relatively small cores of full-time workers and larger sets of part-time workers and subcontractors. The full-time workers are covered by benefit plans, offered job security, and expected to remain with the firm. Part-time workers receive lower wages and few benefits, if any. Similarly, the firm ducks responsibility for workers employed by subcontractors, so it need not offer prevailing wages (those set on federal government contracts), benefits, or secure terms of employment.[51] Union concessions regarding two-tiered wage scales reflect this corporate strategy and structure. Even Japanese firms, long famous for guaranteeing lifetime employment and retirement benefits, have changed their system, putting more than a third of the Japanese workforce into "nonregular" jobs, without guarantees. Some 9 million Japanese workers were ineligible in 2009 for unemployment insurance should they have been laid off.[52]

Labor-intensive oligopolies tend to be large firms with small work sites, and they tend to operate primarily in sales, health care, and finance. Many of these industries, such as banking and insurance, were deregulated, sometimes with infamous results, and others have been subjected to changing federal regulations (e.g., rate ceilings for medical reimbursements), forcing them to become more cost-conscious. Like the capital-intensive firms, these firms create a bifurcated labor force. Each employs a core of full-time workers, often restricted by direct or institutional discrimination against minorities and women. These regular employees provide the base for essential activities. At the top they are notorious for paying themselves abusively high compensation and taking fantastically costly perks. Other workers in these firms, however, do less well, with perhaps one-third of a firm's workers hired on a part-time basis. Wages polarize along similar lines.

Competitive service firms use two clear strategies for increasing flexibility through employment patterns. These firms are usually small, producing specialized goods or services. Some require highly skilled labor and offer services on short-term contracts—industries such as publishing, advertising, and entertainment. Firms increase their flexibility through well-paid independent contractors, such as professional consultants, who can provide the needed service or technical skill. Competitive-industry firms that need workers with low skills seek flexibility through the intensification of labor. Thus, in apparel and textiles, employees often work at home or in sweatshops, with piecework wage rates. Even in clerical work, home-based employment has expanded, and international "outsourcing" of such work as call centers has become standard.[53]

These strategies have heightened the flexibility of business firms. They allow firms to reduce labor costs easily, for example, during short-term downturns in demand—but at the cost of increased unemployment and poverty, imposed through polarized patterns of work and distribution of working time.[54] Instead of the traditional forty-hour workweek, both longer and shorter work weeks are becoming more common. Firms use this bifurcation as another employment strategy to increase flexibility, reduce fixed costs, and improve profits.[55] Fully employed people in relatively good jobs are working longer hours and taking less leisure, either to make stretched ends meet or to keep their jobs in more competitive labor markets. In 2007, according to the American Time Use Survey, full-timers worked long hours: men averaged 8.2 hours a day, 57 hours per week, and women averaged 7.8 hours a day, 55 hours per week. These averages are way up from earlier years.[56]

At the other end of the spectrum, instead of full-time, full-year work, an increasing number of jobs are part-time, temporary, or self-employed, many of them contributing to the new group of poor adults who figure so prominently in the statistics of Chapter 2—underemployed workers. One category is part-time workers, those who would prefer full-time work but cannot obtain it. In the 1980s, of the more than 19 million part-time workers, at least a third, 5.6 million, wanted to work more. In November 2008 at least 7.3 million persons found themselves working part-time but wanting full-time jobs. Many other workers who are inappropriately classified as *voluntary* part-time employees would prefer to work full-time but must care for children or cannot afford the transportation costs.[57]

Temporary work, called contingent and alternative, has also expanded. In February 2005 some 5.7 million people worked at "temporary" positions, some of which can last weeks, months, or years. Increasing employment of "temps" results from a restructuring of the labor force, and it includes the use of a permanent "temporary" force for certain jobs, often without benefits. In January 1985 the White House Office of Management and Budget issued a circular permitting the employment of so-called temporary workers by the federal government; these "contract" workers could be hired for up to four years without benefits (except Social Security). The federal government in the late 1980s employed over three hundred thousand temporary workers in the executive branch alone.[58]

The number of workers who were self-employed, independent "contractors" had steadily decreased from 1950 to 1970, led by reductions in small retail operations, but the self-employed have been increasing in number since 1970. Between 2002 and 2003 the number of businesses constituted by self-employed workers increased by 1 million. Reasons for increases vary from personal to structural. Among structural causes are the deregulation of manufacturing, transportation, and service industries. For example, with deregulation, many previously unionized truckers, working in fleets or directly for shippers, were forced to become independent, non-union, self-employed drivers. Incomes of the self-employed vary widely, but on average they are low. The nearly 7 million child-care "nonemployer businesses" in 2006 averaged just over $12,400 in annual income, while the nearly 21 million self-employed (including the child-care individuals) averaged just under $46,900.[59]

Ignoring for the moment the long-term unemployed and those who have dropped out of the labor market altogether, the other groups who most often fall into poverty are displaced workers, temporary workers, involuntary part-time workers, and full-time, full-year, low-wage earners. The groups overlap, and comparisons are difficult. There are few studies of annual earnings, distribution of working hours, job benefits, and job security of these new forms of employment. The conditions of employment of these workers, especially involuntary part-time and temporary workers, make them likely targets for poverty.

From what do these worsened labor market situations arise? Can we connect the status of the domestic labor market to the global economy? We believe the answer is yes, and we begin by looking at worldwide processes of industrial location.

Industrial Relocation in the International Economy

Contradictory territorial and institutional trends have long been essential in the organization and dynamic reorganization of capitalism. On the one hand, there is centralization of control over capital, and on the other, the spread of trade, production, and markets. Since the 1960s an increase in overseas investment and manufacturing by U.S. corporations has brought about a dramatic geographic spreading of industrial operations. Concurrently, one of the fastest-growing sectors of the economy, corporate services, has concentrated in the industrial world's largest cities, generating employment, attracting foreign investment, and reshaping the geography of economic relations.

One of the earliest, simplest, and clearest models to depict these changes in the structure of the international economy goes by the name the New International Division of Labor (NIDL). From the NIDL perspective, when ownership and control are centralized and activity is dispersed, there are important economic, political, and spatial implications. To draw out these implications, we observe that parts of multidivision industrial corporations fall into three groups: headquarters' operations, which encompass innovation and finance, organization, and engineering activities such as product design; plant-level manufacturing, which requires complex machinery and skilled workers; and unskilled operations and assembly production, which "in principle [require] no qualifications" for the workforce.[60] There is also a residual, of course—underemployment and unemployment for those left behind when industry moves.

These three kinds of activities in the international economy have different locational requirements. The tasks of finance and communication require corporate executives to have access to centralized network nodes. In contrast, simple assembly production may be relocated to remote areas, to ensure easy access to cheap and unorganized labor. Head offices therefore prosper most in a few giant centers (often called "world cities" or "global cities").[61] But at the opposite end, businesses locate their assembly and processing plants in peripheral locations in the Third World to facilitate access to inexpensive, unskilled labor. This pattern of industrial location also leads to increases in operating flexibility and domination over labor. For example, firms use arrangements such as multiple sourcing of factory inputs and even parallel production of the same products in identical factories in more than one country, so as to give credibility to threats of factory shutdowns against striking unions.[62] Firms that spread their factory and assembly sites also aim for ready access to foreign markets. The resulting allocation of tasks, called the spatial division of labor, reflects internal organization of firms and the dispersal of their functions over a varied regional and national terrain.

It is, we repeat, played out in the distributions of work, wages, and unemployment. To some degree there is even a hierarchy of countries, with their ranks corresponding to their functions in the corporate organizational structure. To a remarkable extent, large corporations have uprooted themselves so thoroughly that when imports and exports cross international boundaries, they move to and from "foreign" branches of "domestic" firms.

As corporations adjust to the changing international order, they also initiate changes of significance for America. As they relocate manufacturing and assembly to other nations, they place unskilled and skilled workers in the United States in direct competition with people in Third World, low-wage labor markets. Multinational corporations abuse their dominance and mobility to undermine national as well as municipal political power.[63] Finally, in a counterbalance as manufacturing moves to the global "periphery," corporate control activity creates world cities in the industrialized countries, which perform as centers of growth and power, concentrating skilled white-collar jobs of control and management.

These internationally inspired occupational structures and wage rates generate not only wealth from high-level jobs but also poverty from low-end service jobs in American cities and elsewhere. The loss of high-wage manufacturing is one problem. As we have pointed out, growth of the service sector itself leads to an increase in inequality by generating at the top a large number of well-paying managerial and professional jobs, very few new middle-income jobs, and masses of unstable, low-wage jobs. In an ironic reversal, even low-wage, low-technology *manufacturing* activities now prosper in the "First World," as some manufacturing growth depends on sweatshop conditions and cheap immigrant labor.[64] For routine assembly work, firms seek overseas labor because it is cheap, especially in the Third World, but as workers willing to accept low wages have arrived as immigrants, firms offer this work in American cities, too. A new domestic labor market thus reflects Third World patterns right at home, with more unemployment and lower wages, fewer benefits, and reduced stability of employment.[65] The critical magnet attracting production plants appears to be cheap, unorganized labor, usually workers inexperienced with industrial production.[66] Such locations in America have even included suburbs with large reserves of underemployed women, as well as big-city immigrant and minority ghettos and barrios, enclaves just across the Mexican border, and small towns and rural areas that lie outside the manufacturing belt and are not unionized.[67] Similar job opportunities induced heavy immigration to previously White/Black areas of the Southeast. Mexicans and Central Americans sometimes constitute nearly the entire workforce in meatpacking plants and other low-wage operations. Latin immigrant laborers played major roles in postflood construction in New Orleans. Of the ten metropolitan areas with the fastest-growing Hispanic populations in recent years, eight are in the Southeast (Fort Myers, Charlotte, Raleigh, Nashville, Atlanta, Naples, Lakeland, and Sarasota). Regarding population growth from 2000 to 2004, demographer William Frey reports, "Hispanic, Asian, and Black populations continue to migrate to . . . new destinations. They are increasingly living in suburbs, in rapidly growing job centers in the South and West, and in more affordable areas adjacent to higher-priced coastal metro areas."[68]

Technological change results in the reorganization of production: the value of industrial products declines as automation cuts costs, allowing for an increased volume of nonindustrial activity, including personal services.[69] A few studies of unemployment within this perspective focus on the reduction in the amount of labor required in each successive stage of technological development—"the tendency for smaller increments of employment to be associated with each new 'vintage' of machinery and plant."[70] The fear is that in the context of international competition, levels of capital investment using high-productivity machinery are not sufficient to reach full employment. "An increasingly large section of the population will continue to be expelled, or at least marginalized, from the sphere of economic activity."[71] Important geographic patterns result from such marginalization—so the world contains underdeveloped countries, backward national regions, and impoverished districts in every city. As David Harvey has pointed out, geography thus acts like time, as a means of putting off or pushing out—and possibly resolving—the reckoning needed for adjusting to the imbalances that inevitably occur in market (that is, capitalist) economies.[72]

Some theorists argue that these changes in structure and hierarchy result from more fundamental shifts in the organization of society, based not only on the emergence of new technologies but on social systems associated with particular technological regimes.[73] In the "new wave" there will be new "core" cities and regions, with a corresponding reorganization of national power in the international economy. The United States will not remain the wealthiest country or the generator of new forms of social organization. Perhaps the events of 2008–2009 portend sharp decline, but perhaps the shock to Wall Street and the U.S. economy will lead to changed ways and strong recovery. Crises lead to interesting times.

The global economy is changing in complex ways. Manufacturing continues to be important, but in transformed ways and in new locations. In the 1980s, for example, modern steel making in Fujan, South Korea, in plants imported from Belgium, brought buoyant growth and optimism to what was previously a fishing village. The concomitant collapse of old steel plants virtually destroyed Gary, Indiana, turning it into one of the poorest and most depressed cities in America.[74] What few observers noticed, however, is that steel was soon again produced in Gary, with equipment superior to that in Fujan; production took place in Gary in one of the most modern and efficient plants in the world. But the modern plant did not solve problems for Gary's residents, improve social institutions, or provide incomes for laid-off steel employees, their dependents, and those who worked in the downstream local economy. The new steel plant employed only a small portion of the workers who worked at the old plants. Looking more broadly, by 2009 North America accounts for less than 10 percent of the world's steel production, and the BLS expects that automation will cause further declines in employment.[75]

As in Fujan and Gary, the shape of things to come in *most* places will be greatly influenced not only by technology but also by the way it is applied, and where. That is, many important events will respond to the internationalization of production and the centralization of control. All these changes, if they are not to destroy opportunities for those unlucky enough to be at the bottom of American society, will require new policies to thwart the harmful effects of dislocation, dehumanization, and marginalization of low-income people. In the following sections we explore facets of globalization, with the aim of identifying more focused issues of particular importance to understanding the sources of U.S. poverty.

Globalization, Trade Flows, and Market Saturation

The growing internationalization of capital, commodity, and labor flows is a well-documented trend. Evidence of growing international interdependence is revealed through the briefest examination of data. Until the late 1960s, trade played a relatively small role; imports of goods and services never constituted more than 6 percent of GDP. From 1970 to 2007, imports trebled in relative terms, to 17 percent of GDP.[76] As we have already seen, manufacturing suffered the most: by late 2008, 37 percent of all manufactured goods sold in the United States were imported, double the proportion in 1991, almost four times the proportion in 1978.[77] Figure 3.4 shows how exports have grown rapidly since the mid-1980s and how imports have grown more rapidly, creating a steadily growing trade imbalance.

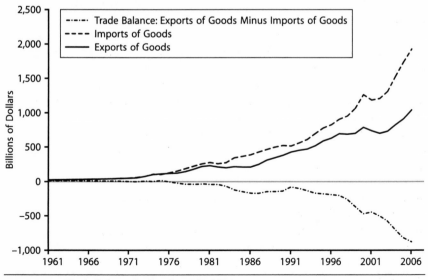

FIGURE 3.4 Trade Balance in Goods, 1961–2006

Source: http://www.census.gov/foreign-trade/statistics/historical/.

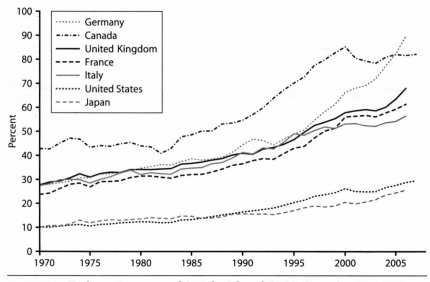

FIGURE 3.5 Trade as a Percentage of GDP for Selected OECD Countries, 1970–2007
Source: OECD.Stat Extracts. Dataset: Macro Trade Indicators. Available at http://stats.oecd.org/Index.aspx.

In other advanced industrial countries the role of imports and exports in national growth has risen as well. Total trade (imports plus exports) for large, wealthy European countries has exploded from just over a quarter of GDP in 1970 to very high levels, facilitated largely by the dropping of intra-European boundaries. In 2006, trade rose to 57 percent of GDP in Italy and 90 percent in Germany. France and the United Kingdom lie between these figures. As Figure 3.5 shows, U.S. trade levels are much lower, a consequence of the country's large land mass, giant domestic market, and relative physical isolation, but U.S. trade too has expanded as a share of total economic activity, roughly trebling from 10 percent of GDP in 1970 to 30 percent in 2006. Only Japan has trade levels comparable with those of the United States—only 26 percent in 2006—a consequence of long-held self-sufficiency policies. (Canada's persistently high trade fits its population and a geography that stretches its cities along the U.S. border.)

In the early years of trade expansion, the industrialized nations traded mostly among themselves, but with the emergence of newly industrializing countries (NICs)—giant economies in India and China, and early industrializers South Korea and Taiwan—trade patterns shifted in location and economic sector. Spread of production led to excess U.S. capacity in mass-production industries, as manufacturers in each country attempted to supply both their own and their neighbors' markets.[78] Then NIC labor began competing for precisely the same type of work but received much lower wages and many fewer social benefits. This placed domestic U.S. labor generally in competition with overseas labor, and in particular it put lower-skilled workers in the United States in competition with overseas labor and internally with one another. In this circumstance the politically weakest labor groups, namely African American and Latino workers, were the losers, and their poverty thus increased.

Competition has come especially from China and India, with large numbers of highly disciplined workers willing to work at extremely low wages, along with generally favorable exchange rates.[79] Pressure has continued to mount from producers in other nations with steeply rising productivity combined with huge, cheap labor pools. American firms face relatively higher unit costs of production, which cannot easily be passed on to consumers since markets are increasingly saturated and competitors also cut costs. Selection among workers for remaining jobs thus becomes tighter, allowing employers to insist on higher qualifications and more rigid screening for positions. As the pressure rises, industry adjusts further. In its adjustment it has dealt out lower wages and more layoffs, reducing the supply of good jobs and indirectly adding to poverty.

Markets for consumer durables (such as automobiles, washing machines, and radios) had already slowed their expansion by the mid-1970s. "This saturation was especially true in the U.S., where in 1979 there was one car for every two residents, compared with one for every four in the early 1950s. Ninety-nine percent of American households had television sets in 1970, compared with 47 percent in 1953. Similarly, more than 99 percent of households had refrigerators, radios, and electric irons, and more than 90 percent had automatic clothes washers, toasters, and vacuum cleaners."[80]

Consumer demand for new products and services subsequently shifted, especially to electronics, where similar levels of saturation are reached quickly even as new products enter the market frequently. Ordinary new products are familiar—microwave ovens, digital cameras, large TV screens, smart phones, and the like. Explosions of spending on real estate, travel, and entertainment involved the occupancy of larger and larger residential units by smaller and smaller households and families, with eating out replacing groceries and home cooking, and air travel used by much larger groups of the population. But even at the peak, these bigger-ticket sorts of consumer spending were restricted to the better-off portions of the population.

In 2008–2009 the false floor collapsed under the expansion, and the explosion in consumption came to a halt. The problem of market saturation has been compounded by the entrance of new competitors into the international market for consumer goods. Many Third World countries pursued policies to encourage the growth of domestic industries. Some, such as those known as the Four Tigers (Hong Kong, Singapore, South Korea, and Taiwan), focused on the development of an export base of mass-produced consumer durables. Others, such as Brazil, Mexico, and Argentina, concentrated on the creation of domestically oriented, mass-production industries and also on mass agricultural exports such as soybeans and beef. One clear consequence was the introduction of competition to markets once well protected for the corporations headquartered in the industrialized countries. These downward pressures did not at first affect headquarters but had an impact on branch plants and subsidiaries. Similarly, lower-level workers were harmed much more than their white-collar contemporaries, and minority workers more than Whites. Only very late in the game, with overall recession, did head office income and employment collapse as well.

The shift in the U.S. economy that began in the 1970s reached one plateau in the early 2000s, when trade balances in goods and services showed imports exceeding exports by values between $60 billion and $70 billion each month. With the shrinkage of global markets and the rapid decline of the U.S. economy, imports shrank drastically from a peak at more than $225 billion midyear 2008 to hardly more than $150 billion by February 2009, so that the trade imbalance diminished to a negative $26 billion. The accumulated deficits end up as fund balances, held mostly by China, obligations of U.S. banks and the U.S. treasury, and, ultimately, debt burdens of U.S. workers, consumers, citizens, and residents.

Estimates of profitability in the economy are notoriously difficult to make. Edward Wolff, whose work on wealth holdings informed Chapter 2, observes that two changes have contributed to a long-run decline in the rate of profit—an increase in the ratio of capital investment to output, as a result of labor-saving technological change, and an increase in "unproductive" labor, due to relatively rapid growth of the workforce in three sectors: wholesale and retail trade; finance, insurance, and real estate; and supervision, in all sectors of the economy.[81]

Internationalization of Finance and (De)regulation: Instability, Speculation, Debt, and Corporate Restructuring

As international commodity flows have changed over three decades, international financial markets have reorganized, imposing additional pressures of increasing competition, uncertainty, and instability on firms, communities, and families. The globalization of finance has weakened the control any one country has over capital circulation. Simultaneously, increased capital flows, reduced financial regulations, and more-developed communication technologies have increased the possibilities for speculative gain and thus opened new ways for firms to make money. In search of higher returns, to meet competition and avoid regulation, corporations bought and sold companies, shifted assets to minimize tax payments, and moved assets across the globe. Finally, in the purely financial sphere, speculators created various new instruments, which played a large role in the recession that began in late 2007. The instruments include "private-equity and hedge funds, money-market funds and auction-rate securities, non-banks such as GE Capital, and new securities such as collateralized debt obligations (CDOs) and credit-default swaps. . . . On the eve of the crash, more capital was flowing through [these instruments] than through the conventional banks."[82] All these strategies that U.S. enterprises use to increase profits have exacerbated poverty in American cities by defunding redistributive programs, by undermining support for them through the promotion of an ideology that celebrates inequality, and by placing the fate of American workers and firms in the hands of foreign capital markets.

Over the decades the internationalization of finance has weakened control by the United States over international exchange and investment. The introduction of the floating dollar, as a way to stabilize the international monetary system, proved to be destabilizing to trade and economic policy. Fluctuations in currency values affect the national economy by affecting capital flows, competitiveness, trade, employment, profits, and debt.[83] Worldwide, daily foreign-exchange transactions doubled between 1979 and 1984, from $75 billion to $150 billion; rose to over $200 billion in 1986; and reached $3.2 trillion by 2007.[84] Only a portion of this enormous volume of foreign exchange provides finance for trade; the bulk is used for speculative transactions. As U.S. investment abroad has increased, so has foreign direct investment in America, but it, too, fluctuates widely, and much foreign investment—just like U.S. corporate investment overseas—consists of the purchase of existing plants and buildings rather than the construction of new ones.[85] Across the globe, businesses find foreign investment convenient for avoiding import and tariff restrictions, getting access to labor supplies with useful skills or low wages, and enjoying the benefits of recruitment incentives offered by local governments. One of the largest challenges in the twenty-first century promises to be the flood of cheap manufactured products from giant low-wage producing areas around the world, many of them organized by U.S.-based firms. Slack activity in U.S. cities of the sort that traditionally absorbed the low-skilled and underskilled workers causes great difficulty for people at the low end of the economy.

Other sources of economic destabilization include shifts in commodity prices, particularly petroleum; rapid private transfers of financial capital previously experienced only by developing countries; the rise of a more unified European market; the emergence of the BRIC economies (Brazil, Russia, India, China) and others; and war spending and disruption, starting with the war in Vietnam, Laos, and Cambodia, later the Persian Gulf War, the long war in Iraq, constant involvement in Palestine, Israel, and other parts of the Middle East, and the continuous war in Afghanistan/Pakistan. The domestic agenda since 1979 has become hostage to congressional and presidential concern about foreign economic affairs, for the first time in American history. U.S. poor people not only suffer from flows of investment capital overseas and shifts away from basic industries that employ unskilled workers but must compete for attention with various overseas preoccupations.

As finance has internationalized, U.S. economic growth (and decline, more so) has brought great social costs—declining average living standards, growing inequality, and increasing poverty. Moreover, this growth, whatever its skewed benefits, was "achieved almost entirely by two manifestly undesirable means." First was the joint explosion of military budgets and the federal deficit, driven both by global political competition and by global financial change. The federal government spent $2.0 trillion more than it collected in taxes and government receipts in the eight years from 1982 to 1989, and another $2.1 trillion from 2002 to 2009.[86] Consumer and business indebtedness also increased, by 2008 beyond the system's capacity. The way we handle exploding debts imposes a double tax on the poor. We reduce service provision to balance the budget, and we abandon programs aimed at correcting inequality, thus, for example, wiping out small budgets that fund salaries of physically or mentally challenged employees in sheltered workshops, throwing those dependent people into deeper debt and despondency. The second undesirable source of growth is distortion and underfunding of civilian research and development.[87] Thus, as the nation failed to renew its industries and push at maximum speed on innovation, enormous debts were poured like diluted cement into the failure-prone foundations of the future. By 2008 the entire system came crashing down.

These changes in the structure of world trade and finance have created additional pressures of increasing competition, uncertainty, and instability, on companies, cities, workers, and their families. The nation divided itself economically and committed economic cannibalism among communities and classes. Corporations relocated production activities, reoriented investment priorities away from production, and as technologies and government regulations permitted, reorganized production itself. In spite of these efforts, corporations have been only partially successful at fighting competition. Many years before the crash, American shares of world trade dropped, profitability and productivity rates declined, and U.S. firms failed to remain competitive in such manufacturing industries as steel, autos, televisions and other consumer electronics, and even semiconductors. These persistent problems all suggest a long-term decline in the competitiveness of some American industries, with corresponding losses of the jobs on which some American communities and large segments of the most vulnerable members of the labor pool depend.[88]

The post-1980 international system finally exploded, "thanks to three simultaneous but distinct developments: deregulation, technological innovation and the growing international mobility of capital."[89] By 2008 the flaws in a system based on financial manipulation rather than production became clear, but the roots of the crisis had been planted nearly thirty years earlier. Although the rate of change accelerated in the twenty-first century, its velocity was high already in the 1980s, when federal tax laws favored restructuring and speculation, the very strategies that have resulted in decreased productive investment, progressive financial collapse, and employee layoffs. When plant closings caught public attention in the 1980s, corporations made money by writing off the estimated value of closed plants against profits made in other units of the corporation. Union Carbide earned $620 million in tax savings by closing chemical plants. United Technologies received $424 million for closing down its computer-equipment subsidiary. For halting domestic production of some aircraft components, TRW was able to write off $142 million in tax liabilities.[90] Each of these transactions had enormous consequences for the workforce and the nation. Other companies use these tactics not only to reduce the size of their workforce but to stall unionization. In some cases, as in the 1984 Playskool shutdown in Chicago, the firm took subsidies aimed at job creation and then shut down without warning, leaving workers and the city to pick up the pieces.[91] In 2009 these earlier tax dodges look like small stuff, as federal transfers are passed out in the hundreds of billions of dollars.

As financial institutions globalized, domestic financial markets (if it makes sense still to call them that) were transformed. Traded volumes of stocks and futures increased. The use of debt to finance mergers and acquisitions, the creation of junk bonds in the early 1980s, the increase in mutual funds, and the gigantic growth of derivative financial instruments all attest to the aggressive competition to make profits, even if only on paper. Between 1983 and 1986, approximately 12,200 companies changed hands. In 1986, mergers, acquisitions, and takeovers amounted to nearly one-fifth of the market value of all traded stock.[92] Already by the mid-1970s "the return on nonfinancial assets had fallen so low in the 'mature' industrial sectors—such as steel, auto, machine tools, apparel, and textiles—that the financial officers who came to dominate the firms in these industries chose to divert their available cash to activities other than manufacturing."[93] The sad results have been evident from 2007 on, and they have led to the virtual collapse of large urban regions.

One of the key problems with U.S. business is the pressure from short-term profit targets. Starting in the 1980s, hostile takeovers and corporate raids, and even the "greenmail" money paid to hostile corporate raiders to forestall takeovers, reduced investments in productive capacity, helping to hollow out American manufacturing. As *Business Week* said, "corporate managers [were] so busy trying to preserve themselves that the entire focus of business [turned] to short-term payoffs . . . [not] spending for plant and equipment, R&D, and job training" as executives were "battling for survival."[94] The emphasis on short-term profits means laying off workers, sacrificing research or capital investment, and selling off assets to build a profit rather than investing in new products. These changes have had dramatic implications for the American standard of living and income inequality. The acquisitions, takeovers, and mergers weed out some unproductive firms to ensure economic efficiency, as the takeover leaders argue, but they also do damage. In 1986, for example, Borg Warner, Goodyear, Holiday, and Potlatch were all targets of corporate raids despite reasonable market performance. In order to pay off junk bonds, otherwise profitable plants were sold and workers lost jobs. Fears of takeovers also prompted corporate restructuring: Union Carbide, following an unsuccessful raid, doubled its debt (to $5.5 billion), sold several profitable businesses, and cut 20 percent of its U.S. payroll.[95] Similarly, Goodyear and USX underwent corporate restructuring, including the sale of assets, plant closures, and employee dismissals, to improve stock performance and ward off future takeover attempts. As Unical chairman Fred Hartley said about the high cost of debt, "Every day we open the door we spend $2 million for interest. Think what that would have done for the U.S. if it had been put into job creation."[96]

This explosive financial activity should have led to regulatory impositions, but in the excitement of market expansion, and lulled by propaganda from market-loving Republican Alan Greenspan at the Federal Reserve and advocacy by Democratic banker Robert Rubin, President Clinton's treasury secretary, federal regulatory agencies failed in their responsibilities. Market activity shifted with truly fantastic speed and volume from production to finance.[97] President George W. Bush appointed Congressman Christopher Cox to head the Security and Exchange Commission, and Cox added to the failure by refusing to appeal court rulings against the regulation of hedge funds and mutual funds. Firms created "a dizzying array of derivative instruments," as they utilized software "wizardry" to allow both "borrowers and savers to unpack and trade all manner of financial risks."[98]

Government tax laws were written to assist corporations and traders to shift from productive investments to quick paper profits by treating interest on debt as a tax deduction while taxing normally the return on equity.[99] Acquiring debt to finance takeovers or stock buy-backs or paying "greenmail" is a less expensive form of financing than equity since, under current tax laws, interest costs are deductible and dividend payments are not.[100]

Federal policies have also promoted restructuring by allowing heightened competitive pressures to bear on firms operating in the United States. Industries that were deregulated include communications, banking, insurance, stock-market transactions, and airlines in the 1970s and trucking, railroads, oil, cable television, intercity buses, and AT&T in the 1980s. Of the numerous changes that occurred in consequence, some were good and many were bad. Firms changed product lines, markets, production organization, and production techniques. In the insurance and banking industries, for example, deregulation resulted in increased diffusion of new technologies, as firms rushed to introduce information technologies driven by the extremely competitive environment into which they were suddenly thrust. Worst of all, deregulation leaves the country without a rudder for steering through international waters. As we saw earlier in this chapter, most of the restructuring in response to deregulation puts enormous pressure on firms to reduce employment, cut wages, and intensify work.

Deregulation of these industries also changed the economics of doing business in various market segments—reducing the profitability of the mass market and of standardized product offerings. This drove firms upmarket to corporate and wealthy customers and to the use of serious market segmentation strategies. For instance, high-priced products such as so-called personal banking are delivered in posh surroundings by highly skilled employees. Low-end "financial" products, in contrast, are produced and delivered by computers and automatic teller machines. Government also privatized public services, sometimes at high social cost, and it reduced benefits to its workforce, not only by letting pay raises lag behind inflation but, as we have seen, by relegating many jobs to "temporary" status and special contracts, without full benefits.

A Comment on Public Policy

Global economic reordering and intensified competition have been followed by industrial change, the shift to the service sector, and a focus on paper profits. Public policymakers, while aiming vaguely to keep America competitive internationally, neglected the long-term needs of manufacturing and shifted the burden of change to employees, those without employment, and ordinary citizens.

We do not mean to suggest that the problems of unemployment and poorly paid jobs would be solved by a return to mass manufacturing. There is no such evidence. Even where reinvestment in manufacturing has revived and where reindustrialization has occurred, the job structures are now more polarized than before. Protected occupations in high-wage craftwork coexist with highly competitive, poorly paid, and regulated occupations, and with increasing numbers of part-time, temporary, or subcontracted jobs. In other cases there are fewer jobs needed to produce the same output.

Federal policymakers remain mired in the past; they need to look to the future. Policies that emphasize trade retaliation will provide only marginal benefits for the poor. Programs that aim at improving the position of capital through tax initiatives, deregulation, and similar benefits are unlikely to build more or better jobs but are likely to destroy job ladders. Supply-side excesses have exacerbated the problems of the poor by freeing business to seek higher returns by destroying jobs, consolidating enterprises, and making profits on currency and tax loopholes rather than by encouraging business to concentrate on the development of productive wealth. As a result, workers' incomes have been sacrificed for short-term capital gains. In the long run, these policies, given the new global order, threaten to bring to American cities conditions reminiscent of the poverty of many Third World nations. The nation needs to return to a strategy of economic planning that will build the necessary infrastructure, both human and physical, to meet the challenge of the new century. This is not a novel proposal. As we see in Chapter 5, the United States was long a leading exponent of economic and resource planning, from the Louisiana Purchase and land-grant colleges to the Marshall Plan and the G.I. Bill. No less is required now.

4

Separate Places

The Changing Shape of the American Metropolis

Poverty is not confined to the lowest-income areas of cities. It has spread across metropolitan regions. In the mid-1990s a representative from Minneapolis to the Minnesota legislature used the word *metropolitics* to propose expanded regional cooperation. The idea was to form an alliance of the Twin Cities with their inner suburbs—to share the burdens of housing for the poor, coordinate sewer construction, pool tax revenues, even to protect farmers against subdivision pressure. By cooperating with the city, nearby municipalities could marshal forces against the privileged, farther-out suburbs.[1] The notion of metropolitics, pursued perhaps most famously with Portland's growth boundary and Toronto's municipal consolidations, fits the new metropolitan reality.[2] Especially in the most populous urban areas, a simple geography no longer applies—it is not just impoverished central cities surrounded by well-to-do suburbs.[3] We can no longer speak the way some people used to of chocolate cities with vanilla suburbs, or of rich doughnuts with empty holes in the middle. Instead, metropolitan geographies are complicated, more like checkerboards, with poor neighborhoods moving outward until more than half of the poorest residents live not in central cities but in the surrounding suburbs.

This situation presents linguistic problems of no small consequence, and the language may reveal lack of understanding. As we noted in Chapter 1, words like *city* and *urban* have come to signify problems not urban in their essence but national or even international, with origins in such maladies as changing industrial fortunes, inequalities of family incomes, and racial discrimination, rather than in the character of a location. Researchers examining school failures invented the ugly word *urbanicity,* pseudoscientific language suggesting that a school's *urbanness* makes its children fail. Those who blame something called "the city" sidestep the need to understand how schools fail, why housing is unaffordable, what makes men and women jobless, and why crime occurs. Such city blamers need not explain why local economies and governments at all levels shortchange poor people who may feel forced to live in central neighborhoods. Nor when urban poverty clones a twin, suburban poverty, do they try to explain it with the word *suburbanicity.* The problem lies not just with our language but with our understanding. Sometimes, in this chapter, we slip and revert to standard linguistic practice. Then we use the words *urban* and *city* to indicate troubled central areas, whether in the city itself or its nearby suburbs, and the word *suburb* to indicate better-off peripheral areas. We beg the reader to remain cautious about the dual use of these freighted terms.

As we know from Chapter 3, some U.S. competitive metropolitan areas answer profitably when the global economy calls. In every case, however, whether the area thrives or falters, it must cope with profound *internal* differences. Suburban wealth and urban poverty—there's that risky usage—have become defining characteristics of American society, so common that we regard them as natural. The continuing waves of subdivision that have extended middle-class suburbs for decades serve to divert attention away from the troubled neighborhoods of Black, Hispanic, and immigrant poor households consigned mainly to central cities and first-ring suburbs. Over recent decades, in periods when labor markets have become more demanding, fewer and fewer men and women living in these unfavored areas have found well-paying full-time jobs. Many of these people lack good schooling and strong skills, and so many of them are incarcerated that the nation's prison population exceeds that of any other time or any other country.

In Chapter 3 we traced metropolitan economic fortunes through four periods—the Great Depression and World War II, the post–World War II decades of rising equality that we call the American Century, the New Gatsby decades of market worship and rising inequality, and finally the times of economic crisis starting in 2007.[4] From the 1970s the economy shifted sharply to services, occupational categories bifurcated throughout the economy, and jobs moved overseas, so while new possibilities for higher wages or promotions to better jobs appeared for some workers, incomes stagnated for the majority. The suburban movement of middle-class African Americans, Latinos, and Asian immigrants, especially since 1990, worked as a political relief valve, lowering the overall ethnic pressure but leaving many central neighborhoods and some suburbs to collapse like worn-out flat tires. Without pumping up, these neighborhoods cannot offer good housing, proper schools, or decent environments. Many of their adults are unhealthy and without hope, and many of their kids can hardly read. The streets may not be safe at night. In nearly every U.S. metropolis, deep and troubling contrasts separate bad residential areas from good ones. The economic crisis has only made things worse.

In this chapter we focus on these *intra*metropolitan differences, tracing them to shifting industrial structures, regional economic differences, new waves of immigration, changing patterns of land values, and biases in public policy. (Chapter 5 treats federal regulations, expenditures, and taxes.) The first section introduces the chapter. The second documents metropolitan trajectories as economies vary region by region, absorbing immigrants, gaining or losing native-born populations, and winning or losing investments and jobs. The third section looks at internal employment patterns, showing shifts from cities to suburbs, growth and collapse of commercial areas, and the rise of low-paid service employment as better-paid manufacturing work vanishes. The fourth section examines changing residential patterns, the dominant pressure of sprawl, the destinations of immigrants, and changing central-city minority areas. Finally, we examine racial discrimination, failing city schools, and concentrated joblessness. What we see as we move from global economy to urban despair is that the bad cards are dealt not just to women, their children, and ethnic and racial minorities, as we saw in Chapter 2, but to select neighborhoods and municipalities as well. People and places suffer.

In the worst cases, in the most depressed neighborhoods of the most troubled regions, nothing masks the misery. New Orleans is a clear example. It has recovered only slowly and partially from the damage of Hurricane Katrina, so the city has lost population, income, jobs, and services. Its failure stemmed not only from hurricane destruction and then incompetent response, but even more from the unpromising pre-disaster situation. New Orleans lay unprotected by an inadequate flood control system, but more to the point, the city's impoverished population of color, its declining economic base, and its bungling, self-seeking political class caught the downside of a nation increasingly complacent about rising levels of inequality. The physical disaster, when it hit, poured putrid water and toxic mud atop the structures of social disaster, to devastate the city's most defenseless residents. Middle-class households, on the contrary, had the means to pick back up, even to prosper, to return from exile, live in areas better protected from flooding, benefit from commercial and public reinvestment, and have jobs.[5] The tragic separations of social class and neighborhood in New Orleans are repeated in many metropolitan areas, though without the insult of the flood added to the injuries of racism and inequality.

Doughnuts and Checkerboards

Patterns of race, class, and citizenship vary considerably from city to city. The Detroit metropolitan area provides one of the country's most visible doughnut patterns, yet even it looks in some ways like a checkerboard. The city once had a booming economy, but no more. Its population peaked at 1.85 million in 1950, but by 2007 had declined by more than half, to 808,000.[6] Detroit has been "one of the nation's most distressed central cities for decades ... by far the most impoverished city in the nation in 2003, with more than one in three residents

TABLE 4.1   DETROIT-AREA FAMILY INCOMES, 2007

	Percentage under $10,000/year	Percentage under $25,000/year	Percentage over $100,000/year
Detroit	15.4	38.3	9.6
Flint	17.2	42.9	4.4
CSA*	5.0	15.8	27.6
CSA without Detroit	3.6	12.7	30.3
CSA without Detroit or Flint	3.3	12.0	30.6

Source: U.S. Census Bureau, American Community Survey, 2007, Selected Economic Characteristics. Available at http://factfinder.census.gov.

*Detroit-Warren-Flint Combined Statistical Area, as defined by the U.S. Census Bureau.

living below the federal poverty line." Detroit "faces the most severe residential segregation between Blacks and Whites of any metropolitan region in the country."[7] Nearly 83 percent of the city's residents are Black, and just over 10 percent are White. Detroit's jobs are extremely decentralized, and it is the metropolis with the "greatest distance between African Americans and jobs."[8] Meanwhile, the surrounding suburban population grew to 4.6 million even as the city tumbled downward with collapsing employment at the big three automakers. In Detroit's metropolitan surroundings, minority populations concentrate in a few centers, mainly Flint. Most suburban areas are nearly all White, so that not counting Detroit, Flint, and Ann Arbor, the Black population of the remaining metropolitan area amounts to less than 10 percent. Accompanying these excessive racial differences, dramatic differences apply also to family and household incomes. In 2007, median income for families in the city of Detroit was about half that of families in the metropolitan area (including Detroit), $33,922 versus $65,560. Table 4.1 contrasts Detroit with its suburbs. In Detroit more than 15 percent of the families are extremely poor, earning less than $10,000 per year, but outside the city, the figure drops below 4 percent. At the other end of the income distribution, more than 30 percent of suburban families earn more than $100,000, but less than 10 percent of city families do. In these ways, it looks like a doughnut with a hole in the middle. But it looks like a checkerboard, too, with its squares marking both race and class. Flint's native Whites (non-Black, non-immigrant) constitute only 42.7 percent of its population, and Flint's median income is even lower than Detroit's. The bottom line in the table subtracts Detroit and Flint (as the "city"), leaving all the rest as "suburb," thus sharpening the contrast in income disparities. All these sad Detroit-area statistics refer to 2007, well before the Big Three automaker meltdown.

An even sharper doughnut example is Rochester, New York, with a metropolitan population of about a million. Over the last half century Whites have headed for the suburbs, leaving Blacks occupying a much diminished city, with Latinos moving in as they abandoned migrant farm labor jobs. Only four municipalities (of twenty-one in the metropolis) have significant minority populations: Rochester itself, two rural townships with prisons, and a third township with an

Indian reservation, poor despite the notion that Native Americans benefit from large-scale gambling income. In a startling example of national patterns of land-use change, even though the region's industrial base collapsed as the photonics industry suffered from severe global competition (e.g., Kodak, Xerox, Bausch and Lomb) and minority underemployment rose, the all-White suburbs continued to sprawl.

Our final example is Washington, D.C. Although middle-class Black populations have moved into the suburbs, and Black elites are members of the government and top law firms, the old form persists. Heavily populated Black neighborhoods have spread out from their tight concentration in South East D.C., but they remain highly concentrated in one segment of the giant metropolis, extending across the border into Maryland's Prince George's County. Prominent Black politicians, attorneys, and others live scattered throughout the suburbs, but most of the outlying tracts have very White populations, while the Black population resides largely in one contiguous set of tracts that extend from the eastern part of the District into the suburbs. In the western suburbs tracts are close to or above 90 percent White, but many of the tracts in the east are 70 to 90 percent Black. There are a few heavily Hispanic tracts in the southwest.

In contrast to these easily depicted geographies of poor center and mainly well-off outskirts, the checkerboard of prosperity and poverty (and of White vs. minority) in many large metropolitan areas is highly complex, so that both cities and suburbs have mixes of racial/ethnic groups and income classes. Yet neighborhood by neighborhood, at that level where people actually sleep, shop, attend school, and walk or play on the sidewalks, sharp geographic variations in income, race, ethnicity, and neighborhood advantage still distinguish daily opportunities and experiences. Variations run across city and suburbs alike. New York City, with nearly 9 million people, and San Francisco, with only three-quarters of a million, each has central neighborhoods dominated by wealthy households but each has very poor districts as well. Each also has poor and minority jurisdictions in the suburbs. In New York the finance bubble gentrified famously poor Black neighborhoods like Harlem and parts of Brooklyn and Queens, and in San Francisco the dot-com boom gentrified the poor Latino Mission District. In both cities the suburbs are generally much better off than the central areas, but in specific outlying zones very poor Blacks and Hispanics dominate. Deeply troubled suburbs in the Bay Area include East Palo Alto, Richmond, large neighborhoods in Oakland, and parts of San Jose, many of these neighborhoods immediately adjacent to some of the wealthiest residential areas in the nation. The New York suburbs are checkered with very poor minority enclaves—some are inner suburban cities themselves, like Newark or Yonkers, while others are old downtowns in farther-out commuter suburbs in Westchester County and Connecticut.

Leaving aside San Francisco, New York, Boston, and a few other cities, in even the most complex metropolitan areas job losses in the center and growth in the surroundings tend to leave city economies stranded. Given the failures of national urban policy, job losses also leave public services without sufficient tax support, pushing cities still further apart from their mostly much better-off suburbs. Government jobs, historically made available as one of the last redoubts for minority employment, get cut and downgraded. For city and inner-suburban residents of color, a cycle of ever-worsening conditions sets in for the economy and public services. These self-reinforcing patterns of division are difficult to reverse.[9]

In Detroit, for example, essential services dried up long before the collapse of the big three carmakers, adding to the burden of insufficient household incomes. Imagine the hospital situation, in the words of Atil Gewande, professor at the Harvard Medical School:

> Sinai-Grace is a classic urban hospital. It has 800 physicians, 700 nurses, and 2,000 other medical personnel to care for a population with the lowest median income of any city in the country. More than a quarter of a million residents are uninsured; 300,000 are on state assistance. Sinai-Grace is not the most cash-strapped hospital in the city—that would be Detroit Receiving Hospital, where a fifth of the patients have no means of payment. But between 2000 and 2003 Sinai-Grace and eight other Detroit hospitals were forced to cut a third of their staff, and the state had to come forward with a $50 million bailout to avert their bankruptcy.[10]

In many metropolitan areas in recent years residential segregation by racial group has become statistically less pronounced, at least among middle-class households. Still, the bulk of social interaction takes place among Whites themselves or among one or another group of people of color, with little crossing of racial or ethnic lines. Indices of segregation for activities such as church attendance and school enrollment remain startlingly high. Not more than one religious congregation in every twenty-five or thirty is racially mixed.[11] Growing numbers of well-off African Americans live in the suburbs of such cities as Washington, D.C., and Atlanta, where their kids sometimes attend integrated public schools, but even in those unusual suburbs with notable minority numbers in the middle class, the internal partitioning of schools districts remains severe. Most ordinary working-class and poor African Americans still live in large, virtually single-race areas. Similar though less intense separations afflict Latinos—who in some areas may be highly suburbanized—and some groups of Asians and other minority residents, including increasing numbers of people living in inner suburbs.

Both cause and consequence of these separations by race and class find themselves reinforced by feelings of fear. Middle-class Whites travel through areas in which they sense danger, but they move protected by private autos or sometimes by suburban trains, via what Martin Jaffe calls "honky tubes" that connect city offices to suburban homes. White commuters rarely venture into contact with life in minority districts.[12] White suburban teenagers often do not visit the city at all, or they conduct hit-and-run forays into entertainment zones. On the other hand, poor people of color, as we observed in Chapter 2, often live isolated in highly circumscribed enclaves. African American, Latino, and poor Asian city teenagers rarely venture into the White suburbs or even into unfamiliar parts of the city itself, places where they feel unwelcome. Grafted on top of historical circumstances, economic differences, and ethnic affinities, the old plagues of ignorance and racism still play a big part. This chapter explores these issues in four more sections, on regional differences, patterns of job location, housing and neighborhoods, and causes that connect poverty and place.

Changing Regional Economies and City Systems

> The past thirty-five years have been kind to idea-producing places, like New York and Boston, and devastating to goods-producing cities, like Cleveland and Detroit.[13]

We begin by examining metropolitan areas as units. Although relationships between regional economic growth and national or even global growth are open to debate, and policies to reduce regional inequality are disputed, there is no doubt that some regions do better and others, worse.[14] The aggregate rate of growth (or decline) in any metropolitan area depends on its own initiative, but perhaps more so on its location vis-à-vis other parts of the nation, its particular industrial structure, and the region's history and long-term trajectory. Metropolitan areas in regions endowed with a healthy portion of industries that enjoy booming demand for their products do relatively well, while those in regions dominated by firms in declining industries do not. Places with innovative, competitive sectors and firms may compete successfully with cheaper production sites overseas, while others may not. Older cities with antiquated streets, bridges, sewer lines, and water treatment plants face heavy repair costs, hence high taxes and relative disinterest from incoming investors. Old cities with lagging industrial sectors may thus be hit doubly hard, with constantly heavy costs for catch-up and falling demand for their exports. So-called global cities may ride high in boom times, but even they can fall hard when the economy heads downward. In this section we examine manufacturing centers and global cities, finishing with a broad comparison of national regions.

Because of its immense territory, giant population, and inward-facing domestic economy, the United States enjoys a network of cities largely independent of outside political and economic forces. Each city (really, metropolis) functions as part of a regional, national, and international economic network of cities. The size of each city's economy, and its population, depends in part on its position in this network, and of course the network itself depends on each of its parts. Thus for centuries London was outsized for England's national market and population because it was the capital of a world empire. Similarly, Buenos Aires was far too large for Argentina's economy or population because it served as the connection to the British Empire and later to America's global reach.[15] Beneath each top internationally connected city lies a network of lesser cities, each dependent on specialized products and services from higher-ranked places, in turn supplying lower-order products and services to cities below. Many cities grow as well with specialties requiring economies of scale, or they grow for highly particular reasons—Detroit for autos, Rochester for photonics, Miami for tourism and its connection to Latin America, Washington for the federal bureaucracy. Economic functions change: Buffalo once prospered as the transportation connection to the West and also as the eastern manufacturer of heavy metal products with access via Great Lakes shipping, but both these advantages faded.

City growth has often depended on specific locational features—access to transportation such as coastal locations or ports on large rivers or lakes, centers of agricultural land, proximity to energy or natural resources, and military advantage. U.S. regional growth has been influenced especially by early development patterns, as immigrant Europeans and enslaved Africans settled first along the Atlantic seaboard but later sought territory to the west. Since World War II a few cities at the top of the global hierarchy have stood out—New York, of course, but also San Francisco and more recently Los Angeles on the other coast, dependent on their financial and military relations to what some call the Pacific Rim Empire. But most cities have grown as centers for processing of agricultural produce, as locations for specialized manufacturing, or as places close to natural resources. The arrangement has shifted as the nation's economy has moved West and South. Ever larger urbanized areas have grown with the self-reinforcing advantages of metropolitan size. Because some declines and other expansions have been so dramatic in recent years, we look separately at manufacturing centers and global cities.

The internal distribution of job loss in every metropolitan area seems to depend on race. As a researcher with the Cleveland Federal Reserve Board wrote in 2006, "race and income are two distinct dimensions of social inclusion."[16] Perhaps the appropriate word is not *inclusion* but *exclusion*. Not too long ago, after taking a loss of 66,000 manufacturing jobs over two decades, Milwaukee rebounded into one of the nation's most robust, revitalizing economies. Nevertheless, after that rebound (in 1991) Milwaukee's official unemployment rate among African Americans was 20.1 percent, not counting people who had given up looking for work or those who were underemployed. The White unemployment rate was only 3.8 percent. Alderman Michael McGee, who started the Black Militia in Milwaukee, summed it up years ago: "Things are not booming in the Black Community. The only new construction is churches, the No. 1 employer is drugs."[17] As we see in the next section, long before the recession that started late in 2007, permanent job losses in manufacturing caused huge increases in Black unemployment. A July 2003 report on Indianapolis provides a telling example: "Autoliv, a Swedish manufacturer of seat belts, is closing a plant and laying off 350 workers, more than 75 percent of them Black. Many are young adults who were hired in the late 1990s when the unemployment rate in Indianapolis was only two percent and Autoliv, to recruit enough workers to expand production, hired young men without high school diplomas."[18]

Manufacturing Centers

As we saw in Chapter 3, the United States lost nearly 5 million manufacturing jobs in about three decades, mainly due to foreign low-wage competition, and the manufacturing workforce dropped from 20 percent of national employment in 1979 to about 11 percent in 2006. At the same time, manufacturers have upgraded skills and productivity so that production has expanded in many parts of the country but with fewer jobs.[19] From 1970 to 1990 there was virtual collapse in many old industrial cities. The city of St. Louis, for example, lost half its manufacturing employees, and Cleveland lost 55 percent.[20] Then came the second decline of the industrial base. Between 1995 and 2005 more than 3 million manufacturing jobs vanished nationally, nearly all after 2000.[21] The losses occurred disproportionately in the Great Lakes states of Illinois, Indiana, Michigan, New York, Ohio, Pennsylvania, and Wisconsin. With the crisis that started in 2007, losses accelerated sharply.[22]

For decades, economic vitality has shifted from the rust-belt and frost-belt cities of the Northeast and Midwest to other countries and the sun belt of the South and West, with such heavy stimulus from federal military expenditures that one prominent scholar refers to the new areas as the "gunbelt."[23] Rust-belt decline and sun-belt/gun-belt growth result from global shifts and outsourcing, technological advances in manufacturing, and changes in the way corporations are organized internally. They fabricate goods with new combinations of skilled and unskilled workers, ship the goods in new ways and on new routes, respond to constant product innovation and changes in consumer demand, employ new technologies, and provide new services. Firms locate offices and factories to adapt to shifts in national political priorities, avoid unions, and take advantage of local tax exemptions and subsidies. From 1969 to 1994, employment in most economic sectors shifted strongly from frost belt to sun belt. Surprisingly, despite sharp contractions in manufacturing employment ever since 1980, *high-skill* manufacturing grew very considerably, adding some employment in all industries and all regions, even where traditional manufacturing employment was rapidly declining.[24] Figure 4.1 maps the country by census regions, showing the change in manufacturing employment from 2000 to 2007.

Table 4.2 shows recent expansions of total employment and declines of manufacturing employment by region of the country, offering dramatic evidence of massive economic and demographic shifts that have continued beyond the 1990s. In every major subregion of the country except East North Central, total nonfarm employment stayed the same or increased from December 2000 to December 2007 (the date of the official onset of the recession). But while employment was stable in the Northeast and Midwest, it increased in the West and increased massively in the South. The "Percent Change" column shows the highest growth rates in the Mountain states, the South Atlantic, and West South Central. The "Change" column shows the quantity of new employment, with virtually all growth either in the South, with nearly 3 million new jobs, or the West, with

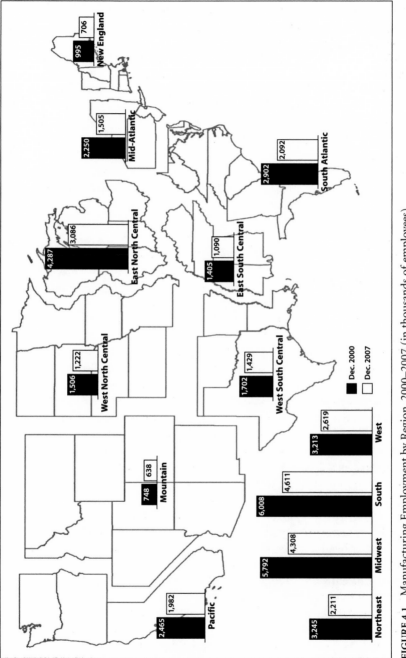

FIGURE 4.1 Manufacturing Employment by Region, 2000–2007 (in thousands of employees)

Source: U.S. Bureau of Labor Statistics, Occupational Employment Statistics.

TABLE 4.2   EMPLOYMENT SHIFTS IN THE UNITED STATES BY REGION, 2000–2007

Region and division	Total nonfarm employment*				Manufacturing employment*			
	2000	2007	Change	Percent change	2000	2007	Change	Percent change
Northeast	25,530	25,740	210	1	3,245	2,211	−1,034	−32
New England	7,073	7,068	−5	0	995	706	−290	−29
Mid-Atlantic	18,457	18,672	215	1	2,250	1,505	−745	−33
Midwest	32,143	31,733	−410	−1	5,792	4,308	−1,485	−26
East North Central	22,239	21,510	−729	−3	4,287	3,086	−1,201	−28
West North Central	9,904	10,223	319	3	1,506	1,222	−284	−19
South	46,743	49,700	2,958	6	6,008	4,611	−1,398	−23
South Atlantic	24,898	26,644	1,746	7	2,902	2,092	−810	−28
East South Central	7,677	7,860	183	2	1,405	1,090	−315	−22
West South Central	14,168	15,197	1,029	7	1,702	1,429	−273	−16
West	29,084	30,622	1,538	5	3,213	2,619	−594	−18
Mountain	8,835	9,809	974	11	748	638	−111	−15
Pacific	20,249	20,813	564	3	2,465	1,982	−483	−20

Source: U.S. Bureau of Labor Statistics.

*Numbers are reported in thousands, as of December of each year, and may not sum due to rounding.

more than 1.5 million new jobs. The story with manufacturing employment is entirely negative, with large percentage declines in every region. In the West jobs fell by well over a half million, in the Northeast by more than a million, and in the Midwest and South by nearly a million and a half each.

During the entire period from 1970 on, employment growth in suburbs and especially fringe areas in the sun belt has dominated. Even during the "urban revival" of the 1980s, suburbs and smaller Metropolitan Statistical Areas (MSAs) grew relatively faster.[25] Manufacturing plants have moved away from the biggest cities of the old industrial heartland, as part of broad regional and global trends. Between 1995 and 2005, service sector jobs increased in all but one of these old manufacturing centers, but generally not enough to offset the loss. In the seven Great Lakes states, 24 metropolitan areas lost jobs, led by Chicago and Detroit.[26] Steel towns in Pennsylvania and Ohio long ago joined the auto cities of Michigan as rust-belt prototypes, and despite revival based on modernized manufacturing in the 1990s, the entire region was hit with collapsing demand for its products in the downturns that began in 2007. The Wall Street malaise quickly spread as thousands of plants lost orders. Shifting fortunes can thin the social and economic fabric that holds communities together, causing poverty to rise and weakening incentives for economic growth.[27]

Ever since the mid-1970s, the job losses of many metropolitan areas have hit workers without much formal education especially hard. Those individual losses in turn have led to community losses marked by out-migration, shrunken tax bases, and reduced services in spite of increased needs. Sometimes job losses for unskilled workers have been matched with job increases in skilled manufacturing, but still the effects have been individually painful, since few laid-off workers themselves have the specialized skills to make the shift. The effects have been collectively destructive, since demands for public expenditures rise to outstrip municipal capacity. Since the 1990s, especially with competition from English-speaking engineers and technical workers in India, China, and elsewhere, competitive losses afflict even the high tech information sector, thus spreading the pain regionally across the country while leaving it focused still on cities but not their suburbs.

As a result of these long-term declines, job displacement is a serious problem, much worse in some regions than others. Although in the 1980s services accounted for an astounding 90 percent of all new jobs,[28] service sector employment grew relatively slowly in the most severely affected job-loss areas—the Northeast and Midwest. There jobs are difficult to find in manufacturing and services, leaving many out of work for the long term.[29] The displacement problem strikes minority workers with particular severity. The auto industry has provided jobs disproportionately for Black workers, so the industry crisis focuses on them. With the slowing of auto plants early in the recession, nearly 20,000 Black auto workers had lost jobs in the year up to November 2008, with the worst still to come.[30] Large numbers of low-skilled workers without much education find themselves without any good options.

In the 1980s displaced workers were most highly concentrated in the East Midwest states (Michigan, Ohio, Indiana, Illinois, and Wisconsin). Other manufacturing areas—the Middle Atlantic states (New York, New Jersey, and Pennsylvania) and the East South Central states (Mississippi, Alabama, Tennessee, and Kentucky)—also had more than their share of displaced workers.[31] These layoffs all had heavy concentrations of lower-skilled minority workers. In more recent economic downturns the geography of displacement has become more complicated, as has the social-class distribution, with many middle-class layoffs when the dot-com bubble burst and many more with the bank failures from 2008 on. Still, the burden falls most heavily on lower-paid, blue-collar, working-class men and women and their families.[32] Mary Chapman notes: "The car companies were hardly multiracial utopias, but they, especially Ford, employed Blacks when many industries would not. Through the decades, the automakers and their higher wage scales provided a route to the middle class for many Black workers, especially those with limited education, and their children."[33]

Further down the urban hierarchy, international competition and corporate restructuring have combined with inappropriate public policy to severely disrupt the economies of cities formerly based on manufacturing.[34] This disruption results from more than the faltering and decline of the industries themselves; even in those places where plants continue in operation, officers and their staffs involved in planning, administration, and financial activities depart to corporate headquarters (in other, fewer cities). These moves, which began during the 1960s and 1970s, continued through the accelerated takeovers and mergers in the 1980s and have extended with globalization, mean that manufacturing cities "lost what little involvement they may have had in the planning, administration, or research and development functions of their industry."[35] These cities are left extremely vulnerable to shifts in market conditions because there is little likelihood of immediate growth in sectors other than traditional manufacturing. Hence the name *rust belt.*

The cities most subject to economic change are those with narrow economic specialization. A city can be highly dependent on an associated set of businesses, a particular complex of industries, such as automobiles in Detroit, optical and office equipment in Rochester, and tires in Akron.[36] Even some metropolitan regions with national corporate headquarters or divisional head offices, such as Cleveland and Milwaukee, have not managed to offset production-job losses in manufacturing by adding new employment in advanced services.[37] Syracuse resisted decline with changes in industrial structure. With their specialization in the manufacturing of machinery and electrical equipment, most firms in Syracuse stayed profitable and some new ones opened—moving to higher technology, shedding basic jobs but adding others, shifting to suburbs, and losing employment much less than in Buffalo, where two large steel plants shut down.[38]

In Upstate New York people suffer severely as their metropolitan centers decline. Upstate includes Buffalo, Rochester, Syracuse, Rome, and Utica, all lying along the Erie Canal just below Lake Ontario, and Binghamton, Elmira, and many smaller cities in New York State's Southern Tier. Pennsylvania cities and rural areas immediately to the south and Ohio to the west suffer similarly, as do areas throughout the broader Northeast region. Pendall and Christopherson find that Upstate incomes grew only half as fast as the nation's in the 1990s and lagged the nation by 11 percent in 2000. Cohorts of workers of the same age, race, and sex, with similar schooling, get lower wages and work fewer hours in Upstate New York. Top-income Upstate households earned less than $75,000 in 1999 compared with more than $81,000 nationally, while poor households saw their relative incomes fall almost 10 percent compared with the nation. Even while poverty rates nationally declined in the 1990s, in Upstate they rose for families, individuals, and children. And even while concentrated poverty declined nationally, it rose Upstate. In these findings we see early warnings that the national "deconcentration" of poverty was about to reverse, revealing—we are afraid—the true nature of U.S. inequality. In one of their most stunning conclusions Pendall and Christopherson point out:

> *Concentrated poverty in Upstate is practically synonymous with city poverty*: 313 of the 575 high-poverty tracts are in Upstate cities. . . . Only 13 small cities among Upstate's 53 cities had no high-poverty tracts. The concentration of poverty in cities is especially troubling because low-income children are segregated into a limited number of school districts. About one-quarter of Upstate's children lived in its cities in 2000, but just over 50 percent of its children below poverty lived in cities.[39]

Global Cities

In many ways the world that urbanist Jane Jacobs wished for has come to pass. Metropolitan economies have increased in importance as nation-states have weakened. Although nation-states still control nearly all military power and regulate human migration as strictly as they can, private corporations and metropolitan interest groups govern much of the world economy and its domestic parts. As the cost and time of communication and transport have declined, geography has strangely become more important and agglomeration economies have made some cities more useful to large corporations and especially convenient for the titans of high finance. Thus we have seen disproportionate growth and wealth in the most highly ranked centers across the globe.[40]

Until about 1980 a major part of regional convergence across the United States came from the catch-up of economic activity played by smaller metropolitan areas. Average wages in small areas increased relative to wages in larger areas, which led to diminished contrasts in metropolitan fortunes and considerable optimism about market-based limits to uneven development. However, since 1980 average metropolitan area wages have diverged, as larger areas have become still richer.[41] At least until the market crash of 2007–2009, larger metropolitan areas prospered because they are more likely to specialize in producer services such as finance, law, publishing, and accounting, as well as corporate management, executive direction, and planning, all functions that expand in line with global prosperity.

In anticipation of these tendencies, in 1966 a book came out titled *The World Cities,* and then sixteen years later a prominent scholar proposed research on "world city formation." Then came the idea of mega-cities, and in 1991 a book called *The Global City.* Since then books and articles on world cities and global cities have come out nonstop, and in 2006 *The Global Cities Reader* republished fifty scholarly articles.[42] In all cases "city" means metropolis, and "world," "global," and of course "mega" cities are nearly always very large. But the idea is not just giant size; it also denotes position in various hierarchies, mostly indicating economic status, but also political and even cultural and ideological status. At the top of all the lists stand those cities that are giant-sized *and* immensely wealthy, by world standards—New York, Tokyo, London, followed by second-ranked cities in terms of both size and wealth, such as Paris, and then by giant, highly influential, but not so wealthy regional leaders such as São Paulo and Seoul.

A frequent index of position in the hierarchy of power and wealth (not just size) used to be the number of headquarters of multinational corporations. But that measure is so highly skewed that only a few cities get onto the list. A more flexible index of hierarchy aims to measure global connections of metropolitan areas based on locations of head offices and branches of advanced producer-service firms. One index lists seven U.S. cities among global cities holding most power—each supported by its metropolitan area economy. New York easily tops the list, followed by Los Angeles, Chicago, and San Francisco; those cities turn out to be ranked in order of their metropolitan populations. Next on the list of cities with hefty service connections come smaller metropolitan areas with special global functions—Miami, the gateway to Latin America; Atlanta, the capital of the new South; and Washington, D.C., the world's dominant political center. Boston, Dallas, Houston, and Seattle, in that order, form the next rank, but each of these cities holds many fewer global connections.[43] Except for New York, each of these top-ranked service centers has fewer international linkages than various foreign counterpart cities, possibly an indication of the declining dominance of the United States in world economic affairs. Even New York, once indisputably the capital city of the global economy, now has to share honors with London, which is smaller economically but more connected internationally, and it faces rising competition from Tokyo and Paris.[44]

Among U.S. cities, how much does sitting atop these pinnacles of global power matter? Answers are contradictory. On the one hand, dominant centers tend to be rich, their economies boosted by finance and financial services (despite periods of severe recession). What manufacturing they have tends to use higher technology and operate with higher productivity. On the other hand, internal inequalities in these more competitive metropolitan areas tend to be pronounced. Even though average wage levels may be higher, so are costs, and the relative position of the poor is often worse. Furthermore, the effects of global dominance on local politics may be important and harmful for the poor, who have not just relatively lower incomes but reduced access and fewer resources. It may be that ordinary neighborhoods in these extraordinary cities have difficulty holding their own.[45]

A few exceptions—the Twin Cities, Denver, Anchorage, Toronto, Mexico City—may prove the rule. Minneapolis–St. Paul serves as headquarters for four giant transnational firms: 3M, General Mills, Target, and Cargill. If theory leads one to expect strong corporate domination, in this case the evidence says that neighborhood politics can resist corporate manipulation of local affairs and the stultifying effects of globalization. This situation contrasts with other cities where corporate control is firmer, as in Atlanta or Cleveland, for example, and according to political scientist Darel Paul it demonstrates the power an opposition can exert so as to slow down the process, to resist elite pressure to "go global." Opposition groups, we see, can "define urban 'success' and 'prestige' in markedly non-global terms."

"Going global" is a politically contested project and far from irresistible. Popular coalitions in Denver and Anchorage have actively impeded local elites' Olympic planning. The Canadian coalition "Bread not Circuses" helped to scuttle Toronto's 2008 Olympic dreams. Peasant farmers near Mexico City protested and eventually blocked construction of a new international airport.

As Paul points out,

> Despite the rhetoric of universal values and collective benefits, subordinate populations know the reality is quite different. Some will enjoy the direct international air flights to global capitals while others will suffer increased noise pollution. Some will find employment with transnational corporations locating in the city while others will lose their jobs with small local firms. Some will profit from industrial incentives while others will pay higher taxes or suffer declining public services. Some will work in redeveloped technology parks while others will lose their homes to local "improvements." Some will welcome the cosmopolitan ethos of a world city while others will lament the erosion of local culture.[46]

The mixed experience suggests that attempts to turn manufacturing centers into global cities may face obstacles not only from the demands of the global economy but also from local forces resisting further maldistribution of the economy's costs and benefits. Even more locally focused remakes may face the same sorts of difficulties. Roberta Gratz talks about "the classic formula of killing a downtown to save it." She observes that big-box projects in New Rochelle, Pittsburgh, New Haven, and Baltimore have been unsuccessful because communities have resisted. Gratz argues that the failure of these projects may "mark the possible end of decades of highly subsidized, developer-driven, national-chain-based projects replacing forlorn downtowns that are nonetheless rich in local history, character and small businesses." Many of these projects have been stopped, she notes, because of "strong coalitions of historic preservationists" who are "invariably on the front lines."[47] In places *without* much remaining small business, the situation is still more bleak.

Resistance or not, levels of inequality have risen rapidly in top-ranked places, which display sharply segmented social structures, with captains of industry and especially kings of finance buying personal services from servants working in the lower orders.[48] Analysis by the Fiscal Policy Institute in New York City shows enormous increases in inequality there through the 1980s and 1990s. The ratio of the average income of the richest and poorest families (the top and bottom quintiles) increased from 7.6 in 1987–1989 to 9.5 in 2004–2006. Even boom towns suffer as they expand, doubly when they contract. Silicon Valley serves as the world's icon for clean, self-generated prosperity, yet the reality is more complex. As one looks carefully, the myths vanish like the morning fog lifting over the Golden Gate. Growth of investment was stimulated partly from "an Italianate agglomeration of small, flexible, cooperating firms," as the myth would have it, but also because of stupendous investment from the Department of Defense; growth of branch plants of giant national industrial firms such as Lockheed Missile and Space, with 20,000 employees; strategic investments by foreign firms such as Korea's Samsung looking for a foothold or for technology transfers;[49] and finally, because of double prosperity offered by suburban advantage in one of the country's fastest-growing metropolitan areas. In its period of rapid growth the miracle development depended on large numbers of bad jobs with low wages, and it produced significant environmental damage.[50] When the downturn punctured the technology bubble in 2002, job loss hit hard even in Silicon Valley.

Theoretical and empirical work emphasizes how regional change is caused as well by the different functional roles that cities play in the international or national economic system.[51] As we saw in the previous chapter, the division of labor results in a hierarchy of cities based on levels of economic specialization, top cities being dominated by higher-order administrative and coordinating functions.[52] Different city roles—that is, different positions in the urban hierarchy—correspond to varying degrees of economic growth.[53] Some cities are more vulnerable than others to the effects of recent economic changes.[54] Top-ranked cities, the most "diversified, advanced-service centers," appear to have benefited most. These cities are highly integrated into the international network of finance and management, and in them are concentrated the control functions of multinational and national corporations.[55] This control involves advanced services, which have grown at all levels of the hierarchy, especially in such national economic capitals as New York, London, and Tokyo. There continues to be very high concentration of the head offices of manufacturing firms in New York and Chicago, and, to a much lesser degree, in half a dozen other U.S. cities.[56] Top cities also have high concentrations of investment banking, corporate law, management consulting, information processing, and other advanced business services, which are increasingly important in the economy. Although they have lost large numbers of jobs in traditional manufacturing, these few cities have rebuilt the foundations of their economies through the growth of advanced services. Corporate service activities give world cities a level of control over their destiny.[57] Thus, the rise of services and the internationalization of production have converged to benefit a select few places.[58] Even direct foreign investment has benefited those few cities in which banking, finance, and related corporate service activities are concentrated, especially the New York region, Chicago, the San Francisco Bay Area, and Los Angeles.[59]

This discussion almost seems to take us off the subject, but it does not. Even in these relatively well off cities, the numbers of poor people are enormous and their misery is increasing. Those who are laid off are not the same ones who get the new good jobs; many of those lucky enough to replace their lost jobs do so at lower pay, and both groups are added to those previously without work or with low wages. If anything, the separation that serves as the main theme of this book is most evident where large, poor, segregated ghettos and barrios sit side by side with booming financial centers.

National Regions and Wage Variation

As evidence on manufacturing centers and global cities suggests, just as household and family incomes have become more unequal in recent years, so have *regional* incomes. Although for many decades researchers observed U.S. regional income convergence, since about 1980 they have found divergence. Past measurement focused on states, but given recent improvements in data, research can focus on metropolitan areas, which, as Matthew Drennan points out, are the "appropriate unit of analysis for studying intranational income inequality" because they "represent single labor markets."[60] For a long time, regional wages converged, as theorists expected. But since 1980 the pattern has shifted, and as in many other parts of the world, regional divergence has been pronounced. Prominent economists, including Gunnar Myrdal, Albert Hirschman, John Romer, and Robert Lucas, have long attributed regional growth and wage differentials to self-reinforcing stimuli—products of the urbanization process itself— rather than to self-equilibrating balances of supply and demand. This idea suggests, and studies find, that larger (and already wealthier) cities will become more prosperous. It also suggests that "pro-active politics may be necessary if the aim is to overcome continuing economic difference between regions."[61]

Regional wage changes have many sources. Recent divergence seems influenced by metropolitan size, the presence of business services, and levels of labor force skills. Since about 1980 the larger the metropolis, the larger the service sector compared with manufacturing, and the more developed the "human capital," then the larger the wage growth.[62]

Powerful regional changes across the United States have been long in the making. In 1950 a third of all employees worked in factories, and more than 70 percent of all manufacturing jobs were concentrated in the metropolitan areas of the Northeast and Midwest,[63] but as national industry was intensely reorganized, the regional shifts were dramatic. The South and West grew more than twice as fast as the Northeast and Midwest regions from 1970 to 1980. Then, from 1979 to 1986, as Table 4.2 shows, employment stagnated in the Midwest, grew slowly in the Northeast, and grew rapidly in the South, the West, and New England. In the next twenty years, manufacturing employment in the older industrial regions of the country declined rapidly.

Moving from place to place is not easy. Americans move more frequently than Europeans, and it is thus often assumed that they find migratory adjustments to economic shifts to be relatively painless. However, despite massive regional imbalances, 56 percent of native-born residents have *never* moved from their birth states and 37 percent live in the community where they were born.[64]

The boom in the South and West and the decline of the Northeast and Midwest were initially attributed to the continued filling of the frontier, the seeking of better climate, the demographic shift to an older population, and investment patterns by corporations or the military.[65] No matter what the cause, this economic volatility most dramatically harmed African Americans in the declining areas, since they had relatively less mobility than Whites, for both social and economic reasons. As a result, as manufacturing jobs moved, African Americans especially were stranded in communities that had no further demand for their talents.[66]

The rise of some cities as opposed to others is also related to what is called the "business climate" provided by local governments and community groups. Businesses avoid some cities that are perceived by business leaders to have anti-growth climates—high taxes, strict site regulations, and strong labor unions, for example.[67] The return movement of firms can be seen as the result of a process of rearrangement of the local political environment, which includes a weakening of pro-labor and pro-neighborhood institutions.[68]

Likewise, some industries have long preferred southern and western cities, where labor unions are weak, with low wages as a result. Southern and western states offer a labor force inhibited by right-to-work legislation, which helps firms avoid unionization of new industrial plants and service industries.[69] At some historical junctions, the presence of large immigrant and minority populations, weakly attached to local politics and therefore relatively defenseless, may weaken opportunities for labor organization. As one researcher said back in 1989, observing economic success despite low wages: "It's very hard to find a Southern city that's not doing well. . . . [Population and industry] trends that have accelerated since the early 1970s have brought much of the nation's urban prosperity to the South. . . . While smokestack industries have been declining in the Northeast and Middle West, manufacturers have been drawn to the South by the area's relatively low wages and antiunion attitudes."[70]

We caution against too much regional specification of industrial and employment change. As a counterexample, take the case of Los Angeles.[71] There one recognizes four familiar, strong elements of the urban economy: a sun-belt city of booming high-tech manufacture; a "control and command" city with a growing, high-finance "downtown"; a rust-belt city of declining heavy manufacturing, in autos and airplanes, for example; and a "Third World" city of sweatshops with immigrant Asian and Latino workers. As this case suggests, analysts should look closely at local industrial structure, not just at the regional averages and trends. Nevertheless, there are justifiable regional generalizations. Regional economic decline is reflected not only in lost jobs and high unemployment but also in involuntary part-time work and low wages.

Where the Jobs Are: Suburbanization and Polycentric Development

The most evident changes in work location since 1980 involve massive decentralization from city centers to suburbs. Researchers represent the complicated metropolitan geography of jobs with various abstract models. There are disagreements, but current trends are pretty clear, with three overlapping patterns of employment. In business districts one finds management, finance, business services, government offices, and an extensive series of ancillary service activities. In the *central* business district (CBD), competition for space is high, so land rents are extremely costly and developers build high to make the floor-area ratio (FAR) as great as possible. Where geology and zoning permit, skyscrapers result. But today the CBD is no longer the dominant employment center. Instead, employment is spread more and more widely, much of it in subcenters. Hence, most large metropolitan areas, once monocentric, are strongly polycentric. As we have seen, job opportunities in these places tend to be highly skewed, with many highly paid professionals depending on poorly paid service workers. As firms disperse, the commute to work becomes much harder for the service workers.

In specially zoned areas of the metropolis, manufacturing employment may occupy a ring surrounding the CBD, located near an airport or seaport, on cheap land with good highway access, or where zoning will allow it for some other reason. Industrial zones—and related railyards—are fewer and farther between than in the past, and in old cities heavy manufacturing sites often stand disused, their large structures rusting before being torn down, with brownfield problems following.

If core management employment concentrates in centers and manufacturing employment on special sites, most employment spreads out in closer connection to the distribution of the residential population—wholesale and retail trade, consumer services including health care, municipal governments, and schools. Employment in these sectors still clusters at enterprise sites (such as a large high school, a mall, or a hospital) and in subcenters that are sometimes built as office parks. With the exception of downtowns and selected subcenters in the very largest metropolitan areas, nearly all places of employment are accessible only by automobile.[72] Low-wage workers confront new difficulties getting to work. Auto ownership is low among African Americans (see Chapter 2), and reverse commutes by transit tend not to work well. Below we examine the more general problem of spatial mismatch, as suburban jobs move out of reach for inner-area populations for a variety of reasons.

How much have things changed, especially in cities famous for sprawl, such as Los Angeles, Atlanta, Las Vegas, and Phoenix? Will current patterns of change persist, and if so, why? In a key study published in 2007, Genevieve Giuliano and her colleagues examined concentrations of employment in the greater Los Angeles area from 1980 to 2000. They asked various questions about how employment is spread across the enormous Los Angeles region, focusing on employment centers, where workers are concentrated. One set of summary statistics appears in Table 4.3.[73] Employment dispersed over the two decades but overall it continues to be remarkably concentrated, so that still more than 70 percent of all employees in the region work on only 10 percent of the land area. The pattern of employment centers in the Los Angeles region has "a remarkable degree of stability" from 1980 to 2000. Jobs are spreading out from the central business core, but even in famously sprawled Los Angeles the largest single employment center is the downtown. Together with adjacent employment centers, downtown L.A. employs about 750,000 people, or 10 percent of metropolitan employment. Outside the core, new employment centers are emerging and growing: employment

TABLE 4.3   PERCENTAGE OF JOBS CONTAINED IN THE DENSEST 10 PERCENT
OF LAND AREA IN THE LOS ANGELES AREA, 1980–2000

County	1980	1990	2000
Los Angeles	73.6	64.0	64.4
Orange	58.7	52.5	50.6
Riverside	85.4	61.4	59.3
San Bernardino	93.5	80.6	78.2
Ventura	69.2	64.6	63.7
All	83.7	74.4	71.1

Source: G. Giuliano, C. Redfearn, A. Agarwal, C. Li, and D. Zhuang, "Employment Concentrations
in Los Angeles, 1980–2000," Environment and Planning A 39, no. 12 (2007): 2935–2957.

on average moves farther from the old core, but it also clusters. In the outer
suburbs, employment growth is rapid and dispersing, but even this dispersed
employment will later cluster into subcenters.

Nationally, as well, metropolitan jobs have dispersed from centers. One study
grouped the 92 largest metropolitan areas by the percentage of jobs inside two
rings, the first radius at three miles, the second at ten miles.[74] Among the areas
with the highest employment density, a few have 25 percent of area employees
working within three miles of the CBD and more than 55 percent of employees
working inside a ten-mile ring. These cities fit on nearly everyone's list of high-
density places—New York, Boston, San Francisco, Pittsburgh, and Portland. But
even in these cities, access to work for the poor can be difficult, made worse for
minority populations because they have not suburbanized along with the jobs.

The list of areas with extremely decentralized employment includes those
with less than 10 percent of employment inside the three-mile ring. Seeing Los
Angeles on the list is no surprise, but perhaps Detroit, St. Louis, and Tampa are
unexpected; in these hollowed-out cities most employment is far out in the suburbs. Nationally, more than a third of people work more than ten miles out. The
Northeast has the least job sprawl, but several western metropolitan areas concentrate their employment (surprise: add Las Vegas to the high-density list!). Job
sprawl is not related to the age of the city. Municipal fragmentation, with lots of
local government, leads to increased job sprawl. Even in places with slightly lower
levels of job dispersal, getting out from the inner areas to the jobs—and for the
job search—presents formidable problems for poor residents.[75] Access to work
depends not only on where the jobs are but also on where people live.

Where People Live

As anyone who has ever bought a house or rented an apartment knows, neighborhood matters. People with a lot of choice, those with resources and good
incomes, move in—that is, they pick areas (usually suburban areas) that have
amenities and are accessible to their needs, and often in the expectation of making money on a housing investment. Those with less choice, but some, with jobs

and incomes that are low but rising, may move *out*—that is, they may escape declining neighborhoods, places with poor services or unsafe streets. The poor usually have little choice at all about where they live.

The layout of metropolitan land uses follows various logics, influenced by politics, social preferences, and economics. Although land-use patterns may vaguely resemble the doughnuts or checkerboards we discussed earlier, they often look disorganized to the untrained eye. Nevertheless, random patterns are rare. Particular needs and goals regulate the location of single-family homes, row houses, and apartments, just as they regulate the locations of retail stores, malls, banks and offices, wholesale and shipping facilities, and storage areas. In nearly all cities around the world, at most times, land uses are denser near the centers, with gradually declining density toward the periphery. Land values are strongly influenced by accessibility, and landowners respond to high values by developing or redeveloping at increased density. In many countries, as densities have been reduced overall by increasing wealth, faster transportation, and instant communication, they have regrouped in minor density peaks rising at various distances from the principal centers. In recent decades residential patterns in U.S. cities have become remarkably less dense at the periphery, as families have shrunk while house sizes and building lots have increased. Even metropolitan areas with stagnant or shrinking populations have extended the spread of urban land on the periphery as households have multiplied and lot sizes have grown. In Rochester, New York, for example, although the metropolitan population has hardly changed since 1970, when it reached a million, the urbanized area has increased enormously. By 2005, the *city* population had declined 37 percent from its peak, but the suburbs had exploded.[76]

Immediately after World War II, large-scale suburban house building and highway construction began, leading to a massive exodus of people from the city. Family preferences for green space, good schools, and rising property values played a part, but commercial pressures and federal policies helped to degrade cities and build up suburbs. The interstate highway system installed 41,000 miles of roads, much of that pavement facilitating travel within metropolitan areas, and the Federal Housing Administration along with the Veterans Administration issued insurance for millions of suburban single-family homes. Immense federal tax expenditures attracted homeowners to the suburbs—they still pay out more than $100 billion per year. Ever since World War II, U.S. suburbanized areas have grown as nowhere else worldwide.

In 1960 central cities held about 29 percent of the country's population. They held the same proportion in 2000 (30 percent). But of course the country grew by more than 80 million people in those forty years, and nonmetropolitan areas lost about 15 million people, so that the suburban population grew enormously, to constitute fully half the nation.[77]

This city-to-suburb movement formed what is still seen as mainstream America, even though it now constitutes far less than a majority—two-adult, White, middle-class suburban families with higher incomes. In fact, 73 percent of the suburban population is White, but they are not all rich, not all happy. California writer Joan Didion has written about Lakewood, a lily-white Los Angeles suburb housing many employees of airplane manufacturers. Lakewood became an icon of troubled suburbs, in a way a measure of rust-belt consequences, as it suffered from widespread teenage sexual abuse and violence.

The national shift outward to the suburbs has been massive, but it has not been uniform. In the 1990s, suburbs grew faster than the central cities in 80 percent of metropolitan areas. Since the year 2000 some central cities have gained, New York prominent among them, but nationally cities still grow less than suburbs.[78] Of the central city population in 2007, 23 percent was African American, and 27 percent was Hispanic. Recently, Whites have moved back in some key cities: 74 central cities gained population in the 1990s, but only 5 (Denver, Atlanta, Memphis, Chicago, and Yonkers, in New York City's first suburban ring) gained enough to offset population losses of the 1980s.[79]

In cities everywhere, residential neighborhoods are defined at least roughly by the characteristics of their residents. As cities change, neighborhoods become differentiated even along occupational lines. Workers in White-ethnic, blue-collar neighborhoods have historically been among the most spatially constrained by the cost and accessibility of urban transportation. Neighborhoods thus reinforce, or reproduce, the different social strata of urban society.[80] Scholars use several statistical indices to measure how different groups are segregated into relatively homogeneous areas, usually according to income or race.[81] Five standard indices measure segregation: isolation, centrality, togetherness, exposure to difference, and intermixtures of various groups.[82] Groups are identified not only by income, race, and ethnicity but also by occupation, "lifestyle" distinctions such as families with or without children or singles or elderly, immigration status, and so on.

When people decide where to live, they consider many things, including job location, housing costs, neighborhood amenities, and the potential for discriminatory resistance by neighbors. As Claude Fischer and his colleagues point out, neighborhood patterns differ regionally (the South vs. the West Coast), among metropolitan areas within regions (Latinos in Phoenix vs. Asians in the Bay Area), in the separation of cities from suburbs, in place-to-place differences (wealthy vs. poor suburbs) and within these jurisdictions, and in segregation that occurs neighborhood by neighborhood. The wealthy have segregated themselves increasingly since 1970 by selecting metropolitan areas, municipalities, and neighborhoods. Segregation of the poorest 20 percent of the metropolitan population increased significantly from 1980 to 1990,[83] and it probably increased again after the census of 2000.

Social Class

Americans are segregated profoundly by class (which we approximate by income). Segregation levels are much higher in the United States than in western Europe,

Canada, or Japan. Americans *expect* neighborhoods to be segregated by income, with the poor in the centers and the better-off in the suburbs, and we all act as though this pattern is natural. In most countries, however, the better-off live in the centers of cities and the poor on the periphery, and the *periphery* is commonly denigrated as containing neighborhoods of the poor.[84] Income groups are typically interspersed in western European neighborhoods, as public provision and rent payments insulate housing from market forces. Volatility and inequality are reduced, limiting the role of housing as a source of exchange value. In the United States, on the contrary, home values constitute the only significant element of wealth for most families, and neighbors nearly always cluster in homogeneous income groups. Furthermore, because localities fund and regulate public schools, an additional opportunity or burden rests on families as they select a place of residence. Suburban municipalities play the game by erecting barriers when they can against undesirables—who would pay lower taxes or who would burden the schools. These are not small matters. The form of the metropolis is in many ways dictated by such concerns, and local governments are dominated by the need to serve private interests of families and households in real estate value and school access.

In a trend that paralleled the expansion of household inequality (see Chapter 2), from 1970 to 1990 most families became more segregated spatially by income (more than 85 percent of the U.S. metropolitan population), though the process differs in declining and growing regions. In regions with declining economies or stagnant or shrinking populations, new suburban construction facilitated segregation as middle-class households, able to afford the higher costs of suburban housing, left bad neighborhoods. Their new amenities included "larger houses, bigger yards and better schools," which act as "magnets . . . into these neighborhoods where they isolate themselves from the economic decline around them." In high-growth metropolitan areas, despite overall suburbanization of minority populations, the segregation of income groups block by block increased via new neighborhood construction, segregation increasing more in areas where overall household inequality expanded fastest.[85]

For a brief time in the 1990s, as we have seen, "economic segregation . . . decreased significantly for all racial and ethnic groups," matching other improvements such as declines in unemployment, poverty, and the concentration of poverty. But then the long-term trend reasserted itself. According to Rebecca Yang and Paul Jargowsky, temporary decreases in spatial inequality were overwhelmed by the continual effects of suburbanization. Even in the go-go years of the 1990s, "metropolitan areas that were suburbanizing more rapidly had smaller declines in economic segregation." As we move toward the second decade of the twenty-first century, further expansions in spatial economic inequality seem likely.[86] One troublesome outcome will likely be further isolation of the poor. Elizabeth Kneebone and Alan Berube note that "poor individuals and families are not evenly distributed across communities or throughout the country.

Instead, they tend to live near one another, clustering in certain neighborhoods and regions. Extremely poor neighborhoods are often home to higher crime rates, underperforming public schools, poor housing and health conditions, as well as limited access to private services and job opportunities. These conditions exacerbate the day-to-day challenges of individual poverty, in effect imposing a "double burden" on the poor population in these neighborhoods."[87]

If it takes a village to raise a child, then when villagers cannot or do not help, children may go astray. Although parents in poverty neighborhoods try to believe that with great individual effort they can safeguard their kids against the neighborhood's demons, the evidence says they are wrong. Poor or problematic neighborhoods exert weaker social control on children, provide more negative role models and inferior peer effects, expose children to crime and violence, deprive them of various opportunities for youth activities, distance them from job opportunities, and inhibit their socialization into the broader society.[88]

Historically in the United States, an ongoing process of acculturation and socioeconomic mobility meant that relative incomes were an important predictor of location for White ethnic minorities, and now they predict location for many new immigrants.[89] As people move up the economic ladder, they leave central city neighborhoods for upgraded, often suburban areas. Levels of ethnic segregation decline in the course of this movement, paralleling the rise in income.[90] This "American Dream" pattern presents a dilemma for policymakers and sociologists alike. No one wants to deprive lower-income people of the opportunity to move up or out, but it is this movement that appears to some to condemn their former communities to persistent poverty and eventually to halt the relocation cycle.[91]

The relationship among ethnic and racial groups in city and suburban neighborhoods varies as the metropolis matures and the society becomes more complex and heterogeneous. In most theories of metropolitan change, this maturation process involves an increase in household incomes. In the course of growth, inner-city zones are seen to "turn over" and move toward "higher and better uses" through a process much like ecological succession in nature. As this happens, residents of central areas are pushed to residential rings further out.[92] This mode of analysis has been applied successfully to explain the location of White ethnic groups, predicting patterns that reflect people's tendency to live in areas with others with similar occupations, incomes, lifestyles, and ethnicity.[93]

Together these observations and findings provide a reasonably sound basis for an accurate description and explanation of metropolitan residential form— once the basic determinants of industrial growth are given. It becomes fairly clear why poor neighborhoods are where they are, and the obstacles to improvement stand out, at one level or another. In one basic way, however, these observations (and the "urban ecology" models on which they are based) fail miserably.[94] They do not account for the persistence of segregation, poverty, and inner-city location for African American workers and their households. This failure points out the need to deal with race explicitly.

Race

Despite marked segregation by income, the most pronounced and persistent characteristic of U.S. residential segregation is not income but race. Levels of income segregation are high, but levels of racial segregation are much higher. Americans commonly recognize certain neighborhoods as *ghettos* and *barrios,* and these terms seem natural, as designations of areas to which residents are *assigned* by race, ethnicity, or skin color.[95] In a brief presentation to the Population Association of America in 2003, John Iceland and his colleagues at the Census Bureau summarized numerous studies of the past few decades, reaching conclusions similar to those of leading sociologists John Logan of Brown University and Douglas Massey of Harvard.[96] Although the landmark housing legislation of the 1960s altered patterns of housing discrimination by outlawing the most blatant methods of exclusion, segregation remains pervasive in the United States. In spite of improvements, African Americans remain the most spatially isolated minority group in U.S. urban areas, Hispanics next.[97] On the average, African American isolation—a measure of the number of people who would have to move their residence to equalize the spatial distribution—is 2.5 times as high as the isolation of Latinos and 10 times higher than for Asians.[98] Peter Marcuse writes that "the clearest divisions of urban space in the United States today are at the extremes," and he notes "the segregation of the poorest, overwhelmingly black, in ghettos," contrasting with "the self-isolation of the rich, in citadels."[99]

Even when income differences do not serve to keep White and African American neighborhoods separate, formal and informal racial restrictions do. Various informal methods operate through the real estate profession, through powerful informal networks, individually imposed rental restrictions, and fear.[100] Formal restrictions exist, too. Large-lot zoning operates to exclude households without enough wealth or income, as do zoning restrictions against rental housing or against apartment buildings, prohibition of industrial housing (including mobile homes), and a variety of other limitations. Through the high correlation of race with income and wealth, these limitations restrict the locational options of minority households. Historically, lease covenants and other legal restrictions directly excluded minority owners or renters; even the Federal Housing Administration prohibited integrated housing developments in the suburbs. Much of the blame for the creation and early enforcement of housing segregation belongs to the federal and municipal governments.[101]

Segregation of Blacks has diminished in recent years, but not much. Levels of racial segregation do diminish for minority group members with higher incomes, but modestly; that is, middle-class Blacks "generally live in more integrated neighborhoods" than do poor Blacks, but the progress has been extremely limited. Studies of African American suburbanization support the conclusion that discrimination still plays a strong role even against those who move out of the city. Suburban movers are steered into selected neighborhoods and resegregated.

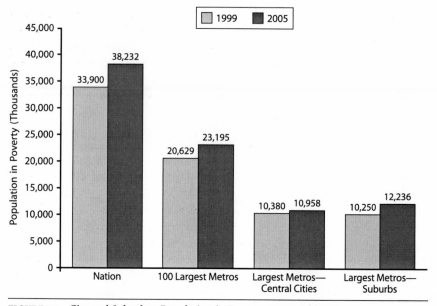

FIGURE 4.2 City and Suburban Population in Poverty, 1999 and 2005

Source: Alan Berube and Elizabeth Kneebone, "Two Steps Back: City and Suburban Poverty Trends, 1999–2005," Brookings Institution, 2006. Available at http://www.brookings.edu/reports/2006/12poverty_berube.aspx.

They pay higher prices for inferior housing and poorer services than do Whites of comparable income levels. Sometimes the move to the suburbs just transfers the segregation to a new location.[102]

By some measures, Latinos have recently become slightly more segregated from Whites, but they are still much less segregated than African Americans. Latino housing patterns depend greatly on immigration—new immigrants with lower incomes, who speak less English, are more segregated. Segregation has been most pronounced in cities with high rates of immigration, in places with a significant rise in the proportion of the population that is Latino. Not all immigrant concentrations lie near the center. In Nassau County on Long Island, for example, poor Latin American workers often earn very low wages (roughly $15,000 a year in 2007), live crowded in doubled-up housing or worse, and encounter hostility and violence. Similar situations confront immigrants in many other metropolitan areas across the country. Indeed, poverty rates in some suburban areas have risen quite dramatically, very likely due to the suburban movement of Blacks and Latinos. Figure 4.2 shows that in the one hundred largest metropolitan areas, the number of poor people in central cities grew 5.6 percent from 1999 to 2005, while in the suburbs the number grew by 19.4 percent. Nationally, growth was 12.8 percent.[103]

An overwhelming percentage of Hispanics—93 percent—live in metropolitan areas. They comprise 16 percent of metropolitan residents, 12 percent of the suburban population, and 21 percent of the central city. Forty-four percent live in suburbs, and 48 percent live in central cities. The segregation of Puerto Ricans provides convincing evidence of the power of racial discrimination. While most Hispanics have traditionally followed the predictions of the urban-ecology model, assimilating culturally and spatially when they have higher incomes, Puerto Ricans have not. They stay highly segregated even when they have high incomes. Although this could conceivably be because Puerto Ricans, from a multi-racial culture, are less averse to settling near African Americans,[104] it is much more likely to be because Whites discriminate against Puerto Ricans, especially those with dark skins.

Urban sociologists and demographers John Logan, Brian Stults, and Reynolds Farley examined the numbers for all metropolitan areas that had at least 2,500 minority residents in 1980 and 2000. They looked at Black/White segregation in 225 areas, Hispanic/White segregation in 210 areas, and Asian/White segregation in 116 areas. Altogether these areas held 77 percent of the nation's White population and 88 percent of the Black population for the Census of 2000. The key statistic is the Index of Dissimilarity (D), the minimum percentage of either group that would have to change census tracts to make the two distributions the same. Thus, in a metropolitan area with 15 percent Asians and 85 percent Whites, the index would tell what percentage of Asians (or Whites) would have to move to give each census tract the same racial composition, that is, 15 percent Asian and 85 percent White.[105] Logan and his colleagues' major findings are that although Black segregation has been declining, Blacks are still *much* more segregated than others, and the already slow rate of decline slowed still further after 1990. During the 1990s Black segregation *increased* in fifteen metropolitan areas, and Asian and Hispanic segregation levels stayed about the same. Segregation levels were higher in the Northeast and Midwest than in the South or West. Larger metropolitan areas are more segregated, as are those where cities are historically surrounded by multiple suburban municipalities, which functioned to exclude Black residents "during the suburban building boom." Demographers use a cutoff of 0.60 for D to mark a high level of segregation. D ranged from a high of 85 in metropolitan Detroit to a low of 20 in Missoula, Montana.[106]

A study of Latino segregation focusing on the 1990s concludes that Latino segregation is increasing, mainly in suburbs, rising toward Black levels just as the latter decline. Puerto Ricans are the most highly segregated, followed by Mexicans and then Cubans. The national statistics are dominated numerically by Mexicans and Mexican Americans, and *their* statistics are dominated by just three areas—Los Angeles, Chicago, and New York—where 83 percent of Latinos live.[107]

Black segregation persists. Despite New York's many population changes, the metropolitan area did not reduce its level of Black/White residential segregation between 1980 and 2000—the level actually rose slightly as measured by the index of dissimilarity. Three explanations all seem to contribute to persistent segregation: socioeconomic disparities, differing preferences, and housing market discrimination. Research shows "white avoidance of areas in which they are not in the majority and especially of areas where Blacks are found in very dominant numbers."[108] Summarizing their nationwide study of metropolitan areas, Logan and his colleagues find no reason to expect any "breakthrough" changes in Black segregation: "demographers continue to wait for signs that large changes in whites' attitudes have had a major impact on the segregation of blacks. . . . Blacks did improve their incomes during the 1990s, and blacks were less segregated in areas in which their incomes were closer to those of whites. But . . . the new factors that could have been expected to accelerate black-white desegregation failed to have much effect."[109] They go on to say: "Without a fundamental reordering of residential processes that would strengthen the potential sources of change, it seems likely that the rate of decline in black-white segregation will remain modest— on the order of 4–5 points per decade, possibly bringing blacks to parity with the current level for Hispanics in the middle of the 21st century."[110]

In the real world, race and income match up. In a 2006 report Brookings urban scholars report on what they call "first suburbs," the older, inner ring of early U.S. suburban development.[111] These suburbs house about a quarter of the nation's metropolitan population and are highly diverse. But their diversity may be a statistical mirage, since each ring of first suburbs is likely to contain two very different kinds of neighborhoods, some strikingly wealthy and white collar, others extremely poor. Some are well established, mainly White, with extremely high real estate prices. Others are mainly Black and Hispanic, with devalued land. Sometimes these dramatic neighborhood variations occur entirely within city boundaries—think of Washington, D.C., with immensely wealthy Georgetown on one side and very poor Anacostia on the other, one overwhelmingly White, the other Black. Cleveland's Shaker Heights is the exception that proves the rule, an anomalous inner suburb, wealthy but intentionally integrated racially, but still contrasting with the usual inner suburbs, with their separate Black and White areas.[112] Across the country many other close-in suburbs display wealth and, typically, Whiteness, while their inner-ring counterparts are the new ghettos and barrios. In many cases these separate suburban jurisdictions in the inner ring, when compared with the central city, have both higher *and* lower levels of median income.[113]

Immigration

Thirty-seven million foreign-born residents (immigrants) live in the United States, the vast majority in metropolitan areas, as shown in Table 4.4. Nearly 20 million immigrants live in just ten metropolitan areas. New York and Los Angeles account for more than a quarter of the country's immigrant population. Add in five more areas—Miami, Chicago, Houston, San Francisco, and Dallas–Fort Worth—and the figure increases to 45 percent. Eighty-five percent of Miami's immigrants are from Latin America. Fifty-two percent of San Francisco's immigrants are from Asia. Of immigrants to the nation since 2000, more than a quarter reside in just three areas: New York, Los Angeles, and Miami. The dominance of these three cities has diminished—of earlier immigrants, they hold more than a third—but it is still pronounced. Nationally, more than half the immigrant population is from

TABLE 4.4   IMMIGRANTS IN METROPOLITAN AREAS, 2005–2007

Area	Total	From Latin America	From Asia	Recent immigrants (entered 2000 or later)
		Immigrant population		
New York	5,271,421	2,645,192	1,382,616	1,116,926
Los Angeles	4,447,658	2,615,153	1,472,943	823,072
Miami	1,993,782	1,696,911	98,718	483,936
Chicago	1,664,624	807,032	392,030	379,081
Houston	1,167,565	815,872	239,791	313,913
Dallas–Fort Worth	1,056,341	722,848	220,158	313,735
San Francisco	1,232,673	397,956	640,314	258,329
Atlanta	646,393	338,649	164,605	228,597
Phoenix	677,615	483,010	91,991	223,785
San Diego	678,357	363,319	224,029	139,091
Total for areas listed above	18,836,429	10,885,942	4,927,195	4,280,465
USA total	37,234,785	19,891,256	9,940,601	9,457,640

Source: U.S. Census Bureau, American Community Survey, 2005–2007, Three-Year Estimates, Selected Social Characteristics in the United States. Available at http://factfinder.census.gov.

Latin America, and more than a quarter from Asia, together totaling 80 percent. In the ten areas listed in Table 4.4, Latinos and Asians account for 84 percent of all immigrants.

Everywhere the geography of immigrant residence has become complex, but nearly everywhere Latinos and Asians are dominant. From 1995 to 2000 more than half of new household heads in the entire United States were Asian and Hispanic, many of them immigrants. From the other side, in 2001, immigrants accounted for 64 percent of all Asian households and over half of Hispanic households. Most Hispanic/Latino immigrants are poor, and more than 90 percent of them live in metropolitan areas, more than a quarter of them highly segregated. The highly segregated Latinos are concentrated in Los Angeles, New York, and Chicago, and as theory would predict, their segregation can be attributed mainly to low education and low income. Residential patterns relate to the job market, and Latino immigrants are especially hurt by the segmented labor market. Like African Americans, they face "globalization and deindustrialization," which "has eliminated millions of low-skilled, high-wage jobs replacing them with low-wage, low-skill service sector jobs."[114] Unfortunately, African Americans and Latino immigrants sometimes struggle for the same jobs.

A study of eighty smaller Metropolitan Statistical Areas (MSAs) found that even though the absolute numbers of immigrants are relatively small, more than three-quarters of these areas *doubled* their immigrant populations. Ninety percent of them had net immigrant inflows between 1970 and 2000.[115] In the South, Latino city growth has been dramatic. Excepting the Miami area, overall numbers of Latinos and the numbers of Latino communities until recently were small. Nevertheless, recent Latino growth rates have soared, above 500 percent in many southern cities. During the 1990s, while the Hispanic population increased nationally by about 58 percent, it trebled in many southern states. In Tennessee the increase was ninefold and in North Carolina, more than tenfold. As in earlier years and elsewhere, most of the recent immigration has been to cities, and the social and political experience has been mixed. Indeed, although Mexicans started working in poultry-processing plants in northern Georgia as long ago as the 1970s, there and elsewhere in the South they have "been accepted as *workers* but not as community *members*."[116]

Asians (both Asian Americans and immigrants), due partly to their relatively small numbers in most areas—and to their relatively high incomes—are much less physically isolated and have higher likelihoods of contact with Whites. The greatest levels of segregation occur in the cities having the largest Asian concentrations, yet even in these cities Asians are much less concentrated than other groups, and some of the concentrations are in good part voluntary. In most areas Asian immigrants settle in no particular community but in a dispersed pattern. Although some Asian immigrant subgroups are poor, especially those from the Philippines and some other Southeast Asian nations, many Asian immigrants are well-to-do. For Los Angeles, real estate operators working in Hong Kong and Taiwan direct wealthy immigrants to enclaves such as suburban Monterey Park (the "Chinese Beverly Hills"). In San Francisco, commuters from suburban dot-com employment and immigrants in wealthy households drove real estate prices and rents up, which drove poor households out.[117] Non-immigrant dot-commers also contributed to the gentrification, of course.

To summarize: overall, while the restructuring of metropolitan residential areas has led to the expansion of minority populations in the suburbs, sometimes very substantially, it has left unchanged many White suburbs and at the same time deepened the isolation of very poor minority areas in the center. African American and Latino suburbanization has come more slowly, less fully, and much later than White suburbanization, and it has ended in many cases in resegregation. These geographic patterns have enormous consequences for politics and public finance at all levels in America, isolating not only rich and poor but dark-skinned people from Whites, and stimulating destructive nativist sentiments, all too frequently ending in racist violence.[118] Suburbanization continues to provide a mechanism for sorting out winners and losers, for assigning to different groups extra benefits and extra costs as the economy gets restructured. Not only do some winners find their way to higher pay (fairly or not), but once there, they solidify their gains by residential separation. As is the case for interfamily distributions of income and wealth (see Chapter 2), geographic distributions of bonuses and deficits is biased against people of color (and against women). Indeed, the production of bias is aided and abetted by the process of geographic separation.

Poverty and Place

The joint effect of the movement of households and the movement of jobs takes us back to the starting point of this book—separation of work, residence, and economic, social, and political life. Now we focus on the high rates of joblessness and poverty among persons of color who live in crowded central-city neighborhoods or, increasingly, in inner suburbs. In this section we show schematically how the global, national, and metropolitan changes discussed above have not only reinforced but actually increased the isolation of very poor African Americans in ghettos. We begin by briefly analyzing the employment conditions of central cities.

Hypersegregation: Concentrated Urban Poverty and Joblessness

Berkeley sociologist Loïc Wacquant offers a new explanation for the persistent concentration of very poor Black households in inner-city or inner-suburban ghettos.[119] Wacquant traces four stages of America's "peculiar institution," which follow one another as a means for exploiting a labor force and isolating its members socially.[120] First comes *chattel slavery,* next the legalistic southern oppression known as *Jim Crow,* third the *Great Migration* and the creation of *Black ghettos* in cities of the North, and finally the partially evacuated but immiserated and *intensified ghetto* combined with *prisons.* As more middle-class Blacks have escaped the ghetto, those left behind, still large in numbers, are pushed still further into an underclass, without hope of improvement. Metropolitan areas have experienced two kinds of dispersal, many to poor inner suburbs and some to the middle-class suburbs—so much so that one scholar refers perhaps hopefully to "melting pot suburbs"[121]—and some central areas have been gentrified. Yet at the same time cities have intensified the segregation and despair of their remaining ghettos and barrios.

Highly concentrated poverty involves at its core some 8 million residents in about 2,500 very poor neighborhoods. For most of the four decades following 1970, concentrations of the very poor have tended to increase. Concentration declined in the 1990s (though not in northeastern cities) but then rose again in cities and inner suburbs.[122] Neighborhoods that are afflicted with high concentrations of poverty impose limits on *all* residents needing access to social, economic and political resources. Large numbers of properties may be vacant and even abandoned. Adult role models may be few and far between. Various forms of criminal behavior may be pervasive.

Looking at race and ethnicity, Wilkes and Iceland report on metropolitan-level *hypersegregation* for 2000, classifying metropolitan areas as racially hypersegregated if they score above 0.60 on at least four of the five standard dimensions of segregation. They examined all metropolitan areas in which a minority group had a population of 1,000 or more. The census shows no hypersegregation for Asians or Native Americans and little for Hispanics but a great deal for Blacks:

> Blacks were hypersegregated in 29 metropolitan areas and . . . levels of segregation experienced by blacks remained significantly higher than those of the other groups. . . .

When we controlled for factors such as income, nativity, region, and economic activity, we found that blacks continued to be significantly more segregated than Hispanics (and Native Americans) on all five dimensions of segregation and were more segregated than were Asians on three out of five dimensions. Contrary to what some may posit, income differentials do not explain levels of hypersegregation, even though they help explain more general patterns of segregation.[123]

Returning to incomes—at the conclusion of the 1990s, scholars discovered a reversal in long-term trends toward the concentration of poverty, and some observers celebrated the reductions. Not only did the number and proportion of neighborhoods with deep poverty decline, but the number and proportion of poor people who lived in those neighborhoods declined, too. (By standard definition, a high-poverty neighborhood is a census tract or zip-code zone with 40 percent or more of its households with income below the poverty line.) "After doubling through the 1970s and 1980s, the poor population living in high-poverty neighborhoods fell by 27% during the 1990s."[124] Looking back, however, we see that the celebration was premature and that the deconcentration, while significant and important, depended not on any solid improvement in skill levels, job structures, income distribution, or policies toward the disadvantaged. Rather, the improvement resulted from the nationwide economic boom, which reduced poverty levels modestly overall and resulted in lower poverty indices for many neighborhoods.[125] No sooner were the good results published, however, when the trends shifted back, toward new and even more intense concentrations and isolation. Nationwide (not just in cities) the number of working poor people living in high-poverty areas increased by 40 percent between 1999 and 2005.[126] In large metropolitan areas changes in concentration of the working poor depended on region: in older industrial areas, mainly in the Midwest and Northeast, concentration increased; in the West, the earlier improvements continued.[127] Although poverty and joblessness do not correlate exactly, their incidences are closely related. Data on Black male joblessness present a sharp picture of concentrations that combine race and income.

The highest concentrations of male joblessness occur in metropolitan areas with large Black populations (and not in the West). Although zones of jobless men have moved out some from city centers since 1980, they are still relatively near the centers. These men have become "more isolated, concentrated, and clustered [into] large, contiguous enclaves." In areas where Blacks constituted high proportions of the population in 1970 (30 percent or more), male joblessness later rose drastically, increasing by more than 17 percent by 2000. In areas with low Black populations (less than 10 percent) the increase was modest, 3 to 5 percent.[128] Robert Wagmiller notes: "Jobless black men occupy a uniquely disadvantaged ecological position in the metropolis: in comparison with other jobless men, they are much less uniformly distributed throughout the metropolis and much more isolated from employed men, they are concentrated in a smaller amount of physical space, and their neighborhoods are more clustered and are located closer to the center of the city."[129]

Table 4.5, compiled from work by Wagmiller, depicts the high concentrations of jobless minority men. In the top part of the table we see that the proportion of neighborhoods (census tracts) with fantastically high levels of joblessness (*where more than half the men have no jobs*) has increased in the fifty largest MSAs. The number of these areas increased fivefold from 1970 to 2000, from less than 1 percent of all census tracts to 4.5 percent. The portion of the total population living in these neighborhoods rose more than sixfold, from half a percent to more than 3 percent, still a small portion, but a growing index of severe problems for some of the neediest members of the society. The proportion of jobless men in the fifty metropolitan areas who live in these extrahigh unemployment areas rose fivefold, from 1.7 percent to 8.4 percent. In 1970 there were 223 of these neighborhoods, with about 690,000 residents. In 2000 there were 2,021 such neighborhoods, with about 6.2 million residents. Of these residents, more than a million were jobless men, joined by 5 million immediate neighbors. In the worst cases, "not only has the number of neighborhoods with low male employment increased dramatically, but large, contiguous [multi-neighborhood] enclaves of concentrated male joblessness have formed as well."[130]

In the bottom part of the table we see that the situation varies drastically depending on race and ethnicity. For Whites, the geographic concentration of unemployed men is minimal. For a start, in 2000 White jobless rates are low, and then only 4 percent of the jobless White men live in such deeply troubled neighborhoods, while 21 percent of jobless Black men do, one in five. Of the White population overall, only 1 percent lives in these neighborhoods, but at the other end of the scale, 12.5 percent of the Black population does, one in eight. That is, a Black person—man, woman, child, employed or not—stands one chance in eight of living in a neighborhood where more than half the employable Black men have no job, and these neighborhoods deliver some of the worst problems our society has to give out. These terrible conditions existed long before the economic meltdown that started in 2007. On this score, Native Americans and Latinos are about half as badly off as Blacks, and Asians are in roughly the same position as Whites. As Wagmiller says:

> Changes in urban economic and social life have disproportionately disadvantaged inner-city residents, particularly less educated black men. Industrial restructuring has undermined the economic competitiveness of the central city, leading to substantial job losses in the manufacturing sector and limited economic opportunities for low-skilled workers. . . . An influx of new immigrants has undermined the labor market position of low-skilled native-born workers . . . [and] progressive suburbanization . . . has concentrated disadvantage in the central city [which segregation further concentrates] in low-income black neighborhoods.[131]

TABLE 4.5   NEIGHBORHOODS WITH LOW MALE EMPLOYMENT IN THE FIFTY LARGEST METROPOLITAN STATISTICAL AREAS IN THE UNITED STATES, BY RACE, 1970–2000

	1970		1980		1990		2000	
	Number	Percent	Number	Percent	Number	Percent	Number	Percent
Neighborhoods with low male employment	223	0.7	1,156	3.2	1,391	3.6	2,021	4.5
Population living in neighborhoods with low male employment								
Total	687,950	0.5	3,145,953	2.1	3,697,683	2.2	6,218,043	3.1
White	443,312	0.4	857,012	0.7	889,174	0.7	1,699,000	1.2
Black	224,615	1.4	2,047,826	10.2	2,447,614	10.7	3,558,266	12.5
Asian			37,070	1.2	80,910	1.3	167,621	1.6
American Indian			15,147	2.2	31,133	3.5	73,282	5.8
Hispanic	55,342	0.7	323,101	2.7	453,064	2.5	1,425,890	4.9
Jobless men in neighborhoods with low male employment								
Total	94,283	1.7	512,238	5.8	629,665	6.6	1,117,215	8.4
White			133,865	3.2	172,643	4.8	318,381	4.1
Black			282,101	16.5	394,445	17.8	598,847	20.9
Asian			4,308	2.5	14,909	3.5	26,221	3.4
American Indian			2,043	5.7	7,046	8.4	15,026	12.0
Hispanic			48,979	6.2	79,335	5.8	262,513	8.7

Source: Robert Wagmiller, "Male Nonemployment in White, Black, Hispanic, and Multiethnic Urban Neighborhoods, 1970–2000," *Urban Affairs Review* 44, no. 1 (2008): 85–125.

Note: Low-male-employment neighborhoods are census tracts where more than half of the men do not have jobs.

Three principal arguments are put forth by students of these situations to explain the extraordinarily high rates of unemployment and underemployment for African American men in central neighborhoods: (1) there is severe discrimination in hiring; (2) educational shortcomings preclude employment as job requirements get stiffer; and (3) the physical distance separating the ghetto and the suburb keeps city workers isolated from areas with multiplying jobs.

Discrimination

As we have argued above, the overall process of urban and metropolitan development has served for decades as a means not only of social and economic advancement for some, but of social and economic separation for all. Just as the suburb has been the avenue for advancement, the central city has become the receptacle for those with few chances. Poor, poorly educated African Americans especially are trapped semipermanently, other ethnic groups temporarily, it seems, and they have limited job opportunities. Although the central-city location still provides special opportunities for some, for these impoverished groups it only adds to the economic, social, and individual inadequacies and constraints they already face.

It is difficult to say where the process begins, as the chicken-egg circle of residential and employment segregation, poor education, and inadequate services is mutually reinforcing. As sociologist Stephen Steinberg has written: "The first thing that needs to be said is that the very existence of a ghetto underclass is prima facie evidence of institutionalized racism. Ultimately, the ghetto underclass is the stepchild of slavery itself, linked to the present by patterns of racial segregation and inequality that are still found in all major institutions."[132]

This residential entrapment situates workers so they are likely to be pushed into job markets that take advantage of these constraints and the workers' limitations, including but not limited to lack of easy access. In a process of labor force segmentation, vulnerable groups must accept work either at less pay or under poorer conditions than they would be expected to in a unified labor market. In the case of African American workers, there is evidence that with the exception of college graduates, most are unable to penetrate higher-wage occupations, no matter how conducive their qualifications or location. Racially based wage differentials have stayed high in cities, for all groups.[133] Surveys show that suburban employers still discriminate against job applicants with darker skins.

Similar findings have been reported for Latino and Southeast Asian immigrants to central cities. The large-scale immigration of poor people from Third World countries after the immigration legislation of 1965 at first fed a process of growth of low-wage industries, with persistent segmentation of immigrant workers into low-wage jobs.[134] More recent immigrants from Mexico and Central America, as we have seen, take low-wage, long-hour jobs not only in agriculture but in construction, manufacturing, commerce, and personal services. Minorities have often been told that if they expect employment at wages comparable to those of Whites, their expectations are too high.

It would be unreasonable to contend that employment, wage, and poverty differentials are entirely functions of race, ethnicity, and discrimination. All analysts agree that other factors enter in important and influential ways, if not directly then at least as intermediate and related causes. One of these factors is education.

Education Mismatch

In 1950 most jobs, 60 percent, did *not* require a high school diploma, and in 1973 still a third were available to those without a diploma. By 2001 those jobs were just about all gone, down to 9 percent. In today's world even factories and trucking firms demand literate and numerate workers. Offices, stores, public agencies, nonprofits, community organizations, and most other employers want job applicants to arrive with formal schooling and good skills. Yet in spite of these stiffening requirements, many young people do not finish high school, and even among the students who stay to graduate, large numbers score unacceptably low in math, science, and reading. When eighth-grade students took the National Assessment of Educational Progress in 2005, many could not deal with the most rudimentary questions, and 43 percent were apparently unable to "understand" science. A quarter to a third of ninth-graders do not graduate from high school in four years. Each high school dropout loses about $260,000 in lifetime earnings and pays about $60,000 less in taxes. Dropouts have much worse health—a 45-year-old dropout has the health of a 65-year-old high school graduate—and dropouts can expect to live nine years less. Once the world leader in higher education, the United States has fallen to seventh in the proportion of young people earning college degrees.[135]

At least 1,700 high schools are "dropout factories," nearly one in ten, according to Bob Balfanz at Johns Hopkins University.[136] The failure numbers rise highest in the cities, harming defenseless individuals and short-changing the society. In Charlotte, San Diego, and Boston, half or more of the students lack basic science concepts. In New York, Houston, Chicago, Cleveland, Los Angeles, and Atlanta, larger proportions are lacking.[137] Cleveland tops the list for school failures, with fewer than one in three graduating on time. In other cities—Memphis, Milwaukee, Columbus, and Chicago—fewer than half the ninth-graders go on to finish high school on time. In fourteen other big-city districts the graduation rates fall between 50 percent and 57 percent: New York, Los Angeles, Orange County (California), Houston, Phoenix, Dallas, Detroit, Forth Worth, Baltimore, Nashville, Las Vegas, Atlanta, Tampa, and Des Moines. The total population of these twenty cities is 29 million, about the same as Canada. Since the measure does not account for children who drop out before ninth grade, the true on-time graduation rates are actually lower.

Going from the city to the suburbs is like moving to a different world. Most suburban public schools have high on-time graduation rates—sometimes 95 percent or higher. Suburban children have much higher rates of college attendance and graduation, so that jobs requiring college degrees are open to them. Jonathan Kozol refers to suburb/city disparities as "savage inequalities," the title of his 1991 book. Nearly every U.S. metropolis has two sets of schools: successful schools for suburban children, and unsuccessful schools for city children and children of broken-down inner suburbs. The high correlations of race with place, and race with jobs and incomes, repeat themselves as race and place correlate with the quality of schooling. Black and Hispanic children, along with the children of some immigrant groups, suffer distinctly and profoundly as they are short-changed by the nation's dual system of public education.

Spatial Lock

Lack of access to jobs is at least a potential problem for many poor metropolitan residents. When the Kerner Commission reported to the White House on urban disturbances in 1968, they coined the term "spatial mismatch" to refer to the physical separation between jobs in the distant suburbs and potential workers who were residents of the ghetto.[138] The mismatch argument rests on several (now familiar) points: that jobs with low educational requirements have nearly vanished with the decline of traditional manufacturing industries, especially in cities; that central-city minority residents were particularly dependent on these (long-declining) industries for work; that these city residents lack access to suburban jobs for want of automobiles and adequate public transport; and finally, that many minority workers are unskilled and therefore poorly matched with high-skill jobs in the service and high-tech sectors, which are available close to home, in the central business district and other metropolitan subcenters. Similar problems confront poor and single-parent households in the inner suburbs, especially those without automobiles.[139]

Skewed racial patterns of automobile ownership help explain why suburban jobs are often beyond the reach of poor city residents. Limited access to automobiles is a key problem in several metropolitan areas, including such global cities as Boston, San Francisco, and Los Angeles, as well as rust-belt cities like Detroit and Cleveland. Nationwide 27 percent of urban households with incomes below $20,000, 22 percent of Black households, and 16 percent of Latino households do not own an automobile. In contrast, 99 percent of households with incomes over $75,000 own a car, as do 95 percent of all White households.[140]

Advocates for the improvement of job accessibility point to several quite different aspects of the problem. Noting the shifting location of jobs, some focus on how residential segregation has denied the same suburban shift to minority households. Others note the failures of transit systems to provide adequate service to "reverse commuters," persons who live in the city but would travel to jobs in the suburbs. Still others focus on lack of access to automobiles. And finally—noting that physical access may not be the problem—some analysts point to employer bias against racial minorities and residents of poor neighborhoods.

In spite of the self-evident nature of many of these issues of transit dependency, a word of caution is necessary. Many analysts who have tried to pinpoint the effects of transit dependency have concluded that it is difficult and probably inappropriate to assign a high proportion of high ghetto unemployment rates to lack of physical access.[141] There may be sufficient jobs near the ghetto, enough at least to even out the discrepancies between White and African American unemployment rates for city residents. The persistent differences in these rates suggest that something else may be the cause.

Yet various methods of access to suburban jobs appear not to help enough either. Federally funded transit programs, for example, aimed specifically at improving bus service to suburban workplaces, gave "little evidence that many jobs were found."[142] Along a slightly different line, a study of African American suburbanization in Cleveland, Detroit, and Philadelphia found that residence in the suburbs does not automatically solve the male employment problem. Likewise, studies of African American teenage unemployment in Chicago suggest that accessibility, though not irrelevant, matters only slightly. Comparable African American and White teenagers fare just as differently when they live next to each other as when they live in areas with dramatic differences in job accessibility.[143] These studies cast serious doubt on the notion that migration to areas of greater employment growth will overcome racial imbalance and racially focused poverty.

The total separateness of the ghetto and barrio from the rest of society is caused by a combination of physical, social, and political isolation. If we aim with a different gun, we may shoot closer to the target. The ghetto and the barrio are symptoms and results of problems. Although the spatial-mismatch hypothesis raises important issues, the deeper problem is not primarily a spatial one. The theory concludes that movement toward jobs would alleviate the problem. It bypasses the problem of discrimination, an issue relevant to both the central-city concentration of African Americans and their access to jobs no matter where they are located. And it bypasses the problem of lack of education and its connection to discrimination. By focusing almost exclusively on distance and accessibility, researchers using this approach arrive at a poor understanding of the problem and recommend insufficient policy.

On the one hand, it would appear absurd to claim that physical isolation in the ghetto or barrio does not hamper residents' ability to search for and keep jobs. On the other, it would be equally absurd to plead for dispersal of the ghetto or barrio as a solution. "Dispersal" of the ghetto or the barrio does not really make sense: the ghetto and barrio represent problems, transmit inequality, and serve as a proxies for many other social processes that seem aimed toward the creation and reinforcement of separate societies.[144] Those problems must be attacked; when they are resolved, physical distance will not be a problem any longer!

The original question was, what significance for job search does ghetto residence have? If racism and discrimination are essential components of restriction from jobs, but their operation cannot be identified by researchers as occurring in overt discriminatory acts in sufficient magnitude to explain such high under-employment rates, then we should suspect that racism and discrimination *use* the ghetto and barrio to restrict employment; they are warehousing areas.

Students of labor market segmentation have long known that at the most basic level (irrespective of education and training) access to jobs depends strongly on personal contacts: plumbers' sons get into the union, others (including their daughters) do not. Word of mouth serves to fill many factory jobs, basic low-skilled jobs, and clerical jobs. The issue is not simply making contact but know-ing the language of the job, observing conventional work practices, and so forth. Even when there are programs of affirmative action, information must flow, personal contacts are influential, and style matters.

William J. Wilson stresses the importance of background supports for job seekers. In the ghetto not only are employee networks thin, but social support and role models are missing.[145] The ghetto and barrio provide only a hollowed-out social structure for informal job contact, conditioning, and training. Young men and women are, in effect, socialized under conditions of deprivation, in which job-related associations are not primary—and sometimes are barely evident.

These ideas have been tested for urban youth, those presumably most sus-ceptible to damage by the absence of such networks. By broadening the defini-tion of accessibility beyond distance from jobs (from city to suburb), to include also density of job-information networks in the city, researchers find that ghetto residence is indeed an inhibitor to job access. In a study of census data for the fifty largest metropolitan areas, Katherine O'Regan and John Quigley have observed that young people, aged 16 to 19, are less likely to find jobs if they live in the ghetto.[146] Their conclusion is based on findings that while social networks provide youth with access to jobs, such networks are often absent in the ghetto. These social networks include the jobs that parents and siblings have, the routes and modes they use to commute, the industries in which they work, and neigh-borhood contacts with other people who are not poor and not African Ameri-can. When these supports are unavailable, the young people are less likely to get jobs and more likely to lose them. The problem is not spatial mismatch but spatial lock.

The changes that have undone and refit the global and national economies have also reworked the shape of American cities. In contrast to an earlier period when urban and suburban growth, of both industries and population, were posi-tively symbiotic, since about 1975 various components of the urban economy have grown and declined in ways that have mixed with neighborhood changes so as to greatly help suburban residents but to deeply harm those left behind in the cities.

Regional economic boom and bust, differential rates of city growth and decline, and a racist-based suburbanization have contributed directly to generate the conditions that create poverty. To be sure, it is possible that on rare, recent occasions suburbanization may have been accompanied by rapid growth of a healthy central city with plentiful jobs and improving neighborhood conditions. In some stagnating regional economies the costs and losses may be widely distributed. More frequently, however, suburban growth has been the flip side of the city's decline and decay, or of a city's division into separate zones of White corporate wealth and African American, Latino, and immigrant Third World–like poverty. White flight (and increasingly minority middle-class flight) has most often left impoverished residents economically stranded, socially separated, and physically locked in isolation, with little political power and few public resources.

5
Rebuilding the American City

In the first edition of this book we advocated changes in national policy to deal with the ills of poverty and neglect in urban areas. We wrote in 1992 that there is a potential cycle for change. It begins with the local problem of urban poverty and central-city decay and then moves to local public recognition, which generates a local response. That response is severely constrained and confounded by the exclusionary obstruction of the privileged suburbs surrounding the cities and by a lack of resources and power. In the best of circumstances, the conflict between attempts to deal locally with the problems of poverty, on the one hand, and lack of resources, on the other, will lead to coalitions and pressures on Congress, the federal judiciary, the White House, and federal agencies. In the face of these pressures, we argued, Congress would pass better federal laws and offer more generous budgets, the executive branch would better regulate the national economy, and industry would develop a more progressive response to competition in the global economy. These changes, in turn, would not only lead to better conditions, such as stronger labor demand, more attention to education, and broad health-care coverage, but also provide the funds for municipalities to make themselves better places to work and live.

We knew that changes of this sort would not happen automatically or easily, and they did not. Changes were tentative and timid in the Clinton administration; in the Bush administration many changes were aimed diametrically in the opposite direction; and during the early Obama administration, despite sympathetic noises, urban concerns have been submerged by worries over the economic crisis, climate change, and global military challenges. We believe the urban concerns merit attention, not only because they are so immediate and serious for the residents of cities and inner suburbs but because urban problems inflict broad national costs.

Even if the government undertakes reforms, however, major changes are unlikely in the short run. Meanwhile, partial reforms are not likely to solve the "poverty problem." Cognizant of these limitations, in this chapter we aim to be practical, to search for means by which—at the least—the serious problems of urban poverty will be written prominently into the political agenda.

We noted in 1992 that local governments would have to become increasingly and deeply engaged in fighting urban poverty. Although some leading local governments—Seattle, San Francisco, Atlanta, and Chicago, for example—took on this challenge, only in 2009 with the incoming Obama administration did the National Conference of Mayors elevate poverty as the central issue for cities. In the face of deepening economic crisis, the mayors' concern goes well beyond the human toll of poverty and inequality. In their preamble the mayors argue that cities are "the engines that drive our national economy." Taking the position that the repositioning of cities' human assets is our most important agenda, the mayors recognize that the nation's fiscal crisis and its ability to overcome the deepening spiral of unemployment and economic shrinkage can be arrested only by bold actions for the restoration of human and physical infrastructure.[1] It is not enough to call for a return to generous, liberal federal policy. Neither our analysis and the recommendations we make below nor the excellent and more detailed proposals of others will stimulate governmental generosity. Advocates need access to the White House basement, where they might push good legislation through Congress, to remake the country in their (and our) better image. They need pressure points in Congress, and they need allies in business firms. But access, points of pressure, and allies all seem unlikely to come into play. Instead, we still believe, better policy to minimize poverty will result only from new political forces, which are now most likely to be rooted in two related national urgencies—the need to reduce urban poverty and inequality, and the need to cope with pressures from the international economy. One purpose of this book is to convince readers that the two urgencies are tied together. If the nation lets the cities and their residents continue to fall, we believe, then the economy will not be able to respond successfully to its international competitors.

When the Clinton administration started, it focused directly on urban programs. As we see below, it developed programs such as Housing Opportunities for People Everywhere (HOPE VI) to reduce the concentration of poverty by tearing down and rearranging public housing to make safer and more sanitary places. In a review in 2004 the Urban Institute called this program "one of the most ambitious urban redevelopment efforts in the nation's history." A national commission had identified some 86,000 "severely distressed" units of the nation's 1.3 million public housing apartments, and in the decade from the program's start to the end of 2002, 63,100 dwelling units were demolished and an additional 20,300 were scheduled for redevelopment.[2] Improvements in public housing and nonprofit affordable housing were laudable, but nevertheless the scale of change was modest compared with the magnitude of the overall housing problem for the poor, and even the HOPE program caused new housing shortages through displacement, a familiar problem from earlier renewal programs. After the Clinton administration left the White House, even this modest pace slowed. Twice in its budget proposals "the Bush administration proposed eliminating funding for the program altogether, citing long delays between grant awards and the completion of ... projects. ... Congress ultimately restored the program for FY 2004, but at a substantially lower level of funding."[3] As we have seen in previous chapters, the nation's worsening income distribution pushed urban development vigorously toward the outer suburbs, and poverty areas spread from the city to inner suburbs. Some cities found that immigrants and back-to-city movers offered relief, but these forms of relief were small or nonexistent in all but a very few cities.

On indirect urban affairs such as improvements in regulation of the national economy, the creation of a progressive climate among industrial firms to respond to global challenges, or seriously redistributive tax and expenditure policy, we were totally wrong. In the Bush years the Republicans turned an already conservative Clintonomics into a reactionary policy on taxation, spending, and financial regulation.[4] The effects on inner urban areas were devastating.

The time is ripe for new ideas. City governments are poor and weak, and although many of them would like to solve the poverty problem, they are unable. The federal government, so distantly separated from urban poverty, is preoccupied with global and national economic and political affairs. But as the problems mount, city officials and community-based organizations will increase their pressures and try to form new political coalitions. Also as the problems mount and threaten national productivity, new solutions will become more attractive to various national groups, such as industrial leaders who fear for their international competitive advantage. If these city-based coalitions can be formed, then inroads can be made to improve some federal policies and transfer some real power to the cities, and a cycle of positive feedback can begin.

The argument proceeds, section by section, through the chapter. In the first section we review the history of federal-local relations in fighting poverty. We begin by pointing out that after years during which federal aid grew, it has drastically declined. Cities are now short of resources and nearly powerless in the face of suburban disparities and economic pressures from big business. The situation is made worse by the rivalries forced on cities by federal programs and their anti-neighborhood bias.[5]

In the second section we provide a selection of proposals for sensible, efficient, and efficacious federal programs to solve the urban poverty crisis. Options for public policy are diverse. The national response to global economic pressures can vary: Japan, France, Germany, Italy, and the Scandinavian countries, for example, have adopted policies considerably different from those taken up in the United States. Even in Britain, where pro-market ideologies have sometimes rivaled the conservative bent of the United States, intercity rivalry is less destructive because national laws and budgets provide a common base for family and urban services.[6] In particular, countries make political choices among technical options to help guide capitalist development. Partly by lack of plan, the United States has chosen regressive policies that guide choice of technology and work arrangements in counterproductive directions, but the country could enact more progressive policies. Reforms could encourage the educating and strengthening of the workforce, from the bottom up. This would be in contrast to the current practice of dividing and further separating labor, destroying opportunity for those at the bottom.

In the third section of this chapter we examine the potential for political support to implement governmental programs. A troubling question concerns sources of political support for these reforms. Of four possibilities, three seem unlikely. The fourth, which stresses the latent strength of grassroots politics in cities, leads us to the last section.

In the fourth and final section of this chapter we focus on strengthening the urban role in the quest for better policy. There we turn briefly to the heart of the matter—how we may work collectively inside cities to gather political support to fight poverty. What are the possibilities for a renewed and revived municipal politics? One way to attack the set of problems treated in this book (poverty, low productivity, social division, and urban decay) is through local, progressive experiments. Success came in earlier decades in several cities—Chicago, Hartford, and Cleveland pursued reforms, along with the more widely discussed but smaller city experiments in Burlington, Santa Monica, and Berkeley.[7] If these experiments were to be multiplied and extended, they could show the way to the needed reconstruction of urban America. There is room for municipal maneuvering, especially within the prospect of improved federal policy toward global competition.

We are more optimistic still. When enough local change takes place, and when more experiments arise from the economic demands and political pressure of impoverished ghetto and barrio populations of African Americans, Latinos, and recent immigrants, they can stimulate coalitions of enlightened mayors and other local advocates to fight for better national policies for raising productivity and improving the U.S. response to global challenges. Once there are better national policies, they will stimulate still better local reforms, and the cycle may reinforce positive change. Clearly, these sorts of optimism stimulated some of the politics that led to the election of a former community organizer to the presidency.

Federal Aid, Municipal Expectations, and Anti-poverty Programs

We open this first section on federal-urban relations with a brief response to conservative pronouncements on the problems of the poor and the central city.

A Note on Neoconservatism

The American city shows a pressing need for more adequate national-level policies. The core of the metropolis is failing. Central cities are falling apart physically, economically, and socially. Whole neighborhoods have fallen apart, the people in them are suffering, and social disorganization threatens entire cities. Far too many people are poor across the nation, not just in the cities and not only when out of work. Their numbers hardly declined even during what the indicators said were economic good times, and in 2008 the numbers in distress skyrocketed, so the situation is tragic. A new generation has reached adulthood in poverty, and the children of that generation are threatened with worse. The gulf between the haves and the have-nots in this country has never been greater, and not withstanding the Obama election, political communication has never been worse. In the few cities with relatively strong economies and steady housing markets in the center—places like Washington, New York, and San Francisco—new strains affect people with ordinary incomes as displacement comes with gentrification. Whole neighborhoods are being displaced in Chicago. In Harlem, Bill Clinton's offices contribute to the gentrification, offering a symbol of the new challenges. Elsewhere in these global cities, real estate costs drove middle-class households to distant suburbs, whose property values then crashed.

Few can doubt that the United States needs a new approach to problems of poverty, nor can they doubt the needs of the central city. It is difficult, therefore, to accept conservatives' arguments that tax cuts for the highest income groups will create jobs and increase opportunities for others, or their argument that the notion of an income gap is a myth. It is hard to believe their theories purporting that the situation will get better by itself. The evidence of the 1980s and 1990s as well as the post-2000 Bush era casts great doubt on claims that problems of poverty will be resolved or even seriously reduced by benefits trickling down from general prosperity, tax cuts, and incentives for the rich. In fact, it is the unleashing of these forces that led to the crash of the global economy, now endangering the entire world economy. Trickling down will not be enough. One hopes for dramatic improvement with the Obama administration, but as we have pointed out, preoccupation with what seem to be even more pressing issues puts city problems on the back burner, or even off the stove.

The conservative argument has been much popularized, but it is false. Most troublesome for our work at this juncture is a tendency in much contemporary discussion to use rhetoric that at once trivializes systematic causes of poverty and magnifies the problems thought to derive from improper individual behavior.[8] To put this bias in context, we borrow ideas from political economist Albert Hirschman, who examined the problem of rhetoric in a broader but closely related context.

The rise of the welfare state in the twentieth century, Hirschman asserts, can be seen as stage three in a protracted zigzag struggle over centuries for the "development of true economic and social citizenship."[9] The first stage was the back-and-forth struggle for civil rights of speech, thought, religion, and justice. Next was the effort to win political rights, by extending the vote, and finally the broader struggle to expand social and economic rights, "recognizing that minimum standards of education, health, economic well-being, and security are basic to the life of a civilized person."[10] Arguments for and against these developments of modern society have used greatly exaggerated rhetoric: progressives extol the advantages of expanded rights, and conservatives warn of the dangers. At each stage there may be progress, followed by attempts to undo the most recent gains. We have just finished a period when what Hirschman calls "reactionary rhetoric" is particularly prominent.

Rhetorical and ideological backlashes stem not simply from gloomy estimates of human capacity, like those made by Edmund Burke on the French Revolution or Thomas Malthus on the utility of starvation for checking the growth of the English working class, nor only from fear by the privileged classes that derives from their being outnumbered by the common people. Support for reaction is provided also by some theoretical predispositions of the social sciences, especially the myth of self-regulating economies, a myth that allows free-market enthusiasts to denounce as strongly "perverse" any effects from progressive interferences with the "natural" laws of supply and demand. It is this unfettered abuse of the rhetoric of supply and demand by hedge fund managers, their investors, and others that has crippled the global economy and wasted enormous resources. The argument that welfare is the cause of poverty is an early and tired example of this sort of reactionary argument, neatly echoing centuries of similar reaction to various stages of progress.[11]

The ideological onslaught of the Reagan, Bush I, and Bush II presidencies against redistributive policies has been widely justified in terms of national economic policy. Although the most negative and racist accompaniments of this policy have usually been kept out of sight, the agendas of those who abuse the theories of free-market economists and other arch-conservative social scientists have sometimes been transparent. The theories lend themselves to this abuse, as is suggested by the quantity of "counterintuitive" reasoning to which we have been subjected. Simulation models are designed to show that "at times programs cause exactly the reverse of desired results," as would be the case, for example, if by providing good housing for the poor the city of Boston attracted impoverished migrants and therefore worsened its average housing conditions. It is claimed that "our efforts to deal with distress themselves increase distress." Conservatives such as Charles Murray argue, "We tried to provide more for the poor and produced more poor instead. We tried to remove the barriers to escape from poverty, and inadvertently built a trap."[12]

These expectations of counterintuitive, reversed, and inadvertent consequences of progressive social policy exist more in the flawed reasoning of the right-wing critics than in reality. Although unanticipated consequences do often result from public (and private) actions, it is important to recognize, as Hirschman points out, that "there is actually nothing certain about such perverse effects."[13]

It is claimed by conservatives, to take but one example, that minimum-wage legislation dries up jobs for the poor by making labor too expensive. But as David Howell and his colleagues point out, "leading economists from seven North American and European countries contend that this conventional wisdom has greatly exaggerated the extent to which the unemployment problem can be blamed on protective labor market institutions and that the case for dismantling the welfare state to fight unemployment rests more on free market ideology than on the empirical evidence."[14] There is in fact little such evidence, and it could be in theory that a higher legal floor to wages would have precisely the intended salutary influence, that is, higher minimums would have "a positive effect on labor productivity and consequently on employment."[15] As the terms of public debate shifted so as to frame a more conservative and less compassionate view, reformers had more and more difficulty defending in public perfectly reasonable attempts (such as the legislation of a higher minimum wage) to improve basic conditions for the poor.

When such extreme rhetoric dominates, good reform is the victim. What is more, throughout history, even legislation purportedly enacted on behalf of the poor has been intended very often by its authors (or been manipulated by others) to the disadvantage of the poor, to control them.[16] It is in this sense, especially in areas such as the administration of welfare, that reactionary sentiment against the poor has been most powerful and most pernicious. Although welfare does provide significant assistance to the poor, it would seem to be designed with hostility in mind. As David Ellwood writes: "Our welfare/income support system seems to be the worst of all worlds. It antagonizes, stigmatizes, isolates and humiliates. It discourages work rather than reinforcing and supporting it. It gives few aids or signals to point people toward self-support. It offers only two real options: work all the time or be on welfare."[17]

The U.S. welfare system and its various counterparts (which we discuss below) leave American cities in much bleaker circumstances than most European cities, where the reversals in social policy are limited and more social services are offered. In the United States a negligent federal government, in the guise of promoting states' rights and home rule, and surrounding itself by claims that localities know best what they need, has used the pressures from a changed international economy to justify turning back decades of progress, to continuously shift power and privilege away from the cities and the poor to the better off in central-city citadels or—mostly—in the suburbs.[18] In these circumstances, it should not be a surprise that cities do not have the capacities or the zeal to adequately address problems of poverty.

We have pervasive evidence that poverty has increased in the United States. That same evidence also suggests that prosperity for the majority of the population is itself threatened by the bad conditions that afflict the poor and debilitate U.S. cities. A poorly educated, inattentive, fearful population reared in the cities is likely to be inefficient, even hostile as a workforce, counterproductive as a citizenry, and dependent. Trickle-down benefits and stricter social control, both conservative suggestions, cannot adequately solve the problem. U.S. jails now hold a higher proportion of the population and larger numbers than is the case for any other country in the world. Building more jails, adding to police budgets, and slamming down on civil rights is the wrong way to go.

In fact, in a whole series of directions U.S. policy has gone awry. Severe and persistent urban poverty is only one manifestation of a soured national project. The solution to problems of urban poverty must be accompanied by solutions to other national problems as well.

To see how conservative arguments are so deeply flawed, we must study the historical evolution of the interconnected activities of the national, state, and local governments in dealing with the economy, poor families, and cities in trouble. We begin by documenting the expansion of the federal role with urban poverty since the beginnings of the 1930s, when national programs first provided assistance to the poor. Although we focus for the most part on specifically urban programs, we wish to leave no doubt about the principal effect of such intervention at the national level. As the statistics presented in earlier chapters demonstrated, and contrary to what conservative theory claims, expansion of federal spending for transfer programs, from Social Security to welfare to health care, resulted in sizable reductions in poverty.[19]

Federal Anti-poverty Policies

There was a long period of progress in federal responsibility for anti-poverty programs. It can be plausibly argued that major social policies were first established even as long as a century ago, to prevent the growth of inequalities. As Lester Thurow, the former dean of the MIT management school, reminds us, Congress established the Interstate Commerce Commission in the 1800s and passed laws against the great commercial trusts "to stop a growing concentration of wealth and to prevent that wealth from being used exploitatively." "The railroads were not to be allowed to exploit their economic advantage over farmers and the oil trust was not to be allowed to exploit the urban consumer. Compulsory education for all was established to create an egalitarian distribution of human capital and more marketable skills in order to prevent large inequalities in earnings. In the 20th century inheritance taxes and progressive income taxes were adopted to lessen inequalities."[20]

These redistributive laws have been systematically eroded, directly by tax cuts for the higher-income groups and program cuts for the poor and indirectly by various increases in regressive taxes for Social Security, flat taxes for Medicare, and sales and real estate taxes that hit hard on renters and households with modest incomes. When poverty spread more widely and threatened the stability of the entire economy, the government shifted the emphasis of its programs from general inequality and comprehensive regulation to the problems of persons with absolute need. The government's first efforts to provide national resources to fight poverty occurred in the Great Depression of the 1930s. As Thurow writes:

"The rising inequalities of the great depression brought Social Security, unemployment insurance and eventually medical insurance for the elderly and the poor to prevent people from falling out of the middle class when confronting unemployment, illness, old age and other harsh facts of life."[21]

National programs were created (the Works Progress Administration, Aid to Families with Dependent Children, Social Security, unemployment insurance, the Civilian Conservation Corps, and others) with the express design of building a broad national safety net to support people, to hold them above poverty and dependency. Within this broad, protective arrangement, local efforts were supported and encouraged to relieve poverty through the provision of better economic opportunity. The federal government concentrated on programs to enhance individual (and therefore family) economic security. Local institutions retained the responsibility for improving the conditions of the places where poverty occurred. A great deal of discretion was left to local government.

The Social Security Act of 1935, which was the heart of the national effort, put into place the basic structure of the American welfare state: general relief for the so-called unemployables, funded by the localities and states; work relief for employables, paid by the federal government; social insurance for pensions for the retired and temporary relief for the jobless; and categorical public assistance for the needy, blind, aged, and children.

The Work Progress Administration, established as a work relief program also in 1935, was designed to cope with a situation of massive unemployment, create national wealth, and provide self-respect through the provision of useful work. As it turned out, the WPA never employed more than 39 percent of the 8 to 11 million unemployed. Moreover, because of hostile management in localities, the make-work nature of the jobs, and the low pay, the morale of many WPA participants did not improve.

Even at the time, top policymakers realized that the American body politic had a very limited capacity to target resources specifically to the poor. As the saying went, "a program for the poor was a poor [politically vulnerable] program." This reluctance to help the "undeserving" poor was seen clearly in state and local responses to the general relief program. Especially hard-hit were the millions of people migrating around the country searching for communities that would give them a chance. In fear of a drain on local resources, many states and cities erected residency requirements as barriers to prevent poor people from staying. California even introduced border checks (serving also as agriculture inspection stations) designed to keep out the riffraff from the Midwest and South. A number of cities introduced stringent vagrancy laws aimed at the drifting poor. As a separate matter, many communities enacted and enforced "sundown laws," which required African Americans to exit before dark.[22]

Local officials also minimized relief expenditures by telling almost everyone—including aging workers without skills, women with dependent children, and the temporarily disabled—that they were employable and thus not eligible for assistance. Similar problems of excessive local control plagued depression-era categorical-assistance programs, particularly the portion concerned with aid to dependent children. Southern states and proponents of "states' rights" won provisions in welfare legislation allowing them to apply prejudicial conditions to exclude recipients. State laws requiring property ownership or the absence of a criminal record permitted many local officials to discriminate against African American or Mexican American households.

Local governments were not eager to administer the welfare state, and they invested much energy in controlling its growth, even by denying benefits to the legally eligible. Despite this and other imperfections, the new programs made progress helping the poor. During the 1930s some 46 million people, 35 percent of the population, received public aid or social insurance at one time or another. Public funds for these programs scarcely existed in 1929; by 1939 they had grown to $5 billion, 27 percent of government expenditures at all levels and 7 percent of the national income.[23] These constituted dramatic improvements in federal capacity to keep individuals functioning in the economy and society.

The essential components of the American welfare state stayed the same for the next three decades, until the civil rights movement brought attention once again to the large numbers of disenfranchised and poor people in the country. The urban riots and rebellions of the 1960s signaled a transition in the national role in fighting poverty. President Lyndon Johnson's declaration of a War on Poverty in 1964, the Moynihan report in 1965 on African American families, and the Kerner Commission's 1968 report on urban unrest were all high-profile government attempts to raise attention to poverty and marshal national resources for addressing it. There was a move away from simply helping poor people toward complementary efforts to alter poor communities.

Rising Expectations for Municipal Power

Faced with riots in Detroit, Los Angeles, Washington, D.C., and most other major cities, the federal government in the mid-1960s tried to focus attention on the problems of poor neighborhoods. Between 1965 and 1969 some 250 people were killed, 12,000 injured, and 83,000 arrested in disorders in dozens of cities. The government responded.[24]

The Kerner Commission (President Johnson's National Advisory Commission on Civil Disorders) investigated the circumstances underlying the African American neighborhood riots of the 1960s. The commission concluded not only that "our nation is moving toward two societies, one black, one white—separate and unequal," but also that "only a greatly enlarged commitment to national action ... can shape a future [for these communities] that is compatible with the historic ideals of American society."[25] The commission called for an end to racial discrimination, and it also called for aggressive federal action to fight unemployment and improve education, housing, and welfare policy at the neighborhood and city level. The report called, for example, for better coordination of the hundreds of employment programs already funded at the local level, as well as the creation of new federal programs to create a million new jobs in communities in both the public and private sectors.[26] Looking back, former senator Fred Harris, one of the members of the commission, noted that "people don't really realize that conditions are so bad for so many people in poverty and—and for African-Americans, and for Hispanics. I think a lot of people say, well, didn't we do all that? ... What we ought to do on the 40th anniversary of the Kerner Report is to get people to see that these problems of race and poverty are still with us. ... Somebody said we may not have all come over on the same boat but we're all in the same boat now."[27]

A popular analogy of the period was to compare poor neighborhoods with colonized, dependent, Third World nations.[28] This concept of the neighborhood as a locus for policymaking was even embodied partially in national legislation. For example, the Model Cities program under the Johnson administration in the mid-1960s required the formation of neighborhood advisory boards for the allocation of federal funds. The Carter administration (a decade later) went even further in attempting to strengthen the role of neighborhoods by establishing a bureau to deal with neighborhood development and autonomy. The Department of Housing and Urban Development (HUD) produced nearly a hundred categorical programs designed specifically for neighborhood revitalization, preservation, economic development, and political and social empowerment.

The funding increases that accompanied these new and expanded activities were truly enormous. As a proportion of all federal outlays, urban program expenditures increased from about 2 percent in 1960 to almost 12 percent in the mid-1970s. In real terms, given a period of rapidly growing federal budgets overall, this represented a gigantic and unprecedented increase in federal transfer payments to cities and their needy residents. There was a vast expansion in programs that were locally run (if often federally administered) for housing, health care, street and highway building and repair, employment and training, and other municipal services.[29] "In New York City federal aid rose from 110 million dollars in fiscal year 1961 to nearly 1.1 billion dollars or about one-sixth of total municipal revenue in 1970. ... In the late 1970s, federal aid to the City approached 2.5 billion dollars annually or about one-fifth the municipal budget."[30]

One major consequence of this explosive growth in municipal activities was a parallel heightening of expectations. City governments or, as we shall see, even neighborhood groups and community organizations would henceforth be expected to deliver goods and services to improve housing, take care of neighborhoods, and provide jobs. Previously weak local public offices, many of them historically hostile to the needs of the poor, were suddenly the great source of assistance. Even though most of the resources originated in federal budgets that provided financial aid to states and municipalities, the public image was of vastly expanded municipal capacity and competence.

This expansion of federal support for city programs manifested a second important characteristic. Federal policymakers hoped that by pulling in disenfranchised groups, they could foster the reconstruction of threatened political and social institutions. To do so, they aimed their efforts at neighborhoods rather than cities overall. The community action programs, with their mandate for "maximum feasible participation," serve as a good example. By galvanizing poor and minority political communities, the federal government hoped to increase the likelihood that locally administered programs would actually meet these groups' needs, and as John Mollenkopf points out, the Democrats hoped to sustain their threatened national coalition.[31] The federal government sought not only to appease minorities' demands for political participation but also to increase the capacity of local governments for addressing localized problems. Nicholas Lemann recalls that the decade of the 1960s really wasn't "a time of faith in big government, but in local affairs": "The War on Poverty looked for solutions to poverty that would be local and diffuse, and would circumvent state and local government and Congress.... Its planners hoped to build public support for it by achieving quick, visible successes."[32]

The increased federal effort in fact aimed at an even more narrow geographic target. In response to claims that big-city political machines practiced intentional bias, and to account for the obvious connections between race and poverty, national policymakers actually bypassed municipal government. A vast array of federal programs was organized to provide services to poor neighborhoods, as though they could be insulated from legally constituted municipal authorities and from the growth and job dynamics of the metropolitan economy. Local governments now also faced neighborhood groups that were federally sponsored, "groups which insisted upon added redistributive service-delivery programs."[33] As sociologist Douglas Yates writes: "Community action was designed as a strategy for fighting city hall, the schools, the housing authority, and the police. It was designed . . . in Washington D.C., to provide creative conflict—to shake up remote and sluggish [city] bureaucracies."[34]

In many respects this approach (eventually) worked. Washington, D.C., is a model of transformation with the rise of Anthony Williams as mayor from 1999 to 2007. Similarly, Edward Rendell began changes in Philadelphia from the bottom to the top. In Seattle, from 1989 to 1997, Mayor Norman Rice pushed government into the neighborhoods with much more collaborative decision making through neighborhood organizations and decentralized city services. In other respects the local focus floundered, and in the end, the combination of struggles for more civil rights, expanded economic opportunities, and increased local authority, accompanied by vastly higher levels of federal financial support, led to the parts adding to less than the whole. As groups pushed simultaneously for rights, jobs, and more political power, there developed several difficulties.

All these programs operated under the general belief that elected municipal government was not trustworthy to deal effectively or in some instances fairly with the needs of depressed communities. From the outset an increase in political power was the central target of the neighborhood movement, so that the fight against poverty was lost in the shuffle. Neighborhood power is an imprecise concept to begin with, and the objectives of those who sought to promote it were unclear. Local businesses, residents, and other interests used the concept to justify narrow, particular pursuits. As Marilyn Landau writes: "Upper-income residents used [neighborhood power] to oppose the location of airports, hospitals, and highways, which provided jobs for lower-income groups. Minorities and labor used the concept to compete for more equitable shares of development projects. Progressives used it to challenge federal support for corporate development of central business districts. In fact, neighborhood became a spatial metaphor for all manner of existing urban conflicts: ethnics vs. blacks; renters vs. landlords; small vs. large property owners."[35]

A variety of coalitions formed, sometimes making allies of neighborhoods and city hall, other times pitting city hall against neighborhoods that were allied with the federal government. Community organizations claimed neighborhood property rights to oppose eminent domain. City planners envisioned decentralized, neighborhood planning to oppose downtown interests. Economic planners sought "substantive alternatives to traditional commercial revitalization, as in Russell's industrial conversion plans for Detroit."[36]

In the end, both citywide and neighborhood programs and budgets expanded. Inroads were made against poverty and urban decay, as we saw in Chapter 2. But then disaster struck, from two sources. First, there was programmatic ineptitude and failure. Most notably, the sub–city hall efforts were not successful. "Members of Congress, mayors, governors, and Cabinet secretaries" were angered, and "hundreds of separate anti-poverty organizations run largely by inexperienced people . . . practically guaranteed . . . failures."[37] These programs, in retrospect, transferred little power to poor people in neighborhoods, helped little with economic development, and provided precious few votes for a reconstructed, liberal Democratic majority. The second and bigger force for undoing these attempts at urban improvement and poverty reduction, however, was systematic, and it drew its negative strength from the process of suburbanization of employment opportunities and solvent taxpayers, the increasing pressures of global economic challenges, and the big turnaround those changes engendered in federal politics.

Our view is that there is a need to resurrect the notion of community development at the neighborhood level. Organized community development corporations, as Avis Vidal has shown, can be creative in developing businesses, housing, and community services far more effectively than city bureaucracies that allocate services by ward or district.[38] Nongovernmental, community-based organizations can provide an equalizing effect that can alter the fortunes of low-income communities. Community development organizations such as the Spanish Speaking Unity Council in Oakland, California, act as community corporations to obtain resources from public and private sources to alter the physical and economic circumstances of poor communities. The council in the last two decades has been able to provide housing and new businesses and even participate in the design and development of a major metropolitan transportation center that has transformed the community. Myriad similar programs operate across the nation—in Kansas City, Minneapolis, San Francisco, and New York.[39] In all these places strong organizations were built at the community level and operate to provide political leverage and promote economic improvement. A national effort is needed at this point to generate new social and economic programs designed to transition community residents and their physical spaces into new environmental and other industrial forms. If this is not done, many communities and people will be left behind as the national economy is dramatically altered.

The Federal Retreat

One important result of the energetic attempts in the 1960s and 1970s to reduce poverty, assist cities and neighborhoods, and transform local politics (and rebuild the Democratic Party coalition) was an increase in expectations. As the proliferation of programs, activities, and funds led to more involvement, it also created the perception that local government is obligated to take a direct responsibility for alleviating poverty and other socioeconomic ills. It is then ironic but predictable that while local institutions were given the mantle of responsibility for solving problems, they were provided with no independent source of resources and no autonomous authority to deal with them. They were allowed no fundamental improvements in municipal organization, increase in taxing power, extension of boundary lines (to annex suburbs), or augmentation of regulatory powers vis-à-vis private corporations. As a consequence, once the political interest in Washington turned away from cities and the flow of federal resources started to run dry, city governments found themselves struggling.

Political developments and social achievements led indeed to high expectations, and then crashed. As Jonathan Walters has written, the Great Society that "bestowed so many programs upon urban areas was by the late 1970s pouring nearly sixty billion dollars a year into cities for . . . housing assistance and mass transit, job training, water projects and block grants of seemingly infinite variety."[40] Boston, for example, which got only $10,000 from the federal government in 1960, garnered $90 million in 1980. How could expectations not rise? Then, only six years later, federal transfers were cut back down to $36 million.[41]

If there was ever a recipe for municipal disaster, this was it. The federal cutbacks actually had begun earlier. Ever since the Nixon-Ford administration (1968–1976), there had been a progression of cutbacks in federal aid, an attempt to reduce taxes, reduce the commitment to expanding civil rights for minorities and women, and slash the size and scope of Washington's transfer payments to poor people and places. The size of the reduction was so dramatic that it has been much publicized and well studied. Here we mention only a few illustrative details.

Investment in national infrastructure dropped as a proportion of GNP by one quarter from 1975 to 1990. Investment in education fell 28 percent (compared with GNP) from 1980 to 1990. The Reagan budgets by 1985 reduced outright spending on unemployment programs by 17 percent, and they cut Aid for Families with Dependent Children (AFDC) expenditures by 14 percent.[42] The administration also lumped twenty-nine categorical education grants targeted toward low-income students—which had increased from $1 billion in 1965 to $3.4 billion in 1980—into one block grant, reduced the budget by 24 percent, and loosened the reporting requirements, thereby weakening the focus on the needs of poor children.[43] The administration successfully scaled back the Urban Development Action Grant (UDAG) program by two-thirds, from a high of $675 million in 1981 to only $216 million in 1988, an even more drastic cut when inflation is factored in, and then did away with the UDAG program altogether. Since the peak in the 1970s, federal aid for low- and moderate-income housing has been drastically cut. For example, in 1980, HUD's housing program budget was $55.7 billion; by 1987 this had been reduced to $15.2 billion. In 1980, social spending consumed 54.3 of all government spending; by 1986 this had been reduced to 47.6 percent of total government expenditures.[44] According to one estimate, aid to needy communities (excluding grants for payments to individuals) was slashed 23.5 percent between 1980 and 1985.[45]

To cut transfer payments, the Reagan administration moved consciously to shift responsibilities but not resources to local governments and the nonprofit sector for "local" problems. Accompanied by reduced federal taxation, this strategy ostensibly would allow localities the opportunity to fulfill voters' desires more directly and more efficiently, using, if they wished, expanded local resource bases.[46] Local officials would do better, it was argued, with minimal federal intervention.

Progress in fighting poverty since the 1930s was not completely undone by any means, but the trend downward was clear. The responsibility for dealing with serious urban poverty was indeed transferred out of the federal realm. The Clinton administration took a far more aggressive approach to aiding cities and increasing funds. One measure of federal attention to cities is the HUD budget. In 1993, when Henry Cisneros was HUD secretary, the new HOPE VI program was funded at $5 billion, then a big increase. By 1999, with Andrew Cuomo at the helm of HUD, the budget had increased to $25 billion, and HUD had introduced a host of other new programs, with emphasis on the redevelopment of public housing and community economic development. Programs included community empowerment funds to equalize capital access for low-income communities, budgeting money to make cities more competitive with suburbs.[47] The approach was aimed essentially at the place, with supports for people. One contradictory consequence of this strategy was to "gentrify" ghettos and increase housing costs, thereby displacing traditional residents. Nonetheless, improvements in communities stimulated investment and attracted both new immigrants and aging suburbanites to return to the central city. Notably, these changes accompanied broader changes that reduced regulatory control over the national economy, leading to the redistribution of benefits from the poor and middle class to the rich. And after these starts by the Clinton administration, cities were later cast adrift. Cities have been left in a dismal situation indeed, as observers now agree.

Debates on National Policy

To prepare this section, we catalogued numerous proposals for more constructive national policies regarding urban poverty. Although in the early 1990s, somewhat to our surprise, we found a solid core of agreement among scholars, politicians, and business leaders,[48] twenty years later there does not seem to be a whole lot of agreement. Earlier there was even a modicum of agreement between the liberal Kerner Commission and the conservative American Enterprise Institute, each paying attention to the need for effort on employment, education, welfare, and health.[49] Today conservatives take a very different tack. The Reason Foundation suggests that there should be little market intervention or regulation, using Houston as a shining example, and the Heritage Foundation favors tax cuts and opposes federal involvement in urban affairs, observing that "the pro-growth elements of President Bush's tax cut plan should be viewed only as the first step in effective tax reform."[50] To the extent any agreement exists, it may originate in fear that problems of poverty have extended beyond small, isolated areas and that pathologies normally thought to be restricted to the long-term poor now afflict many more—the homeless, the jobless, and others in despair. If a community of poverty produces illness, poor education, negative attitudes, and therefore poor work habits and low productivity, it is sure eventually to cause problems for the country as a whole. Inasmuch as urban poverty is closely associated with collapsing and devalued housing, streets, bridges, utility systems, and other components of infrastructure, it also symbolizes (and results from) a huge drag on productivity and industrial flexibility nationally. These problems go far beyond urban poverty, but they are closely connected.

In earlier chapters we argued how changes in the economy and failures in policy generate poverty. Here we wish to point out how rising poverty generates difficulties throughout the economy and hampers the development of sound overall policy. To work, economic policy and anti-poverty policy must complement one another.

Anti-poverty policy cannot function without an array of positive changes in several directions. In our view, improvements are required in three major groups of policies. These will also counteract problems with education, productivity, and global competitiveness. The three changes are improved industrial policy, expanded opportunity for education, and increased family support. Successful programs and policies exist in each group in the United States, although for some programs, examples are best borrowed from other countries.

Better U.S. policy would result not only in rehabilitated cities, more equal income distribution, and less poverty in the cities and inner suburbs, but also in a reconstructed economy and society, which would compete more effectively overseas. Most of the proposals we discuss reentered public debate with the election of Barack Obama, an oddity after almost three decades when progressive ideas were rarely taken seriously by the federal government. We make no claims of originality, and we leave the particulars of federal policy to be worked out in public debate, which, as we write, rages in newspapers, journals, and on the internet, as a liberal White House gingerly proposes changes, and conservatives, driven apparently by the Republican "base," demand more business as usual. Despite capturing the presidency and sizable majorities in the House of Representatives and Senate, the Democratic Party hardly seems a voice for the future, as its ideas lag far behind the requirements of the age.

Industrial Policy

In the face of severe recession and for many in the United States an undeclared depression, there is a continuing attempt to compete with lower-cost producers in other countries, as American firms respond to the increased "flexible" globalization of labor and technology. American industry is no longer national but global both in organization and in commitments, with few ties to the nation. The global financial collapse of 2008–2009 demonstrated the imperfections and the interconnectivity of global financial and industrial markets. Workers all over the world have suffered as shallow, selfish, and unregulated use of financial tools and methods led to collapse. This global economy collapsed precisely because global firms and finance put down no roots in any locality and lack any sensitivity to supplies of local resources or needs for the generation of real wealth.

Political economists have long known that private firms, including and perhaps especially the largest financial corporations, act destructively unless governed by appropriate rules, restrictions, and regulations. The notion of a truly "free" market is nonsense to anyone but an ideologue acting to protect special privilege. Similarly, "free" trade is a mantra used by nation-states to protect and project the interests of their residents, but especially their manufacturers, exporters, importers, investors, and bankers. Free trade works fine for firms and workers in dominant nations, when those nations write the global rules based on biased agendas such as the "Washington Consensus" and when they patrol the trade routes with unquestioned military power. But the advantages can wither. U.S. hegemony has been squandered with wasteful spending and high debt, adventurous and fantastically expensive wars, theft of wealth by a tiny band of financial "wizards," and lack of investment in a more educated labor force. Hegemony faces pressures brought on by cheaper international shipment of goods and the almost cost-free communication via internet. The waste and pressures have flipped the tail of the imperial dragon. Incompetent leaders like George W. Bush or hard-right, self-indulgents like Dick Cheney or former defense secretary Donald Rumsfeld appear to believe not only that might is right but also that the privilege of power is earned and that the power of the mighty goes unchallenged. As Paul Krugman put it in 2007, "The [conservative] movement's politicization of everything, the way it values political loyalty above all else, creates a culture of cronyism and corruption that has pervaded everything the Bush administration does, from the failed reconstruction of Iraq to the hapless response to Hurricane Katrina. The multiple failures of the Bush administration are what happens when the government is run by a movement that is dedicated to policies that are against most Americans' interests and must try to compensate for that inherent weakness through deception, distraction, and the distribution of largesse to its supporters."[51] Most surprising is the large numbers of people who are taken in by these leaders' claims.

From Adam Smith on, political philosophers and economists have understood the need for regulatory frameworks. Even from within the normally market-worshiping economics profession, the most brilliant voices of recent years—including Nobel Prize winners Amartya Sen, Joseph Stiglitz, and Paul Krugman—focus on the damages of inequality and the need for regulatory regimes that limit the options, channel the greed, and more consciously organize markets for the benefit of entire societies, perhaps even the whole globe.[52]

In the context of new challenges, the first goal for global firms is to cut costs by reducing wages, demanding harder work, reducing benefits, replacing skilled workers with machines that put them out of work, and if that does not succeed, then taking funds out of U.S. production entirely, investing either in financial affairs or in overseas plants. As we saw in Chapter 3, this deindustrialization process is the option many, perhaps a majority, of large American corporations have chosen, and it has resulted in depressed wages, unemployment, and reduced incomes.[53] Industrial policy that allows or even encourages this sort of negative change on the part of firms or industries has turned out to be counterproductive. At best, these sorts of industrial adaptations make firms more competitive in the short run. In the long run the firms are less likely to stay competitive. Without adequate pay and training, workers become less, not more, productive. Without heavy investment in both social and productive infrastructure, such as schooling and the sort of technical equipment that requires highly qualified workers, American industry loses in nose-to-nose competition with foreign industry, even when foreign workers are better paid.

American industry can encourage labor force development and build new wealth based on the quality of its human capital. If there were improvements in the metropolitan economic environment, better skills would mean that American labor could compete with any in the world. A high and pressing demand for labor is the fundamental condition for reduction in poverty. Good labor policy must be emphasized, in particular, because there are contrary forces.[54] High labor demand can be a problem for business in the short run, as it can raise wages and therefore production costs and puts pressure on profits. Industrial policy must resolve this problem.

A growing demand for labor was, of course, one of the components of the rapid economic growth and decline in poverty during most of the early post–World War II period. The principal reason these thirty years can be celebrated as the "American Century" is that the standard of living rose rapidly while poverty fell, especially in the 1960s and early 1970s. The strong demand for basic labor improved the distribution of income, supported families, and tended to reduce poverty. The Democratic Party under Barack Obama wants to build strong employment and wage growth as a political and economic objective. No matter what approach is taken, it is important that improved labor pools and increased technology do not add to the number of people who cannot participate in the economy. No one who worries seriously about reducing poverty forgets that there must be growth in the number of jobs that pay decent wages.[55] The problem is, there are as many ways to generate jobs as there are to run the economy. Consequently, analysts and politicians have great difficulty agreeing on how to stimulate the growth of well-paying jobs. They even have difficulty agreeing that it is possible to do so.[56]

The question is not whether the United States needs an industrial policy. As an editor of *Business Week* once put it: "Every country has an industrial policy, and the United States is no exception. The only question is whether we will choose to make it explicit and effective."[57] Put slightly differently, the question is, what kind of industrial policy is appropriate? Even in benign economic circumstances, when the Treasury and the Federal Reserve are not distributing hundreds of billions of dollars to banks, insurance companies, brokerage houses, and automobile manufacturers, the government establishes industrial policies. Consider these individual actions: the Treasury devalues the dollar, Congress rewrites the tax code and raises the minimum wage, the Defense Department selects a technology or a contractor, the Federal Communications Commission establishes a competitive process for determining who will manufacture high-resolution television, and the Environmental Protection Agency establishes rules governing imports under NAFTA from Mexico. These elements of an unconscious, implicit industrial policy benefit some companies and industries and not others, redistribute the tax burden, tilt the advantages of competition, and result in "billions of dollars of revenues and productivity lost or gained."[58] We must add to this the large distortions caused by the transfer of productive energy from the domestic economy into a hugely bloated military budget.

Long before the current crisis, leading economists and industrialists estimated that faulty industrial policy causes losses by American companies that amount to hundreds of billions of dollars annually: a 1991 estimate added up $6 billion from counterfeiting and more from patent violation, $9 billion from inappropriate export controls, $36 billion in underpaid U.S. taxes by Japanese companies, and $51 billion from the low U.S. savings rate. The same analysts added $60 billion for drug abuse, $100 billion for remedial education, and finally, $300 billion in waste from the U.S. tort system.[59] According to Robert Eisner, a past president of the American Economics Association, in the 1990s it would have taken $50 billion to replace and repair bridges and $26 billion to bring highways back to standard, with another $14 billion for environmental cleanup, plus $9 billion for education funding, $4 billion for public housing, and $130 billion for other problems.[60] Summing these up, former labor secretary Robert Reich came up with a separate estimate of the deficit in physical and human infrastructure, not counting pollution abatement, at $600 billion each year throughout the 1990s.[61] These are heavy business costs, to be borne by the nation, all estimated long before the deep economic crises of the twenty-first century. In 2009 the American Society of Civil Engineers estimated that $1.7 trillion would be necessary just to stabilize the condition of the nation's core infrastructure. The federal Department of Transportation estimates a $461 billion "backlog of needed road, highway, and bridge repair and improvements," and the ASCE says that in place of some of these repairs, "U.S. motorists spend at least $54 billion a year in repairs and operating costs because of poor road conditions."[62] A different sort of calculation estimates the penalty paid by lack of investment in education. An achievement gap reduces gross domestic product by $3 billion to $5 billion *per day*, trillions of dollars each year: "The persistence of these educational achievement gaps imposes on the United States the economic equivalent of a permanent national recession."[63]

There are alternatives to poor industrial policy. Although market economies produce unavoidable ups and downs, experiences in various western European countries and Japan demonstrate that a mixed-capitalist, social-democratic society can manage its economy to produce long-run growth (or at least stability) while basic services and benefits continue to be provided. The key lies in a constant push to improve the quality of the labor force by increasing labor's commitment to the job, increasing the level of benefits, and using enhanced skills to raise productivity. The increased skills must be accompanied by technological innovation and investment, and education must be designed to match the new possibilities.

Although in the current dismay over bad U.S. industrial policy most signs are negative, it is good to remember that positive policy is not unknown to the United States. Elements of industrial policy to improve the labor force have worked in the past. Immediately following World War II, the G.I. Bill of Rights "greatly broadened and deepened the intellectual capital of the nation. It created a new generation of homeowners and stake-holders in the society. And perhaps most significantly, it more than paid for itself through its contribution to the nation's economic growth and welfare."[64]

The G.I. Bill was "far-sighted, far-reaching, and effective" as a promoter of economic development, and it did not work alone. Other elements of an implicit national industrial policy complemented it. The 1956 Highway Act built 42,500 miles of freeways, and the Education Act that followed the launching of the Soviet space satellite Sputnik gave a boost to schools and universities in general. The federal government also stimulated the development of civilian technologies through sponsorship of military work in computer science and in other spin-offs from military research. Federal guidance and subsidies of transportation, higher education, and research led to the creation of an "invaluable base of structural and human capital for further industrial growth." The Rural Electrification Act offered low-interest loans that changed the structure of the American countryside and led to enormous gains in agricultural productivity. Numerous other federal policies focused on stabilizing farm incomes and production, resulting in giant productivity gains and cost efficiencies that put U.S. agriculture and much of the U.S. workforce in an enviable competitive position worldwide.[65]

All aspects of industrial policy are important to anti-poverty efforts, but one in particular is more directly related to our quest to challenge the roots of urban decay. This is the rebuilding of physical infrastructure, which could reduce the intensity of geographically concentrated poverty by resuscitating the decayed capacities for production and life support of older cities. We take transportation as an example. Until recently, backbone infrastructure such as interstate transportation has typically been the responsibility of the government. Long before the interstate highway system, the government gave high priority to a national railroad system in the nineteenth century because it seemed likely to catalyze economic development. One tangible aspect of "industrial policy" then was public subsidy, the land grants that allowed huge private real estate profits to railroad investors. The policy had results: in spite of robber baron thievery, the railroads stimulated iron and steel industry development, and that spilled over into other industries. The success was repeated almost a century later with the interstate highways, suburban beneficiaries perhaps being the new robber barons. Looking ahead, we observe interest nationally in pursuing policies to wean the nation from its dependence on oil, reduce auto movement and congestion, build more compact and safer cities, improve rail passenger service, and improve the organization and delivery of health care and education. The Obama administration has a strong electoral mandate for such far-reaching reforms, and these new industrial foci can alter the opportunity structures for new entrants to the labor force with the potential to lower the barriers for the poor so they can become participants in a growing and changing economy, much as occurred in the post–World War II era.

Even with this mandate the administration and the Congress show no willingness to practice conscious national planning. That failure to organize to plan is all the more shocking in the face of the mounting problems: Realistic estimates indicate that the United States will at least have to double its spending to maintain infrastructure over the next ten years. Moreover, this estimate does not include the resources for developing new high-tech infrastructure systems necessary to meet the needs of the twenty-first century.

The specific magnitudes are daunting: the interstate highway system needs repairs of 2,000 road miles each year, and more than 250,000 bridges (half those in the country) must be heavily repaired or replaced, at an estimated cost of $2.2 trillion.[66] Highway projects that rebuild old infrastructure can create more new jobs than building new roads. The nation will have to rebuild its infrastructure entirely for electric autos, solar heating and lighting, and more passive energy techniques and technologies. The cores of older metropolitan areas, which suffer antiquated sewer, water, and other utility systems, as well as widespread need for replacement or rehabilitation of buildings, streets, factories, and the majority of those bridges, require massive work. A program to mend and maintain would allow the nation to invest in fast-start job-training programs for jobs that require only modest skill levels. These efforts are now under way in a piecemeal fashion and should be developed in a manner that places a premium on fixing the labor pools as well as fixing the streets. Local governments can be developers of new infrastructure that merges many of the people-versus-place debates. This moves us to the second group of government policies, which is focused more directly on people.

Education Programs

Before we examine education directly, we want to consider general principles that should apply to all essential services to citizens (and, we believe, to resident aliens as well). Probably the most important principle is that service provision should be "universal." That is, recipients should be offered services regardless of their wealth, income, or other personal qualifiers. Services, in general, should not be available only to the poor. Eligibility should not be means-tested. One example of an important service that is *not* means-tested is comprehensive health care, notably not available in the United States except in the strictly bounded example of participants in a large, comprehensive health-maintenance organization such as the Kaiser Plan. Another, which used to be available to large portions of the U.S. urban population but is not available to most central-city families now, is high-quality public education, which includes preschool and public colleges and universities in addition to primary and secondary schools. Such services provide support to families, children, and adults, and they work both directly and indirectly to improve the distribution of income and reduce poverty.

There is a crucial difference between services that are at least in theory offered to and used by all citizens (such as public schools in the suburbs) and services that are offered to or used by only the poor (such as city public hospitals). When there is a means test, so that no one with too much income or wealth can get the service, then the recipients are stigmatized, public effort is likely to be reduced, and the quality of service is likely to be inferior. Sometimes recipients or their relatives are even forced into poverty, as in the case of subsidized medical services available only after couples have used up their savings and even home-ownership investments. Look at the case of central-city public schools. Many upper-middle-class residents in large central cities now find a better alternative in the private school. Families' decisions to send children to costly private schools, in response to inadequate public schools, ends up stigmatizing public school students, leads to weakened public support and therefore reduced public school budgets, and leads ultimately to inferior education for the poor.[67] The society is separated. In 2009, when Manhattan parents were hit with Wall Street losses, many enrolled their children for the first time in public schools, and then they objected to being treated like everyone else.[68] The gulf increases. To suggest possibilities for better policy, we review briefly three proposals for central-city schools.

Public support for improved schools is not lacking. Polls find that improved schooling ranks as a very high priority. A May 1991 *Newsweek* poll indicated that over two-thirds of Americans, regardless of race, believe they "should focus most of their energy on improving education."[69] A poll in 2009 came to a similar conclusion and sought the source of the problem: "Lack of funding for schools tops the list of 'biggest problems facing schools' for the sixth year in a row."[70] A 2009 CBS/*New York Times* poll found that Americans think education is the second most important activity for the president and Congress to focus on, after health care (and the economy, which was assumed to be the most important and so was not included in the poll).

We examine three proposals—community schools, early education, and work-study. Once again, as in the case of mutually reinforcing industrial and anti-poverty policies, here we see the mutually reinforcing capacity of investments in education and in community building. Good schools can add to individual opportunity, and they can also build community. Not least of all, the school is important because it can contribute a set of intellectual resources to assist in community transformation. Teachers and administrators can become advocates for community involvement and provide the continuing presence necessary to bring about reform in individuals, families, and neighborhoods. In addition, schools now have a significant number of minority persons in leadership positions, to provide role models, personal bridges from the isolated community to the outside world, and spokespersons.

Reforms are emerging in a number of cities. In post-Katrina New Orleans, Superintendent Paul Vallas made the school an important part of the community, fighting "an all-fronts, total-war strategy on what is certainly this city's most deep-rooted social problem. 'You begin to make the schools community centers,' he said. 'The whole objective here is to keep the schools open through the dinner hour, and keep schools open 11 months out of the year.'"[71] Aggressive remodeling of school systems in Philadelphia (where Vallas was earlier), Chicago, New York, and other cities follow from the belief that the combination of good governance and the coupling of education with the total community can alter outcomes for students and their parents with potentially dramatic improvements for the total community.[72] Evidence over the decades, from similar efforts undertaken in various districts, suggests caution. The imbalance with successful suburban districts is of overwhelming importance. Most suburbs get steady, reliable, strong support of the sort required from community leaders as well as voters, and they are required to provide extra schooling to much smaller portions of their children.[73] In smaller communities highly successful public schools involve families, community members, school staff, and students in making decisions.[74] Nevertheless, these big-city efforts represent positive use of the only significant governmental institution available to communities. Most city neighborhoods have no prominent physical public institutions other than schools and fire stations. Many libraries, playgrounds, and other neighborhood facilities are shut or on short hours or—in the worst cases—have been long abandoned, even from as long ago as the 1960s or 1970s.

Schools can also provide a new means of delivering social and community services. A number of school districts coordinate family social services ranging from employment and training to drug abuse counseling. These schools can be a new platform for community revitalization. City school districts can also increase the length of the school year, in effect adding an entire year to the average inner-city child's twelve years of education. Such a change could make an enormous difference in raising skill levels of minority students, increasing their competitive abilities and closing the achievement gap.

Federal funding is needed to support such community schools. Community education grants would assist urban school districts to develop community delivery systems. These grants would assist school districts to develop longer school years and coordinate community service programs, ranging from recreation to employment and training, family planning, drug counseling, economic development, and related family and community services. School districts, local governments, and nonprofit agencies affiliated with local colleges would get comprehensive planning grants to design community-school plans. These districts would receive multiyear funding based on the plan, which would include the allocation of local taxes and partnerships with nonprofit, charitable, and private business groups. There have been minor efforts in the U.S. Department of Education to move in these directions. Several competitive grant programs have supported community schools. We are suggesting that community-based and community-supported education become a national effort sustained by substantial resources.

The second major program should be in early education. The evidence is overwhelming that the earlier a boy or girl reaches school, the sooner he or she will be in a position to learn and contribute. Early childhood education is a good investment for the total society. Findings from Head Start and similar programs suggest enormous potential in reducing school failure, providing safe and secure child care, gaining access to parents for their education and training, and early screening of potential health and related problems. Opportunities for poor children could be appreciably improved by high-quality early education and child-care programs.

Recent research suggests that Head Start reduced the mortality rates for 5- to 9-year-old children from causes that could have been affected by the participation in Head Start when they were 3- and 4-year-olds. HS provides health and dental services to children and families who might otherwise not have them. Parents who participate in HS are found to have greater quality of life satisfaction; increased confidence in coping skills; and decreased feelings of anxiety, depression, and sickness. HS children are at least eight percentage points more likely to have had their immunizations than those children who did not attend preschool.[75]

A study of six hundred Head Start graduates in San Bernardino County, California, concludes that the society gains about nine dollars for every dollar spent. Head Start children do better on achievement tests, repeat grades less often, use less special education, and have higher graduation rates.[76] More local employment opportunities lie here, too.

Our third recommendation for federal education policy is the creation of a linkage between schools and workplaces. In an effort to reduce the fragile connection between work and school for many disadvantaged young persons, a national work experience program should be developed to allow a consortium of firms in each city to design in-school, after-school, and cooperative education programs for youth. School work-experience programs would operate like college work-study programs. Students would be allowed to complete part-time work at certified nonprofit groups, government agencies, and business firms. The school district would match employees' salaries up to an amount established statewide. The federal government would match the funds of states in implementing these programs, which would be developed in conjunction with national business organizations such as the National Alliance of Business and various minority business associations. These business organizations would establish local partners for the program and develop business education councils in communities where they do not exist or need strengthening. Experiments run by individual industrialists have been successful.

The National Security Agency offers two Baltimore-Washington programs for high school students, a work-study program in business computing or office technology and a vocational/technology program for students in graphic arts or manufacturing. The students are paid, get sick leave, and are promised entry-level jobs on graduation.[77] These kinds of programs need broader, national-level support.

The work-experience scheme would allow for the development of apprenticeships in small and new emerging fields such as computer technology and biotechnology. Participants would receive the minimum wage, allowing them to avoid other, less academically related jobs that take time from their studies. The scheme would be administered centrally, students would receive school credit, and they would be evaluated by work supervisors and school counselors. Teachers participating in the program would be awarded fellowships, funded jointly by the government and industry, for summer experience with the students' employers. The teachers would also gain experience in the business or industry into which they are sending their students. The business participants would gain a clearer picture of the student population. This program would forge new, stronger relationships among school, business, and community.

Prison education programs, which were cut out in the 1980s before the massive increases in nonviolent crime imprisonment, must be reopened and strengthened. The magnitude of the prison problem and its racial bias are deeply threatening. In March 2009 the Pew Center on the States released a report titled *One in 31: The Long Reach of American Corrections*. The title reflects the report's primary finding, that 1 of every 31 U.S. citizens is under some form of correctional control. Particularly alarming is the finding that 1 in 18 men fall into this category and that 1 in 11 of all African Americans are currently under some form of correctional control. The Pew report shows that total state and federal spending on corrections systems has grown by 303 percent in the past two decades. "That growth has outpaced spending on elementary and secondary education (205 percent), transportation (82 percent), higher education (125 percent) and public assistance (9 percent)."[78] A principal element in growth of the prison population is recidivism. Considerable evidence suggests that prison education programs reduce recidivism substantially. Prison schooling combined with post-release programs provide stronger benefits to both prisoners and society. A paper from the John Jay criminology program at the City University of New York reports studies showing that recidivism declines between 7 percent and 46 percent when there are prison-education and post-release programs.[79] Almost a third of adult Black and Latino males who are already parents are in prison; when they are released, especially after long sentences (as in "three strikes" cases), they are unskilled and aimed in the wrong direction, likely dangerous to the community. All current policies add to their frustration by denying them employment and even voting rights rather than allowing them to rehabilitate themselves and prepare for gainful employment and adult roles in society. In most prisons more money is spent on gym equipment than education. Post-release felons without highly unusual ties to well-off families are unable to do any more than sink into vagrancy, homelessness, or crime.[80] If there were decent programs aiming at teaching competitive skills and offering degrees, prisoners would emerge with higher self-esteem and greater potential to maintain a family—thus reducing poverty for them and their families and reducing recidivism.

We propose a program for state prisons with partial federal funding to provide an assessment of skills and aptitude of all people entering prison. The prison, in concert with local school districts, community colleges, and local colleges and universities, would offer courses of instruction to inmates on a voluntary basis and be remunerated by the state at the same cost per pupil as for any other child or adult. In essence, prisoners requiring remedial elementary or secondary education would have funding up to the same levels as children in the same district or community college students. For postsecondary education, the subsidy for students would be provided with a federal matching grant. In many instances volunteer teachers would be required to make the budgets work. University students, retirees, and others could fill this void.[81] With the advent of closed-circuit television and online computer-based college courses, on- and off-campus approaches can be integrated for inmates at low cost. The costs of providing prison education are low, but the costs of not providing it are high and growing.

Such innovative programs require leadership even more than money, but they need both. A few programs are already in place. They need the added impetus of national recognition, networking, and support so that even more creative local options will be designed.

Family Support

The third group of policies to be improved involves "transfer payments." Transfers can include such items as monthly checks to the elderly and family support payments to parents with children, programs for dependent adults, Medicare, Social Security, and many others. As we saw in Chapter 2, existing transfer programs improve the distribution of income, and they also work directly to reduce poverty of whole classes of people. Transfer programs work in other ways as well. Some, lobbied for ferociously by many who are well-to-do, include payments to giant banks and auto companies, as the public learned in 2009.

It is important, once again, to note the crucial difference between universal payments, which are not restricted to those in need, and means-tested payments, which are. Actual programs may be a mix. Social Security is a good example of a program that is close to universal. With few exceptions, payments go to all elderly persons, regardless of need. No one is excluded for being too well-off. Actually, retirees who paid in more get larger monthly checks. Nevertheless, the payments that go to poor people provide much more assistance in proportion to their incomes and more, also, in proportion to their contributions. Some people, perhaps influenced still by FDR's claims when the program was founded, see Social Security as an enforced personal savings system, with no transfers involved. Others see the system with two parts, one that taxes current workers and one that transfers funds to the elderly. To us, this rendition seems closer to the truth, since Congress sets tax rates and payment rates, which are subject to heavy debate.[82]

Political support for universal programs tends to be broad, despite the political right wing's persistent overall attack on the very idea of government and taxes. Public schools, parks, public libraries, and other public provisions suffer when tax pressures are high or when strict limits to taxes are contrived, as in Proposition 13 in California, but for the most part people see these provisions as public goods that everyone deserves. We do not charge kids to go to school—and most Americans think charging would be an absurd idea.

When transfer payments are universal, then opposition to the inclusion of poor people as recipients is minimized. Nor is any stigma attached to the receipt of the transfer. The efficiency of administration is high because the bureaucracy requires minimal checking for rule compliance or guarding against fraud. Furthermore, what recipients do with their money, or how they behave in general, is their own business.

These principles are important when we consider our proposals for family support programs. Universal family support policies are found to be generally sound and workable in almost all European nations, Japan, Australia, and Canada. Given the unforeseen growth in the number of female-headed households in the United States, precisely the group that is in or is headed most surely for persistent poverty, a move to provide support without stigma makes sense. The transfers can be reinforced considerably by strict enforcement of fathers' financial responsibility.

A family support program could be administered in large part through the Earned Income Tax Credit, introduced by President Nixon and already on the books and functioning. "In 1993, President Clinton and Congress doubled the size of the EITC as the centerpiece of Clinton's strategy to ensure that a minimum-wage worker could support himself or herself and family with full-time work. The 1993 expansion also created a small credit for very low-income workers without children at home."[83] The EITC could be made more generous and also modified to allow an additional tax write-off for each minor dependent. Families could elect to receive the credit as a direct payment, a refund on their taxes, or a deduction against their withholding, using financial vehicles easily understood by all Americans. These innovations would provide at least a supplement—better yet, an alternative to welfare and poverty—helping families to cope quickly with unemployment and reducing many social costs. The country has begun to move in these directions. "During the past 20 years, many states and localities have enacted versions of the federal credit to benefit their own residents. Meanwhile, a new generation of local leaders has emerged to publicize the availability of the EITC and related tax credits for lower-income families and neighborhoods, and to argue for progressive federal tax policies."[84]

Although limited family support programs have functioned since the mid-1960s and transfers have "reduced the extent of both poverty and income disparity,"[85] the welfare system was subject to widespread criticism, culminating in Clinton's "end to welfare as we know it." The massive underemployment beginning in 2009 extended the borders of poverty to include more and more of the "deserving poor," so it may become politically possible (and surely better) to merge the entire welfare system with Social Security and EITC, removing completely the ideas of remediation, social control, and tests of worthiness. Coupled with broad family support, such administrative changes would be salutary. Eligible participants would sign up for benefits in the same way they apply for Social Security disability benefits. Even here it is possible to avoid a stigmatizing means test. Because most employees, even young teenagers working odd jobs, contribute to Social Security, most eligible participants (or their spouses prior to divorce) would have already made contributions and already be enrolled, and this includes the vast majority of the poor. Various changes in the assignment of benefits to spouses and children would facilitate increased responsibility. Financing would be possible inside the system, with rather small modifications to the top taxable limit, to the tax rate, and to the reimbursement schedules.[86]

There exists no comprehensive family support program for dependent adults, but one is badly needed. Those who choose to register for health problems, disability, drug addiction, or other causes could either be placed in a group setting, as current policy often provides, or remain with parents, relatives, or adult foster care. The caregiver would receive an allowance for providing the care, once again as either a supplementary Social Security benefit or an EITC benefit. Similar approaches have been proposed for many of the homeless.[87] Adult care programs in many states already have some of these features. We wish to encourage communal and family settings, without making halfway houses and group homes the only alternative.

How much would these combined programs for family support cost? Not much more than the current welfare system, and the funding base is already in place. It merely replaces the form of payment and vastly simplifies the administration. Most important, however, is the chance to remove the counterproductive stigma of welfare.

A crucial complement to these family support programs is improved healthcare policy. More than 45 million Americans had no health insurance as the Obama administration entered office, and many others are not covered adequately. With the recession, the numbers of uninsured people rose. It is estimated that one-third of the population in any given year is at one time or another without any coverage.[88] Notably, many part-time workers, a large group, are intentionally hired at less than full-time so firms can avoid health insurance premiums. (Even the federal government has used this escape clause.) For those without insurance, illness often threatens and it can lead to poverty.

There are ways to deal effectively with the problem of health care. We must either incorporate a minimum health premium for all workers, require a health plan for all employers and the self-employed, or establish a national health plan. A growing majority believe that all Americans should be covered by basic and catastrophic health insurance. In the absence of a national care plan, this approach would operate as workers' compensation does now. Employers would have the option of providing coverage or paying into the state medical insurance pool fund. The self-employed would be required to file with their state tax forms and pay premiums with taxes. Those without jobs would have premiums paid from state and federal funds. Health care would be available to all, regardless of the source of the premium.

With the disappearance of compulsory military service in 1973, the opportunity for many Americans to be engaged in useful public work to connect themselves to the nation and to others in their peer group was reduced. Those individuals who opt to go to the Peace Corps, Teach for America, or other programs now under the umbrella of AmeriCorps are building a new foundation for Americans of every age to give back and learn to live together in service. An expanded program would both help reestablish the notion of *civitas* and help create an avenue for all who want to escape the bounds of their parochial settings, be it a gang or small-town small-mindedness, to become larger people than their immediate circumstances might allow.

Political Support

It would be unrealistic to ignore questions about programs and laws promoting affirmative action. Different in nature from the three groups of anti-poverty policies we have just discussed, affirmative action is, most unfortunately, still an essential requirement in the United States. Where redress is required, especially where discrimination persists, there can be no substitute for rules that push in the direction of fairness. The women's movement and the civil rights movement keep pushing because women, on the one hand, and minority men, women, and children, on the other, suffered from discrimination in housing, employment, and public institutions, and they still do. As we write, four Supreme Court justices oppose affirmative action with firm hostility, and the Chief Justice seems to misread U.S. race history. We hope their positions will be overcome as the nation's politics swing back from three decades of reaction. We do not take space here to elaborate how we think affirmative action should work, nor do we specify how it may overlap, integrate with, or supplement policies for industry, education, or family support. Affirmative action, nevertheless, is part of the discussion that will have to continue as federal policies are reformed and probably beyond.[89]

The reader will observe that we have left out two other crucial policies that must be developed specifically with the very poor in mind. The first is a national emergency employment program. We would propose a youth service corps.[90] We leave the discussion for elsewhere. The second group includes programs for personal rehabilitation, counseling, job placement services, drug treatment, and the like. These remedial programs are absolutely necessary, and we expect they will be forthcoming in cities, once there is positive action on national policies for industry, education, and family support.

In the next section we turn to a difficult set of questions. Even if economists, political scientists, planners, and various policymakers can agree on the policies to reduce poverty, that agreement provides no guarantee the policies will be enacted. There remain big issues of implementation. Questions of political support are essential. So, before turning (in the last section of the chapter) to treat specific questions, we investigate four alternative arenas for potential political support.

Sources of Political Support

Who can make these federal changes happen? Americans agree that reforms are required, not only to fight poverty but also to reposition the United States as an effective overseas competitor, but they do not agree on how to get there. We consider four approaches. The first two would be dictated from the top down because they depend on the interests of either corporate America or the managers of the still-reforming Democratic Party coalition. The second two depend on pressure from the bottom up, either from the new suburban constituencies or, more likely, from the central city itself. These four approaches are not mutually exclusive, and they might even be supportive.

National Cross-Sector Coalition Building

The first instance of potential support for the four major groups of anti-poverty and pro-city policies comes from the leadership of some of the country's largest corporations. At first, large corporations would seem to occupy an unlikely corner of the political economy for the expression of such liberal sentiments. One finds, however, considerable support for reform. There is nothing unusual about this interest of business in finding ways to implement better federal policy, given clear self-interest in shifting the rising costs of social expenditures from private, corporate accounts to the government, and given great fear of the explosive growth of an unproductive workforce. This desire to shift from the direct accounts of the corporation to the indirect accounts of the government (to be paid through taxation or inflation) does not arise from corporate worry about either the problems of the poor or the difficulties of central cities. Instead, the desire grows from the pressure pushing on corporations to cut their operating costs in the face of ever rising costs of employee selection, training, health care, and retirement benefits. Even the largest of corporations are finding it difficult to train qualified workers from among the many who lack adequate basic educations, or to tax their profits enough to meet heavy costs for health care and retirement. Auto workers, automakers, and their linked businesses have been the most prominent in sacrificing profits, earnings, and fringe benefits. As late as February 2009, *The Economist* assumed firms and jobs would be saved,[91] and although some are able to keep their jobs, many are not.

Evidence of interest in reform on the part of big corporations has to do with costs for health care. Consider the public statement on corporate needs for health care, made in 1985 by Joseph Califano, who had been secretary of Health, Education, and Welfare in the 1960s in the Johnson administration. While working for the Chrysler Corporation, Califano stressed the importance of expanded federal programs for national health insurance, especially the provision of financing. After findings by Chrysler that 25 percent of its health costs were probably due to inefficiency and waste, and that caps on payments by Medicare and state plans were ineffective in reducing costs, Califano called on Congress "to create a national commission to develop health policy to cut costs without reducing care."[92] In 1985 this represented a notable turnaround in an almost solid corporate wall of opposition to any increases in public efforts to improve the provision of health care, and especially against any nationalization. Twenty-five years later, when Chrysler was forced to declare bankruptcy despite heavy federal lending, health-care costs were surely a pertinent concern. Even insurance companies worry about masses of uninsured people creating problems for the companies.[93] Much of the discussion surrounding the Big Three automakers points to new consciousness of shared responsibilities. Further evidence of remarkable turnarounds comes from a 2008 Reuters survey that showed more than half of doctors supporting national health insurance and less than a third opposing it.[94]

The negative effects on business of poor public education has also been on the agenda for twenty-five years or longer, emerging strongly again now. The discussions are not yet highly focused, but they are getting clearer. In a 1980s report to President Reagan from his Commission on National Productivity, chairperson and Hewlett Packard chief executive officer John Young and his coauthors laid great stress on the liabilities of a weak public educational system. They sounded a clear warning about corporate losses being caused by public schools that are inferior to those in Japan and other important international competitors. The biggest problems were then in inner-city schools, which, of course, many poor children attend. These schools suffer most, they pointed out, from the scissors movement of budget cutting and growing numbers of students in need of extra support.[95] Endless anecdotal evidence reveals that large corporations have had difficulty selecting new employees despite huge numbers of job applicants. The New York Telephone Company, for example, found in 1987 that "only 3,619 of 22,800 applicants have passed the examinations, intended to test skills including vocabulary, number relationships and problem-solving for jobs ranging from telephone operator to service representative." Not only did the telephone company turn down 86 percent of its applicants for lack of rudimentary literacy and numeracy skills, but that bad experience was shared by brokerage houses, secretarial services, and other employers who found applicants "without a strong background—grammar, spelling, language." A leading bank that interviewed five hundred applicants every week reported hiring only about 3 percent.[96] Thirty years later, the evidence has hardly changed. Although federal education law may aim to raise basic skill levels of all children, we are "not lifting 21st-century skills for the new economy." The gap between Black and White 17-year-olds can be understood "as the rough equivalent of two and three years' worth of learning."[97] Thanks to studies by a foundation set up by former secretary of state Colin Powell and his wife, Alma Johnson, that same gap can now be demonstrated clearly in statistics that for the first time show how far central cities lag behind their suburbs in high school graduation rates.[98]

Of course, these interests by big business in a liberal, even progressive agenda are greatly tempered by the realization that the proposed programs cost money, and that funding must one way or another be a draw-down on receipts otherwise available for profits and private reinvestment. Real conflicts arise between the broad national interests of corporations and their narrow industrial or company interests. Corporate officers are often hard-calculating people who look at short-term company bottom lines. What they see as most desirable is the possibility of *shifting* costs, by having the responsibilities taken up by the general public so that their own individual taxes (corporate and personal) will increase less than proportionately.

These leaders know that in the long run they and their businesses will benefit from national cost sharing and the relatively wide guarantees to higher productivity that are provided by better education, health, and other social programs, because they will be less expensive than the alternatives. There are ample statistics to show that teachers are cheaper than jailers, even if we do not count the increased productivity due to learning and positive attitudes. Economic regulations in the United States, however, do not encourage corporations to plan for the long run. And private cost reductions and enhanced business productivity need long-term plans. The hoped-for cost transfers, from corporations to the state, will be a difficult change, especially without risk of higher taxes on profits. The lack of outright progress to move these programs ahead through political channels, in spite of the positive evidence, is explained in good part by this conundrum.

A second hesitation on the part of big business is its own historical connection with the Republican Party, as well as its old antagonisms toward organized labor. Unfortunately, the connection with the Republicans lumps big business leaders in a political alliance with reactionary rather than progressive economic interests; they appear unsympathetic to technological and organizational innovation, xenophobic in their reactions to both U.S. investment overseas and foreign investment in the United States, and, worst of all for the case at hand, hostile to nearly all forms of public expenditure. Perhaps most unfortunately, they rely for political support on those who deride careful thought, science, and evidence. We hope corporate leaders will not sleep in the bed arch-conservatives have made, for as long as they do they will fail to resist much of the political hostility toward the increased public taxation and expenditure required for education, training, health, and retirement. This hostility is encouraged by the negative politics of racism, sexism, selfishness, and fear that has so dominated the Republican strategy since the 1980s. Although party *leaders* have shown signs that they wish to set up a broader tent, and defections like those of senators James Jeffords of Vermont and Arlen Specter of Pennsylvania might be expected to push them in more moderate directions, primary elections remain heavily influenced by well-funded conservative zealots who work to keep the ideological tent very small. From resistance to the first Obama stimulus legislation in February 2009, one sees that progressive interests among corporations and their leaders by no means represent the interests of all corporations or all corporate leaders. Clearly, some businesses expect to continue to benefit from the availability of an unskilled, defenseless, and poorly paid workforce.

We argue that various business interests do seem likely to consider new approaches, but they seem very unlikely to provide either the initiative or the main political pressure for better policies.

Creating New Friends

The more widespread expectation is that innovation will come through new policies designed and implemented in Washington by the revived Democratic Party that helped elect Barack Obama. The leadership that survives in the old base of the Ted Kennedy Democratic Party is the favored candidate for setting up the new agenda. The old coalition that grew from the New Deal included unions and other working-class, ethnic Whites in city neighborhoods or inner suburbs, as well as minorities, public employees, city administrations, and a variety of unaffiliated liberals.[99] A political coalition of groups like these could lead to new strong, clear proposals for federal solutions to the problems of poverty and the central city, of the sort we presented in the section above.

Many in these groups see the solution of core-city problems as an environmental issue because rebuilding inner cities can reduce urban sprawl and with it the nation's carbon footprint. Segments of the women's movement have long stressed the penalties associated with suburban life. Political revival is building on energy put forth by both the women's movement and the environmental movement, whose interests are in many cases compatible with those of the old liberal coalition. This is far from an unreasonable approach, particularly given the presumption, among most political scientists, that national, not local, governments have a better record of promoting social reform. The Obama White House is the obvious place to start.

The technical possibilities of a liberal, top-down solution to the problems of poverty and urban decline must be balanced against a considerable quantity of negative political evidence. Most obviously, there is the failure of the Democrats, including the more liberal wing of the party that has now captured both the White House and the Congress. But the prospects for solutions to the problems of poverty have to be examined through the lens of a nation reeling in debt and an economy that is failing. Even in periods of economic recovery, heavy job losses and strong international competition take a heavy toll. Many analysts see in this economic failure a key role played by unproductive and disorganized metropolitan economies, which must pick up the bills for inefficiencies associated with severe geographic inequalities.

Apart from various social, economic, and political influences, the collapse of economic growth suggests new allegiances, which have long been undermined by physical forces that separate old partners. Most important has been the massive suburban movement of the White working class. Our argument is similar to the one regarding corporate support. To be sure, many of the interests that once made up a winning liberal coalition would welcome more constructive policy to fight poverty, even reforms that imposed costs. They would also support reconstruction of the central city. They would even be joined by some business partners who would support the formation of a new smart-growth coalition. Some real estate developers, and corporate leaders such as Microsoft's Bill Gates, see the solving of national and global problems as the role of the United States at this point in history. This coalition understands that America's best war against terrorism is to live up to the nation's ideals of social and economic progress and to be a beacon of hope for the world. The Bush policies of might-over-right they see as flawed and failed. They propose to form a national coalition to generate new energy, restrain global warming, and promote social justice agendas as the new national weapon against totalitarianism. It is an open question whether enough elements of the old coalition will come together again. It is hard to predict whether the new Democratic leadership led by Nancy Pelosi will forge a compact with the Obama administration. We believe such a new source of pressure could help push for the ample programs needed to reduce poverty and restructure cities.

Re-creating a National Mission

Recent studies of the evolution of the metropolis have speculated about changes in the suburban community. Observers note, for example, that conservatives in Orange County (in the greater Los Angeles area) are intrigued with planning as a technique for controlling the real estate market and protecting settled areas against the pressures of metropolitan growth. The initial moves aim defensively to protect privilege, but they may lead to other forms of cooperation. Elsewhere families and single women with children, as well as the elderly, having moved earlier to the suburbs, now frequently find themselves burdened by expensive suburban houses with high taxes; the houses are difficult to convert to multiple units, hard to reach by bus, and located far away from specialized services and the cultural diversity offered by towns and cities. City planners have long recognized a serious need for central-city services and culture, efficient transit, and a variety of flexibilities, as the suburban population and its needs change.[100] As we saw in Chapter 4, "suburbs," that is, areas outside the jurisdiction of the "central city," also now house more than half the officially poor metropolitan population as well as dramatically increased minority populations. The way these areas fit into the calculation may in the near future be radically different from the fit in the past.

However, it would take a huge stretch of the imagination to expect that the base or even a substantial part of the base of a new urban political strength could be built on suburban unrest. Even if the national economic pie is smaller, the suburban slice is large and its influence still bigger. Even if the costs of urban decay, inner-ring suburban collapse, and poverty mount and drag on national productivity, the connection to reduced suburban incomes and well-being is complicated because nonpoor suburban households still represent the majority of American households. At the same time, new suburbanites, especially immigrants, minorities, and younger suburban dwellers, are asking for the rebuilding of the suburbs to make them less auto-dependent. Reflecting these interests, many new light-rail projects stretch well into the suburbs. The American Recovery and Reinvestment Act of 2009 allocates $6.9 billion for investment in local transit projects.[101] Still, it is quite possible for suburbs to avoid not only most urban problems but also the responsibility for them. Suburban taxes may be high, but so are many suburban incomes and services. Gridlock may block suburban streets and highways, but at least most residents have cars and places they can afford to go. Environmental reform, the women's movement, and even parts of the civil rights movement—as well as a relatively detached sympathy for the problems of the poor residents of central cities (and inner suburbs)—will surely drive numerous suburban constituents into support of anti-poverty and pro-city reforms. But we should not expect the driving force for reform to come entirely from suburban areas, and we should continue to work with the progressive coalitions in Congress to revamp suburban agendas. This leaves us with one good option to lead the others.

Forging a New Urban Coalition

It is, of course, to the central city itself that we turn to find the greatest support for national policies aimed at reducing poverty and improving conditions of living in the central city. We now lay out the patterns by which we think central cities, particularly city halls, can build coalitions to create national pressure for an improved federal agenda.

Rebuilding the American City

Cities and city governments can modify the process of political and economic modernization to move away from the separations we have observed. We look at three urban options. The first is municipal experimentation with progressive reform. We ask if innovation is possible, whether any is taking place, and what benefits local reforms may offer to the poor. The second option for municipalities would stretch this approach a bit, using local reforms to transform federal practice. Might specific reforms and reform movements find responsive chords in the federal bureaucracy? Is it possible to fit municipal reforms into federal lawmaking? Can these changes lead to reinforcement, support, and perhaps further reform? As we have noted, the third option is already under way through the National Conference of Mayors, which is building a coalition based on the potential for urban reform. (An additional element, reform of state government constitutional provisions to *enable* municipal reform, is amply discussed by Gerald Frug and David Barron in *City Bound*.)

What is required in all three cases may be thought of as an increase in collective capacity. Collective capacity, not individual or area development, must be built as the vehicle to fight poverty. Local institutions are needed to serve as the political and social platform for confronting poverty. Local government is the best place to start since it has the dual virtues of being part of the national political structure and being politically closest to the community that requires assistance.[102] From the family to the neighborhood, the city, the state, and the federal government, effort must be put on building coalitions that connect across these lines. The most abundant evidence of that collective capacity, and the ability to "connect" new interests, arises from studies of municipal innovations.

Possibilities for Local Reform

In his studies of "progressive cities" Pierre Clavel demonstrates not only that many U.S. municipal governments have successfully experimented with reforms but also that they have done so despite adverse regional and national (and international) economic conditions.[103] As others have documented, profound municipal reforms have been enacted as radicals have taken power in various cities around the world. Voters in São Paulo, liberated after two decades of national military dictatorship but still badly burdened by conservative national politics, elected leftist Luisa Erundina as mayor in 1989, the same year that voters in Porto Alegre established their famous system of participatory budgeting.[104] A decade later,

> in October 2000, left-wing parties elected mayors in 29 of the 62 most important cities in Brazil, including giant São Paulo with a 61 percent majority. They won 775 municipal elections in all, taking more than a quarter of Brazil's cities and towns. The strongest left-wing party, the Workers' Party (in Portuguese, the *Partido dos Trabalhadores*—PT), held on to the five city halls it won in the 1996 election and added 12 more. The remarkable case of Porto Alegre, where the PT ... won its fourth consecutive four-year term of office with 66 percent of the vote, may have been the example that spurred people to vote for change elsewhere.[105]

In other Latin American countries progressive municipal governments and their institutions have succeeded even while national reforms have gone wanting. Amid the terrible violence throughout war-torn Colombia, city governments with progressive mayors in Bogotá and Medellín have made great strides in housing, transportation, public works, and services to the poor.[106] In Britain local elections in the 1980s almost put left-wing members of the Labor Party into dominant majorities on metropolitan councils in a number of counties, including London, Sheffield, Leeds, and the West Midlands. With widespread support they enacted a variety of reforms in areas of employment, housing, and public services.[107] Perhaps one of the most memorable reforms was the Greater London Council's provision of highly subsidized public transportation, which the leader of the council used for his commute to work.[108] Cities throughout western Europe have had Communist and Socialist city governments since the end of World War II. As in the well-known case of "Red" Bologna, many of these cities are widely admired for their reforms—sometimes with supportive leftist national governments, sometimes despite conservative national rule. Xavier de Souza Briggs suggests that a coalition of local municipal forces worldwide might forge a new path to local democracy and generate new responses to local dilemmas.[109]

U.S. cities have been part of this movement, but in a less hospitable environment, given the prominence of conservative officials at the state and federal levels. There were early experiments, and new progressive reforms began in the 1970s, some of which have survived intact, others leaving important legacies. Progressives won notable elections in Cleveland, Hartford, Burlington, Madison, Santa Monica, and Berkeley in the 1970s, in addition to Boston and Chicago.[110] Later reformers have instituted changes, too. Mayor Gavin Newsome of San Francisco, first elected in 2003, signed Health Choices in 2007, a city-level plan for universal health care; directed the city clerk to issue marriage licenses to same-sex couples; signed the city on to the Kyoto Protocol; and has moved to redevelop neighborhoods.[111] The U.S. Conference of Mayors Climate Protection Agreement has 944 cities as signatories.[112] Mayors and coalitions can institute practical reforms, and they can provide symbols of progress, in both ways offering models for other cities to help residents get better housing, improve health care, and make public services more accessible. They have also found ways to stimulate business to provide more and better-paid jobs.

Some look to cities to innovate because "local governments have more room to maneuver than is commonly assumed."[113] Others examine local potential for economic action, similarly observing that "because of the major changes in the international economy, rather than in spite of them," localities can successfully pursue economic development.[114] John Logan and Todd Swanstrom argue that "a great deal more discretion exists ... than is commonly believed. Many cities have more options to forge ... development and to allocate costs and benefits among social groups than they have been willing to consider."[115] During conservative periods, when national governments withdraw, cities may become freer to design their own solutions to local problems, and they often do so.[116]

When grassroots, neighborhood-based political movements work with coalitions to get hold of the instruments of legitimate power, such as the mayor's office or the city council, then four kinds of intensely local progress are possible: altering the agenda for public debate, relating closely to neighborhood groups for support and then nourishing them, pulling diverse members into a municipal coalition, and finally, building a core of experts to manage reform in a way that responds to the base and also the coalition's diversity. These are not just theoretical prospects; they are activities and results that have been observed in practice.[117] Even after progressive moments pass, many of the reforms stick.

In Burlington, Vermont, for example, Mayor Bernard Sanders made much of his socialist preferences, giving the city a voice to dispute "the claims of businessmen and developers" in efforts to influence economic policy, leading to real gains for "city working class and anti-development interests." In Santa Monica, California, a coalition pushing for rent control gained the upper hand in debate. They set a construction moratorium at their first council meeting, established new task forces to review projects, and took control of the process of development.[118] In Berkeley, radical coalitions, even when without a majority on the city council, used the ample California initiative process to move ahead on proposals for rent control, reorganization of the police force, a takeover of utilities, and an ordinance for neighborhood protection, all of which shifted the emphasis of public policy to benefit the poor. These efforts "brought out the vote ... and dramatized popular support." After a period of success the balance shifted and "liberals" increased their power versus the Berkeley Citizens Action "progressives," but over the long run, progressive institutions and political inclinations survived.[119] In Burlington, Sanders gained support from neighborhood groups when he opposed the city planning board, which favored development projects and a new and threatening highway. In Boston, a Rainbow Coalition base that organized around mayoral challenger Mel King, to the left of newly elected mayor Raymond Flynn, provided Flynn the leverage to undertake progressive reforms, including improved housing policies and new demands on developers for "link-age" fees to provide funds for housing and social services. In Cleveland, Mayor Dennis Kucinich and Planning Commissioner Norman Krumholz were backed by neighborhood interests when they disrupted the suburban-dominated met-ropolitan transportation committee so as to garner a larger share of funds for inner-city, flexible transportation, and also when they sued the private utility company to keep down inner-city rates.[120]

Expanding politically to build a local coalition beyond just neighborhood interests, what Clavel and Wiewel call "transcending the base," is more difficult. Although in Santa Monica, for example, leaders of a progressive government were able to negotiate the interests of their rent-control coalition around broad, common goals with homeowners and developers, they were not confronted with the most serious problems of poverty and race.[121]

Most divisive is the issue of race. In Cleveland and Boston, White mayors stumbled on this difficult issue. In the first case, when race-baiting crept into populist reformer Kucinich's reelection campaign, it "destroyed his chances of uniting the city's Black and White working class neighborhoods against the banks" and lost him the election. Nevertheless, although "by the 1990s the city ... had moved away from social concerns in favor of a bricks and mortar approach," it managed to accommodate neighborhood interests, saw community development corporations (CDCs) create the Cleveland Housing Network, and broadened support for progressive initiatives.[122] In the case of Boston, Flynn was attacked from his left for his tepid approach to problems of minorities. In Hart-ford, Connecticut, progressive city council president Nick Carbone built inter-racial coalitions in the 1970s to control development and to demand jobs for city residents from developers and large employers. Although Carbone lost the elec-tion in 1979 and "the city council majority fell into a period of reaction and stalemate," one result of the changes "was that Puerto Rican and African Ameri-can representation ... became dominant in the 1990s." Yet race remains a key division, even in cities with large Black or Latino populations.

In many cities a core of officials and managers have experimented and found ways to stay in office, move ahead with a progressive agenda, increase public participation, and incorporate the interests of their support groups. It is no small matter that management style was able to change to break down bureaucratic obstacles. It was a real achievement to modify city practice to fit better the "infor-mal and often highly charged styles of street organizing," thus building solid connections between city hall and previously disenfranchised poor neighbor-hoods. More important, these changes went further, bridging class and race lines and bringing the bureaucrats themselves into contact with their constituency. Managers, planners, and other city officials testify that they find their vision of the world permanently changed, their viewpoint now originating not just in their own, relatively privileged neighborhoods, experiences, and official positions, but in the neighborhoods of people who are poor.

These kinds of municipal innovations are widespread. They demonstrate a store of unused economic leverage, a political strength of organized communities, and a source of new social ideas. As their numbers increase, and as they connect, they will form an important part of the attack on poverty.

Influencing Federal Policy

It is one thing to claim and give evidence that to improve conditions for the poor there is considerable latitude for municipal experimentation with progressive change. It is quite another, however, to envision local experimentation being supported from outside (by changes in state constitutional provisions for cities or with funding from improved federal policy, for example). We now provide some evidence that this kind of support exists in limited amounts, but first we must give a cautionary note.

A remarkable instance of the opposite of support—implacable national government hostility to progressive municipal reform—came in the 1980s in response to success from municipal reformers in Britain. For the Thatcher government, these reforms were too much, and in order to quash them, the government changed national laws and abolished not just the offending councils but all county councils in the country—like hitting a fly with a sledgehammer. The progressive local governments were put out of business.[123] The Thatcher government represented the extreme right wing, and its anti-Labor municipal reorganization was an extreme gesture.[124] The Reagan presidency, at the same time as Thatcher, challenged progressive municipal rule in the United States. Most federal opposition takes the form of budgetary reductions and diversion of finances. These sorts of denial of federal support, as we have seen, reached an art form during the Bush presidency after 2000. Generally, new practices do not disappear along with the ouster of the reformers. The ideas stay on in collective memories, and until legislation or regulation changes them back, they continue in practice, expected by the beneficiaries.[125] Indeed, many reforms of the leftist Greater London Council did stick. In the case of U.S. cities, although reform may be more difficult initially to enact than in Britain, once in place it may be harder to remove because of various constitutional limitations.[126] The effects of federal pressures are more diffuse and indirect, filtered as they are through the autonomy of state governments, under which all municipal charters are issued (with the exception of Washington, D.C.).

More positive expectations came, of course, with Barack Obama's election, about which time will tell. But even in nationally conservative climates, positive evidence appears. We note two experiences, efforts to combat homelessness and to provide affordable housing, to demonstrate that even in unlikely circumstances local action can have broad national consequences. These two cases, documented by housing consultant Emily Paradise Achtenberg, show how local grievances can affect local politics, whose proponents can mount statewide coalitions, which in turn move to challenge and change federal housing regulations and legislation. These federal changes in turn alter the environment for local programs. Local changes start the cycle again; if improvements are seen, then the cycle may move in progressive sweeps across the landscape. These experiences illustrate André Gorz's idea about the importance of reforms that empower, which stimulate pressures for further reform.

The attractive Northgate-Greenfield Apartments in Burlington, Vermont, were built nearly four decades ago on the shore of Lake Champlain. At the end of the 1980s three hundred thirty-six mostly poor families in these subsidized units were threatened with the removal of federal rent limitations and prohibitive rent increases because the developer wanted to prepay his mortgage.[127] Tenants organized to stop the prepayment and got the city to back them. Because it involved the largest residential property in Vermont, the project attracted attention, and so did the developer, who owned half a dozen other projects and was visible because he was active in Vermont's ski industry. Tenants, activists, and politicians formed a task force eventually incorporated as Northgate Non-Profit, which found a partner in the statewide, equity-raising group called Housing Vermont, and which worked with Vermont Housing and Conservation, a state-wide trust fund, and with various other state and city agencies to get financing and issue tax-exempt bonds for affordable housing.

At the same time, these groups worked with others nationally to decide how to influence bill writing and then how to use the federal Emergency Low Income Housing Preservation Act of 1987. This act provided a moratorium on conversion that would remove the federal restrictions and allowed community (social) ownership, even though the bill was originally written to help subsidized developers get new federal money to stay in their projects as private owners. Reformers later influenced the 1990 amendment to this act.[128] The Burlington people also worked to get a rehabilitation grant from HUD. The pressures from the residents, the city, and the activists were effective. The developer decided to sell to the tenants and the community, not just the Burlington property but all his projects, and Northgate became the first prepayment housing project nationally "to be transferred to community-based non-profit sponsored ownership." Neighborhood and municipal initiative got results.

Another project, five hundred units in Somerville, Massachusetts, a working-class suburb of Boston, became eligible for prepayment in 1989. A majority of the tenants were poor and a third were elderly. The project represented a big portion (about 20 percent) of Somerville's affordable housing stock. Once again, reformers and residents found themselves initially very weak compared with a disinterested landlord who thought tenants insubstantial and therefore not worth bargaining with. But later, by joining with other local forces and taking their case statewide (during Governor Dukakis's presidential campaign) and to HUD, the tenants won against even three powerful developers who were New York partners, including the developer of Battery Park City.[129]

At the national level the political activities required to save eight hundred apartments hardly seem eventful. Even should a highly unlikely nationwide rescue have taken place, with all 360,000 housing units being saved from decontrol, housing reformers would still have been a long way from what was then necessary to make a dent in the problems of housing shortages, and they would not have cut deeply into urban poverty.[130] The problems are worse now. There remain all the rest of the housing problems, and then problems with jobs, incomes, education, and more. Although it would be a major achievement to guarantee decent and affordable housing for perhaps a million persons, even that number would be insufficient.

Nevertheless, these cases provide instructive examples of how local interests and actions can lead to modified federal programs, providing a new base for local action. In order to make the Burlington and Somerville cases national, reformers participated in meetings of officials from various cities, in conferences of developers, housing specialists, and advocacy activists, as well as in negotiating sessions and lobbying efforts in Washington. This is how groups connect, how they change legislation, how coalitions get built, and how they move ahead with their agendas. The success of progressive forces in saving housing in spite of a hostile administration in Washington should be encouraging.

Examples abound of efforts in housing, local economic development, and even welfare reform, in which local officials and reformers attempt to modify federal law and administrative practice. For many years, these efforts were promoted and documented by the Conference on State and Local Progressive Policies, at which local politicians, administrators, planners, and activist reformers met annually. Information is now disseminated through various national organizations, such as the Planners Network, and it is analyzed to influence federal policy through such groups as the Poverty and Race Research Action Council.[131]

Efforts in these areas are extremely important, and they comprise the second element in a national strategy for attacking urban poverty, leading the way to the design of better programs and keeping political constituencies interested and involved. But still, these scattered improvements in federal policy do not change the major policies.

Local Coalitions and National Political Change

Now we must be more speculative because there is less experience. We look at two questions. The first asks whether coalitions and networks of localities can work to shift the center of power from national to state and local levels. This, after all, is one of the stated purposes of reforms in federal-local relations pushed by the Nixon, Reagan, and Bush administrations, and it is one that should be taken seriously by progressive reformers. The greater the local power, in theory, the more resources will be allocated to pressing domestic priorities. Instead, given excessive federal power, the federal budget expands almost crazily through taxation, tax expenditures, and inflationary bag holding (especially for war spending, corporate bailouts, and—most recently—banking transfers) while school and city budgets suffer from taxpayer revolt. The sentiment is captured by a bumper sticker: "Budgets for Schools, Bake Sales for Bombs." With an increase in local power, a strong but now missing domestic and minority representation of central-city voters, women, and people of color could form on all levels of national politics.

The second question is broader still. Can networks of municipal reform governments change the *entire* federal agenda? They would have to make the case that better policies will not only help cities (and poor people elsewhere) but also assist in the reconstruction of national productivity and the regaining of international competitiveness.

On the first question, of shifting power to the cities, it is clear that some kinds of policies, particularly those that are geographically sensitive, ought to be under the control of municipalities, others not. The idea is that matters should be handled at the lowest competent level. In the European Union "subsidiarity" governs relations between the union and member states, and many planners view regional and municipal affairs through a similar lens, using the same term. The Obama administration has spoken in similar terms. Changes that bring about better industrial policy, an educational policy worthy of the name, and the provision of basic family services ought to be enacted at the national level. Municipal authority, however, should exert more influence on the pattern of economic and physical development, on the redistributive effect of municipal services, and especially on the effort to support troubled neighborhoods. Municipal governments and affiliated community-based organizations will play an important role. They have the greatest sensitivity to the nature of their problems, the ability to involve residents in finding solutions, and the capacity to deliver where aid is needed.

Simple geographic proximity raises the possibility for effective voting blocs of poor people or minorities in local elections, and it facilitates their oppositional activity versus landlords, downtown businesses, and not-too-distant neighborhoods.[132] In spite of all the evidence of separation, we do not live in a world of total alienation, where the notion of social responsibility is discarded in the face of the most obvious need. Instead, we live in a real world, still influenced by social forces. At the municipal level the abstractions of the real estate market become inflated rents and homeless families, the esoterics of labor markets turn into jobless men, poorly paid women, and hungry children, and the mysteries of fiscal austerity translate into closed hospitals, unfunded halfway houses, and sidewalks filled with hopeless people. These bitter realities are not part of the America anyone wants, but they confront even unaffected people with unavoidable aspects of life at the local level. They are also the basis for rising demands for more municipal authority.

The distinct worsening of poverty in the 1980s and again in the first decade of the 2000s has built up pressures from the disruption of urban life. Harvard law professor Gerald Frug wrote about "municipal liberation," to speculate how an expansion of local political and economic power can be envisioned as a means of facilitating more widespread and higher levels of participation, as a counterpart to the increasing alienation of modern corporate bureaucratic society.[133]

Frug argues that there is an enormous potential for local action, even on matters of economic development, which is undermined by traditional assumptions of municipal incapacity and by a web of weakening legal-political constraints. Political economists Christopher and Hazel Gunn have called for communities to "reclaim capital" by undertaking democratic initiatives in economic development.[134] Providing considerable support for Frug's political and legal theories, the Gunns point out that there are ways for communities to gain financial resources, to build assets, and even to constrain the free actions of corporations.

We support these ideas because they suggest that the separation and polarization associated with poverty in cities may be countered. Rising demands will lead to new ways of building more effective municipal power. These ideas have not yet spread widely, but in some big cities progressive municipal politics have moved in these directions. One prominent example is Chicago, where Mayor Harold Washington took a coalition of neighborhood groups into office, and where he challenged the interests of suburbs and downtown business by involving many who had been disenfranchised. Washington built solid political support in the country's most separated African American community and used it brilliantly to form a coalition with other progressive neighborhood forces.[135] His tragic death in 1987 left many reforms intact but denied the city of the sort of leadership needed for undertaking deep change.

Two efforts undertaken in Chicago before Washington's death deserve our attention. The first is that the city itself established an economic development policy that refused simply to respond to external, corporate stimuli. In Ann Markusen's words, they chose instead to "build on the basics" by working inside the city to transform the floundering steel industry, by working with existing small manufacturers to maintain or increase employment and improve productivity, and by making demands on corporations already in place.[136] Noting changes in the global economy, the city government worked to cut deals directly with foreign corporations. It also worked to provide jobs for city residents and to direct municipal purchases toward city producers and suppliers. The city even sued Playskool when it shut down a plant, dropping employees from their jobs in apparent violation of contract involving an earlier city loan.[137]

Second, the city worked intensely with neighborhood groups to turn the focus of public assistance away from subsidies to large, downtown businesses. Robert Mier, the city's commissioner of economic development (and later assistant to the mayor for all economic affairs) was able to build on his earlier founding of the Center for Urban Economic Development, which provided assistance to grass-roots and neighborhood groups. Other members of Washington's central group also came from the neighborhoods. Mier's chief assistant, Robert Giloth, had been a neighborhood organizer and a builder of coalitions. He and Ann Shlay document one of the more unusual fights, over a world's fair.[138] Financial interests wanted the fair, arguably as a means of channeling large city subsidies into renewal of a railyard area adjacent to downtown, to facilitate inexpensive but profitable real estate expansion. There was, of course, interest by local businesses in the profits to be made from the brief boom the fair would provide. The neighborhoods, on the other hand, according to analysis by groups by then working inside city hall, were convinced that benefits from the fair would be short term and outweighed in the long run by city debt and higher taxes. In the new, more participatory style and content of Chicago politics established by Washington's two electoral victories, city hall needed only to proclaim neutrality, and in the ensuing debate the neighborhoods won. In this and many similar decisions, over sports stadiums, street and highway investments, business taxes and linkage fees, what was saved on the conventional subsidies to large businesses could be transferred into city expenditures for housing, neighborhood improvement, public services, and the protection of existing jobs in small businesses throughout the city.[139] The coalition was fought against by downtown business, but Mayor Washington held it together and enlisted a grudging cooperation.

Changes in Chicago took on a different and more progressive quality than changes now taking place in many cities not only because of the special capabilities of the mayor himself, but because the challenge to business as usual and the corporate agenda came from residents and neighborhoods—especially from the working-class and poor neighborhoods—as they exercised their franchise to support a set of leaders who returned the favor.

On the second question, that of forming national coalitions, we can say much less, but we can be equally hopeful, again illustrating our case with examples from Chicago. Harold Washington had been in Congress. To be sure, as mayor his attention was mostly focused on the city, building his base, keeping the coalition together, staying in office, and strengthening real municipal power. But he left some time for larger affairs, and one of the objectives he shared with others was an attack on national politics through coalitions of city leaders. We think such a coalition becomes more likely as city changes continue.

We admit that, to the disappointment of many observers, African American and Latino mayors often have not acted progressively but instead have simply reaped the fruits of office or worked in traditional ways with the old political machines. But as competition for office expands and minority candidates vie against one another, the emergence of a progressive option seems more likely.[140]

Where does this leave us? Cities and especially the poor people who live in them are beset with problems not of their own making. Hostile economic forces from the outside seem relentless, and political tendencies at the national level are unpromising. City governments and neighborhood groups have experimented successfully with reforms, and they have even managed to influence some federal policy for the better. But this leaves them well short of the capacity they need for cutting into persistent and debilitating poverty. Many will conclude that this is the end of the story: maybe this is also the end of the American dream, and the country will begin a long decline marked by the deterioration of its cities and the abandonment of its poor.

We are not so pessimistic. A few city leaders have found strength in this adversity. They may find it possible to use this strength, with support from organized neighborhoods of ordinary residents, to build multi-city coalitions, adding to their numbers and their potential influence. These coalitions, we envision, would be based first on the interests of the poor, people of color, and the many others who still live and work in the cities and their close-in suburbs. They might be joined by American corporations, the many who are threatened not only by external competition but also by a weak domestic base for productivity growth. At some point these coalitions may turn around the trajectory of federal politics, command a revival of American generosity, and show that a dream for one is a dream for all.

Notes

CHAPTER 1. THE END OF AN ERA: DIVIDED WE FALL

1. Blakely and Snyder, *Fortress America*.

2. The numbers are for 1999, from the Census of 2000.

3. Michael Bloomberg, Op-Ed, *New York Times*, February 28, 2008.

4. *Southern Burlington County N.A.A.C.P. v. Township of Mount Laurel*, 67 N.J. 151 (1975) (Mount Laurel I); *Southern Burlington County N.A.A.C.P. v. Township of Mount Laurel*, 92 N.J. 158 (1983) (Mount Laurel II); *Hills v. Gautreaux* 425 U.S. 284 (1976). Personal stories in *Class Matters*, intro. Bill Keller, reveal the growing gaps.

5. Goldsmith, "From the Metropolis to Globalization."

6. Daniel Brook, "Extreme Inequality," *Nation*, April 7, 2008, quoting David Kay Johnston, *Free Lunch* (2008).

7. Goldsmith, "Ghetto as a Resource."

8. "Plutocracy Reborn," *Nation*, June 30, 2008, pp. 24–25.

9. Wallerstein, "Citizens All?" p. 650.

10. Castells, "European Cities."

11. AFDC—Aid to Families with Dependent Children. TANF—Temporary Assistance to Needy Families.

12. Blakely and Snyder, *Fortress America*.

13. Davis, "Shared Equity Homeownership"; Clavel and Deppe, "Innovation in Urban Policy."

14. Gladwell, "Risk Pool," quoting Jennifer Klein, a labor historian at Yale University.

15. UAW leader Walter Reuther urged federal health and retirement benefits but was defeated by Detroit's hostility to "socialism." See full discussion in Chapter 2. Roger Lowenstein, "Siphoning G.M.'s Future," *New York Times*, Op-Ed, July 10, 2008.

16. As Jimmy Carter's inflation czar, Alfred Kahn (chairman, Council on Wage and Price Stability), points out, the financing of benefits with employment taxes instead of

progressive taxes on income and inheritance handicaps companies in international competition. "The Optimal Way to Finance Employee Benefits," *Ithaca Journal,* 19 July 2007.

17. John Judis, "Arnold's Dilemma," *California Monthly* 117, no. 1 (January–February 2006): 20–25.

18. Gilmore, *Golden Gulag.*

19. Fineman, "Dependency and Social Debt," focuses on the particular burdens on women of poverty and inequality in the United States by examining how the society defines and then stigmatizes dependency. See also Nussbaum, "Poverty and Human Functioning," and Sen, "Conceptualizing and Measuring Poverty." In contrast to Nussbaum's criticism, see Cox and Alm, "Off the Books," for contrary (and doubtful) evidence of constant technological progress and improvements in work and leisure conditions in the United States.

20. Anthropologist Oscar Lewis, economist Everett Hagen, psychologist David McClelland, and political scientist Daniel Lerner published landmark studies c. 1960.

21. Rieder, *Canarsie,* quoted in Edsall, "Race," p. 58. The ethnocentricity of such opin-
ions, described in a study of a White ethnic Brooklyn neighborhood, was starkly revealed in the Bensonhurst case, in which a White mob chased an unknown and innocent Black man to his death. See other examples in Edsall, "Race."

22. Works by Charles Valentine, Eleanor Leacock, and Elliot Liebow in the late 1960s.

23. Anne Barnard, "Latinos Recall Pattern of Attacks before Killing," *New York Times,* January 8, 2009; Kirk Semple, "A Killing in a Town Where Latinos Sense Hate," *New York Times,* November 14, 2008. An online Times Topics section treats Marcelo Lucero, the murder victim; see http://topics.nytimes.com/topics/reference/timestopics/people/l/marcelo _lucero/index.html.

24. Dedrick Muhammad, "Race and Extreme Inequality," *Nation,* June 30, 2008.

25. Feagin, *Racist America;* Feagin, Vera, and Batur, *White Racism.*

26. Bonilla-Silva, *Racism without Racists.*

27. Bobo, Kluegel, and Smith, "Laissez-Faire Racism."

28. Bobo and Zubrinsky, "Attitudes toward Residential Integration"; Bonilla-Silva, *Racism without Racists.*

29. Bonilla-Silva, *Racism without Racists.*

30. Linda Greenhouse, "Justices, Voting 5–4, Limit the Use of Race in Integration Plans," *New York Times,* June 29, 2007.

31. On this argument, that bad personal choices and behavior are present but deriva-
tive of bad social (economic) situations, see Wilson, "Social Theory and the Concept 'Underclass.'" Also see Cosby and Poussaint, *Come On, People.*

32. Women eagerly joined the federal program to encourage them to marry, only to confront impossible barriers of discrimination, physical isolation, and poverty. The program was part of the Bush II effort to consolidate "welfare reform." Boo, "Marriage Cure."

33. Sampson and Wilson, "Toward a Theory of Race, Crime, and Urban Inequality," p. 186.

34. Mead, "Expectations and Welfare Work," pp. 249–250.

35. See Ewen and Matthews, "Families Forgotten."

36. Perkins, *Confessions of an Economic Hit Man.*

37. In several significant places, which Pierre Clavel calls progressive cities, local politics has been strongly redistributive. See Clavel, *Progressive City.* Also see Paul, "Local Politics," which shows how Minneapolis politics resists inequality-producing effects of globalization.

38. For a similarly pessimistic interpretation, see Darity and Myers, *Persistent Disparity;* Beneria, "Crisis of Care"; and Neckerman and Torche, "Inequality."

39. It is well known that poverty increases stress in adults. Martha Farah finds that poverty reduces working-memory size and therefore learning by children. Gary Evans and Michelle Schamberg relate memory to stress. "I am just a poor boy though my story's seldom told: Neuroscience and Social Deprivation," *Economist*, April 4, 2009.

40. Caldeira, *City of Walls*.

41. Marmot and Wilkinson, *Social Determinants of Health*. This inference is tentative in part because when material standards are so highly influenced by social position (the rich have more power and get better standards), researchers cannot distinguish the two effects. See Marmot and Wilkinson, *Social Determinants of Health*, especially chs. 1, 12, 14, and 16. The main critics of Wilkinson's thesis of social inequality as a determinant of health take issue with his focus on social capital instead of income inequality and its corollary that inequality affects the affluent as well as the poor. See Lynch et al., "Income Inequality and Mortality"; Muntaner and Lynch, "Income Inequality"; Muntaner, Lynch, and Smith, "Social Capital"; and Blakely et al., "Income inequality and Mortality."

42. Hacker, *Great Risk Shift*, p. 5.

43. U.S. Centers for Disease Control, National Vital Statistics Report, revised March 2007, available at http://www.cdc.gov/; Daniel Goleman, "Black Scientists Study the 'Pose' of the Inner City," *New York Times*, April 21, 1992. For numerous similar examples, see the collection by Harvard public health professor Nancy Krieger, "The Public Health Disparities Geocoding Project," available at http://www.hsph.harvard.edu/thegeocodingproject.

44. Hacker, *Great Risk Shift*, pp. 5–6, emphasis added. Wilkinson finds that among the richest twenty-five or thirty countries, there is *no* such correlation. That is, health status of the population on average does *not* improve with average incomes. In health terms it does one good to be at the top of one's national income *distribution*, but among industrialized countries it matters little whether one's national *average* income is higher than the average incomes of other nations.

45. Marmot et al., "Health and the Psychosocial Environment"; Wilkinson, "Ourselves and Others," pp. 341–342.

46. Daley et al., "Income Inequality and Homicide," graph in Marmot and Wilkinson, *Social Determinants of Health*, p. 346. Such cross-section analysis is always subject to many qualifiers, since neither causation nor intervening factors are stipulated, but the results are nonetheless striking.

47. Fajunzylber et al., "Inequality and Violent Crime," graph in Marmot and Wilkinson, *Social Determinants of Health*, p. 347.

48. In 2008 the Supreme Court upheld an Indiana law requiring voters to show photo identification, sure to disenfranchise more of the poor. U.S. Census Bureau, Table A-7, "Reported Voting Rates in Congressional Election Years by Selected Characteristics: November 1966 to 2002," available at http://www.census.gov/hhes/www/socdemo/voting/publications/historical/tabA-7.xls. See Katrina vanden Heuvel, "Just Democracy," *Nation*, July 21–28, 2008; Lynette Holloway, "Low Voter Turnout Cited by School Board Foes," *New York Times*, June 7, 1999; Lori Yaklin, Michigan Education Report, "Consolidate School Elections with General Elections," fall 1999, available at http://www.educationreport.org/; and Shields and Goidel, "Participation Rates."

49. Voting rates among *eligible* voters have not declined since 1972, but among the resident population they have fallen because noncitizens and ineligible felons, who earlier constituted about 2 percent of the voting-age population, by 2004 had increased to nearly 10 percent nationally, 21 percent in California. For voting rates 1948 to 2000, see McDonald and Popkin, "Myth of the Vanishing Point." Daniel Brook quotes Justice Brandeis while reviewing Michael Thompson, *The Politics of Inequality*, in "Extreme Inequality," *Nation*, April 7, 2008.

50. Patricia Williams, "Colorstruck," *Nation,* April 23, 2007.

51. Many if not most other countries claim to have relatively unitary histories of language, cultures, ethnicity, even race. The long list includes even those countries throughout Africa, Asia, Latin America, and the Middle East whose borders, once drawn by European invaders, often violate historic ethnic boundaries. Most claims of ethnic, linguistic, racial, and cultural purity collapse when tested against careful historical evidence—witness movements for regional autonomy in France and Spain, for example, and regional conflicts in former colonies such as Bolivia, where Europeans and Andean peoples have such different histories, or Senegal, where Christians, Animists, and Muslims teach their children in markedly different school systems.

52. Against "identity" politics and the massive scholarly production of culture studies, which emphasize race, ethnicity, gender, sexual orientation, and other crucially significant identities as bases for solidarity, proponents of "class" politics sometimes point to a declining significance for race—as William J. Wilson, *Declining Significance of Race,* once put it. For a discussion of these disputes, see Robert S. Boynton, "The Plot against Equality," a review of Walter Benn Michaels, *The Trouble with Diversity: How We Learned to Love Identity and Ignore Inequality* (2006), *Nation,* December 25, 2006.

53. Census 2000: forty-eight cities, not quite half of the one hundred largest, had majority minority populations. Throughout the book, when dates and sources for population figures and the like are not cited, the reference is the U.S. Census of Population and Housing for 2000, available at http://www.census.gov/prod/cen2000/index.html.

54. The ten cities are Hialeah, Detroit, Miami, Santa Ana, Newark, El Paso, Honolulu, Birmingham, Oakland, and Jersey City, listed in Katz and Lang, *Redefining Urban and Suburban America,* vol. 1, Table 8-2, p. 142.

55. Between 2000 and 2006, San Francisco, Boston, Seattle, and five other of the largest fifty cities saw the White *share* of their populations increase, stimulating now familiar interethnic disputes over gentrification—but this turnaround hardly constitutes neighborhood mixing. Conor Dougherty, "The End of White Flight," *Wall Street Journal,* July 18, 2008.

56. Katz and Lang, *Redefining Urban and Suburban America,* vol. 1, contains several chapters examining this phenomenon. William Frey, a leading demographer, has examined city/suburb ethnic (or "racial") differences, suggesting that there are some metropolitan areas with "melting pot" suburbs, other metro areas north and south that are largely White/ Black, and still others(nationwide) that are largely White. See Frey, "Diversity Spread Out."

57. Census 2000. In 2005 Gary was 10.2% White and 82.6% Black, and Hispanic was not listed (U.S. Bureau of the Census, American Community Survey, 2006).

58. The Census Bureau handles this sort of problem by defining Primary and Consolidated, or ordinary and "Combined," Metropolitan Areas for the largest, most complex urban regions with populations of over 1 million people and containing at least two Metropolitan Statistical Areas (MSAs). Thus Gary is one of three primary areas in the greater Chicago metropolis, just as Santa Rosa is one of six primary areas in the greater San Francisco Bay Area metropolis.

59. Frey, "Diversity Spread Out."

60. The Los Angeles metropolis includes four MSAs, which differ considerably in their ethnic makeup: the Asian population is nearly 14 percent in Los Angeles and Orange County, but only 4–6 percent in Riverside and Ventura; the Black population is 7–8 percent in Los Angeles and Riverside, but only 1–2 percent in Orange and Ventura counties. See Frey, "Diversity Spread Out."

61. Transfer of municipal power *among* White ethnic groups constitutes a subject on its own. On "whiteness," see Guglielmo and Salerno, *Are Italians White?;* Ignatiev, *How the Irish Became White;* and Brodkin, *How the Jews Became White Folks.*

62. Sadly, even what many believe to be positive about the War on Drugs is not. That is, the "war" does not reduce drug use. See Goldsmith, "Drug War and Inner-City Neighborhoods."

63. The warnings were out, but they were ignored. See Javier Silva, "A House of Cards: Refinancing the American Dream," Demos Policy Brief, January 2005, available at http://www.aecf.org/KnowledgeCenter/Publications.aspx?pubguid=%7BF04C3F95-1356-447B-BE31-6ABB48974646%7D, and "State of the Nation's Housing 2006," Harvard University, Joint Center for Housing Studies, 2006, available at http://www.jchs.harvard.edu/publications/markets/son2006/index.htm.

64. *Governing* (April 1991): 29.

65. Kate Zernike, "Violent Crime Rising Sharply in Some Cities," *New York Times,* February 12, 2006.

66. According to economist Robert Frank, "America's Great Economic U-Turn," *Wall Street Journal,* May 15, 2008.

67. See Kohn, *Brave New Neighborhoods.*

68. Blakely and Snyder, *Fortress America.*

69. Alfonzo, "Mall in a Former Life."

70. The CEO of one of the top McMansion builders in the country, who makes his megamillion profits because the income gap is growing, worries aloud that the government seems to favor "the creation of more wealth for the wealthy." That wealth for a few means the CEO has plenty of buyers for his $665,000 suburban homes. John Gertner, "Chasing Ground," *New York Times Magazine,* October 16, 2005.

71. "Plutocracy Reborn," *Nation,* June 30, 2008, pp. 24–25.

72. See http://www.forbes.com/static/pvp2005/LIRXC25.html.

73. For income decline, see U.S. Census Bureau, Historical Income Tables, Families, available at http://www.census.gov/hhes/www/income/histinc/incfamdet.html. For living wages, see Alternatives Federal Credit Union, *Living Wage Chart 2009,* available at http://www.alternatives.org/livingwagechart2009.html.

74. Neocons also mislead by obscuring the racist roots of their policies. In 1981 the powerful Republican strategist Lee Atwater explained his party's "Southern strategy" with alarming candor. The policy first opposed the Voting Rights Act but later the public rhetoric turned to economic benefits. Still, as Atwater explained, White voters were persuaded because "a byproduct . . . is blacks get hurt worse than whites." Paul Krugman, "Bigger than Bush," *New York Times,* January 1, 2009. Also see Goldsmith, "Resisting the Reality of Race."

75. See Lefeber and Vietorisz, "Meaning of Social Efficiency." Louis Uchitelle, "Economists Warm to Government Spending but Debate Its Form," *New York Times,* January 7, 2009, finds that although mainstream economists finally agree with "progressives" that Keynesian public spending is necessary in a recession, they advocate a quick return to Reaganomics, with minimization of taxes, regulations, and public spending. Harvard economist Martin Feldstein, a top Reagan adviser, proposed spending on worn-out military supplies and equipment. But Jonathan Chait, author of *The Big Con,* points out that "a handful of fanatical ideologues, along with a somewhat larger number of men who stand to gain a fortune from supply-side policies, relentlessly enforce the faith." *New York Times,* Op-Ed, October 9, 2007.

76. Ronald Reagan's Housing and Urban Development secretary, Samuel Pierce, once informed inquisitive Cornell University students that "nothing in the Constitution" requires HUD or any other federal agency to help poor people satisfy their housing needs.

CHAPTER 2. SEPARATE ASSETS: RACE, GENDER, AND OTHER DIMENSIONS OF POVERTY

1. Smeeding, "Poor People in Rich Nations," Tables 1 and 2. Statisticians dispute measurement techniques: for example, for 2005, the Census Bureau released twelve alternative measures, eleven showing higher than official poverty, and the National Academy of Sciences also calculated a higher rate. See "How the Census Bureau Measures Poverty," available at http://www.census.gov/hhes/www/poverty/povdef.html, and *Measuring Poverty: A New Approach*, available at http://www.nap.edu/openbook.php?record_id=4759&page=1.

2. Ideology really does not matter; detailed calculations are provided by the Internal Revenue Service, the Congressional Budget Office, and the Census Bureau. See the response of Gary Burtless, head of economic studies at the Brookings Institution, to Alan Reynolds, of the Cato Institute, "Has U.S. Income Inequality *Really* Increased?" Brookings Institution, January 11, 2009.

3. Stephan R. Weisman, "In China, People See Paulson and Think of Goldman," World Business, *New York Times,* September 22, 2006.

4. Galbraith, *Tenured Professor.*

5. *New York Times,* March 16, 1989.

6. Anthony Lewis, *New York Times,* March 9, 1989.

7. Joel Stashenko, "Kaye Prepared to Sue for Judicial Raises," *New York Law Journal,* April 10, 2007. In 2008 judges became eligible for $5,000 bonus payments and six weeks of annual vacation. Typical U.S. workers are entitled to only two weeks, and many feel compelled to take even less.

8. In 2005 federal judges earned between $162,000 and $172,000, plus hefty medical, pension, and vacation benefits. In 2004 median household income was just over $44,000.

9. Paul Krugman, "Feeling No Pain," *New York Times,* March 6, 2006.

10. Frank and Cook, *Winner-Take-All Society;* also see Frank, *Falling Behind.*

11. Rose, *American Profile Poster.* See discussion of the BLS standard below.

12. Smeeding, "Poor People in Rich Nations."

13. William J. Grinker, reported by Josh Barbanel, *New York Times,* April 2, 1989, p. 6E.

14. Paul Krugman, "Poverty Is Poison," *New York Times,* Op-Ed, February 18, 2008.

15. Nineteen forty-seven was the first year the Census Bureau started using the Gini coefficient to measure income inequality. See David Johnston, "Income Gap Is Widening, Data Shows," *New York Times,* March 29, 2007.

16. U.S. Census Bureau, Historical Income Tables—Households: Table H-2, available at http://www.census.gov/hhes/www/income/histinc/h02ar.html. A comparison of after-tax average incomes of the rich and the poor reveals that in the last quarter century the gulf separating the top quintile from the bottom has expanded by more than half. Shapiro and Friedman, "New CBO Data Indicate Growth in Long-Term Income Inequality Continues," Center on Budget and Policy Priorities, January 30, 2006, available at http://www.cbpp .org/cms/?fa=view&id=1001. The multiple grew from 6.6 in 1979 to 9.8 in 2003. W. Michael Cox and Richard Alm, economists with the Federal Reserve Bank of Dallas, acknowledge the shifting income shares that favor the richest quintile but recommend using household *consumption* expenditures rather than income, resulting in much smaller gaps separating quintiles. Unfortunately, Cox and Alm do not extend their analysis to show trends over time. "You Are What You Spend," *New York Times,* February 10, 2008.

17. Harrison and Bluestone, *Great U-Turn.* Alderson et al., "Exactly How Has Income Inequality Changed?" using Luxembourg Income Study data, show that except for Sweden and Canada, similar polarization has occurred in nearly all OECD countries, most notably

in Britain. The German Institute for Economic Research reports that the middle class, defined as workers making between 70 percent and 150 percent of the median, shrank from 62 percent to 54 percent of the workforce between 2000 and 2007. Carter Dougherty and Katrin Bennhold, "Squeezed in Europe," *New York Times,* May 1, 2008.

18. Census definitions: a *family* is a group living together, related by marriage, adoption, or blood. A *household* (the subject of Figure 2.1) is all persons in the same dwelling unit. Taking taxes and subsidies into account changes the distribution very little.

19. Prominent economists of every political persuasion agree that inequality has been rising for at least a quarter century. As Burtless points out in a scathing response to Reynolds (see note 2), ideology really does not matter because the facts are so abundant and because dispassionate, detailed calculations come from the IRS, the Congressional Budget Office, and the Census Bureau.

20. Wealth statistics normally do not include the present value of pensions or Social Security. Wolff, "Wealth Holdings," p. 160, concludes that although pensions (thought of in terms of their net present value) add to the wealth disparity, Social Security benefits work in the other direction, for a net effect of zero. For the majority, wealth consists of homes (minus mortgage debt) and automobiles.

21. Paul Krugman, "America the Polarized," *New York Times Magazine,* January 4, 2002. Wolff examines changes from 1983 to 2004 in "Recent Trends in Household Wealth" (especially the chart on p. 12).

22. See Wolff, "Recent Trends in Household Wealth."

23. The Gini coefficient, which varies from zero to one, measures the percent deviation from a uniform distribution in which each household would receive the same income.

24. $6,380 in 1967, inflated to $20,952 in 1986.

25. Warren, "Growing Threat"; 94.2 percent were middle class.

26. Census definitions of "race" are increasingly nuanced, reflecting the Census Bureau's growing attention to racial complexity. Like adding a "Kosher" section to the international food aisle, the categorical distinctions are less about cultural sensitivity than about utility and precision counting. Throughout this book the categories are simplified for clarity, but the Census allows respondents to check multiple boxes, and there is now a whole separate category for Hispanics. Consequently, it is possible to tabulate any number of combinations of racial composition, all with or without a Hispanic overlay (one could, for example, identify as White/Asian-non-Hispanic). In Table 2.6 "Black," "White," and "Hispanic" refer to those who self-identified as only Black, only White, or only Hispanic. The omission of those who self-identified in such combined categories as Black/Asian results in insignificant statistical variation.

27. See, e.g., Briggs, "Power and Limits of Place."

28. U.S. Census Bureau, Historical Income Tables—Families, Table F-5, Race and Hispanic Origin of Householder—Families by Median and Mean Income: 1947 to 2007, available at http://www.census.gov/hhes/www/income/histinc/f05.html. In 2007 CPI-U-RS dollars the median family income was $61,355 for all races, $64,427 for White alone, $69,937 for White alone not Hispanic, $40,222 for Black alone or in combination, $40,143 for Black alone, $76,606 for Asian alone or in combination, $77,133 for Asian alone, $70,454 for Asian and Pacific Islander, and $40,566 for Hispanic, all races.

29. Quoted in Katha Pollitt, "Tough Luck, Ladies," *Nation,* June 25, 2007. The Supreme Court shocked observers when it ruled against Lilly Ledbetter in 2008. When she retired, Ledbetter discovered she had been paid illegally low, "$6,700 a year less than the lowest man at her level." Although it agreed that the pay was discriminatory, the Court denied relief, ruling that she had to have complained of the discrimination within six months of her first

paycheck, an impossibility since pay is a private matter. Congress subsequently strengthened the law.

30. Oliver and Shapiro, *Black Wealth/White Wealth,* p. 97.

31. The U.S. Census Bureau calculates Gini ratios for American households as part of the "Annual Social and Economic Supplement" to the Current Population Survey. For 2007, the Gini ratio for the nation overall was 0.443. Among White households, the ratio was 0.433. The ratio among Asians was 0.414, among Hispanics 0.432, and among Blacks, the most unequal group, 0.472.

32. Ford Fessenden, "Subprime Mortgages Concentrated in City's Minority Neighborhoods," *New York Times,* October 15, 2007. Investigations revealed that unscrupulous lenders pushed these highly costly and risky mortgages on minority borrowers. U.S. House, Subcommittees on Housing and Community Opportunities and Financial Institutions and Credit, *Protecting Homeowners: Preventing Abusive Lending While Preserving Access to Credit,* testimony of Allen J. Fishbein, 108th Cong., 1st sess., 2003, 3.

33. In 1988 the ratio between White married-couple and Black or Hispanic female-headed household wealth was more than 80 to 1. See 1st edition (*Separate Societies: Poverty and Inequality in U.S. Cities* [Philadelphia: Temple University Press, 1992]), Fig. 2.7.

34. When underemployment (see Table 2.5) reached staggeringly high rates in 2009— 17 percent or higher from September on—minority workers suffered much more than White workers.

35. Kennickell, "Rolling Tide"; more precisely, 19 percent vs. 54 percent.

36. Dowd, *Against the Conventional Wisdom.*

37. Orshansky, "Who Are the Poor?" quoted in Fisher, "Development of the Orshansky Poverty Thresholds."

38. Brown, "Designing Cities for People."

39. The BLS stopped providing figures in 1981. See Rose, *American Profile Poster,* pp. 7–8. For a thorough historical discussion, see Fisher, "Development of the Orshansky Poverty Thresholds." Also see U.S. Bureau of the Census, "Effects of Government Taxes and Transfers."

40. Acs and Turner, "Making Work Pay Enough."

41. Census "families" exclude households composed of single individuals or entirely unrelated people.

42. U.S. Bureau of Labor Statistics, "Profile of the Working Poor."

43. Perry and Blumberg, "Health Insurance for Low-Income Working Families."

44. As of October 2008, Congress renamed the program SNAP, the Supplemental Nutrition Assistance Program. George Orwell lives on!

45. Boushey et al., "Understanding Low-Wage Work."

46. Simms, "Weathering Job Loss."

47. Boushey et al., "Understanding Low-Wage Work."

48. See Zedlewski et al., "New Safety Net."

49. Oppressive laboring conditions and labor relations are not things of some ancient past, and they may be on the rise again. See the 1979 movie *Norma Rae,* which depicts working conditions in textile plants, and the 2008 book by Greenhouse, *The Big Squeeze: Tough Times for the American Worker.*

50. Burtless, ed., *Future of Lousy Jobs,* p. 2. In Chapters 3 and 4 we discuss debates among statisticians and economists about the reasons for falling wages.

51. Harrison and Gorham, "What Happened to Black Wages." Annual wage levels are measured by standardizing part-time and full-time earnings.

52. Roughly 60 percent of the workforce lives in higher-minimum-wage states, many with cost-of-living indexing.

53. For comparison of methods of defining better and worse jobs, see "Pulling Apart: Wage Growth in Good Jobs and Bad Jobs" (Fig. 2) and other portions of Boushey et al., "Understanding Low-Wage Work."

54. Levitan and Shapiro, *Working but Poor*, Fig. 2, p. 17. In the economic recovery after September 2004, U.S. employers added lower-wage jobs at 150 percent the rate they added higher-wage jobs. "The results aren't necessarily surprising. Shaken by a sharp slowdown in business spending, the bursting of the stock market bubble, the Sept. 11 attacks, war and corporate scandals, CEOs have been cautious about hiring workers. It stands to reason that firms would be much more comfortable adding a $6-an-hour job vs. a $30-an-hour one." Barbara Hagenbaugh and Barbara Hansen, "Low-Wage Jobs Rise at Faster Pace," *USA Today*, June 30, 2004.

55. *Still Working Hard, Still Falling Short*, the October 2008 report of the Working Poor Families Project, available at http://www.workingpoorfamilies.org/pdfs/NatReport08.pdf.

56. The BLS stopped calculating underemployment rates during the Nixon administration. The rates in inner cities sometimes ran as high as 75 percent. See Spring, Harrison, and Vietorisz," Crisis of the Underemployed."

57. In both cases the cities are overwhelmingly Black and the suburbs White. Among the few Whites in St. Louis, the unemployment rate was only 1.4 percent.

58. Boston, *Race*, pp. 82ff., analyzes data from a detailed supplement on occupational mobility, training, experience, and job tenure in the January 1983 *Current Population Survey* of the U.S. Bureau of the Census.

59. Boston, *Race*, p. 133.

60. Bernstein and Kornbluh, "Running Faster to Stay in Place," p. 7, available at http://www.newamerica.net/files/nafmigration/archive/Doc_File_2437_1.pdf.

61. See, e.g., Beneria, *Gender* and "Crisis of Care."

62. Sheets et al., *Impact of Service Industries*.

63. U.S. Census Bureau, Current Population Survey, Annual Social and Economic Supplements, Historical Poverty Tables—Families, Table 4. Poverty Status of Families, by Type of Family, Presence of Related Children, Race, and Hispanic Origin: 1959 to 2007. Available at http://www.census.gov/hhes/www/poverty/histpov/hstpov4.xls.

64. Sheets et al., *Impact of Service Industries*, Table 3-6, p. 42; Falk and Lyson, *High Tech*, Table 5-1, pp. 107–130.

65. Information from Laura Foo, *Asian American Women* (Ford Foundation, 2003), cited in Werschkul and Williams, "2004 National Overview Report."

66. Schoen et al., "US Health System Performance," citing G. F. Anderson et al., "Health Care Spending."

67. Frank Green, "Health Care System Leaves Poor to Suffer," available at http://www.commondreams.org/views04/0811-05htm, quoted in *Baltimore Sun*, August 11, 2004.

68. Gardner and Vishwasrao, "Physician Quality and Health Care."

69. Guy Boulton, "Hospital Discourages Poor," *Milwaukee Journal*, December 9, 2006, available at http://jsonline.com/story/index.aspx?id=540345.

70. Evidence suggests that higher "sin taxes" reduce smoking: http://www.tobaccofreekids.org/reports/prices/.

71. Rose, "Army Aids Those Too Fat to Enlist."

72. U.S. Centers for Disease Control, reported in Ferguson, "Growing Problem."

73. Boardman et al., "Race Differentials in Obesity."

74. Nord et al., "Household Food Security."

75. Nord et al., "Household Food Security."

76. Nord et al., "Household Food Security."

77. Nord et al., "Household Food Security."

78. MacDorman and Mathews, "Recent Trends in Infant Mortality."

79. MacDorman and Mathews, "Recent Trends in Infant Mortality."

80. Zweig, *What's Class Got to Do with It?*

81. Since about 1990, most research on "persistent poverty" has focused on rural areas, using county-level data to identify *places* with high percentages of poverty households for more than one census period. See, e.g., Miller et al., "Persistent Poverty and Place."

82. Erickson et al., *Enduring Challenge of Concentrated Poverty.*

83. For a study of persistent urban poverty in Britain, see Blanden, "Bucking the Trend."

CHAPTER 3. SEPARATE OPPORTUNITIES: COMPETITION VERSUS INCLUSION—THE INTERNATIONAL DIMENSIONS OF AMERICAN URBAN POVERTY

1. Bluestone et al., *Urban Experience,* p. 143. See also Friedman, *World Is Flat.*

2. William Greider, "A Globalization Offensive," *Nation,* January 29, 2007: "critics of the global system have been pinned down by multinational business and finance."

3. Quoted in Greider, "Globalization Offensive."

4. Fukuyama, *End of History.* Evidence suggests that economic expansion does *not* necessarily bring democracy. China's market expanded, but its political system remains tightly closed. Furthermore, markets almost automatically generate inequality. Patricia Cohen, "An Unexpected Odd Couple: Free Markets and Freedom," *New York Times,* June 14, 2007.

5. Hayek, *Road to Serfdom.*

6. In early 2009, for example, eight persons died and thousands took sick from salmonella in peanut butter that the Food and Drug Administration had allowed on the market despite its own findings of violations years earlier following a whistle-blower's warning. Michael Moss, "Safety Net Missed Problems at Peanut Plant," *New York Times,* February 9, 2009.

7. David Stockman, director of the Bureau of the Budget (now the Office of Management and Budget), apologized in 1986 in *Triumph of Politics.*

8. Radio talk-show host Rush Limbaugh says, "Tax cuts are the surest and quickest way to create permanent jobs and cause an economy to rebound," and admonishes us to "cut the U.S. corporate tax rate . . . in half. Suspend the capital gains tax for a year [to be later] reimposed at 10%. Then get out of the way!" "My Bipartisan Stimulus," *Wall Street Journal,* Op-Ed, January 29, 2009. In May 2009 former vice president Dick Cheney said that Limbaugh represented the Republican line better than the former secretary of state, Colin Powell, Cheney's long-term former colleague.

9. Quoted by Patricia Cohen, "An Unexpected Odd Couple," *New York Times,* June 14, 2007. Years earlier, when the elite Trilateral Commission contemplated conflict between capitalism and democracy, they recommended less of the latter. Crozier et al., *Crisis of Democracy;* Goldsmith, "Giant Corporations."

10. Signs of conflict: President Obama complained forcefully and suggested limits on compensation for executives who receive federal bailout billions, but these gestures seem more for publicity than for the economy. The well-compensated CEO of Netflix suggested that the government instead increase the top marginal income tax rates to 50 percent. Reed Hastings, "Please Raise My Taxes," *New York Times,* Op-Ed, February 6, 2009. The following week the White House did propose higher taxes, but only to 38 percent at the upper margin.

11. The expanding split of wage/salary levels separates college graduates from the rest. In the knowledge economy, formal education matters, but still the great majority of young people do not get four-year college degrees.

12. Drennan, "Decline and Rise," pp. 25–26.

13. Hazel Henderson, author of *The Politics of the Solar Age: Alternatives to Economics,* quoted in *New York Times,* April 6, 1989.

14. Louis Uchitelle, "To Mend the Flaws in Trade," *New York Times,* January 30, 2007, notes the vigorous debate on globalization, citing Dani Rodrik, *Has Globalization Gone Too Far?*; Jeffrey Frieden, *Global Capitalism*; Martin Wolf, *Why Globalization Works*; and Peter Singer, *One World.* U.S. small-arms exports total more than $500 million annually. Mvemba Phelzo Dixolele and Rachel Stohl, "The Toll of Small Arms," *New York Times,* September 5, 2006.

15. Quoted by Uchitelle, "To Mend the Flaws."

16. Quoted by Uchitelle, "To Mend the Flaws."

17. The backlash words are Uchitelle's, in "To Mend the Flaws."

18. Steven Greenhouse and David Leonhardt, "Real Wages Fail to Match a Rise in Productivity," *New York Times,* August 28, 2006.

19. Ranney, *Global Decisions.* On the other face of this coin, globalization imposes economic troubles on underdeveloped countries.

20. William J. Broad, "U.S. Is Losing Its Dominance in the Sciences," *New York Times,* May 3, 2004.

21. O'Connor, *Fiscal Crisis,* pp. 104–151. Radice, "Capital, Labor and the State."

22. The assumption of much of the debt by foreign powers, especially China, helped postpone the reckoning, as discussed below. See Rivlin and Sawhill, "Deficits and Debt."

23. Peter S. Goodman, "Is a Lean Economy Turning Mean?" *New York Times,* March 2, 2008.

24. Harrison, *Lean and Mean.*

25. Congressional Budget Office, "What Accounts for the Decline in Manufacturing Employment?" Economic and Budget Issue Brief, February 18, 2004, Washington, D.C.

26. Bivens, "Shifting Blame."

27. Harry J. Holzer, an economist at Georgetown University, quoted in Erik Eckholm, "Plight Deepens for Black Men, Studies Warn," *New York Times,* March 20, 2006.

28. Quoted by Goodman, "Is a Lean Economy Turning Mean?"

29. Richmond *Times-Dispatch,* November 11, 2008.

30. *New York Times,* editorial, February 6, 2009. The editorial also claimed that unemployment rose "among virtually all demographic groups."

31. U.S. Census Bureau, American Community Survey (ACS), available at http://www.census.gov/acs/www/, has estimates for 2005–2007.

32. Mayer, "Union Membership Trends." Sam Hananel, "Union Membership Rises," *Ithaca Journal,* January 31, 2009.

33. For example, the U.S. Supreme Court allowed a fish-packing plant to continue to operate like a plantation, separating low-paid Alaskan and Filipino workers from well-paid Whites, allowing even this racially based absence of promotion ladders. *New York Times,* June 6, 1989.

34. Liming and Wolf, "Job Outlook by Education," chart 18, gives Bureau of Labor Statistics (BLS) projections for rapidly growing occupations. The very low wage categories of home health and personal care aides add almost a million jobs.

35. Bluestone and Harrison, *Deindustrialization,* estimate that 22 million jobs were lost between 1969 and 1976. The quotation is from Herz, "Worker Displacement," p. 3.

36. U.S. Bureau of Labor Statistics, Economic News Release, "Displaced Workers Summary," August 20, 2008, available at http://www.bls.gov/news.release/disp.nr0.htm.

37. Herz, "Worker Displacement," p. 3.

38. Office of Technology Assessment, *Technology and Structural Unemployment*, Fig. 1.6, p. 9.

39. Frank and Freeman, "Distributional Consequences," cited in Bluestone and Harrison, *Deindustrialization*, p. 45.

40. See Pendall and Christopherson, "Losing Ground."

41. Burnstein, *Discrimination*.

42. The growth of services is often attributed to the natural evolution of an advanced country or increased demand for services by dual-earner families and working singles with less time or more discretionary income. The first approach, the postindustrial view, assumes that services can continue to grow within the United States even without industrial production. For critiques of this assumption, see Walker, "Geographical Organization," and Cohen and Zysman, *Manufacturing Matters*. The second perspective is criticized by Harrison and Bluestone, *Great U-Turn*, p. 74. On the other hand, in at least some cities (e.g., New York), service provision is the *dominant* export. See Drennan, "Local Economy" and *Econometric Model*.

43. Storper and Walker, *Capitalist Imperative*.

44. "Decoupled: Companies' and Countries' Prosperity," *Economist*, February 25, 2006.

45. Mollenkopf and Castells, *Dual City*.

46. The literature on labor market segmentation (LMS) is voluminous and contentious. Employers create barriers to entry so as to stabilize and control labor, while workers try to protect themselves against other (potential) workers as well as against employers. "Virtually all labour market studies have shown that the labour market is segmented in some sense." Leontaridi, "Segmented Labour Markets."

47. Boston, "Segmented Labor Markets," found that upward mobility from one sector of employment to another was enhanced most by education and held back most by being Black.

48. Harrison and Bluestone, *Great U-Turn*. On privatization, see Starr, *Limits of Privatization*; Warner, "Market-Based Governance"; and Warner and Hefetz, "Rural-Urban Differences."

49. Associated Press, "Obama Repealing 4 Bush Orders Unions Opposed," available at http://www.newsmax.com/politics/obama_unions/2009/01/29/176594.htm.

50. The BLS refers to "contingent and alternative employment arrangements," noted in U.S. Bureau of Labor Statistics, News Release, February 2005, available at http://www.bls.gov/news.release/conemp.nr0.htm. Christopherson, "Emerging Patterns," discusses oligopolies, competitive firms, and part-time work.

51. "Prevailing" wages on construction projects that use federal funds are set by the Davis-Bacon Act.

52. Martin Fackler, "In Japan, New Jobless May Lack Safety Net," *New York Times*, February 8, 2009.

53. Holman et al., *Global Call Center Report*.

54. Appelbaum, "Restructuring Work."

55. Gorz, *Critique of Economic Reason*.

56. U.S. Bureau of Labor Statistics, "American Time Use Survey Summary," Economic News Release, June 25, 2008, available at http://www.bls.gov/news.release/atus.nr0.htm, and Peter T. Kilborn, "The Work Week Grows," *New York Times*, June 3, 1990, pp. E1 and E3. Nearly one-quarter of all full-time workers were on the job 49 hours or more each week in

1989, up from about 18 percent in 1970. In 1989 more than 44 percent of male executives worked these long weeks.

57. As of April 2009, U-6 (underemployment) is 15.8 percent (the highest on record) and U-3 (official unemployment) is 8.9 percent (the highest since December 1983; see Table 2.5). The BLS provides data on discouraged workers in its Table A-13, available at http://www.bls.gov/webapps/legacy/cpsatab13.htm.

58. Numbers of temp workers fluctuate. The BLS reported that as of February 2005, "contingent and alternative" employment constituted between 1.4 and 4.1 percent of the total workforce, depending on definitions, down from 2.2 to 4.9 percent in 1995 and comparable to 1.7 to 4.5 percent in 2001. U.S. Bureau of Labor Statistics, News Release, July 27, 2005, available at http://www.bls.gov/news.release/conemp.nr0.htm.

59. U.S. Census Bureau, Joint Release, U.S. Department of Housing and Urban Development: New Residential Sales, July 31, 2008. Available at http://www.census.gov/const/newressales.pdf.

60. Hymer, *Multinational Corporation,* notes Alfred Marshall's analysis of functional divisions c. 1900. See the February 2009 posting by the London School of Economics: http://www.lse.ac.uk/collections/geographyAndEnvironment/research/newidol.htm.

61. Friedmann and Wolff, "World City." Sassen, *Global City.*

62. Bluestone and Harrison, *Deindustrialization.*

63. For a recent exposé about bribery, economic control, and even the toppling of elected governments, see Perkins, *Confessions of an Economic Hit Man.*

64. Portes and Walton, *Labor, Class, and the International System.* Sassen, "Informal Economy."

65. As argued in Chapter 5, these domestic Third World patterns are at least in part a consequence of conscious public policy. See Goldsmith, "Bringing the Third World Home."

66. Storper and Walker, *Capitalist Imperative.* Fernández-Kelly, *For We Are Sold.*

67. Scott, *Metropolis,* pp. 210–211.

68. Frey, "Diversity Spread Out."

69. Maire, "Le chómage zéro, c'est possible," quoted in Gorz, *Critique of Economic Reason,* p. 6.

70. Freeman et al., *Unemployment and Technical Innovation.*

71. Gorz, *Critique of Economic Reason,* p. 5.

72. Much of Harvey's work has examined these sorts of geographical imbalances. See Harvey, "Right to the City," "Geopolitics of Capitalism," and *Condition of Postmodernity.*

73. Perez, "Structural Change"; Freeman et al., *Unemployment and Technical Innovation.*

74. The comparison of Fujan and Gary was made by historian Bruce Cummings ("Archeology, Descent, Emergence: Japan in American Hegemony in the 20th Century," lecture for the Program on International Studies in Planning, Cornell University, May 3, 1991).

75. World Steel Review, February 2009, available at http://www.steelonthenet.com/production.html. As production declines in the United States and western Europe, China is the only country with growth: see http://www.issb.co.uk/issb/files/image/jpeg/key_global crude.jpg. The BLS analyzes production trends: see http://www.bls.gov/oco/cg/cgs014.htm.

76. Imports of goods and services data are from http://www.gpoaccess.gov/eop/tables09.html, Table B-25.

77. Louis Uchitelle, "'Buy America' in Stimulus (Good Luck with That)," *New York Times,* February 20, 2009, available at http://www.nytimes.com/2009/02/21/business/21buy.html.

78. Bluestone and Harrison, *Deindustrialization.* Piore and Sabel, *Second Industrial Divide.*

79. Evidence about productivity growth rates must be treated with great caution since data are highly sensitive to definitional and measurement error.

80. Piore and Sabel, *Second Industrial Divide,* pp. 184–185.

81. Wolff, review of Moseley, *Falling Rate of Profit.*

82. "The Uneven Contest," *Economist,* January 22, 2009.

83. Kolko, *Restructuring the World Economy,* p. 215.

84. Bank for International Settlements, "Triennial Central Bank Survey," December 2007, Table B.1, available at http://www.bis.org/publ/rpfxf07t.pdf.

85. Sassen-Koob, "Recomposition and Peripheralization."

86. Historical Tables, Budget of the United States Government, Fiscal Year 2009, Table 1.3, "Summary of Receipts, Outlays, and Surpluses or Deficits, in constant (FY 2000) Dollars," available at http://www.whitehouse.gov/omb/budget/fy2009/pdf/hist.pdf; and Kolko, *Restructuring the World Economy,* pp. 73–77.

87. Harrison and Bluestone, *Great U-Turn,* p. 17.

88. Cohen et al., "Competitiveness"; Cohen and Zysman, *Manufacturing Matters.* Thurow and Tyson, "Adjusting the U.S. Trade Imbalance."

89. "Taming the Beast," *Economist,* October 9, 2008.

90. "Industry Cleans House," *Business Week,* 1985, p. 33, cited in Harrison and Bluestone, *Great U-Turn,* p. 55.

91. Hasbro, based in Rhode Island, acquired Playskool. Giloth and Mier, "Spatial Change and Social Justice."

92. Dobrzynski and Bieger, "For Better or for Worse?" *Business Week,* January 12, 1987, p. 38.

93. Harrison and Bluestone, *Great U-Turn,* p. 54.

94. *Business Week,* November 24, 1986, p. 86.

95. *Business Week,* November 24, 1986, pp. 93–94.

96. Unical acquired a $4 billion debt to forestall a takeover; *Business Week,* November 24, 1986, p. 86.

97. Olpadwala and Mansury, "Finance and Production."

98. "The Uneven Contest," *Economist,* January 22, 2009.

99. That is, taxing both corporate profits and dividend payments.

100. "Deal Mania," *Business Week,* November 24, 1986.

CHAPTER 4. SEPARATE PLACES: THE CHANGING SHAPE OF THE AMERICAN METROPOLIS

1. The legislator was Myron Orfield, who published *Metropolitics* in 1997. The word *metropolitics* was used in 1952 by J. S. Gow, writing on Pittsburgh, then infrequently until reintroduced by Orfield.

2. Jun, "Portland's Smart Growth Policies"; White, "Sprawl."

3. From 80 to 83 percent of the nation's population lived in metropolitan areas in 2000—the variation depends on changing census definitions. In 2007 around 25 percent of the nation's population lived in the nine metropolitan areas with populations of more than 5 million: New York, Los Angeles, Chicago, Washington-Baltimore, San Francisco, Philadelphia, Boston, Detroit, and Dallas–Fort Worth.

4. See Crump and Merrett, "Scales of Struggle," on Regulation School periodicity: rise (1937–1954), prosperity (1955–1970), and crisis (1971–1990), corresponding roughly to changes in labor laws, shifts in corporate power versus labor, and increases in the scale of conflict, from local to national to global.

5. Edward J. Blakely, "Thank You from New Orleans," *Chicago Tribune,* December 23, 2008.

6. These population figures and the income figures to follow are from before the steep decline of the auto industry in 2009.

7. Grengs, "Job Accessibility."

8. Grengs, "Job Accessibility."

9. Even in San Francisco and New York, as in nearly every populous central city in the country, middle-class White families with school-age children avoid city public schools— they use parochial schools or private schools, or live in the suburbs.

10. Gewande, "Checklist," p. 92.

11. "If we define a racially mixed congregation as one where no one racial group is 80 percent or more of the congregation, just 7.5 percent of the over 300,000 religious congregations in the United States are racially mixed. For Christian congregations, which form over 90 percent of congregations in the United States, the percentage that are racially mixed drops to five and a half. Of this small percentage, approximately half of the congregations are mixed only temporarily, during the time they are in transition from one group to another." DeYoung et al., *United by Faith,* p. 2.

12. Martin Jaffe, "Viewpoint," *Planning Magazine,* March 1989, p. 53.

13. Glaeser and Ponzetto, "Death of Distance."

14. Martin, "National Growth."

15. Vapñarsky, "On Rank-Size Distributions of Cities."

16. Eberts et al., "Dashboard Indicators."

17. *New York Times,* March 19, 1991, p. A16.

18. Louis Uchitelle, "Blacks Lose Better Jobs Faster as Middle-Class Work Drops," *New York Times,* July 12, 2003.

19. Orr and Deitz, "Leaner, More Skilled."

20. Wilson and Wouters, "Spatiality and Growth Discourse."

21. Many more jobs were lost, but they were replaced by new jobs, leaving the net difference at about 3 million. From the 1979 peak to January 2004, manufacturing employment dropped by 5.2 million nationally.

22. From the U.S. Bureau of Labor Statistics March 2009 Employment Situation Summary: "Since the recession began in December 2007, 5.1 million jobs have been lost, with almost two-thirds (3.3 million) of the decrease occurring in the last 5 months."

23. Markusen, *Rise of the Gunbelt.* Gordon et al., "Metropolitan and Non-metropolitan Employment Trends," note that "Denver sees a lot of frost, and Seattle, Portland and San Francisco do not get much sun. Perhaps a West-East distinction might be more accurate. However, the idea behind the division is less in terms of geography and climate than in economic structure and dynamics." They get the climate wrong, since most of the San Francisco *metropolitan* population gets sunshine.

24. Orr and Deitz, "Leaner, More Skilled."

25. Gordon et al., "Metropolitan and Non-metropolitan Employment Trends."

26. These seven states accounted for 37.5 percent of the national job loss, highest in Michigan. Friedhoff and Wial, "Bearing the Brunt."

27. In the 1990s larger and younger manufacturing establishments prospered relatively in rust-belt cities, with high rates of job creation matching job loss. Faberman, "Job Flows."

28. Thurow, "Regional Transformation."

29. There are exceptions, such as the New York region. See Drennan, "Decline and Rise."

30. Scott and Dorsey, "Economic Snapshot."

31. Markusen and Carlson, "Deindustrialization in the American Midwest."

32. White-collar workers are hit, too. "This recession is throwing the city's most educated workers out of their jobs at a rapid rate. And while unemployment rates remain higher for workers with less education, the gap is quickly narrowing. In the past year, the number of city residents with at least a bachelor's degree who are collecting unemployment benefits has risen about 135 percent, an analysis of state labor statistics shows—nearly twice the rate of increase for people who did not finish high school." Patrick McGeehan, "This Time, Slump Hits Well-Educated, Too," New York Times, April 4, 2009.

33. Mary Chapman, "Black Workers in Auto Plants Losing Ground," New York Times, December 30, 2008.

34. Some production centers, especially industrial-military places such as San Diego and San Antonio, have benefited as military contracts have countered potential regional decline and provided the basis for future growth. See Markusen et al., High Tech America, and Markusen, Rise of the Gunbelt.

35. Noyelle, "Advanced Services," p. 156.

36. San Jose suffers from its specialization in electronics, but the case is analytically weak since the city is part of the greater San Francisco metropolis.

37. Goldsmith, "Poverty and Profit." Stanback and Noyelle, Cities in Transition.

38. Crandall, "Decline in Manufacturing Jobs."

39. Pendall and Christopherson, "Losing Ground" (emphasis added).

40. Sassen, "Locating Cities on Global Circuits." See also Jacobs, Cities and the Wealth of Nations. As is often remarked, the city-reinforcing effects of cheaper transport seem counter to intuition.

41. Drennan et al., "Interruption of Income Convergence." Drennan, "Possible Sources of Wage Divergence."

42. The bibliography is long, including Friedmann, "World City Hypothesis"; Friedmann and Wolff, "World City Formation"; Sassen, Global City; Abu-Lughod, New York, Chicago, Los Angeles; Scott, Global City-Regions; King, Global Cities; Fainstein, City Builders; and Knox and Sussman, "World Cities in a World System." In 2006 Routledge put out the Global Cities Reader (ed. Brenner and Keil). One sees little control on definitions, purpose, or cause and effect.

43. Taylor and Lang, "U.S. Cities." New York, London, and Tokyo dominate for stock markets, but there is a lessening of spatial concentration among forty-five cities worldwide. U.S. stock market rankings: New York, Chicago, Los Angeles, followed by San Francisco, Miami, Atlanta, and Washington, D.C. Also see Poon et al., "Rank Size Distribution."

44. Taylor and Lang, "U.S. Cities."

45. For a summary of research on how elites in old manufacturing centers such as St. Louis, Cleveland, and Indianapolis use "growth discourse" to support their global-city agendas, see Wilson and Wouters, "Spatiality."

46. Paul, "Local Politics." The Little Apple is fifteenth in metro population and eighth in exports and has large Somali and Hmong populations, that is, it seems "global." Unfortunately, the literature most engaged with researching world cities has been particularly lacking in its analyses of politics. John Friedmann, Saskia Sassen, and Peter Taylor have authored pioneering work.

47. Roberta Brandes Gratz, "Preserving the Urban Dynamic," Nation, April 23, 2001.

48. Sassen has long emphasized this king and pauper image of the global city. Boschken, following Sassen, says that "global cities lead the way in having both the highest average incomes in the United States and the highest percentage of families below the national

poverty line." Boschken, "Global Cities." Drennan et al., "Interruption of Income Convergence," and others have shown that despite severe inequalities, wages for the working class and poor rose in leading cities, above those of lower-ranked cities. States with very high costs of living see a reflection in high percentages of families unable to meet budget requirements. California has the largest number—2 million people living in families with incomes below basic budget amounts. Allegretto, "Basic Family Budgets."

49. Gray et al., "New Industrial Cities?"

50. Gray et al., "New Industrial Cities?" and Sachs, "Virtual Ecology."

51. Mollenkopf, "Paths toward the Post Industrial Service City," builds on classical theories of hierarchies or systems of cities.

52. See Glickman, "Cities"; Rodriguez and Feagin, "Urban Specialization"; Stanback and Noyelle, *Cities in Transition*; and Cohen, "New International Division of Labor."

53. Pred, *City Systems.*

54. Noyelle, "Advanced Services."

55. See also Noyelle and Stanback, *Economic Transformation.* Top-ranked cities also tend to have more technical innovation, and the higher a city sits in the urban hierarchy, the younger are its industries. See Thompson, "National System of Cities."

56. Scott, *Metropolis.*

57. Cohen, "New International Division of Labor," and Noyelle, "Advanced Services."

58. See Friedmann and Wolff, "World City Formation"; Cohen, "New International Division of Labor"; and Noyelle and Stanback, *Economic Transformation.* According to Stanback and Noyelle, there are only four national nodal cities in the United States—New York, Los Angeles, San Francisco, and Chicago.

59. Noyelle, "Advanced Services."

60. Drennan, "Possible Sources of Wage Divergence," examines all 276 metropolitan areas: 248 Metropolitan Statistical Areas (MSAs), 17 Consolidated Metropolitan Statistical Areas (CMSAs), and 11 New England County Metropolitan Statistical Areas (NECMAs). (The Census and the Office of Management and Budget changed MSA definitions in 2003.) Also see Drennan et al., "Interruption of Income Convergence," 1996.

61. Button, "Infrastructure Investment."

62. Drennan, "Possible Sources of Wage Divergence." Miller and Gene, "Alternative Regional Specification," offer what might seem to be contrary findings but are not, with regional convergence for regions similar to metropolitan areas but over the entire period 1969–1997. Freeman, "Sources of Fluctuations in Regional Growth," refers to a "supply-side" approach, citing classic studies by Borts and Stein, and Muth, whereby cities attract workers with climate, safety, schools, health services, and the like. But he believes population growth is responsive to job growth rather than the other way around.

63. Barbara Hagenbaugh, "U.S. Manufacturing Jobs Fading Away Fast," *USA Today,* December 12, 2002. Kasarda, "Jobs."

64. Sam Roberts, "Data Show Steady Drop in Americans on the Move," *New York Times,* December 21, 2008.

65. Markusen et al., *High Tech America*; Stanback and Noyelle, *Cities in Transition*; and Bergman, *Local Economies.*

66. Phillips and Vidal, "Growth and Restructuring," p. 303, suspect that poor migrants to growing cities may displace workers already there, and Salinas, "Urban Growth," p. 261, found that moves south or west actually *reduced* a worker's probability of upward mobility!

67. Goodman, *Last Entrepreneurs.*

68. This was true of the Northeast in the 1980s. Harrison, "Regional Restructuring."

69. Mollenkopf, "Paths toward the Post Industrial Service City."

70. Edward Bergman, University of North Carolina, quoted in "The South Has Its Second Cities, and They Thrive," *New York Times*, April 23, 1989. Also see Glickman and Glasmeier, "International Economy."

71. The example comes from Soja, *Postmodern Geographies*.

72. Other exceptions include shops, offices, or schools in small cities or villages, to which a small number of employees walk, or those accessible by bus or streetcar in medium-sized cities.

73. Giuliano et al., "Employment Concentrations," provide excellent summaries of theories and evidence followed by interpretation of the Los Angeles data. The maps show little shrinkage if any in employment in the core but much growth outside, with Los Angeles County still totally dominant. Earlier dispersal in Orange County is now concentrated in larger, growing, and increasingly dense employment centers. The more peripheral counties are still dispersed but are likely to concentrate as they grow.

74. Glaeser, Kahn, and Chu, *Job Sprawl*, list 100 areas, but 8 were subordinate parts of larger CMSAs.

75. See Brueckner et al., "Local Labor Markets," and Brueckner and Zenou, "Space and Unemployment."

76. See Pendall, Goldsmith, and Esnard, "Thinning Rochester." The metro population fell 2 percent in 1970–1990, then rose 4 percent by 2005. The *city* population declined 37 percent from a peak of 330,000 in 1950 to 207,000 in 2005.

77. In 2003 the Census changed the definitions, no longer recognizing central cities but rather identifying "principal" cities in metropolitan areas. In 2000 the metropolitan population outside central cities was 146 million, and outside principal cities, 140 million.

78. Katz and Lang, *Redefining Urban and Suburban America*, vol. 1, intro.

79. Katz and Lang, *Redefining Urban and Suburban America*, vol. 1, intro.

80. See Abrahamson, *Urban Enclaves*.

81. The Brazilian political scientist Lucio Kowarick, a leading student of urban affairs, focuses on exclusion. See, for example, Catholic Church, *São Paulo*, and Kowarick, *Social Struggles and the City*. Also see Caldeira, *City of Walls*. Blakely and Snyder, *Fortress America*, focus on the gated community as a means of exclusion.

82. See Massey and Denton, *American Apartheid*, and Iceland et al., "Class Differences."

83. Fischer et al., "Distinguishing the Geographic Levels," note that segregation of the *very* poor would show even larger increases.

84. See Fishman, *Bourgeois Utopias*, for discussion of the historical English denigration of the periphery, the place for cemeteries, thieves, and prostitutes. In today's world, signs of convergence appear, as middle-class suburbs, often "gated," appear in many countries, and in the United States there are exceptions, where the rich live not only in the suburbs but also in the centers. Yet strong differences persist.

85. Watson, "Metropolitan Growth."

86. Yang and Jargowsky, "Suburban Development." They measure inequality by the neighborhood sorting index (NSI) and suburbanization by density gradient, population density, homogeneity of new growth, the number of local governments (to measure exclusion), and job-travel time for central-city residents (to measure inaccessibility).

87. Kneebone and Berube, *Reversal of Fortune*.

88. Galster and Santiago, "What's the 'Hood Got to Do with It?" These effects are drawn from the literature and are tentative. Holloway and Mulherin, "Effect of Adolescent Neighborhood Poverty," offer theory and evidence to argue that adolescents growing up in poor neighborhoods suffer lasting bad effects on their chances of getting good jobs. Despite these negative neighborhood effects, low-income parents think their own positive influence can prove sufficient.

89. Massey, "Ethnic Residential Segregation."

90. See Massey and Denton, "Hypersegregation," and Clark, "Residential Segregation."

91. This is an important component of W. J. Wilson's argument in *Truly Disadvantaged*.

92. The human (or urban) ecology school, including "social area analysis," analyzes racial and ethnic group location by socioeconomic status, with an almost organic conception of cities in which the dynamics of urban form are tied to processes that generate "efficient" or functional outcomes.

93. Berry and Kasarda, *Contemporary Urban Ecology*, discuss models of "factorial ecology."

94. Even most urban ecology proponents admit that the theory fails to explain why African Americans are located where they are and, more importantly, why they have not been able to move to other locations as rapidly as Whites as their incomes rise.

95. On use of these terms, see Wacquant, "Three Pernicious Premises." Also see Gans, "Deconstructing the Underclass."

96. Iceland et al., "Class Differences." The standard source is Massey and Denton, *American Apartheid*. Literally scores of other findings appear in monographs on the Census, done every decade.

97. "Black self-segregation plays a statistically significant, albeit minor role in explaining housing segregation," as Ihlanfeldt and Scafidi point out in "Black Self-segregation," adding, "The best known measure of housing segregation between blacks and whites is the dissimilarity index, which indicates the share of either racial group that would have to move to obtain an even distribution of the two groups across locations. While this index has tended to decline over time in most places, these declines have been modest in magnitude."

98. Frey and Farley, "Latino, Asian, and Black Segregation," report that for the twenty-three metro areas with the largest black populations, the average value of the index fell from 78.8 in 1980 to 74.5 in 1990.

99. Marcuse, "Shifting Meaning of the Black Ghetto."

100. Yinger, *Closed Doors*.

101. Goldsmith, "Ghetto as a Resource."

102. Clay, "Process of Black Suburbanization."

103. Berube and Kneebone, *Two Steps Back*, and Eyal Press, "The New Suburban Poverty," *Nation*, April 23, 2007.

104. Massey and Denton, "Trends in Residential Segregation," p. 803.

105. The percentages of White movers and Asian movers are identical. A census tract has about 4,200 residents.

106. Logan et al., "Segregation of Minorities," citing works by Keating and Good. Various studies have shown low degrees of voluntary segregation by minorities and high degrees of White preference for small numbers of Black neighbors or none at all. Using data from a major study of Atlanta, Boston, Detroit, and Los Angeles, Adelman, "Neighborhood Opportunities," concluded that "African-American homeowners are forced to buy in segregated neighborhoods."

107. Velez and Martin, "Latino Segregation Patterns."

108. Rosenbaum and Argeros, "Holding the Line."

109. Logan et al., "Segregation of Minorities," p. 19.

110. Logan et al., "Segregation of Minorities," p. 20.

111. Puentes and Warren, "One-Fifth of America," look at "first suburbs" surrounding fifty-two "major or center cities."

112. Keating and Bier, "Greater Cleveland's First Suburbs Consortium."

113. Berube and Kneebone, *Two Steps Back*.

114. Velez and Martin, "Latino Segregation Patterns."

115. Norman, "Bright Lights, Little Cities."

116. Winders, "Changing Politics."

117. Pamuk, "Geography of Immigrant Clusters."

118. On violence, see Chapter 2. Local legislatures pass laws hostile to immigrants, laws that are sometimes reversed, sometimes upheld in the courts. See Julia Preston, "In Reversal, Courts Uphold Local Immigration Laws," *New York Times*, February 10, 2008, and Damien Café, "Facing Local Demand, States Take New Tack on Illegal Immigration," *New York Times*, June 9, 2008. On the immigration experience, see "Remade in America: The Newest Immigrants and Their Impact," various items, *New York Times*, 2009, available at http://projects .nytimes.com/immigration/.

119. See Wacquant, "From Slavery to Mass Incarceration."

120. The explanation would apply not only to literal descendants of Africans enslaved in the United States but also to dark-skinned people, including Latinos (some Dominicans, Puerto Ricans, Cubans, and Haitians).

121. Frey, "Melting Pot Suburbs."

122. Holloway and Mulherin, "Effect of Adolescent Neighborhood Poverty."

123. Wilkes and Iceland, "Hypersegregation."

124. Kneebone and Berube, *Reversal of Fortune*. Deep poverty here means that 40 percent of the neighborhood's households are officially poor. Jargowsky, "Stunning Progress," notes that the most dramatic declines of the 1990s were in Midwest rust-belt metros and the South.

125. Iceland, "Why Concentrated Poverty Fell."

126. The working poor are defined here as those who receive payments from the Earned Income Tax Credit, the EITC.

127. Kneebone and Berube, *Reversal of Fortune*.

128. Wagmiller, "Changing Geography of Male Joblessness."

129. Wagmiller, "Race and the Spatial Segregation of Jobless Men."

130. Wagmiller, "Male Nonemployment."

131. Wagmiller, "Male Nonemployment," cites many authorities in this concluding paragraph.

132. Steinberg, "Turning Back,'" p. 149.

133. Lichter, "Racial Differences."

134. Freedman, "Urban Labor Markets."

135. Of every 100 ninth-graders nationally, 68 graduate on time, 40 enroll immediately in college, 27 are still enrolled as sophomores, and 18 graduate from college within six years. *Measuring Up, 2006: The National Report Card on Higher Education*, September 7, 2006, http://measuringup.highereducation.org/, has several useful reports and files, including a national overview and state reports. Science test data for 2002 from the National Center for Higher Education Management Systems, cited in *USA Today*, November 14, 2006. Sable and Garofano, "Public Elementary and Secondary School Student Enrollment." On earnings, see Henry Levin and Nigel Holmes, "America's Learning Deficit," *New York Times*, November 6, 2005. On global rankings for ages 25–35, see Young, National Center for Public Policy and Higher Education, cited in Tamar Lewin, "Report Finds U.S. Students Lagging in Finishing College," *New York Times*, September 7, 2006.

136. Nancy Zuckerbrod, "More Than 1 in 10 U.S. High Schools Are 'Dropout Factories,'" Associated Press, October 29, 2007.

137. Diana Jean Schemo, "Most Students in Big Cities Lag Badly in Basic Science," *New York Times*, November 16, 2006.

138. Kerner Commission, *Report*, p. 278.

139. Grengs, "Does Public Transit Counteract the Segregation of Carless Households?"

140. For incomes, see Pucher and Renne, "Socioeconomics of Urban Travel"; for race, see National Household Travel Survey, 2001, available at http://nhts.ornl.gov/index.shtml.

141. Leonard, "Interaction," pp. 3–6. Mayer and Jencks, "Growing Up," review dozens of studies and conclude that "the 'spatial mismatch' hypothesis . . . fail[s] to match the evidence." Also see Ellwood, "Spatial Mismatch."

142. Meyer and Gómez-Ibáñez, *Autos, Transit and Cities*, p. 231, cited in Leonard, "Interaction," p. 5.

143. Ellwood, "Spatial Mismatch."

144. It was these notions that gave rise to the enormous controversy among researchers and policymakers when Kain and Persky first presented "Alternatives to the Gilded Ghetto." See Goldsmith, "Ghetto as a Resource."

145. Wilson, *Truly Disadvantaged*.

146. O'Regan and Quigley, "Labor Market Access."

CHAPTER 5. REBUILDING THE AMERICAN CITY

1. The U.S. Conference of Mayors held the 2008 Mayors' Action Forum on Poverty in Los Angeles, September 23–24, 2008. The conference presented a "National Action Agenda on Poverty for the Next President of the United States" in which it identified poverty as a serious issue facing cities, one that requires national solutions.

2. "Since 1992, HUD has awarded 446 HOPE VI grants in 166 cities. As of the end of 2002, 15 of 165 funded HOPE VI programs were fully complete (U.S. GAO 2003b). The billions of federal dollars allocated for HOPE VI have leveraged billions more in other public, private, and philanthropic investments." Popkin et al., "Decade of HOPE VI."

3. Popkin et al., "Decade of HOPE VI."

4. Clintonomics are sometimes called Rubinomics, after Treasury Secretary Robert Rubin, who came to the Clinton White House from Goldman Sachs and whose many protégés have joined the Obama economics team.

5. Kantor, "Case for a National Urban Policy"; Goldsmith, "Drug War and Inner-City Neighborhoods."

6. Agnew, "Market Relations"; Boaden, *Urban Policy Making*; and Kantor, "Case for a National Urban Policy," p. 408.

7. Clavel, *Progressive City*.

8. Phillips, *Politics of Rich and Poor*, and Stockman, *Triumph of Politics*, expose evidence of the do-nothing, laissez-faire, benign-neglect approach to problems of the poor that was so popular among conservatives in the Reagan administration.

9. The term is from T. H. Marshall's 1949 lecture, cited by Hirschman, *Rhetoric of Reaction*.

10. Hirschman, *Rhetoric of Reaction*, p. 63.

11. See comments on Charles Murray, *Losing Ground*, by Hirschman, *Rhetoric of Reaction*, pp. 29–32.

12. Forrester, "Counterintuitive Behavior"; Glazer, *Limits of Social Policy*; and Murray, *Losing Ground*, all quoted by Hirschman, *Rhetoric of Reaction*, ch. 2. Hirschman, pp. 29–30, comments on Murray: "almost any idea that has been out of view for a long time has a good chance of being mistaken for an original insight."

13. Hirschman, *Rhetoric of Reaction*.

14. Howell, *Fighting Unemployment*.

15. Hirschman, *Rhetoric of Reaction.*

16. Piven and Cloward, *Regulating the Poor.* Note also the "we/they" dichotomy suggested in the quotation by Murray in the text just above.

17. Ellwood, *Poor Support,* p. 137.

18. *Citadel* is the word used by Peter Marcuse in "The Enclave, the Citadel, and the Ghetto."

19. Ellwood, *Poor Support,* p. 159, points out that the federal focus has moved about, from individuals, to communities, and back to individuals, but he and others also leave no doubt about the effectiveness of transfer payments.

20. Thurow, "Surge in Inequality," p. 36.

21. Thurow, "Surge in Inequality," p. 36.

22. Loewen, *Sundown Towns,* p. 3.

23. Patterson, *America's Struggle against Poverty,* pp. 60–76.

24. Herbers, "Kerner Report," p. 20.

25. Kerner Commission, *Report,* p. 221.

26. Kerner Commission, *Report,* p. 223.

27. Bill Moyers interview, March 28, 2008.

28. Blauner, *Racial Oppression*; Goldsmith, "Ghetto as a Resource."

29. Goldsmith and Derian, "Is There an Urban Policy?" The increase from 1967 to 1978 was eightfold.

30. Brecher and Horton, *Setting Municipal Priorities,* p. 11.

31. Mollenkopf, *Contested City.*

32. Lemann, "Unfinished War."

33. Peterson, *City Limits,* pp. 212–213.

34. Yates, *Ungovernable City,* p. 51.

35. Landau, *Race, Poverty and the Cities,* p. 37.

36. Landau, *Race, Poverty and the Cities,* p. 37; see Luria and Russell, *Rational Reindustrialization.*

37. Lemann, "Unfinished War."

38. Vidal, "Beyond Housing."

39. Vidal, "Beyond Housing."

40. Walters, "Cities on Their Own," p. 29.

41. By the 2000s, to make matters worse, the limited resources available to cities had usually been turned to other matters, such as competition for business growth. Walters, "Cities on Their Own," pp. 27–32.

42. Quigley and Rubinfeld, *American Domestic Priorities,* p. 97.

43. Quigley and Rubinfeld, *American Domestic Priorities,* pp. 127–128; this consolidation was done with the Educational Consolidation and Improvement Act of 1981.

44. U.S. Department of Commerce, *Statistical Abstracts of the United States,* 1989 edition.

45. McGeary and Lynn, *Urban Change and Poverty,* p. 298.

46. Palmer and Sawhill, *Reagan Experiment,* pp. 10–11.

47. Michael Janofsky, "HUD Asks Money for Housing and Jobs for Urban Homeless," *New York Times,* February 2, 1998.

48. Leading poverty scholars Wilson, Ellwood, Moynihan, and Katz, as well as leading business spokespersons and others coming from various political directions, all agreed that on *this* score policies advocated by Social Democrats (or Democratic Socialists?) were correct.

49. Sandefur, of the Institute for Research on Poverty, points to the importance of these four areas, in "Blacks, Hispanics, American Indians," pp. 57–68; for a conservative statement, see Peterson, *New Urban Reality,* pp. 24–29.

50. Heritage Foundation, "Issues: Transportation and Smart Growth," available at http://www.heritage.org/Research/SmartGrowth/index.cfm.

51. Krugman, *Conscience of a Liberal*, p. 12.

52. Polanyi, *Great Transformation*, long ago offered powerful illustrations of how social rules always govern markets. Krugman, *Conscience of a Liberal*.

53. Blakely, *Planning Local Economic Development*, p. 34.

54. Although perhaps no one says explicitly that a high demand for workers is *not* an important requirement for an improved distribution of income and a reduction of poverty, many avoid mentioning it.

55. In the debates on ghetto underdevelopment in the 1970s, otherwise differing analysts agreed on this point. See, for example, the reviews by Goldsmith, "Ghetto as a Resource," and Harrison, "Ghetto Economic Development."

56. Ellwood, *Poor Support*.

57. William Holstein, editor of *Business Week*, lecture at Cornell University, quoted in a project report to Alan McAdams by Bayer et al., "Project USA," p. 58.

58. Bayer et al., "Project USA," p. 56.

59. The figures are from President's Commission on Industrial Competitiveness, *Global Competition*; the National Academy of Sciences; the Internal Revenue Service; economist Gary Jufbauer of Georgetown University; and Peter Huber of the Manhattan Institute, all cited in Bayer et al., "Project USA," p. 56.

60. Eisner, "Our Real Deficits," p. 135.

61. Reich, "Real Economy."

62. EIR Economics Staff, "Scope of the U.S. Infrastructure Deficit," p. 14.

63. McKinsey & Company, Social Sector Office, "Economic Impact of the Achievement Gap."

64. Bayer et al., "Project USA," p. 56.

65. Bayer et al., "Project USA," pp. 57–58, 61. Unless otherwise noted, this is the source for information on industrial policy.

66. *Economist*, February 17, 2009, p. 32.

67. This bad effect is aside from the debates about the public *funding* of private schools. It is worth noting that considerable public aid to these (relatively privileged) private schools is already provided. Aside from books, health services, and other benefits, in New York State, for example, public school districts are *required* to pay for buses to transport private school children, and they must do this even when they do not bus their own students!

68. Comments posted on the *New York Times* Web site in response to Teri Karush Rogers, "The Sudden Charm of Public School," *New York Times*, April 5, 2009.

69. *Newsweek*, May 6, 1991, p. 31.

70. From the 40th Annual PDK/Gallup Poll.

71. Adam Nossiter, "A Tamer of Schools Has Plan in New Orleans," *New York Times*, September 27, 2007.

72. "In the first week of school, Mr. Vallas's bunkerlike command post was buzzing with activity well after quitting time. His own plans are delivered in short, staccato bursts; he is brimming not so much with optimism as with projects. The strategy is hardly new. Mr. Vallas put elements of it into effect in the much larger cities he served previously. Yet the scale of it, in New Orleans, will have to be much bigger because of the greater poverty here. Considerably more than half the children here will require this total approach, he said, unlike in Chicago, say, where the figure would have been closer to a third." Nossiter, "Tamer of Schools." Also see Paul Tough, "A Teachable Moment," *New York Times Magazine*, August 14, 2008.

73. Goldsmith, "Any Fix for Urban Schools?"

74. In Ithaca, New York, for example, the Alternative Community School, a member of the National Coalition of Essential Schools, is directed by an advisory board of parents, community members, school staff, and students.

75. NHSA, "Head Start Benefits."

76. NHSA, "Head Start Benefits."

77. National Security Agency, "Opportunities for You," a list of work-study opportunities for high school students with the NSA, is regularly updated with new listings, available at http://www.nsa.gov/careers/opportunities_4_u/index.shtml.

78. Urhan et al., *One in 31.*

79. "Newark Mayor: Black Leaders Must Innovate," *NPR Morning Edition,* August 8, 2006. Also see Gaes, "Impact of Prison Education Programs."

80. Rukus, "San Francisco's Reentry Strategy."

81. The Cornell (University) Prison Education Program is one such pilot operating with great success. See http://www.sce.cornell.edu/sce/cpep.php.

82. The Republican right wing tried to privatize Social Security, but that "reform" is a dead letter after the Wall Street collapse. The combination of Social Security taxes and payments is regressive—the rich pay lower proportional taxes but get higher absolute transfers.

83. Hotz and Scholz, "Earned Income Tax Credit," quoted in Holt, "Earned Income Tax Credit at Age 30."

84. Holt, "Earned Income Tax Credit at Age 30."

85. Danziger, "Antipoverty Policy," quoted in Sandefur, "Blacks, Hispanics, American Indians," p. 67.

86. Labor Secretary Robert Reich estimated in 1991 that taxing all income from Social Security, raising the payroll tax ceiling by $10,000, and increasing by one-half percent the contributions by married persons would increase the yield by $700 billion per year (in 1991 terms). "Real Economy."

87. Rossi and Wright, "Urban Homeless."

88. For racial breakdowns, see Beal et al., "Closing the Divide."

89. We note W. J. Wilson's caution about race-specific policies, but we find racial discrimination so thoroughly woven through the social fabric that we cannot see how programs of affirmative action can be avoided if fairness is to be achieved. The problem, as Wilson points out, is to make it work for the poor. Wilson, *Truly Disadvantaged.*

90. See, for example, Goldsmith and Vietorisz, "Operation Bootstrap."

91. *Economist,* February 6, 2009.

92. *New York Times,* May 6, 1985, p. 23.

93. Kevin Sack, "With Son in Remission, Family Looks for Coverage," *New York Times,* April 20, 2009.

94. Reuters, "Doctors Support Universal Health Care: Survey," March 31, 2008, available at http://www.reuters.com/article/idUSN31432035.

95. President's Commission on Industrial Competitiveness, *Global Competition.*

96. Elizabeth Neuffer, "Poor Skills Cited in New York Entry-Level Applicants," *New York Times,* July 4, 1987, p. 29.

97. Sam Dillon, "'No Child' Law Is Not Closing a Racial Gap," *New York Times,* April 29, 2009.

98. Swanson, "Closing the Graduation Gap."

99. Minorities, specifically Black Americans, were uniformly excluded from New Deal benefits, through all the northern urban exclusions documented in earlier chapters and also through exclusions designed to satisfy White southerners.

100. Hayden, *Redesigning the American Dream.*

101. Title XII of H.R. 1 (2009) also allocates $8 billion for investment for intercity high-speed rail.

102. In a discussion with Gerald Frug at a Cornell University seminar, May 2, 2009, it was pointed out that in many western European countries, unlike the United States, mayors often seize national power, either through ex officio appointments or because their municipal positions serve as ladders to national political prominence.

103. Clavel, *Progressive City;* Clavel, *Progressive Cities and Neighborhood Planning;* and Clavel, "Progressive City as Planning History."

104. Goldsmith, "São Paulo as a World City."

105. Goldsmith and Vainer, "Participatory Budgeting."

106. On Bogotá and Medellín, see Vega, "Internal Displacement and Urbanization." On Latin American cities more generally, see Chavez and Goldfrank, "Left in the City," and various works by Martim Smolka, including Smolka and Larangeira, "Informality and Poverty in Latin American Urban Policies."

107. Bennington, "Local Economic Strategies."

108. See Clavel, *Progressive Cities and Neighborhood Planning.*

109. Briggs, *Democracy as Problem-Solving.*

110. Clavel, "Progressive City as Planning History."

111. The city's authority for same-sex marriage was reversed by the state supreme court, and the issue later shifted to state-level politics.

112. U.S. Conference of Mayors, "Climate Protection Agreement," 2008.

113. Clavel and Kleniewski, "Space for Progressive Local Policy," p. 20.

114. Blakely, *Planning Local Economic Development,* p. 50.

115. Logan and Swanstrom, *Beyond City Limits,* pp. 5–6.

116. Clavel and Wiewel, *Harold Washington and the Neighborhoods.* City freedom to innovate is strictly limited by state constitutions, as Frug and Barron show in *City Bound.*

117. We constructed this set of four from a longer list in Clavel and Wiewel, *Harold Washington and the Neighborhoods,* pp. 19–30. Unless noted otherwise, all the information and the citations in this subsection are from that source.

118. Shearer, "In Search of Equal Partnerships."

119. When a "longtime BCA state legislator and ally and moved into the mayoralty in 2002, [he] governed as a 'progressive' rather than BCA [Berkeley Citizens Action] leader." Clavel, "Progressive City as Planning History."

120. Krumholz and Forester, *Making Equity Planning Work.*

121. Clavel, "Progressive City as Planning History."

122. Clavel, "Progressive City as Planning History."

123. Livingstone, *If Voting Changed Anything.*

124. So outraged was the prime minister at the head of the Greater London Council that she sold the county hall to a Japanese entertainment company.

125. This is a point made by Clavel in various places.

126. Fainstein, "Economics, Politics, and Development Policy." See also Fainstein, *City Builders.*

127. Achtenberg, "Preserving Expiring Use Projects" and "Federally-Assisted Housing."

128. The Federal Low Income Housing Preservation and Resident Homeownership Act of 1990.

129. See also Davis, *Affordable City.*

130. Achtenberg judged it unlikely that even a majority of the threatened housing would be saved, because of the enormously high costs of paying off the windfall profits, which federal legislation promised to the landlords.

131. Web sites for these organizations: http://www.prrac.org/ and http://www.plannersnetwork.org/.

132. See Davis, *Contested Ground.*

133. Frug, "City as a Legal Concept."

134. Gunn and Gunn, *Reclaiming Capital.*

135. See Mier et al., "Strategic Planning."

136. Markusen, "Steel and Southeast Chicago."

137. Giloth and Mier, "Spatial Change and Social Justice."

138. Shlay and Giloth, "Social Organization."

139. Information from our conversations with Robert Mier.

140. See Mier et al., "African-American Elected Officials."

Bibliography

Abrahamson, Mark. *Urban Enclaves: Identity and Place in America.* New York: St. Martin's Press, 1996.

Abu-Lughod, Janet L. *New York, Chicago, Los Angeles: America's Global Cities.* Minneapolis: University of Minnesota Press, 1999.

Achtenberg, Emily Paradise. "Federally-Assisted Housing in Conflict: Privatization or Preservation?" In *A Right to Housing: Foundation for a New Social Agenda,* ed. Rachel G. Bratt, Michael E. Stone, and Chester Hartman. Philadelphia: Temple University Press, 2006.

———. "Preserving Expiring Use Projects: Strategies for Social Ownership and Permanent Affordability." Photocopy, unpublished manuscript. Cambridge, Mass., May 22, 1991.

Acs, Gregory, and Margery Austin Turner. "Making Work Pay Enough: A Decent Standard of Living for Working Families." Urban Institute. July 16, 2008. Available at http://www.urban.org/publications/411710.html.

Adams, Terry K., Greg J. Duncan, and Willard L. Rogers. "The Persistence of Urban Poverty." In *Quiet Riots: Race and Poverty in the United States,* ed. Fred R. Harris and Roger W. Wilkins, 78–99. New York: Pantheon, 1988.

Adelman, Robert M. "Neighborhood Opportunities, Race, and Class: The Black Middle Class and Residential Segregation." *City & Community* 3, no. 1 (2004): 43–63.

Agnew, J. A. "Market Relations and Locational Conflict in Cross-National Perspective." In *Urbanization and Conflict in Market Societies,* ed. K. R. Cox, 128–143. Chicago: Maaroufa Press, 1978.

Alderson, Arthur S., Jason Beckfield, and François Nielsen. "Exactly How Has Income Inequality Changed? Patterns of Distributional Change in Core Societies." *Luxembourg Income Study Working Papers,* May 2005.

Alfonzo, Mariela. "A Mall in a Former Life: How Converting Former Malls into Mixed-Use Neighborhoods Impacts Sense of Community." Ph.D. dissertation, University of California, Irvine, 2007.

Allegretto, Sylvia A. "Basic Family Budgets: Working Families' Incomes Often Fail to Meet Living Expenses around the US." Economic Policy Institute, September 1, 2005.

Alternatives Federal Credit Union. *Alternatives Federal Credit Union Living Wage Study (2007): Living Wage Chart 2007*. 2009. Available at http://www.alternatives.org/livingwagechart 2009.html.

Appelbaum, E. "Restructuring Work: Temporary, Part-Time and At-Home Employment." In *Computer Chips and Paper Clips: Technology and Women's Employment*, ed. Heidi Hartmann. Washington, D.C.: National Academy Press, 1986.

Ashton, Patrick J. "Urbanization and the Dynamics of Suburban Development under Capitalism." In *Marxism and the Metropolis: New Perspectives in Urban Political Economy*, ed. W. K. Tabb and L. Sawers, 54–81. New York: Oxford University Press, 1984.

Assaad, Ragui. "Structured Labour Markets: The Case of the Construction Sector in Egypt." Ph.D. dissertation, Cornell University, 1990.

Babcock, Blair. *Unfairly Structured Cities*. Oxford: Basil Blackwell, 1984.

Bailey, Thomas, and Roger Waldinger. "The Changing Ethnic/Racial Division of Labor." In *Dual City: Restructuring New York*, ed. John Hull Mollenkopf and Manuel Castells, 43–78. New York: Russell Sage Foundation, 1991.

Bane, Mary Jo, and Paul Jargowsky. "Urban Poverty Areas: Basic Questions Concerning Prevalence, Growth, and Dynamics." Paper prepared for the Center for Health and Human Resource Policy, John F. Kennedy School of Government, Harvard University, Cambridge, Mass., February 28, 1988.

Banfield, Edward C. *The Unheavenly City: The Nature and Future of Our Urban Crisis*. Boston: Little, Brown, 1968.

Baran, Barbara. "Technological Innovation and Deregulation: The Transformation of the Labor Process in the Insurance Industries." Working paper, Berkeley Roundtable on the International Economy, University of California, Berkeley, 1985.

Bauer, David. "The Question of Foreign Investment." *New York Affairs* 6, no. 2 (1982): 52–58.

Baumol, William J., Sue Anne Batey Blackman, and Edward N. Wolff. *Productivity and American Leadership: The Long View*. Cambridge, Mass.: MIT Press, 1989.

Bayer, Michael, Lynn Little, and Stephen Silver, eds. "Project U.S.A.: A Study of American Competitiveness and What Must Be Done to Restore It." Report prepared for the Graduate School of Management, Cornell University, Ithaca, N.Y., June 15, 1991.

Beal, Anne, Michelle Doty, Susan Hernandez, Katherine Shea, and Karen Davis. "Closing the Divide: How Medical Homes Promote Equity in Health Care; Results from the Commonwealth Fund 2006 Health Care Quality Survey." *Health Policy, Health Reform, and Performance Improvement* 62 (June 27, 2007). Available at http://www.wafp.org/documents/closingthedivide.pdf.

Beckford, George. *Persistent Poverty: Underdevelopment in Plantation Economies*. New York: Oxford University Press, 1972.

Beneria, Lourdes. "The Crisis of Care, International Migration and the Capabilities Approach: Implications for Policy." Working Paper no. 4-07. Mario Einaudi Center for International Studies, Cornell University, June 2007.

———. *Gender, Development and Globalization: Economics as if All People Mattered*. New York: Routledge, 2003.

Bennington, John. "Local Economic Strategies." *Local Economy* 1 (1986): 7–24.

Bergman, Edward, ed. *Local Economies in Transition*. Durham, N.C.: Duke University Press, 1986.

Bernstein, Jared, and Karen Kornbluh. "Running Faster to Stay in Place: The Growth of Family Work Hours and Incomes." Washington, D.C.: New America Foundation, 2005. Available at http://www.newamerica.net/files/nafmigration/archive/Doc_File_2437_1.pdf.

Berry, Brian J., and John D. Kasarda. *Contemporary Urban Ecology*. New York: Macmillan, 1977.

Berube, Alan, Bruce Katz, and Robert E. Lang. *Redefining Urban and Suburban America: Evidence from Census 2000, Volume 2*. Washington, D.C.: Brookings Institution Press, 2005.

Berube, Alan, and Elizabeth Kneebone. *Two Steps Back: City and Suburban Poverty Trends, 1999–2005.* Washington, D.C.: Brookings Institution, 2006.

Bivens, Josh. "Shifting Blame for Manufacturing Job Loss: Effects of Rising Trade Deficit Should Not Be Ignored." Briefing Paper. Economic Policy Institute, Washington, D.C., April 2004.

Blackburn, McKinley L., David E. Bloom, and Richard B. Freeman. "The Declining Economic Position of Less Skilled American Men." In *A Future of Lousy Jobs: The Changing Structure of U.S. Wages,* ed. Gary Burtless, 31–67. Washington, D.C.: Brookings Institution, 1990.

Blakely, Edward J. *Planning Local Economic Development: Theory and Practice.* Newbury Park, Calif.: Sage, 1989.

Blakely, Edward J., and Mary Gail Snyder. *Fortress America: Gated Communities in the United States.* Washington, D.C.: Brookings Institution Press, 1999.

Blakely, Tony, Alistair Woodward, Oliver Razum, Nancy A. Ross, Michael Wolfson, Jean Marie Berthelot, James Dunn, George Kaplan, and John Lynch. "Income Inequality and Mortality in Canada and the United States." *British Medical Journal* 321, no. 7275 (December 16, 2000): 1532–1534.

Blanden, Jo. "'Bucking the Trend': What Enables Those Who Are Disadvantaged to Succeed Later in Life?" Working Paper no. 31, Department for Work and Pensions. Department of Economics, University of Surrey, and the Center for Economic Performance, LSE. 2006. Available at http://research.dwp.gov.uk/asd/asd5/WP31.pdf.

Blauner, Robert. *Racial Oppression in America.* New York: Harper and Row, 1972.

Bluestone, Barry, and Bennett Harrison. *The Deindustrialization of America: Plant Closings, Community Abandonment, and the Dismantling of Basic Industry.* New York: Basic Books, 1982.

Bluestone, Barry, Mary Huff Stevenson, and Russell Williams. *The Urban Experience: Economics, Society, and Public Policy.* Oxford: Oxford University Press, 2000.

Boaden, N. *Urban Policy Making.* Cambridge: Cambridge University Press, 1971.

Boardman, Jason D., Jarron M. Saint Onge, Rogers G. Richard, and Justin T. Denney. "Race Differentials in Obesity: The Impact of Place." *Journal of Health and Social Behavior* 46 (September 2005): 229–243.

Bobo, Lawrence, James R. Kluegel, and Ryan A. Smith, "Laissez-Faire Racism: The Crystallization of a 'Kindler, Gentler' Anti-Black Ideology." Russell Sage Foundation, June 1996.

Bobo, Lawrence, and Camille L. Zubrinsky. "Attitudes toward Residential Integration: Perceived Status Differences, Mere In-Group Preference, or Racial Prejudice?" *Social Forces* 74 (1996): 883–909.

Bonilla-Silva, Eduardo. *Racism without Racists: Color-Blind Racism and the Persistence of Racial Inequality in the United States.* Lanham, Md.: Rowman and Littlefield, 2003.

Boo, Katherine. "The Marriage Cure." *New Yorker,* August 18, 2003.

Boschken, Herman L. "Global Cities, Systemic Power and Upper-Middle-Class Influence." Paper presented at the annual meeting of the American Political Science Association, Boston, 2002.

Boston, Thomas. *Race, Class, and Conservatism.* Boston: Allen and Unwin, 1988.

———. "Segmented Labor Markets: New Evidence from a Study of Four Race-Gender Groups." *Industrial and Labor Relations Review* 44, no. 1 (1990): 99–115.

Botwinick, Howard J. *Wage Differentials and the Competition of Capitals.* Princeton, N.J.: Princeton University Press, 1992.

Boushey, Heather, Shawn Fremstad, Rachel Gragg, and Margy Waller. "Understanding Low-Wage Work in the United States." The Mobility Agenda, March 2007. Available at http://www.mobilityagenda.org/lowwagework.pdf.

Bradbury, Katherine L., and Lynne E. Browne. "Black Men in the Labor Market." *New England Economic Review* 18 (March–April 1986): 32–42.

Brecher, Charles, and Raymond D. Horton, eds. *Setting Municipal Priorities*. New York: New York University Press, 1989.

Brenner, Neil, and Roger Keil, eds. *The Global Cities Reader*. Routledge Urban Reader Series. London: Routledge, 2006.

Briggs, Xavier de Souza. *Democracy as Problem Solving: Civic Capacity in Communities across the Globe*. Cambridge, Mass.: MIT Press, 2008.

———. "The Power and Limits of Place: New Directions for Housing Mobility and Research on Neighborhoods." In *Poverty and Race in America: The Emerging Agendas*, ed. Chester Hartman, 168–172. Lanham, Md.: Lexington Books, 2006.

Brodkin, Karen. *How Jews Became White Folks and What That Says about Race in America*. New Brunswick, N.J.: Rutgers University Press, 1998.

Brown, Lester R. "Designing Cities for People Rather Than Cars." May 15, 2007. Available at http://postcarboncities.net/node/186.

Brueckner, Jan K., Jacques-François Thisse, and Yves Zenou. "Local Labor Markets, Job Matching, and Urban Location." *International Economic Review* 43 (2002): 155–171.

Brueckner, Jan K., and Yves Zenou. "Space and Unemployment: The Labor-Market Effects of Spatial Mismatch." *Journal of Labor Economics* 21 (2003): 242–246.

Burns, L. "The Urban Income Distribution." *Regional Science and Urban Economics* 5 (1975): 465–485.

Burnstein, Paul. *Discrimination, Jobs, and Politics*. Chicago: University of Chicago Press, 1985.

Burtless, Gary, ed. *A Future of Lousy Jobs: The Changing Structure of US Wages*. Washington, D.C.: Brookings Institution, 1990.

Button, K. J. "Infrastructure Investment, Endogenous Growth and Economic Convergence." *Annals of Regional Science* 32, no. 1 (1998): 145–162.

Caldeira, Teresa Pires do Rio. *City of Walls: Crime, Segregation, and Citizenship in São Paulo*. Berkeley: University of California Press, 2000.

Campaign for Tobacco-Free Kids. *Higher Cigarette Taxes: Reduce Smoking, Save Lives, Save Money*. February 19, 2009. Available at http://www.tobaccofreekids.org/reports/prices/.

Caro, Robert. *The Power Broker*. New York: Knopf, 1974.

Castells, M. "European Cities, the Informational Society, and the Global Economy." *New Left Review* 204 (March–April 1994): 18–32.

Catholic Church. Comissão Justiça e Paz de São Paulo. *São Paulo: Growth and Poverty*. London: Bowerdeen Press, 1978.

Chait, John. *The Big Con: Crackpot Economics and the Fleecing of America*. New York: Houghton Mifflin, 2007.

Chall, Daniel. "New York City's 'Skills Mismatch.'" *Federal Reserve Bank of New York Quarterly Review* 10 (Spring 1985): 20–27.

Chandler, Alfred. *The Visible Hand: The Managerial Revolution in American Business*. Cambridge, Mass.: Belknap Press, 1977.

Chavez, Daniel, and Benjamin Goldfrank. "The Left in the City: Progressive and Participatory Governments in Latin America." Latin American Bureau, 2004.

Christopherson, Susan. "Emerging Patterns of Work in the U.S." Paper presented to the OECD Working Group on Technological Change and Human Resources, Columbia University, New York, September 1988.

Clark, W.A.V. "Residential Segregation in American Cities: A Review and Interpretation." *Population Research and Policy Review* 5 (1986): 95–127.

Clavel, Pierre. *Progressive Cities and Neighborhood Planning, 1969–2005*. Ithaca, N.Y.: Cornell Library, Division of Rare and Manuscripts Collections. 2005. Online materials available at http://www.aap.cornell.edu/crp/research/pcnp/index.cfm.

———. *The Progressive City*. New Brunswick, N.J.: Rutgers University Press, 1986.

———. "The Progressive City as Planning History." Paper presented at the Society for American City and Regional Planning History, October 2007.

Clavel, Pierre, and Maile Deppe. "Innovation in Urban Policy: Movement and Incorporation in City Administration and Community Development." *Policy Studies Journal* 27, no. 1 (1999): 129–146.

Clavel, Pierre, and Nancy Kleniewski. "Space for Progressive Local Policy: Examples from the United States and the United Kingdom." In *Beyond the City Limits: Urban Policy and Economic Restructuring in Comparative Perspective,* ed. John R. Logan and Todd Swanstrom, 199–234. Philadelphia: Temple University Press, 1990.

Clavel, Pierre, and Wim Wiewel. *Harold Washington and the Neighborhoods: Progressive City Government in Chicago, 1983–1987.* New Brunswick, N.J.: Rutgers University Press, 1991.

Clay, Phillip L. "The Process of Black Suburbanization." *Urban Affairs Quarterly* 14, no. 6 (1979): 405–424.

Coates, Robert C. *A Street Is Not a Home.* Buffalo: Prometheus Books, 1990.

Cohen, Robert B. "The New International Division of Labor, Multinational Corporations and Urban Hierarchy." In *Urbanization and Urban Planning in Capitalist Society,* ed. Michael Dear and Allen J. Scott, 287–315. London: Methuen, 1981.

Cohen, Stephen, D. Teece, L. Tyson, and J. Zysman. "Competitiveness." Working Paper no. 8. Berkeley Roundtable on International Competitiveness, Berkeley, Calif., 1985.

Cohen, Stephen, and John Zysman. *Manufacturing Matters: The Myth of the Post-industrial Economy.* New York: Basic Books, 1987.

Congressional Budget Office. "What Accounts for the Decline in Manufacturing Employment?" Economic and Budget Issue Brief, February 18, 2004.

Cosby, Bill, and Alvin F. Poussaint. *Come On, People: On the Path from Victims to Victors.* Nashville, Tenn.: Nelson, 2007.

Council of Economic Advisors. *Economic Report of the President, 1991.* Washington, D.C.: U.S. Government Printing Office, 1991.

Cox, Michael W. and Richard Alm. "Off the Books." *Reason,* August/September 2002.

Crandall, Robert W. "The Decline in Manufacturing Jobs in the Syracuse Metropolitan Area." Brookings Institution, Washington, D.C., March 6, 2003.

———. "The Migration of U.S. Manufacturing and Its Impact on the Buffalo Metropolitan Area." Brookings Institution, Washington, D.C., July 6, 2002.

Crozier, Michel, Samuel Huntington, Joji Watanuki. *The Crisis of Democracy: Report on the Governability of Democracies to the Trilateral Commission.* New York: New York University Press, 1975.

Crump, Jeff R., and Christopher D. Merrett. "Scales of Struggle: Economic Restructuring in the U.S. Midwest." *Annals of the Association of American Geographers* 88, no. 3 (September 1998): 496–515.

Cummings, Bruce. "Archeology, Descent, Emergence: Japan in American Hegemony in the 20th Century." Lecture for the Program on International Studies in Planning, Cornell University, May 3, 1991.

Daly, M., M. Wilson, and S. Vasdev. "Income Inequality and Homicide Rates in Canada and the United States." *Canadian Journal of Criminology* 43 (2001): 219–236.

Daniels, Peter W. "New Office in the Suburbs." In *Suburban Growth: Geographical Process at the Edge of the Western City,* ed. J. E. Johnson, 177–200. Chichester, U.K.: Wiley, 1974.

Danziger, Sheldon H. "Antipoverty Policy and Welfare Reform." Paper presented at the Rockefeller Foundation Conference on Welfare Reform, Williamsburg, Va., February 16–18, 1988.

Darity, William A. "Racial Inequality in the Managerial Age: An Alternative Vision to the NRC Report." *American Economic Review* 80, no. 2 (1990): 247–251.

Darity, William A., Jr., and Samuel L. Myers Jr. *Persistent Disparity: Race and Economic Inequality in the United States since 1945.* Cheltenham, U.K.: Edward Elgar, 1998.

Davis, John Emmeus. *The Affordable City: Towards a Third-Sector Housing Policy.* Philadelphia: Temple University Press, 1994.

———. *Contested Ground: Collective Action and the Urban Neighborhood.* Ithaca, N.Y.: Cornell University Press, 1991.

———. "Shared Equity Homeownership: The Changing Landscape of Resale-Restricted, Owner-Occupied Housing National Housing." National Housing Institute, 2006.

Dear, Michael, and Jennifer Wolch. *Landscapes of Despair: From Deinstitutionalization to Homelessness.* Princeton, N.J.: Princeton University Press, 1987.

DeGiovanni, Frank. "Patterns of Change in Housing Market Activity in Revitalizing Neighborhoods." *Journal of the American Planning Association* 49 (Winter 1983): 22–39.

DeYoung, Curtiss Paul, Michael O. Emerson, George Yancey, and Karen Chai Kim. *United by Faith: The Multiracial Congregation as an Answer to the Problem of Race.* New York: Oxford University Press, 2003.

Dowd, Douglas. *Against the Conventional Wisdom: A Primer for Current Economic Controversies and Proposals.* Boulder, Colo.: Westview, 1997.

Drennan, Matthew P. "The Decline and Rise of the New York Economy." In *Dual City: Restructuring New York,* ed. John Hull Mollenkopf and Manuel Castells, 25–41. New York: Russell Sage Foundation, 1991.

———. *An Econometric Model of the New York City Region.* New York: New York University Press, 1985.

———. "The Local Economy." In *Setting Municipal Priorities,* 1990 volume, ed. Charles Brecher and Raymond D. Horton, 27–49. New York: New York University Press, 1989.

———. "Possible Sources of Wage Divergence among Metropolitan Areas of the United States." Paper presented at the Western Regional Science Association Meeting, San Diego, 2005.

Drennan, Matthew P., Emanuel Tobier, and Jonathan Lewis. "The Interruption of Income Convergence and Income Growth in Large Cities in the 1980s." *Urban Studies* 33, no. 1 (1996): 63–82.

Duncan, Greg J. *Years of Poverty, Years of Plenty: The Changing Economic Fortunes of American Workers and Families.* Ann Arbor: Survey Research Center, Institute for Social Research, University of Michigan, 1984.

Eargle, Judith. *Household Wealth and Asset Ownership: 1988.* Current Population Reports, Household Economic Studies, Series P-70, no. 22. Washington, D.C.: U.S. Department of Commerce, Bureau of the Census, 1990.

Eberts, Randall, George Erickcek, and Jack Kleinhenz. "Dashboard Indicators for the Northeast Ohio Economy." Working Paper. Fund for Our Economic Future, April 2006.

Edsall, Thomas Byrne. "Race." *Atlantic Monthly* (May 1991): 53–86.

EIR Economics Staff. "Scope of the U.S. Infrastructure Deficit." *Executive Intelligence Review* 34 (August 17, 2007).

Eisner, Robert. "Our Real Deficits." *Journal of the American Planning Association* 57, no. 2 (1991): 131–135.

Ellwood, David. *Poor Support: Poverty in the American Family.* New York: Basic Books, 1988.

———. "The Spatial Mismatch Hypothesis: Are There Teenage Jobs Missing in the Ghetto?" In *The Black Youth Employment Crisis,* ed. R. Freeman and H. Holzer, 147–190. Chicago: University of Chicago Press, 1986.

Erickson, David, Carolina Reid, Lisa Nelson, Anne O'Shaughnessey, and Alan Berube. *The Enduring Challenge of Concentrated Poverty in America.* Washington, D.C.: Federal Reserve System and Brookings Institution, 2008.

Ewen, Danielle, and Hannah Matthews. "Families Forgotten: Administration's Priorities Put Child Care Low on List." Clasp.org and the National Priorities Project, February 2007. Available at http://www.clasp.org/admin/site/publications/files/0341.pdf.

Faberman, R. Jason. "Job Flows, Establishment Characteristics, and Labor Market Dynamics in the US Rust Belt Region." *Monthly Labor Review* (September 2002): 3–10.

Fainstein, Norman I. "The Underclass/Mismatch Hypothesis as an Explanation for Black Economic Deprivation." *Politics and Society* 15, no. 4 (1986–1987): 403–451.

Fainstein, Susan S. *The City Builders: Property Development in New York and London, 1980–2000.* Lawrence: University Press of Kansas, 2001.

———. "Economics, Politics, and Development Policy: The Convergence of New York and London." In *Beyond the City Limits: Urban Policy and Economic Restructuring in Comparative Perspective,* ed. John R. Logan and Todd Swanstrom, 119–149. Philadelphia: Temple University Press, 1990.

Fajnzylber, P., D. Lederman, and N. Loayza. "Inequality and Violent Crime." *Journal of Law and Economics* 45, no. 1 (2002): 1–40.

Falk, William W., and Thomas A. Lyson. *High Tech, Low Tech, No Tech: Recent Industrial and Occupational Change in the South.* Albany: State University of New York Press, 1988.

Farley, Reynolds, and Steven Schecterman. "The Social and Economic Status of Blacks: Does It Vary by Size of Metropolis?" Photocopy. Population Studies Center, University of Michigan, Ann Arbor, June 1990.

Feagin, Joe R. *Racist America: Roots, Current Realities, and Future Reparations.* New York: Routledge, 2000.

Feagin, Joe R., Hernán Vera, and Pinar Batur. *White Racism.* New York: Routledge, 2001.

Ferguson, Mary. "A Growing Problem: Race Class and Obesity among American Women." In *Race, Class and America at the Millennium,* [2000?]. Available at http://journalism.nyu.edu/pubzone/race_class/race.htm.

Fernández-Kelly, María Patricia. *For We Are Sold, I and My People: Women and Industry in Mexico's Frontier.* Albany: State University of New York Press, 1983.

Fineman, Martha. "Dependency and Social Debt." In *Poverty and Inequality,* ed. David B. Grunsky and Ravi Kanbur, 133–150. Stanford, Calif.: Stanford University Press, 2006.

———. *The Illusion of Equality.* Chicago: University of Chicago Press, 1991.

Fischer, Claude S., Gretchen Stockmayer, John Stiles, and Michael Hout. "Distinguishing the Geographic Levels and Social Dimensions of U.S. Metropolitan Segregation, 1960–2000." *Demography* 41, no. 1 (February 2004): 37–59.

Fisher, Gordon M. "The Development of the Orshansky Poverty Thresholds and Their Subsequent History as the Official U.S. Poverty Measure." September 1997. U.S. Census Bureau. Available at http://www.census.gov/hhes/www/povmeas/papers/orshansky.html.

Fishman, Robert. *Bourgeois Utopias: The Rise and Fall of Suburbia.* New York: Basic Books, 2007.

Foley, Donald. "The Suburbanization of Administrative Offices in the San Francisco Bay Area." Research Report no. 10. Real Estate Research Program, Berkeley, Calif., 1957.

Forrester, Jay W. "Counterintuitive Behavior of Social Systems." *Technology Review,* 73, no. 3 (1971): 52–68.

Frank, Robert H. *Falling Behind: How Rising Inequality Harms the Middle Class.* Berkeley: University of California Press, 2007.

Frank, Robert H., and Philip J. Cook. *The Winner-Take-All Society: How More and More Americans Compete for Ever Fewer and Bigger Prizes, Encouraging Economic Waste, Income Inequality, and Impoverished Cultural Life.* New York: Free Press, 1995.

Frank, Robert, and Richard Freeman. "The Distributional Consequences of Direct Foreign Investment." In *The Impact of International Trade and Investment on Employment: A Conference of the U.S. Department of Labor,* ed. William Dewald, 153–176. Washington, D.C.: U.S. Government Printing Office, 1978.

Freedman, Marcia. "Urban Labor Markets and Ethnicity: Segments and Shelters Reexamined." In *Urban Ethnicity in the United States: New Immigrants and Old Minorities,* ed. L. Maldonado and J. Moore, 145–165. Urban Affairs Annual Reviews, vol. 29. Beverly Hills, Calif.: Sage, 1985.

Freeman, Christopher, John Clark, and Luc Soete. *Unemployment and Technical Innovation: A Study of Long Waves and Economic Development.* Westport, Conn.: Greenwood Press, 1982.

Freeman, Donald G. "Sources of Fluctuations in Regional Growth." *Annals of Regional Science* 35, no. 2 (2001): 249.

Freeman, R. B., and B. Hall. "Permanent Homelessness in America?" *Population Research and Policy Review* 6, no. 1 (1987): 3–27.

Frey, William H. "Diversity Spread Out: Metropolitan Shifts in Hispanic, Asian, and Black Populations since 2000." Brookings Institution, Washington, D.C., March 2006.

———. "Melting Pot Suburbs: A Census 2000 Study of Urban Diversity." Brookings Institution, Washington, D.C., June 2001.

Frey, William, and Reynolds Farley. "Latino, Asian, and Black Segregation in U.S. Metropolitan Areas: Are Multiethnic Metros Different?" *Demography* 33, no. 1 (1996): 35–50.

Friedhoff, Alec, and Howard Wial. "Bearing the Brunt: Manufacturing Job Loss in the Great Lakes Region, 1995–2005." Brookings Institution, Washington, D.C., July 2006.

Friedman, Thomas. *The World Is Flat.* New York: Farrar, Straus and Giroux, 2005.

Friedmann, John. "The World City Hypothesis." *Development and Change* 17, no. 1 (January 1986): 69–83.

Friedmann, John, and Goetz Wolff. "World City Formation: An Agenda for Research and Action." *International Journal of Urban and Regional Research* 6 (1982): 309–344.

Frobel, Folker, Jurgen Heinrichs, and Otto Kreye. *The New International Division of Labor: Structural Unemployment in Industrialized Countries and Industrialization in Developing Countries.* Cambridge: Cambridge University Press, 1980.

Frug, Gerald. "The City as a Legal Concept." *Harvard Law Review* 93, no. 6 (1980): 1059–1154.

———. *City Making: Building Communities without Building Walls.* Princeton, N.J.: Princeton University Press, 2001.

Frug, Gerald E., and David J. Barron. *City Bound: How States Stifle Urban Innovation.* Ithaca, N.Y.: Cornell University Press, 2008.

Fukuyama, Francis. *The End of History and the End of Man.* New York: Free Press, 1992.

Fulton, P. "Public Transportation: Solving the Commuting Problem?" *Transportation Research Record* 928 (1983): 3.

Gaes, Gerald G. "The Impact of Prison Education Programs on Post-release Outcomes." Paper presented at the Reentry Roundtable on Education, Washington, D.C., March 31–April 1, 2008.

Galbraith, John Kenneth. *A Tenured Professor: A Novel.* Boston: Houghton Mifflin, 1990.

Galster, George C., and Anna M. Santiago. "What's the 'Hood Got to Do with It? Parental Perceptions about How Neighborhood Mechanisms Affect Their Children." *Journal of Urban Affairs* 28, no. 3 (June 2006): 201–226.

Gans, Herbert J. "Deconstructing the Underclass: The Term's Dangers as a Planning Concept." *Journal of the American Planning Association* 56, no. 3 (1990).

———. "Uses and Misuses of Concepts in American Social Science Research: Variations on Loïc Wacquant's Theme of 'Three Pernicious Premises in the Study of the American Ghetto.'" *International Journal of Urban and Regional Research* 21, no. 3 (September 1997): 504–507.

Gardner, Lara, and Sharmila Vishwasrao. "Physician Quality and Health Care for the Poor and Uninsured." Working Papers no. 6001. Department of Economics, College of Business, Florida Atlantic University, 2007.

Garofalo, Gaspar, and Michael S. Fogarty. "Urban Income Distribution: The Urban Hierarchy-Inequality Hypothesis." *Review of Economics and Statistics* 61, no. 3 (1979): 381–388.

Gewande, Atil. "The Checklist." *New Yorker,* December 10, 2007.

Gilder, George. *Wealth and Poverty.* New York: Basic Books, 1981.

Gilmore, Ruth. *Golden Gulag: Prisons, Surplus, Crisis, and Opposition in Globalizing California.* Berkeley: University of California Press, 2007.

Giloth, Robert P., and Robert Mier. "Spatial Change and Social Justice: Alternative Economic Development in Chicago." In *Economic Restructuring and Political Response,* ed. Robert A. Beauregard, 181–208. Urban Affairs Annual Reviews, vol. 34. Beverly Hills, Calif.: Sage, 1989.

Giuliano, Genevieve, Christian Redfearn, Ajay Agarwal, Chen Li, and Duan Zhuang. "Employment Concentrations in Los Angeles, 1980–2000." *Environment and Planning A* 39, no. 12 (2007): 2935–2957.

Gladwell, Malcolm. "Risk Pool." *New Yorker,* August 28, 2006.

Glaeser, Edward L., Matthew Kahn, and Chenghuan Chu. *Job Sprawl: Employment Location in U.S. Metropolitan Areas.* Washington, D.C.: Brookings Institution, 2001.

Glaeser, Edward L., and Giacomo A. M. Ponzetto. "Did the Death of Distance Hurt Detroit and Help New York?" WP-2007–08. A. Alfred Taubman Center for State and Local Government, Harvard University, Cambridge, Mass., 2007.

Glazer, Nathan. *The Limits of Social Policy.* Cambridge, Mass.: Harvard University Press, 1990.

Glickman, Norman J. "Cities and the International Division of Labor." Working Paper no. 31. Lyndon B. Johnson School of Public Affairs, University of Texas, Austin, 1985.

Glickman, Norman J., and Amy K. Glasmeier. "The International Economy and the American South." In *Deindustrialization and Regional Economic Transformation: The Experience of the United States,* ed. Lloyd Rodwin and Hidehiko Sazanami, 60–80. Boston: Unwin Hyman, 1989.

Glickman, Norman J., and Douglas P. Woodward. *The New Competitors: How Foreign Investors Are Changing the U.S. Economy.* New York: Basic Books, 1989.

Goddard, J. B. *Office Location in Urban and Regional Development.* London: Oxford University Press, 1975.

Gold, Steven D. "State Fiscal Conditions." In *Urban Change and Poverty,* ed. Michael G. H. McGeary and Laurence E. Lynn, 284–307. Washington, D.C.: National Academy Press, 1988.

Goldsmith, William W. "Any Fix for Urban Schools?" *Journal of Urban Affairs* 25, no. 1 (2003): 107–111.

———. "Bringing the Third World Home: Enterprise Zones." *Working Papers Magazine* 9, no. 2 (1982): 24–30.

———. "The Drug War and Inner-City Neighborhoods." In *The Oxford Handbook of Urban Economics and Planning,* ed. Kieran Donaghy and Nancy Brooks. Oxford University Press, forthcoming.

———. "From the Metropolis to Globalization: The Dialectics of Race in Urban Form." In *Globalizing Cities: A New Spatial Order?* ed. Peter Marcuse and Ronald van Kempen, 37–55. Malden, Mass.: Blackwell, 2000.

———. "The Ghetto as a Resource for Black America." *Journal of the American Institute of Planners* 40, no. 1 (1974): 17–30.

———. "Giant Corporations Breed Bureaucracy and Big Government." *In These Times,* no. 15 (1978).

———. "Poverty and Profit in Urban Growth and Decline." In *Race, Poverty and the Urban Underclass,* ed. Clement Cottingham, 35–59. Lexington, Mass.: Heath, 1982.

———. "Resisting the Reality of Race: Land Use, Social Justice, and the Metropolitan Economy." Lincoln Institute of Land Policy, Cambridge, Mass., 1999.

———. "São Paulo as a World City: Industry, Misery, and Resistance." In *Social Struggles and the City: The Case of São Paulo,* ed. Lucio Kowarick, 13–30. New York: Monthly Review Press, 1994.

Goldsmith, William W., and Michael Derian. "Is There an Urban Policy?" *Journal of Regional Science* 19 (1979): 93–198.

Goldsmith, William W., and Harvey Jacobs. "The Improbability of Urban Policy: The Case of the United States." *Journal of the American Planning Association* 48, no. 1 (1982): 53–66.

Goldsmith, William W., and Mario Rothschild. "The Effect of Regional Specialization on Local Economic Activity: A Study of Chile." *Papers of the Regional Science Association* 31 (1974): 183–201.

Goldsmith, William W., and Carlos B. Vainer. "Participatory Budgeting and Power Politics in Porto Alegre." *Landlines* 13, no. 1 (2001): 7–9.

Goldsmith, William W., and Thomas Vietorisz. "Operation Bootstrap, Industrial Autonomy, and a Parallel Economy for Puerto Rico." *International Regional Science Review* 4, no. 1 (1979): 1–22.

Goodman, Robert. *The Last Entrepreneurs: America's Regional Wars for Jobs and Dollars.* New York: Simon and Schuster, 1979.

Gordon, David M. "Capitalist Development and the History of American Cities." In *Marxism and the Metropolis: New Perspectives in Urban Political Economy,* ed. W. K. Tabb and L. Sawers, 21–53. New York: Oxford University Press, 1984.

———. "The Global Economy: New Edifice or Crumbling Foundation?" *New Left Review* 168 (March–April 1988): 24–64.

Gordon, Peter, Harry W. Richardson, and Gang Yu. "Metropolitan and Non-metropolitan Employment Trends in the US: Recent Evidence and Implications." *Urban Studies* 35, no. 7 (1998): 1037–1057.

Gorz, André. *Strategy for Labor: A Radical Proposal.* Boston: Beacon Press, 1967.

Gray, Mia, Elyse Golob, Ann Markusen, and Sam Ock Park. "New Industrial Cities? The Four Faces of Silicon Valley." *Review of Radical Political Economics* 30, no. 4 (1998): 1–28.

Greenhouse, Steven. *The Big Squeeze: Tough Times for the American Worker.* New York: Knopf, 2008.

Greenstein, Robert, and Scott Barancik. *Drifting Apart: New Findings on Growing Income Disparities between the Rich, the Poor, and the Middle Class.* Washington, D.C.: Center on Budget and Policy Priorities, 1990.

Grengs, Joe. "Does Public Transit Counteract the Segregation of Carless Households? Measuring Spatial Patterns of Accessibility." *Transportation Research Board* 1753 (2001): 3–10, online January 31, 2007. Available at http://trb.metapress.com/content/a6723h2443t74060/.

———. "Job Accessibility and the Modal Mismatch in Detroit." *Journal of Transport Geography* 18, no. 1 (January 2010): 42–54. Available at http://dx.doi.org/10.1016/j.jtrangeo.2009.01.012.

Grier, Eunice, and George Grier. *Minorities in Suburbia: A Mid-1980's Update.* Washington, D.C.: Urban Institute, 1988.

Guglielmo, Jennifer, and Salvatore Salerno, eds. *Are Italians White? How Race Is Made in America.* New York: Routledge, 2003.

Gunn, Christopher, and Hazel Dayton Gunn. *Reclaiming Capital: Democratic Initiatives and Community Development.* Ithaca, N.Y.: Cornell University Press, 1991.

Hacker, Jacob. *The Great Risk Shift: The Assault on American Jobs, Families, Health Care, and Retirement—and How You Can Fight Back.* Oxford: Oxford University Press, 2006.

Hagen, Everett Einar. *Economics of Development.* Homewood, Ill.: Irwin, 1968.

Harrison, Bennett. "Ghetto Economic Development: A Survey." *Journal of Economic Literature* 12 (1974): 1–37.

———. *Lean and Mean: Why Large Corporations Will Continue to Dominate the Global Economy.* New York: Basic Books, 1994.

———. "Regional Restructuring and 'Good Business Climate': The Economic Transformation of New England since World War II." In *Sunbelt/Snowbelt: Urban Development and Regional Restructuring,* ed. Larry Sawers and William K. Tabb, 48–96. New York: Oxford University Press, 1984.

Harrison, Bennett, and Barry Bluestone. *The Great U-Turn: Corporate Restructuring and the Polarizing of America.* New York: Basic Books, 1988.

Harrison, Bennett, and Lucy Gorham. "What Happened to Black Wages in the 1980s: Family Incomes, Individual Earnings, and the Growth of the African American Middle Class." Working Paper no. 90-1. Carnegie Mellon University School of Urban and Public Affairs, Pittsburgh, 1990.

Hartman, Chester. "Comment on 'Neighborhood Revitalization and Displacement': A Review of the Evidence." *Journal of the American Planning Association* 45 (October 1979): 488–491.

Harvey, David. *The Condition of Postmodernity: An Enquiry into the Origins of Cultural Change.* Oxford: Blackwell, 1990.

———. "The Geopolitics of Capitalism." In *Social Relations and Spatial Structure,* ed. Derek Gregory and John Urry. New York: St. Martin's Press, 1985.

———. *The Limits to Capital.* Chicago: University of Chicago Press, 1982.

———. "The Right to the City." *New Left Review* 53 (September–October 2008): 24–39.

Haworth, C. T., J. Long, and D. Rasmussen. "Income Distribution, City Size, and Urban Growth." *Urban Studies* 15, no. 1 (1978): 1–7.

Hayden, Dolores. *Redesigning the American Dream: The Future of Housing, Work, and Family Life.* New York: Norton, 1984.

Hayek, Friedrich von. *The Road to Serfdom.* Chicago: University of Chicago Press, 1944.

Health Affairs. "Health Care Spending and Use of Information Technology in OECD Countries." *Health Affairs* (May–June 2006): 819–831.

Henderson, Hazel. *The Politics of the Solar Age: Alternatives to Economics.* Garden City, N.Y.: Anchor Press, Doubleday, 1981.

Herbers, John. "The Kerner Report: A Journalist's View." In *Quiet Riots: Race and Poverty in the United States,* ed. Fred R. Harris and Roger W. Wilkins, 16–26. New York: Pantheon, 1988.

Herz, Diane E. "Worker Displacement Still Common in the Late 1980s." *Monthly Labor Review* 14, no. 5 (1991): 3–9.

Hill, Edward W., and Thomas Bier. "Economic Restructuring, Earnings, Occupations, and Housing Values in Cleveland." *Economic Development Quarterly* 3, no. 2 (1989): 123–144.

Hill, Polly. *The Migrant Cocoa Farmers of Southern Ghana: A Study in Rural Capitalism.* Cambridge: Cambridge University Press, 1963.

Hirsch, B. "Income Distribution, City Size, and Urban Growth: A Reexamination." *Urban Studies* 19 (February 1982): 71–74.

Hirsch, Seev. *Location of Industry and International Competitiveness.* Oxford: Clarendon Press, 1967.

Hirschman, Albert O. *The Rhetoric of Reaction: Perversity, Futility, Jeopardy.* Cambridge, Mass.: Harvard University Press, 1991.

Holloway, Steven, and Stephen Mulherin. "The Effect of Adolescent Neighborhood Poverty on Adult Employment." *Journal of Urban Affairs* 26, no. 4 (October 2004): 427–454.

Holman, David, Rosemary Batt, and Ursula Holtgrewe. *The Global Call Center Report: International Perspectives on Management and Employment.* Ithaca, N.Y.: DigitalCommons@ILR, 2007.

Holt, Steve. "The Earned Income Tax Credit at Age 30: What We Know." Brookings Institution, Washington, D.C., February 2006.

Hoos, I. *Automation in the Office.* Washington, D.C.: Public Affairs Press, 1961.

Howell, David R. *Fighting Unemployment: The Limits of Free Market Orthodoxy.* Oxford: Oxford University Press, 2005.

Hymer, Stephen. *The Multinational Corporation: A Radical Approach.* Ed. Robert Cohen et al. Cambridge: Cambridge University Press, 1979.

Iceland, John. *Poverty in America: Handbook.* Berkeley: University of California Press, 2003.

———. "Why Concentrated Poverty Fell in the United States in the 1990s." Population Reference Bureau, August 2005.

Iceland, John, Cicely Sharpe, and Erika Steinmetz. "Class Differences in African American Residential Patterns in US Metropolitan Areas: 1990–2000." *Social Science Research* 34, no. 1 (March 2005): 252–256.

Iceland, John, Daniel H. Weinberg, and Erika Steinmetz. *U.S. Census Bureau, Series CENSR-3: Racial and Ethnic Residential Segregation in the United States: 1980–2000.* Washington, D.C.: U.S. Government Printing Office, 2002.

Ignatiev, Noel. *How the Irish Became White.* New York: Routledge, 1995.

Ihlanfeldt, Keith, and Benjamin Scafidi. "Black Self-Segregation as a Cause of Housing Segregation: Evidence from the Multi-city Study of Urban Inequality." *Journal of Urban Economics* 51, no. 2 (2002): 366–390.

Jackson, Kenneth. *Crabgrass Frontier: The Suburbanization of the United States.* New York: Oxford University Press, 1985.

Jacobs, Jane. *Cities and the Wealth of Nations.* New York: Random House, 1984.

Jargowsky, Paul A. "Stunning Progress, Hidden Problems: The Dramatic Decline of Concentrated Poverty in the 1990s." Brookings Institution, Washington, D.C., 2003.

Jargowsky, Paul A., and Mary Jo Bane. "Ghetto Poverty: Basic Questions." In *Inner City Poverty in the United States,* ed. Laurence E. Lynn and G. H. McGeary. Washington, D.C.: National Academy Press, 1990.

Jaynes, Gerald D., and Robin M. Williams Jr., eds. *A Common Destiny: Blacks in American Society.* Washington, D.C.: National Academy Press, 1989.

Jenkins, R. "Divisions over the International Division of Labor." *Capital and Class* 22 (Spring 1984): 28–57.

Jones, D., and R. Hall. "Office Suburbanization in the United States." *Town and County Planning* 40 (1972): 470–473.

Jun, Myung-Jin. "Are Portland's Smart Growth Policies Related to Reduced Automobile Dependence?" *Journal of Planning Education and Research* 28, no. 1 (2008): 100–107.

Kain, John F., and Joseph Persky. "Alternatives to the Gilded Ghetto." Discussion Paper no. 21. Program on Regional and Urban Economics, Harvard University, Cambridge, Mass., 1968.

Kantor, Paul. "A Case for a National Urban Policy: Governmentalization of Economic Dependency." *Urban Affairs Quarterly* 26, no. 3 (1990): 394–415.

Kasarda, John. "Jobs, Migration and Emerging Urban Mismatches." In *Urban Change and Poverty,* ed. Michael G. H. McGeary and L. E. Lynn Jr., 148–198. Washington, D.C.: National Academy Press, 1988.

———. "Urban Industrial Transition and the Underclass." *Annals of the American Academy of Political and Social Science* 501 (January 1989): 26–47.

Katz, Bruce, and Robert E. Lang. *Redefining Urban and Suburban America: Evidence from Census 2000, Volume 1.* Washington, D.C.: Brookings Institution Press, 2003.

Kawachi, Ichiro, Bruce P. Kennedy, and Richard G. Wilkinson. *The Society and Population Health Reader, Vol. 1: Income Inequality and Health.* New York: New Press, 1999.

Keating W. D., and T. Bier. "Greater Cleveland's First Suburbs Consortium: Fighting Sprawl and Suburban Decline." *Housing Policy Debate* 19, no. 3 (2008): 457–477.

Kennickell, Arthur B. "A Rolling Tide: Changes in the Distribution of Wealth in the U.S., 1989–2001." Finance and Economics Discussion Series 2003–24. Board of Governors of the Federal Reserve System (U.S.), 2003.

Kerner Commission. *Report of the National Advisory Commission on Civil Disorders.* New York: Dutton, 1968.

King, Anthony D. *Global Cities: Post-imperialism and the Internationalization of London.* International Library of Sociology. London: Routledge, 1990.

Kneebone, Elizabeth, and Alan Berube. *Reversal of Fortune: A New Look at Concentrated Poverty in the 2000s.* Washington, D.C.: Brookings Institution, 2008.

Knox, Taylor, and Gerald Sussman. "World Cities in a World System." *Journal of the American Planning Association* 62, no. 4 (1996): 541.

Kohn, Margaret. *Brave New Neighborhoods: The Privatization of Public Space.* New York: Routledge, 2004.

Kolko, Joyce. *Restructuring the World Economy.* New York: Pantheon, 1988.

Kowarick, Lúcio, ed. *Social Struggles and the City: The Case of São Paulo.* Trans. William H. Fisher and Kevin Mundy. New York: Monthly Review Press, 1994.

Krieger, Nancy, ed. *Embodying Inequality: Epidemologic Perspectives.* New York: Baywood, 2005.

Krugman, Paul. *The Conscience of a Liberal.* New York: Norton, 2009.

Krumholz, Norman, and John Forester. *Making Equity Planning Work: Leadership in the Public Sector.* Philadelphia: Temple University Press, 1990.

Lall, Betty, ed. "Economic Dislocation and Job Loss." Extension and Public-Service Division, New York State School of Industrial Relations, Metropolitan District, Cornell University, 1985.

Landau, Madeline. *Race, Poverty and the Cities: Hyperinnovation in Complex Policy Systems.* Berkeley: Institute for Governmental Studies, University of California, 1988.

Landis, John. "The Future of America's Central Cities." Working Paper no. 486. Institute of Urban and Regional Development, Berkeley, Calif., 1988.

Lawrence, R. *Can America Compete?* Washington, D.C.: Brookings Institution, 1984.

Leacock, Eleanor Burke, ed. *The Culture of Poverty: A Critique.* New York: Simon and Schuster, 1971.

Lefeber, Louis, and Thomas Vietorisz. "The Meaning of Social Efficiency." *Review of Political Economy* 19 (2007): 139–164.

Lemann, Nicholas. *The Promised Land.* New York: Knopf, 1991.

———. "The Unfinished War." *Atlantic Monthly* (January 1989): 37–56.

Leonard, Jonathan S. "The Interaction of Residential Segregation and Employment Discrimination." NBER Working Paper no. 1274. National Bureau of Economic Research, Cambridge, Mass., 1984.

Leontaridi, Marianthi Rannia. "Segmented Labour Markets: Theory and Evidence." *Journal of Economic Surveys* 12, no. 1 (1998): 63–102.

Lerner, Daniel. *The Passing of Traditional Society: Modernizing the Middle East.* New York: Free Press of Glencoe, 1958.

Levitan, Sar, and Isaac Shapiro. *Working but Poor: America's Contradictions.* Baltimore: Johns Hopkins University Press, 1987.

Lewis, Oscar. *Five Families: Mexican Case Studies in the Culture of Poverty.* New York: Basic Books, 1959.

Lichter, D. T. "Racial Differences in Underemployment in American Cities." *American Journal of Sociology* 93 (January 1988): 771–792.

Liebow, Elliot. *Tally's Corner: A Study of Negro Street Corner Men.* Boston: Little, Brown, 1967.

Liming, Drew, and Michael Wolf. "Job Outlook by Education: 2006–2016." BLS Employment Projections, Fall 2008.

Linder, Staffan. *An Essay on Trade and Transformation.* New York: Wiley, 1961.

Lipietz, Alain. "Imperialism or the Beast of the Apocalypse." *Capital and Class* 22 (Spring 1984): 81–109.

Livingstone, Ken. *If Voting Changed Anything, They'd Abolish It.* Glasgow: Fontana Paperbacks, 1987.

Loewen, James W. *Sundown Towns: A Hidden Dimension of American Racism.* New York: New Press, 2005.

Logan, John, and Harvey Molotch. *Urban Fortunes: The Political Economy of Place.* Berkeley: University of California Press, 1987.

Logan, John R., Brian J. Stults, and Reynolds Farley. "Segregation of Minorities in the Metropolis: Two Decades of Change." *Demography* 41, no. 1 (2002): 1–22.

Logan, John R., and Todd Swanstrom, eds. *Beyond the City Limits: Urban Policy and Economic Restructuring in Comparative Perspective.* Philadelphia: Temple University Press, 1990.

Loveman, G. W., and Chris Tilly. "Good Jobs or Bad Jobs: What Does the Evidence Say?" *New England Economic Review* 20 (January–February 1988): 46–65.

Luria, Dan, and Jack Russell. *Rational Reindustrialization: An Economic Development Agenda for Detroit.* Detroit: Widgetripper Press, 1981.

Lynch, J. W., G. D. Smith, G. A. Kaplan, and J. S. House. "Income Inequality and Mortality: Importance to Health of Individual Income, Psychosocial Environment, or Material Conditions." *British Medical Journal* 320, no. 7243 (2000): 1200–1204.

Lynn, Laurence E., and G. H. McGeary. *Inner City Poverty in the United States.* Washington, D.C.: National Academy Press, 1990.

MacDorman, M. F., and T. J. Mathews. "Recent Trends in Infant Mortality in the United States." Centers for Disease Control and Prevention. NCHS Data Brief no. 9, October 2008. Available at http://www.cdc.gov/nchs/data/databriefs/db09.htm.

Maire, Edmond. "Le chômage zéro, c'est possible." *Alternatives économiques* 48 (June 1987).

Mangum, Garth L., Stephen L. Mangum, and Andrew M. Sum. *The Persistence of Poverty in the United States.* Baltimore: Johns Hopkins University Press, 2003.

Marcuse, Peter. "The Enclave, the Citadel, and the Ghetto: What Has Changed in the Post-Fordist US City." *Urban Affairs Review* 33, no. 2 (1997): 228–264.

———. "Gentrification, Abandonment, and Displacement: Connections, Causes, and Policy Responses in New York City." *Journal of Urban Contemporary Law* 28 (1985): 195–240.

———. "The Shifting Meaning of the Black Ghetto in the United States." In *Of States and Cities: The Partitioning of Urban Space,* ed. Peter Marcuse and Ronald van Kempen, 109–142. New York: Oxford University Press, 2002.

Markusen, Ann R. *The Rise of the Gunbelt: The Military Remapping of Industrial America.* New York: Oxford University Press, 1991.

———. "Steel and Southeast Chicago: Reasons and Opportunities for Industrial Renewal." Research Report to the Mayor's Task Force on Steel and Southeast Chicago. Center for Urban Affairs and Policy Research, Northwestern University, Evanston, Ill., November 1985.

Markusen, Ann R., and Virginia Carlson. "Deindustrialization in the American Midwest: Causes and Responses." In *Deindustrialization and Regional Economic Transformation,* ed. Lloyd Rodwin and Hidehiko Sazanami, 29–59. Boston: Unwin Hyman, 1989.

Markusen, Ann R., Peter Hall, and Amy Glasmeier. *High Tech America: The What, How, Where, and Why of the Sunrise Industries.* Boston: Allen and Unwin, 1986.

Marmot, Michael, John Siegrist, and Tores Theorell. "Health and the Psychosocial Environment at Work." In *Social Determinants of Health,* ed. Michael Marmot and Richard G. Wilkinson, 97–130. New York: Oxford University Press, 2006.

Marmot, Michael, and Richard Wilkinson, eds. *Social Determinants of Health.* Oxford: Oxford University Press, 2006.

Marris, Peter. *Community Planning and Conceptions of Change.* London: Routledge and Kegan Paul, 1982.

Martin, Ron. "National Growth versus Spatial Equality? A Cautionary Note on the New 'Trade-off' Thinking in Regional Policy Discourse." *Regional Science Policy and Practice* 1, no. 1 (November 2008): 3–13.

Massey, Douglas. "Ethnic Residential Segregation: A Theoretical Synthesis and Empirical Review." *Sociology and Social Research* 69, no. 3 (1985): 315–350.

Massey, Douglas, and Nancy Denton. *American Apartheid: Segregation and the Making of the Underclass.* Cambridge, Mass.: Harvard University Press, 1998.

————. "Hypersegregation in U.S. Metropolitan Areas: Black and Hispanic Segregation along Five Dimensions." *Demography* 26, no. 3 (1989): 373–389.

————. "Trends in Residential Segregation of Blacks, Hispanics and Asians, 1970–1980." *American Sociological Review* 52, no. 6 (1987): 802–825.

Mayer, Gerald. "Union Membership Trends in the United States." CRS Report for Congress, August 31, 2004. Available at http://digitalcommons.ilr.cornell.edu/cgi/viewcontent.cgi?article=1176&context=key_workplace.

Mayer, Susan, and Christopher Jencks. "Growing Up in Poor Neighborhoods: How Much Does It Matter?" *Science* (March 17, 1989): 1441–1447.

McClelland, David C. *The Achieving Society.* Princeton, N.J.: Van Nostrand, 1961.

McDonald, Michael P., and Samuel L. Popkin. "The Myth of the Vanishing Point." *American Political Science Review* 95, no. 4 (December 2001): 963–974.

McGeary, Michael G. H., and Laurence E. Lynn, eds. *Urban Change and Poverty.* Washington, D.C.: National Academy Press, 1988.

McKenzie, Richard. *Competing Visions: The Political Conflict over America's Economic Future.* Washington, D.C.: Cato Institute, 1985.

McKinsey & Company, Social Sector Office. "The Economic Impact of the Achievement Gap." April 2009.

Mead, Lawrence M. "Expectations and Welfare Work: WIN in New York State." *Polity* 23, no. 2 (Winter 1985): 224–252.

Meyer, John, and José Gómez-Ibáñez. *Autos, Transit, and Cities.* Cambridge, Mass.: Harvard University Press, 1981.

Mier, Robert E., Joan Fitzgerald, and Lewis Randolph. "African-American Elected Officials and the Future of Progressive Political Movements." In *Economic Development Policy Formation: Experiences in the United States and the United Kingdom,* ed. David Fasenfest. New York: St. Martin's Press, 1992.

Mier, Robert, K. J. Moe, and I. Sherr. "Strategic Planning and the Pursuit of Reform, Economic Development, and Equity." *Journal of the American Planning Association* 52 (1986): 299–309.

Miller, Jon R., and Ismail Gene. "Alternative Regional Specification and Convergence of U.S. Regional Growth Rates." *Annals of Regional Science* 39, no. 2 (June 2005): 241–252.

Miller, Kathleen K., Mindy S. Crandall, and Bruce A. Weber. "Persistent Poverty and Place: How Do Persistent Poverty and Poverty Demographics Vary across the Rural-Urban Continuum?" *Measuring Rural Diversity, November 21–22, 2002.* Washington, D.C.: U.S. Department of Agriculture, Southern Rural Development Center and Farm Foundation, 2002.

Miller, Vincent P., and John M. Quigley. "Segregation by Racial and Demographic Group: Evidence from the San Francisco Bay Area." *Urban Studies* 27, no. 1 (1990): 3–21.

Mincy, Ronald. "Industrial Restructuring, Dynamic Events and the Racial Composition of Concentrated Poverty." Paper prepared for the Social Science Research Council, New York, September 12, 1988.

Mishel, Lawrence, and David M. Frankel. *The State of Working America.* 1990–1991 edition. Armonk, N.Y.: M. E. Sharpe, 1991.

Mollenkopf, John H. *The Contested City.* Princeton, N.J.: Princeton University Press, 1983.

————. "Paths toward the Post Industrial Service City: The Northeast and the Southwest." In *Cities under Stress: The Fiscal Crises of Urban America,* ed. R. W. Burchell and D. Listokin, 77–112. New Brunswick, N.J.: Center for Urban Policy Research, Rutgers University, 1981.

Mollenkopf, John H., and Manuel Castells, ed. *Dual City: Restructuring New York.* New York: Russell Sage Foundation, 1991.

Muntaner, C., and J. Lynch. "Income Inequality, Social Cohesion, and Class Relations: A Critique of Wilkinson's Neo-Durkheimian Research Program." *International Journal of Health Services: Planning, Administration, Evaluation* 29, no. 1 (1999): 59–81.

Muntaner, C., J. Lynch, and G. D. Smith. "Social Capital, Disorganized Communities, and the Third Way: Understanding the Retreat from Structural Inequalities in Epidemiology and Public Health." *International Journal of Health Services: Planning, Administration, Evaluation* 31, no. 2 (2001): 213–237.

Murray, Charles. *Losing Ground: American Social Policy.* New York: Basic Books, 1984.

National Center for Public Policy and Higher Education. *Measuring Up, 2006: The National Report Card on Higher Education.* September 7, 2006. Available at http://measuringup .highereducation.org/.

Nazroo, James Y., and David R. Williams. "The Social Determination of Ethnic/Racial Inequalities in Health." In *Social Determinants of Health,* ed. Michael Marmot and Richard G. Wilkinson, 238–266. New York: Oxford University Press, 2006.

Neckerman, Kathryn M., and Florencia Torche. "Inequality: Causes and Consequences." *Annual Review of Sociology* 33 (2007): 335–357.

Nelson, Kirstin. "Labor Demand, Labor Supply and the Suburbanization of Low-Wage Office Work." In *Production, Work and Territory: The Geographical Anatomy of Industrial Capitalism,* ed. Allen J. Scott and Michael Storper, 149–171. Boston: Allen and Unwin, 1986.

New York Times and Bill Keller. *Class Matters.* New York: Times Books, 2005.

NHSA. "Benefits of Head Start and Early Head Start Programs." October 8, 2009. Available at http://www.nhsa.org/research/head_start_benefits.

Noble, David F. *America by Design: Science, Technology, and the Rise of Corporate Capitalism.* Oxford: Oxford University Press, 1977.

Nord, Mark, Margaret Andrews, and Steven Carlson. "Household Food Security in the United States, 2005." *Economic Research Service.* November 2006. Available at http://www.ers.usda .gov/Publications/ERR29/.

Norman, Jon Robin. "Bright Lights, Little Cities: Understanding Change in American Small Cities from 1970 to 2000." Ph.D. dissertation, University of California, Berkeley, 2007.

Noyelle, Thierry J. "Advanced Services in the System of Cities." In *Local Economies in Transition: Policy Realities and Development Potentials,* ed. Edward Bergman, 143–164. Durham, N.C.: Duke University Press, 1986.

Noyelle, Thierry J., and Thomas M. Stanback. *The Economic Transformation of American Cities.* Totowa, N.J.: Rowman and Allenheld, 1984.

Nussbaum, Martha. "Poverty and Human Functioning: Capabilities as Fundamental Entitlements." In *Poverty and Inequality,* ed. David B. Grunsky and Ravi Kanbur, 47–75. Stanford, Calif.: Stanford University Press, 2006.

O'Connor, James. *The Fiscal Crisis of the State.* New York: St. Martin's Press, 1973.

Office of Technology Assessment (OTA). *Technology and Structural Unemployment: Re-employing Displaced Adults.* Washington, D.C.: U.S. Government Printing Office, 1986.

Oliver, Melvin L., and Thomas M. Shapiro. *Black Wealth/White Wealth: A New Perspective on Racial Inequality.* 2nd ed. New York: Routledge, 2006.

Olpadwala, Porus, and Yuri Mansury. "Finance and Production in the United States, 1928–2001: An Empirical Note." In *Capture and Exclude: Developing Economies and the Poor in Global Finance,* ed. Amiya Kumar Bagchi and Gary A. Dymski. Delhi: Tulika Books, 2007.

O'Regan, Katherine M., and John M. Quigley. "Labor Market Access and Labor Market Outcomes for Urban Youth." *Regional Science and Urban Economics* 21, no. 2 (1991): 227–294.

Orfield, Myron. *Metropolitics: A Regional Agenda for Community and Stability.* Washington, D.C.: Brookings Institution Press, 1997.

Organisation for Economic Co-operation and Development (OECD). "Analysis of Fiscal Policies." *OECD Economic Outlook* 48 (1990): 113–116.

———. *OECD Economic Outlook: Historical Statistics, 1960–1988.* Paris: OECD, 1989.

Orr, James, and Richard Deitz. "A Leaner, More Skilled U.S. Manufacturing Workforce." *Current Issues in Economics and Finance* 12, no. 2 (February–March 2006).

Orshansky, Mollie. "Children of the Poor." *Social Security Bulletin* 26, no. 7 (July 1963): 3–13.

———. "Counting the Poor: Another Look at the Poverty Profile." *Social Security Bulletin* 28, no. 1 (January 1965): 3–29. Reprinted in *Social Security Bulletin* 51, no. 10 (October 1988): 25–51.

Palmer, John, and Isabel Sawhill. *The Reagan Experiment.* Washington, D.C.: Urban Institute Press, 1982.

Pamuk, Ayse. "Geography of Immigrant Clusters in Global Cities: A Case Study of San Francisco, 2000." *International Journal of Urban and Regional Research* 28, no. 2 (June 2004): 287–307.

Patterson, James T. *America's Struggle against Poverty, 1900–1985.* Cambridge, Mass.: Harvard University Press, 1986.

Paul, Darel E. "The Local Politics of 'Going Global': Making and Unmaking Minneapolis–St Paul as a World City." *Urban Studies* 42, no. 12 (2005): 2103–2122.

Pendall, Rolf, and Susan Christopherson. "Losing Ground: Income and Poverty in Upstate New York, 1980–2000." Brookings Institution Survey Series. September 2004.

Pendall, Rolf, William W. Goldsmith, and Ann-Margaret Esnard. "Thinning Rochester: Yesterday's Solutions, Today's Urban Sprawl." Working Paper. Lincoln Institute of Land Policy, Cambridge, Mass., 2001.

Perez, Carlota. "Structural Change and Assimilation of New Technologies in the Economic and Social Systems." *Futures* 15, no. 5 (1983): 357–375.

Perkins, John. *Confessions of an Economic Hit Man.* New York: Penguin, 2005.

Perlman, Janice E. *The Myth of Marginality: Urban Poverty and Politics in Rio de Janeiro.* Berkeley: University of California Press, 1976.

Perna, Nicholas S. "The Shift from Manufacturing to Services: A Concerned View." *New England Economic Review* 9 (January–February 1987): 30–38.

Perry, Cynthia, and Linda J. Blumberg. "Health Insurance for Low-Income Working Families—Summary." Urban Institute. July 16, 2008. Available at http://www.urban.org/publications/411717.html.

Peterson, Paul E. *City Limits.* Chicago: University of Chicago Press, 1981.

———, ed. *The New Urban Reality.* Washington, D.C.: Brookings Institution, 1985.

Phillips, Kevin. *The Politics of Rich and Poor: Wealth and the American Electorate in the Reagan Aftermath.* New York: Random House, 1990.

Phillips, Robin S., and Avis C. Vidal. "The Growth and Restructuring of Metropolitan Economies: The Context for Economic Development Policy." *Journal of the American Planning Association* 49, no. 3 (1983): 291–306.

Piore, Michael, and Charles Sabel. *The Second Industrial Divide: Possibilities for Prosperity.* New York: Basic Books, 1984.

Piven, Francis, and Richard Cloward. *Regulating the Poor: The Functions of Public Welfare.* New York: Pantheon, 1971.

Polanyi, Karl. *The Great Transformation: The Political and Economic Origins of Our Time.* Boston: Beacon Press, 2001.

Poon, Jessie P. H., Bradly Eldredge, and David Yeung. "Rank Size Distribution of International Financial Centers." *International Regional Science Review* 27, no. 4 (2004): 411–430.

Popkin, Susan, Bruce Katz, Mary K. Cunningham, Karen D. Brown, Jeremy Gustafson, and Margery Austin Turner. "A Decade of HOPE VI: Research Findings and Policy Challenges." Urban Institute, May 2004.

Portes, Alejandro, and John Walton. *Labor, Class, and the International System.* New York: Academic Press, 1981.

Pred, Alan. *City Systems in Advanced Economies.* New York: Wiley, 1977.

President's Commission on Industrial Competitiveness. *Global Competition: The New Reality.* Washington, D.C.: U.S. Government Printing Office, 1985.

Pucher, John, and John L. Renne. "Socioeconomics of Urban Travel: Evidence from the 2001 NHTS." *Transportation Quarterly* 57, no. 3 (2003): 49–77.

Puentes, Robert, and David Warren. "One-Fifth of America: A Comprehensive Guide to America's First Suburbs." Brookings Institution, Washington, D.C., 2006.

Quigley, John, and Daniel Rubinfeld. *American Domestic Priorities.* Berkeley: University of California Press, 1985.

Rabin, Yale. "Metropolitan Decentralization, Transit Dependence, and the Employment Isolation of Central City Black Workers." Paper prepared for Symposium on the Role of Housing Mobility in Achieving Equal Opportunity for Minorities, Urban Institute, Washington, D.C., April 21–22, 1988.

Radice, Hugo. "Capital, Labor and the State in the World Economy." Lecture presented at Cornell University, Ithaca, N.Y., September 1987.

Ranney, David. *Global Decisions, Local Collisions: Urban Life in the New World Order.* Philadelphia: Temple University Press, 2003.

Reich, Robert B. "The Real Economy." *Atlantic Monthly* (February 1991): 35–52.

Reynolds, Alan. "Has U.S. Income Inequality Really Increased?" Policy Analysis no. 586. Cato Institute, January 8, 2007. Available at http://www.cato.org/pub_display.php?pub_id=6880.

Rieder, Jonathan. *Canarsie: The Jews and Italians of Brooklyn against Liberalism.* Cambridge, Mass: Harvard University Press, 1985.

Rivlin, Alice, and Isabel Sawhill. "Why Deficits and Debt Render the United States Vulnerable." Brookings Institution, Washington, D.C., February 21, 2007.

Roberts, Brandon, and Deborah Povich. "Still Working Hard, Still Falling Short." Working Poor Families Project, October 2008. Available at http://www.workingpoorfamilies.org/pdfs/NatReport08.pdf.

Rodriguez, N. P., and J. R. Feagin. "Urban Specialization in the World System: An Investigation of Historical Cases." *Urban Affairs Quarterly* 22, no. 2 (1986): 187–220.

Rose, Julie. "Army Aids Those Too Fat to Enlist." *National Public Radio,* March 23, 2009.

Rose, Stephen J. *The American Profile Poster: Who Owns What, Who Makes How Much, Who Works Where, and Who Lives with Whom.* New York: Pantheon, 1986.

Rosenbaum, E., and G. Argeros. "Holding the Line: Housing Turnover and the Persistence of Racial/Ethnic Segregation in New York City." *Journal of Urban Affairs* 27, no. 3 (2005): 261–281.

Rossi, Peter H., and James D. Wright. "The Urban Homeless: A Portrait of Urban Dislocation." *Annals of the American Academy of Political and Social Sciences* 501 (1989): 132–142.

Rukus, Joseph. "San Francisco's Reentry Strategy: Using Economic Equity to Reduce Recidivism." Master's thesis, Cornell University, 2009.

Rymarowicz, L., and D. Zimmerman. *The Effect of Federal Tax and Budget Policies in the 1980s on the State-Local Sector.* Washington, D.C.: Congressional Research Service, 1986.

Sable, Jennifer, and Anthony Garofano. *Public Elementary and Secondary School Student Enrollment, High School Completions, and Staff from the Common Core of Data: School Year 2005–06.* Washington, D.C.: National Center for Education Statistics, Institute of Education Sciences, U.S. Department of Education, 2007. Available at http://purl.access.gpo.gov/GPO/LPS83116.

Sachs, Aaron. "Virtual Ecology: A Brief Environmental History of Silicon Valley." *World Watch Magazine* (January–February 1999).

Salinas, Patricia. "Subemployment and the Urban Underclass: A Policy Research Report." Paper distributed by Graduate Program in Community and Regional Planning, University of Texas, Austin, 1980.

———. "Urban Growth, Subemployment, and Mobility." In *Local Economies in Transition: Policy Realities and Development Potentials,* ed. E. M. Bergman, 248–270. Durham, N.C.: Duke University Press, 1986.

Sampson, Robert J., and William Julius Wilson. "Toward a Theory of Race, Crime, and Urban Inequality." In *Race, Crime, and Justice: A Reader,* ed. Shaun L. Gabbidon and Helen Taylor Greene, 177–190. New York: Routledge, 2005.

Sandefur, Gary D. "Blacks, Hispanics, American Indians, and Poverty—and What Worked." In *Quiet Riots: Race and Poverty in the United States,* ed. Fred R. Harris and Roger W. Wilkins, 46–74. New York: Pantheon, 1988.

Sassen, Saskia. *The Global City: New York, London, Tokyo.* Princeton, N.J.: Princeton University Press, 2000.

———. "The Informal Economy." In *Dual City: Restructuring New York,* ed. John H. Mollenkopf and Manuel Castells, 79–102. New York: Russell Sage Foundation, 1991.

———. "Locating Cities on Global Circuits." *Environment and Urbanization* 14, no. 1 (2002): 13–30.

———. *The Mobility of Labor and Capital: A Study in International Investment and Labor Flow.* Cambridge: Cambridge University Press, 1988.

Sassen-Koob, Saskia. "The New Labor Demand in Global Cities." In *Cities in Transformation: Class, Capital, and the State,* ed. Michael Smith, 139–171. Urban Affairs Annual Reviews, vol. 26. Beverly Hills, Calif.: Sage, 1984.

———. "Recomposition and Peripheralization at the Core." *Contemporary Marxism* 5 (1982): 88–100.

Sawers, Larry, and William Tabb, eds. *Sunbelt/Snowbelt: Urban Development and Regional Restructuring.* New York: Oxford University Press, 1984.

Saxenian, Anna Lee. "The Cheshire Cat's Grin: Innovation, Regional Development and the Cambridge Case." *Economy and Society* 18, no. 4 (November 1989): 448–477.

Schill, Michael H., and Richard P. Nathan. *Revitalizing America's Cities: Neighborhood Reinvestment and Displacement.* Albany: State University of New York Press, 1983.

Schoen, Cathy, Karen Davis, Sabrina K. H. How, and Stephen C. Schoenbaum. "US Health System Performance: A National Scorecard." *U.S. Health System* 25, no. 6 (2006). Available at http://content.healthaffairs.org/cgi/content/abstract/25/6/w457.

Schulman, S. "Discrimination, Human Capital, and Black-White Unemployment: Evidence from Cities." *Journal of Human Resources* 22, no. 3 (1987): 361–376.

Scott, Allen. *Metropolis: From the Division of Labor to Urban Form.* Berkeley: University of California Press, 1988.

———, ed. *Global City-Regions: Trends, Theory, Policy.* Cambridge: Oxford University Press, 2001.

Scott, Allen J., and Michael Storper. "Production, Work, Territory: Contemporary Realities and Theoretical Tasks." In *Production, Work, and Territory: The Geographical Anatomy of Industrial Capitalism,* ed. Allen Scott and Michael Storper, 3–15. Boston: Allen and Unwin, 1986.

Scott, Robert E., and Christian Dorsey. "Economic Snapshot: African Americans Are Especially at Risk in the Auto Crisis." Economic Policy Institute, December 5, 2008.

Sen, Amatya. "Conceptualizing and Measuring Poverty." In *Poverty and Inequality,* ed. David B. Grunsky and Ravi Kanbur, 30–46. Stanford, Calif.: Stanford University Press, 2006.

Shaikh, Anwar. "Laws of Production and Laws of Algebra: Humbug 11." In *Growth, Profits and Property: Essays in the Revival of Political Economy,* ed. Edward J. Nell, 80–95. Cambridge: Cambridge University Press, 1980.

Shearer, Derek. "In Search of Equal Partnerships: Prospects for Progressive Urban Policy in the 1990s." In *Unequal Partnerships: The Political Economy of Urban Redevelopment in Postwar America,* ed. Gregory D. Squires, 289–307. New Brunswick, N.J.: Rutgers University Press, 1989.

Sheets, Robert, Stephen Nord, and John Phelps. *The Impact of Service Industries on Underemployment in Metropolitan Economies.* Lexington, Mass.: Lexington Books, 1987.

Shields, Todd G., and Robert K. Goidel. "Participation Rates, Socioeconomic Class Biases, and Congressional Elections: A Crossvalidation." *American Journal of Political Science* 41, no. 2 (April 1997): 683–691.

Shlay, Anne B., and Robert P. Giloth. "Social Organization of a Land Based Elite: The Case of the Failed Chicago 1992 World's Fair." *Journal of Urban Affairs* 9, no. 4 (1986): 305–324.

Silvestri, Gary, and John Lukasiewicz. "Projections of Occupational Employment, 1988–2000." *Monthly Labor Review* 112, no. 11 (November 1988): 42–65.

Simms, Margaret. "Weathering Job Loss: Unemployment Insurance." Urban Institute, July 16, 2008.

Singer, Paul T. *Economia política da urbanizaçao* [Political Economy of Urbanization]. São Paulo: Editora Brasiliense, 1973.

Smeeding, Timothy M. "Poor People in Rich Nations: The United States in Comparative Perspective." Luxembourg Income Study Working Paper no. 419. October 2005. Available at http://ssrn.com/abstract=835506.

Smolka, Martim, and Adriana de A. Larangeira. "Informality and Poverty in Latin American Urban Policies." In *The New Global Frontier: Urbanization, Poverty and Environment in the 21st Century*, ed. George Martine, Gordon McGranahan, and Mark Montgomery, 99–114. Sterling, Va.: Earthscan, 2008.

Soja, Edward W. "Economic Restructuring and the Internationalization of the Los Angeles Region." In *The Capitalist City*, ed. M. P. Smith and J. R. Feagin, 178–198. New York: Basil Blackwell, 1987.

———. *Postmodern Geographies: The Reassertion of Space in Critical Social Theory*. London: Verso, 1987.

Solloway, Michele R. "Labor and Health Policy in the 1990s: Meeting the Challenge of a Changing Economy." Ph.D. dissertation, University of California, Berkeley, 1991.

Sowell, Thomas. *A Conflict of Visions*. New York: Morrow, 1987.

Spring, William, Bennett Harrison, and Thomas Vietorisz. "Crisis of the Underemployed." *New York Times Magazine*, November 5, 1972.

Stanback, Thomas. *Understanding the Service Economy: Employment, Productivity, Location*. Baltimore: Johns Hopkins University Press, 1979.

Stanback, Thomas M., and Richard Knight. *Suburbanization and the City*. New York: Allanheld, Osmun, 1976.

Stanback, Thomas, and Thierry Noyelle. *Cities in Transition*. Totowa, N.J.: Rowman and Allanheld, 1982.

Starr, Paul. *The Limits of Privatization*. Washington, D.C.: Economic Policy Institute, 1987.

Steinberg, Stephen. *Turning Back: The Retreat from Racial Justice in American Thought and Policy*. Boston: Beacon Press, 1995.

———. "The Underclass: A Case of Color Blindness." *New Politics* 11, no. 3 (1989): 142–166.

Stockman, David Allan. *The Triumph of Politics: How the Reagan Revolution Failed*. New York: Harper and Row, 1986.

Stone, Michael. "Housing and the American Economy: A Marxist Perspective." In *Urban and Regional Planning in an Age of Austerity*, ed. Pierre Clavel, John Forester, and William W. Goldsmith, 81–108. New York: Pergamon Press, 1980.

Storper, Michael, and Richard Walker. *The Capitalist Imperative: Territory, Technology and Industrial Growth*. Oxford: Basil Blackwell, 1989.

Swanson, Christopher B. "Closing the Graduation Gap." America's Promise Alliance and the Bill and Melinda Gates Foundation, April 2009.

Tanzer, Michael. *The Political Economy of International Oil and the Underdeveloped Countries*. Boston: Beacon Press, 1969.

Taylor, Peter J., and Robert E. Lang. "U.S. Cities in the 'World City Network.'" Brookings Institution, February 2005.

Thompson, Wilbur. "The National System of Cities as an Object of Public Policy." *Urban Studies* 9, no. 1 (1972): 99–116.

Thurow, Lester C. "Regional Transformation and the Service Activities." In *Deindustrialization and Regional Economic Transformation: The Experience of the United States*, ed. Lloyd Rodwin and Hidehiko Sazanami, 179–198. Boston: Unwin Hyman, 1989.

————. "Surge in Inequality." *Scientific American* 256, no. 5 (1987): 30–37.

Thurow, Lester C., and L. Tyson. "Adjusting the U.S. Trade Imbalance: A Black Hole in the World Economy." Working Paper no. 24. Berkeley Roundtable on the International Economy, University of California, Berkeley, 1987.

Tobin, G. A., ed. *Divided Neighborhoods: Changing Patterns of Racial Segregation.* Urban Affairs Annual Reviews, vol. 32. Newbury Park, Calif.: Sage, 1987.

Tumminia, A. E. "Locational Factors for the Office Function of Industry." Masters' thesis, Columbia University, 1953.

Turner, Margery, and Michael Fix. "Opportunities Denied, Opportunities Diminished." Urban Institute, Washington, D.C., May 1991.

Urhan, Susan, et al. *One in 31: The Long Reach of American Corrections.* Washington, D.C.: Pew Center on the States, 2009.

U.S. Bureau of Labor Statistics. *Employment and Earnings* 38, no. 4 (April 1991). Washington, D.C.: U.S. Government Printing Office.

————. "A Profile of the Working Poor, 2003." March 2005. Available at http://www.bls.gov/cps/cpswp2003.pdf.

U.S. Bureau of the Census. *American Community Survey (ACS).* Available at http://www.census.gov/acs/www/.

————. *Current Population Survey.* Washington, D.C., 1990; computer tape, 1991.

————. *Current Population Survey, Money Income and Poverty Status in the United States.* Series P-60. Washington, D.C.: U.S. Government Printing Office [various years].

————. *Demographic State of the Nation.* Washington, D.C.: U.S. Government Printing Office, 1990.

————. "The Effects of Government Taxes and Transfers on Income and Poverty: 2004." February 14, 2006. Available at http://www.census.gov/hhes/www/poverty/effect2004/effectofgovtandt2004.pdf.

————. *Statistical Abstracts of the United States.* Washington, D.C.: U.S. Government Printing Office, 1989.

U.S. Conference of Mayors. "Climate Protection Agreement." Chicago, 2005. Available at http://usmayors.org/climateprotection/documents/mcpAgreement.pdf.

U.S. Congress. House Committee on Ways and Means. *Overview of Entitlement Programs: Green Book, 1991.* Washington, D.C.: U.S. Government Printing Office, 1991.

————. House Select Committee on Children, Youth and Families. *Barriers and Opportunities for America's Young Black Men.* Hearing, 101st Cong., 1st sess., July 25, 1989. Washington, D.C.: U.S. Government Printing Office, 1989.

————. House Subcommittees on Housing and Community Opportunities and Financial Institutions and Credit. *Protecting Homeowners: Preventing Abusive Lending While Preserving Access to Credit.* Testimony of Allen J. Fishbein. 108th Cong., 1st sess., November 5, 2003.

————. Joint Economic Committee. *Falling Behind: The Growing Income Gap in America.* Washington, D.C.: U.S. Government Printing Office, 1991.

U.S. Public Health Service. *Health, United States.* Washington, D.C.: U.S. Government Printing Office, 1990.

Valentine, Charles A. *Culture and Poverty: Critique and Counter-Proposals.* Chicago: University of Chicago Press, 1968.

Vapñarsky, Cesar A. "On Rank-Size Distributions of Cities: An Ecological Approach." *Economic Development and Cultural Change* 17, no. 4 (July 1969): 584–595.

Vega, Adriana. "Internal Displacement and Urbanization in Colombia: Policy Challenges for a Country in Conflict." Master's thesis, Cornell University, forthcoming.

Velez, William, and Michael Martin. "Latino Segregation Patterns in Metro Areas, 2000." Paper presented at the Annual Meeting of the American Sociological Association, San Francisco, 2004.

Vergara, Camilo Jose. "Big Apple Follies." *Planning* 57, no. 7 (1991): 28.

Vidal, Avis. "Beyond Housing: Growing Community Development Systems." Urban Institute, July 2005.

Vietorisz, Thomas. "Global Information." Unpublished manuscript. Ithaca, N.Y., 1991.

Vietorisz, Thomas, William Goldsmith, and Robert Mier. "Urban Poverty Strategies: A Comparison of Latin America and the United States." School of Architecture and Urban Planning, University of California, Los Angeles, 1975.

Vietorisz, Thomas, Bennett Harrison, and Robert Mier. "Full Employment at Living Wages." *Annals of the American Academy of Political and Social Sciences* 418 (March 1975): 94–107.

Wacquant, Loïc J. D. "From Slavery to Mass Incarceration: Rethinking the 'Race' Question in the US." *New Left Review* 13 (January–February 2002): 41–60.

———. "Three Pernicious Premises in the Study of the American Ghetto." *International Journal of Urban and Regional Research* 21, no. 2 (1991): 341–353.

———. "Urban Outcasts: Stigma and Division in the Black American Ghetto and the French Urban Periphery." *International Journal of Urban and Regional Research* 17, no. 3 (1993): 366–383.

Wagmiller, Robert L. "The Changing Geography of Male Joblessness in Urban America: 1970 to 2000." *Housing Policy Debate* 19, no. 1 (2008): 93–135.

———. "Male Nonemployment in White, Black, Hispanic, and Multiethnic Neighborhoods, 1970–2000." *Urban Affairs Review* 44, no. 1 (2008): 85–125.

———. "Race and the Spatial Segregation of Jobless Men in Urban America." *Demography* 44, no. 3 (2007): 539–562.

Walker, Richard. "The Geographical Organization of Production Systems." *Environment and Planning: Society and Space* 6 (1988): 377–408.

———. "A Theory of Suburbanization: Capitalism and the Construction of Urban Space in the U.S." In *Urbanization and Urban Planning in a Capitalist Society,* ed. Michael Dear and A. J. Scott, 383–429. London: Methuen, 1981.

Wallerstein, Immanuel. "Citizens All? Citizens Some! The Making of the Citizen." *Comparative Studies in Society and History* 45, no. 4 (October 2003): 650–679.

Walters, Jonathan. "Cities on Their Own." *Governing* 4, no. 7 (1991): 26–32.

Warner, Mildred E. "Market-Based Governance and the Challenge for Rural Governments: U.S. Trends." *Social Policy and Administration: An International Journal of Policy and Research* 40, no. 6 (2006): 612–631.

Warner, Mildred, and A. Hefetz. 2003. "Rural-Urban Differences in Privatization: Limits to the Competitive State." *Environment and Planning C: Government and Policy* 21, no. 5 (2005): 703–718.

Warren, Elizabeth. "The Growing Threat to Middle Class Families." *Brooklyn Law Review* (April 2003). Available at http://www.nacba.org/files/new_in_debate/GrowingThreatMiddle ClassFamilies.pdf.

Watkins, Alfred J. *The Practice of Urban Economics.* Sage Library of Social Research, vol. 107. Beverly Hills, Calif.: Sage, 1980.

Watson, Tara. "Metropolitan Growth, Inequality, and Neighborhood Segregation by Income." Brookings-Wharton Papers on Urban Affairs, 2006.

Wehler, Cheryl. *Survey on Childhood Hunger.* Washington, D.C.: Food Research and Action Center, Community Childhood Hunger Identification Project, 1991.

Weinstein, Bernard L., and Robert E. Firestine. *Regional Growth and Decline in the United States: The Rise of the Sunbelt and the Decline of the Northeast.* New York: Praeger, 1978.

Werschkul, Misha, and Erica Williams. "The 2004 National Overview Report: The Status of Women in the States." Ed. Amy Caiazza and April Shaw. Institute for Women's Policy Research, November 2004. Available at http://www.iwpr.org/States2004/PDFs/National .pdf.

White, Richard. "Sprawl: The View from Toronto." *Journal of Planning History* 8 (2009): 274–283.

Wilger, Robert J. "Black-White Residential Segregation in 1980." Ph.D. dissertation, University of Michigan, 1988.

Wilkes, Rima, and John Iceland. "Hypersegregation in the Twenty-First Century." *Demography* 41, no. 1 (2004): 23–36.

Wilkinson, Richard G. "Ourselves and Others—for Better or Worse: Social Vulnerability." In *Social Determinants of Health,* ed. Michael Marmot and Richard G. Wilkinson, 341–358. New York: Oxford University Press, 2006.

Williamson, Jeffrey G. "Productivity and American Leadership: A Review Article." *Journal of Economic Literature* 29, no. 1 (1991): 51–68.

Williamson, Jeffrey G., and Peter G. Lindert. *American Inequality: A Macroeconomic History.* New York: Academic Press, 1980.

Wilson, David, and Jared Wouters. "Spatiality and Growth Discourse: The Restructuring of America's Rust Belt Cities." *Journal of Urban Affairs* 25, no. 2 (2003): 123–138.

Wilson, Patricia. "The New Maquiladoras: Flexible Manufacturing and Local Linkages." In *The Maquiladora Industry: Economic Solution or Problem?* ed. Khosrow Fatemi. New York: Praeger, 1990.

Wilson, William J. *The Declining Significance of Race: Blacks and Changing American Institutions.* Chicago: University of Chicago Press, 1978.

———. "Social Theory and the Concept 'Underclass.'" In *Poverty and Inequality,* ed. David Grusky and Rabi Kanbur, 103–116. Stanford, Calif.: Stanford University Press, 2006.

———. *The Truly Disadvantaged: The Inner City, the Underclass, and Public Policy.* Chicago: University of Chicago Press, 1987.

———. "The Underclass: Issues, Perspectives, and Public Policy." *Annals of the American Academy of Political and Social Sciences* 501 (1989): 182–192.

Winders, Jamie. "Changing Politics of Race and Region: Latino Migration to the US South." *Progress in Human Geography* 29, no. 6 (2005): 683–699.

Wolff, Edward N. "Recent Trends in Household Wealth in the United States: Rising Debt and the Middle-Class Squeeze." Working Paper no. 502. Levy Economics Institute of Bard College, June 2007.

———. "Review of *The Falling Rate of Profit in the Postwar United States Economy.*" *Journal of Economic Literature* 31, no. 2 (1993): 895–896.

———. "Wealth Holdings and Poverty Status in the U.S." *Review of Income and Wealth* 36, no. 2 (1990): 143–165.

Working Seminar on Family and American Welfare Policy. *The New Consensus on Family and Welfare.* Washington, D.C.: American Enterprise Institute for Public Policy Research, 1987.

Yang, Rebecca, and Paul A. Jargowsky. "Suburban Development and Economic Segregation in the 1990s." *Urban Affairs* 28, no. 3 (June 2006): 253–273.

Yates, Daniel. *The Ungovernable City.* Cambridge, Mass.: MIT Press, 1977.

Yinger, John. *Closed Doors, Opportunities Lost: The Continuing Costs of Housing Discrimination.* New York: Russell Sage Foundation, 1995.

Zedlewski, Sheila R., Ajay Chaudry, and Margaret Simms. "A New Safety Net for Low-Income Families." Urban Institute, July 16, 2008. Available at http://www.urban.org/publications/411738.html.

Zweig, Michael, ed. *What's Class Got to Do with It? American Society in the Twenty-First Century.* Ithaca, N.Y.: Cornell University Press, 2004.

Index

William W. Goldsmith is Professor of City and Regional Planning and Director of the Program on International Studies in Planning at Cornell University. He has taught throughout Latin America, and during the Clinton Administration he served on the EPA Clean Air Act Advisory Board.

Edward J. Blakely is Honorary Professor of Urban Policy in the U.S. Studies Centre at the University of Sydney. He ran for Mayor of Oakland, California, in 1998, was Dean of Urban Planning at the University of Southern California (1994–1999) and Dean of the Milano Graduate School at The New School in New York (1999–2003), and most recently served as recovery czar for New Orleans after Hurricane Katrina.